Journey with No Maps

SANDRA DJWA

Journey with No Maps

A Life of P.K. Page

MCGILL-QUEEN'S UNIVERSITY PRESS

Montreal & Kingston • London • Ithaca

© McGill-Queen's University Press 2012

ISBN 978-0-7735-4061-3 (cloth)
ISBN 978-0-7735-4191-7 (paper)

Legal deposit third quarter 2012
Bibliothèque nationale du Québec

First paperback edition 2013
Printed in Canada on acid-free paper

This book was first published with the help of a grant
from the Canadian Federation for the Humanities and
Social Sciences, through the Aid to Scholarly Publications
Program, using funds provided by the Social Sciences
and Humanities Research Council of Canada.

McGill-Queen's University Press acknowledges the support
of the Canada Council for the Arts for our publishing
program. We also acknowledge the financial support of
the Government of Canada through the Canada Book
Fund for our publishing activities.

Library and Archives Canada Cataloguing in Publication

Djwa, Sandra, 1939–
Journey with no maps : a life of P. K. Page / Sandra Djwa.

Includes bibliographical references and index.
ISBN 978-0-7735-4061-3 (bnd)
ISBN 978-0-7735-4191-7 (pbk)

1. Page, P. K. (Patricia Kathleen), 1916–2010. 2. Poets,
Canadian (English)–20th century–Biography. I. Title.

PS8531.A34Z52 2012
C811'.54
C2012-904093-2

This book was designed and typeset by studio oneonone
in Sabon 10/13

To my husband Lalit Srivastava (1932–2012),
who kept good company with this book
for more than a decade

Contents

Illustrations   ix

Preface   xiii

 1 Beginnings, 1884–1927   3

 2 Calgary: Intimations, 1928–1934   24

 3 England: Discovering Modernism, 1934–1935   37

 4 Saint John: Apprenticeship, 1935–1941   46

 5 Montreal: Art and Life, 1941–1944   69

 6 Halifax and Victoria: Loss, 1944–1946   93

 7 Ottawa: Recovery, 1946–1953   108

 8 Australia: The Journey Out, 1953–1956   136

 9 Brazil: Exotic Worlds, 1957–1959   161

10 Mexico: New Maps, 1960–1964   177

11 Victoria: Finding Oneself, 1964–1969   199

12 Victoria: Inner Events, 1970–1979   221

13 Victoria: Transformations, 1980–1989   247

14 Victoria: Acclaim, 1990–1999   268

15 Victoria: Endings, 2000–2010   292

Acknowledgments   323

Notes   327

Bibliography   381

Index   395

Illustrations

COLOUR PLATES

1 Detail from a photograph of "Patty" Page as a child. Courtesy of Library and Archives Canada (LAC) and Page Estate. Watercolour of "The Joy" from *Wisdom from Nonsense Land*, a booklet for children. The verses are written by Lionel Page and the illustrations are by Rose Page circa 1918. Courtesy of Wendy Page and the Page Estate.

2 *Fiesta*, an oil painting by P.K. Irwin of a carnival, circa 1959–60. August 1960. Reprinted with the permission of Sandra Djwa and the Page Estate. Photographer: Lisa Hartley Photography.

3 *Pat Page, 1940*, an oil painting by Miller Brittain, Saint John, New Brunswick. Reprinted with permission from a private collector, Toronto. Photographer: Michael Cullen.

4 *Woman's Room*, an oil painting by P.K. Irwin of her dressing room. Brazil, circa 25 March 1959. Reprinted with the permission of Sandra Djwa and the Page Estate. Photographer: Lisa Hartley Photography. Vancouver, British Columbia.

5 *A Kind of Osmosis*, a painting of the cosmic egg by P.K. Irwin. Mexico, 5 August 1960. Reprinted with the permission of the Page Estate and the Art Gallery of Ontario.

6 Pat and Arthur Irwin, circa 1980s. Courtesy of LAC and the Page Estate.

7 Photograph of lunch in honour of Ted Hughes at the Deep Cove Chalet. Sidney, British Columbia, 12 August 1993. Photographer: Beverly Koffel.

BLACK-AND-WHITE ILLUSTRATIONS

Lionel Page as a homesteader, Red Deer, Alberta. Courtesy of LAC and the Page Estate. 7

Rose Page as a young woman. Courtesy of LAC and the Page Estate. 8

Patty Page as a baby with her mother Rose. Courtesy of LAC and the Page Estate. 9

Patty the tomboy with father Lionel and brother Michael. Courtesy of LAC and the Page Estate. 18

Detail from a "Baby Party," Pat Page and Phil Golding (in bonnets). Rothesay, New Brunswick, circa 1936–37. Courtesy of George Teed. 47

Pat on cruise with parents, circa 1938. Courtesy of LAC and the Page Estate. 52

Ted Campbell's studio, Saint John, circa 1940. Courtesy of LAC and the Page Estate. 63

The *Preview* group. Courtesy of LAC and the Page Estate. 79

Pat Page and F.R. Scott. Courtesy of Queen's University Archives and William Toye. 87

Pat Page, photo portrait, Teresa Studios. Probably taken in Halifax or Victoria in 1944–46. Courtesy of Queen's University Archives and William Toye. 94

Pat Page during her time at the National Film Commission. Courtesy of LAC and the Page Estate. 109

Mrs Arthur Irwin at the Canadian Embassy in Brazil. Courtesy of LAC
and the Page Estate. 163

Octagon. S. Djwa. 231

P.K. Irwin, black-and-white octagonal series, *Tree of Life.* Reprinted
with the permission of the owner, Dorothea Adaskin, Victoria, British
Columbia. 233

P.K. Page performing "Me Tembro" in Victoria, British Columbia,
12 May 1984. Photographer: Marilyn Bowering. 254

Photograph after Doris Lessing's address to the Canadian Club,
26 March 1984. Elizabeth Smart, Doris Lessing, Martha Butterfield,
P.K. Page, Michael Ondaatje. Photographer: David Young. 258

P.K. Page and Margaret Atwood, University of Victoria, 1980s.
Courtesy of Margaret Atwood and the Page Estate; University of
Victoria Photographic Services. 261

Unless the Eye Catch Fire performance at the Belfry Theatre, Victoria,
British Columbia, May 1994. Courtesy of LAC and the Page Estate.
271

P.K. awarded the Companion of the Order of Canada, February 1999.
289

P.K. Page's last public reading from *You Are Here* at the Winchester
Art Gallery, April 2009. Photographer: Don Denton. 309

Plate 1
Photograph of "Patty" Page as a child.
Watercolour of "Joy" from *Wisdom from Nonsense Land*,
a book for children.

Plate 2
Fiesta, an oil painting by P.K. Irwin of a carnival, circa 1959–60.

Plate 3
Pat Page, *1940*, by Miller Brittain, Saint John, New Brunswick.

Plate 4
Woman's Room, an oil painting of her dressing room by P.K. Irwin.

Plate 5
A Kind of Osmosis, a painting of the cosmic egg by P.K. Irwin.

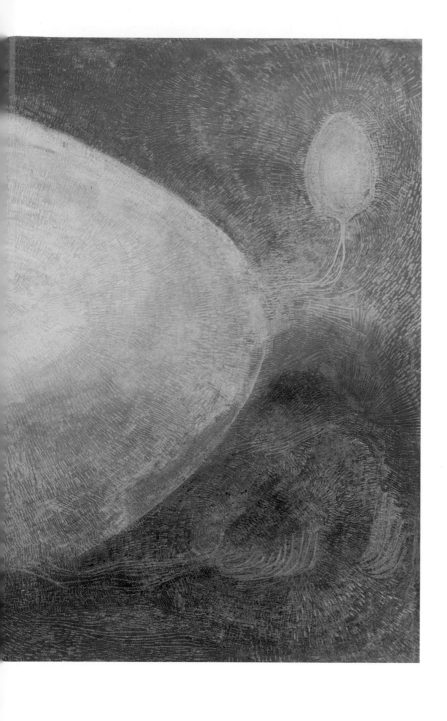

Plate 6
Pat and Arthur Irwin, circa 1980s.

Plate 7
Lunch in honour of Ted Hughes at the Deep Cove Chalet, Sidney, British Columbia.
From left to right: Patrick Lane, Lorna Crozier, Marilyn Bowering, Michael Elcock,
Stephen Reid, Christine Tanner, Ted Hughes, P.K. Page, Susan Musgrave.

Preface

For a woman born near the start of the twentieth century, life was a journey with no maps because so much changed during her lifetime – the right to vote, to gain higher education, to pursue a career or to marry, and, if married, to choose whether to have children. This is the story of an extraordinary woman who recognized the choices offered by modern life and successfully navigated a number of paths as poet, lover, wife, artist, and spiritual being. Simultaneously she told her own story – and the larger woman's journey that it represented – in poems, short stories, diaries, and librettos. During the 1950s and after, she began to draw and paint, recording aspects of her life in visual art.

I met P.K. Page in April 1970 when she gave her first public poetry reading to my students in English at Simon Fraser University. Three years later we met again at a Banff conference for poets and critics. As a group of us, including F.R. Scott, the poet and constitutional lawyer, stood together in the Calgary airport waiting for our separate planes, Scott gestured towards Page and quipped, "We're the post-view of *Preview*. You should write on us." *Preview* was the Montreal "little mag" that helped launch literary modernism in Canada.

In 1986 I published Scott's biography, *The Politics of the Imagination*, a public life that alluded briefly to the "fellow poet" he loved. In the intervening years both Scott and Page have died, expectations for biographical writing have deepened, and there has been a new understanding of the woman's quest. In this book, I pick up the story again but now from the perspective of a young woman on the Canadian prairie with a yearning to write poetry.

Sandra Djwa
West Vancouver

I am traveller. I have a destination but no maps. Others perhaps have reached that destination already, still others are on their way. But none has had to go from here before – nor will again. One's route is one's own. One's journey unique. What I will find at the end I can barely guess. What lies on the way is unknown.
P.K. Page, "Traveller, Conjuror, Journeyman," 1970

There are four ways to write a woman's life: the woman herself may tell it, in what she chooses to call an autobiography; she may tell it in what she chooses to call fiction; a biographer, woman or man, may write the woman's life in what is called a biography; or the woman may write her own life in advance of living it, unconsciously, and without recognizing or naming the process.
Carolyn G. Heilbrun, *Writing a Woman's Life*, 1988

What one wants most in one's life is to write well.
P.K. Page, *B.C. Book World*, 1991

Beginnings, 1884–1927

One evening in the mid-1980s, I heard P.K. Page read from her poem "Ancestors" at the old Duthie's Bookstore on Robson Street in Vancouver. She stood on stage with her head flung back, her resonant voice invoking figures of power – ancestors, she said, clothed in scarlet, purple, and black. Now the last of her line, a woman without children, she is expected to give an account of her life. In this version of the story she is rescued, just in the nick of time, by clattering gypsy ancestors with "flashing knives" that put the respectable lot "to rout." But in real life, as Page told poet Tom Marshall, who read the poem as autobiography, she didn't have gypsy ancestors and the sequence of poems that included this one "are not about me – except very indirectly."[1]

The poem was based on a dream in which generation upon generation of Page's family, in a "cavernous theatre," filled endless rows of seats: "Men with arrogant Roman faces, / women like thoroughbred horses / held in check."

> These were the people for whom
> I had lived in exemplary fashion,
> had not let down,
> for whom I'd refrained from evil,
> borne pain with grace.
> And now they were here – resurrected –
> the damned demanding dead ...[2]

The poem's "arrogant Roman faces" and "old brocade" suggest the aesthetic Whitehouses and her mother's side of the family – great-great-grandfather Robert Whitehouse was a silk merchant. Other references to "thorough-bred horses" and "Brasso" suggest the land-owning Pages of

Essex, her father's family. Her father, Lionel Page, was an officer in Lord Strathcona's Horse, and in the military barracks of her childhood home, his batman was always cleaning Page's boots or polishing up his brass. To be sure, not all of the details are strictly autobiographical. While P.K. Page did not have gypsy ancestors, as a child she had longed to run away to a gypsy camp. Yet the strong emotion of the last stanza is compelling. The poet has been raised to feel an overpowering sense of duty to "the damned demanding dead" – the Pages and the Whitehouses. Although both sets of ancestors helped to shape her character it was her father, Lionel Page, who had the strongest influence.

The Pages of Essex can be traced back to the early eighteenth century, but the first of P.K. Page's ancestors that we can place surely was her grandfather, Henry James Page, born in 1856. Henry was the son of a well-to-do landowner with a thousand acres, but as a middle son he could expect little from his family; so he went into "trade," setting himself up as a brewer in Frodingham, in the North Riding of Yorkshire. According to the British national census, on 4 April 1881 the twenty-five-year old Henry Page was a visitor at 22 Graham Road, Broadwater, Sussex, the household of Emma Augusta Jones, the widow of Lieutenant Winchester Jones of the King's Royal Rifles, formerly of Bray, Wicklow County, Ireland. Mrs Jones had three daughters: Elizabeth, Charlotte, and Augusta. When the girls were in London they rode their horses on Rotten Row, where they were known as "the handsome Miss Jones, the beautiful Miss Jones and the pretty Miss Jones."[3] Henry was courting the pretty Miss Jones, Augusta. In 1883 they were married, and by December 1884 they had a son, Lionel Frank. But by 1886 Henry was dead, killed in a shooting accident, leaving his wife with very little money and a small boy to raise.

Augusta's relations with the Page family were cool (perhaps because of her Irish background), and they offered little support. She moved back into her mother's household, along with her sister Lizzie (Elizabeth Graham), who had recently divorced her husband and had one child, Violet.[4] According to Lionel Page, to save money the two sisters soon set up house with one of Lizzie's friends, Mrs Patrick Campbell, whose husband had left to seek work in Australia after their second child was born. This would have been in the late 1880s before Mrs Campbell's career as an actress took off.[5]

Page later spoke of the close relationship between his family and Mrs Campbell during his early childhood, when the three women were independently raising four children of almost the same age.[6] Lizzie supported her family by writing serials and articles, and Mrs Campbell supported hers through acting, with growing celebrity. Years later, in 1914, an infatuated Bernard Shaw created the role of Eliza Doolittle for her in *Pygmalion*. Little information is available on the Jones sisters or on Mrs Patrick's private life during this time, but Lionel Page clearly spent some formative years of his childhood among accomplished, unconventional women. Even in 1897, when he was a teenager, the Page, Jones, and Campbell families were all listed as neighbours in the same London square, Glebe Place. He brought from this environment a strong sense of duty, a store of music-hall ballads, and a great sense of fun, including a talent for mimicking: for a time he had a Yorkshire nanny, whose accent he could mimic perfectly. But childhood penury had instilled an obsessive sense of economy: nothing was to be wasted or thrown away that could still be used. And early adversity had helped him throw off much of the snobbishness of his father's class, the landed gentry. His character was strongly egalitarian. Even years later, when he was a senior officer in the army, his men said that Lionel Page treated everyone the same, from private to brigadier.

During his childhood there were occasional visits to his father's family. Sepia photographs from the period show a small boy and his mother visiting the large Page farms. The Pages, solidly grouped, stand beside several large beautiful horses – the family was a strong supporter of the Essex Hunt, and Page became a keen horseman. He attended Fairseat School in Kent for some years,[7] and when he was thirteen, in 1897, the Page relatives paid for him to attend Berkhamsted School for Boys in Hertfordshire for the next six years.

Founded in 1541, the school had achieved a fine reputation by the late nineteenth century for its training in classics and its strong discipline. In 1892 the headmaster, Dr Thomas C. Fry, instituted a Cadet Corps in which the students were trained in arms and participated in a field day at Aldershot.[8] Page liked Berkhamsted, where he acquired some military skills, including map reading and orientation (which he later taught his daughter Pat). On graduating, he longed to join the cavalry; but when he wrote the stiff exams for the Royal Military College at Sandhurst, he failed. Candidates frequently did fail, but the young Page could not wait another year to try again – his mother's finances presumably would not permit it. Luckily, another opportunity beckoned.

Before the turn of the century the governor general of Canada, the Marquess of Lorne, had sent back glowing accounts of Canada's fertile prairies, "God's country." In 1901–02 Dr Fry established a branch of the school, called Berkhamsted Farm, in Red Deer, near Calgary. The farm was intended to train graduates of Berkhamsted School to homestead on the prairies, and in the spring of 1903 a group of the school's young graduates, Lionel Page included, embarked for Canada.

Despite a rail link and incorporation in 1901, the settlement of Red Deer was in the backwoods, with a population of less than two hundred. The Blackfoot, the local Native people, were a strong presence, and except for a few houses and municipal buildings, most settlers lived some distance from their neighbours in log houses with sod roofs and bare mud floors. At Berkhamsted Farm, conditions were only somewhat better. The main house – a two-storey wood frame with a wide verandah – was converted to accommodate prospective students, with dormitory cubicles for eight men. They cleaned barns, tended to the horses and cows, and learned to sow crops and harvest. Canada must have been a bitter cultural shock. But as the students became proficient, they received a small stipend.

Most, like Page, stayed for only a year and then staked a claim to a tract of land. Page settled on land two miles east of Red Deer Post Office, for which he paid $25 per acre, which suggests that he had come into some family money. Like many bachelor settlers, he decided to become a rancher rather than a homesteader because the soil was poor and it was easier for a man to get started in a small way on a ranch than on a farm. The custom was to put up a shack and corrals but to allow the cattle and horses to range for miles around.[9] Page, a superb horseman, could break and train wild horses and breed them, and he had good relations with the Sarcee people, from whom he obtained ponies or "cayuses." Even so, it was a difficult and lonely life, especially for a cultivated young man, and before long he was desperate to return to England. He bought a one-way ticket, but (he told his children) no sooner had he arrived in England than he knew he had to get back to Canada.[10] Without a profession or independent means, he had no place in a class-dominated society; and, equally likely, he missed the freedom of the Canadian prairies. In any event, he returned to the ranch at Red Deer. Later, in 1907, he brought his mother Augusta to the settlement.

There are scattered references to the young man, now twenty-three, playing cricket on the Pine Lake team, and joining up as a voluntary trooper in 1907 with the 15th Canadian Light Horse. That same year he attended summer training for the military at Sarcee Camp near Calgary, close to the Sarcee Reserve, a landscape that was to shape his daughter's imagination. The 15th Canadian Light Horse was later replaced by the 35th Central Alberta Horse, Non-Permanent Active Militia, and Page

Lionel Page as a homesteader, Red Deer, Alberta.

became a reserve officer, receiving his first commission in December 1911. He was finally getting closer to the cavalry, the profession he had wanted.

In 1912, because of a tremendous land boom in Red Deer, Page sold the ranch at a profit but retained his mother's house. He then went into partnership with C.H. Chapman, and they later purchased a building that was operated as a garage. Page recognized that the automobile would soon replace the horse, but he made his move a little too early. A depression intervened and land prices fell. By February 1914 the partnership was dissolved and his finances took a dive. Lionel Page was now almost thirty. He was a forthright, attractive man, tall and dark-haired, at ease with all kinds of people and part of an active social circle. It was in Red Deer, probably in the spring of 1914, that he met Rose Laura Whitehouse, a charming Englishwoman a year younger. She was visiting

Rose Page as a young woman.

her brother Frank, the manager of the local Imperial Bank of Commerce. Rose had classic features with a beautiful mouth, grey eyes, and long chestnut hair. She looked, as her daughter fondly recalled, like the heroine in a romance novel.

Rose was spontaneous, affectionate, and amusing – if a little spoiled – the product of a finishing school in Switzerland and an artistic family. Her grandfather had made money in the silk trade; but her father, Robert Whitehouse, was more interested in collecting *objets d'art* than in maintaining the family business. As a result, his children – four boys and two girls – were obliged to make their own way. The bank manager was the oldest son, Frank. Next came Beatrice ("Bibbi"), a bluestocking, who completed the requirements for a degree at Cambridge in the 1890s when so few women did (women were denied the degree until the 1920s). She trained as a nurse to earn her living. A middle son, Robert,

Patty Page as a baby with her mother Rose.

distributed little Blue Books – cheap, portable editions of popular classics – and was a part-time singer in the D'Oyly Carte Opera Company.
Two younger brothers left England for careers in Australia and India,
respectively. Rose was the cosseted and highly protected baby of the
family, subject to injunctions from her siblings that "Baby couldn't" and
"Baby shouldn't." Undoubtedly, she had been sent to Canada to contract a good marriage. Perhaps because of this, her brother Frank (who
as bank manager knew the state of Lionel Page's overdraft) forbade the
match.[11] But despite his objections, "Baby could" and, before her return
to England, Rose and Lionel became secretly engaged.

When the First World War broke out in August 1914, Page promptly
joined up. On 21 August 1914 he left for Valcartier Camp, Quebec, with
the volunteers of the first Canadian contingent. Page, together with the
"beloved Padré" of Quebec, Canon F.G. Scott (the father of poet F.R.
Scott), embarked for England with the First Division of the Canadian

Expeditionary Force. By October he was confirmed as a lieutenant with the 5th Battalion in the second brigade that went to France. He was a natural leader – intelligent, courageous, unpretentious, and at ease with his men in a period when the norm with officers was a stuffy superiority. His first major engagement was at St Julien in April 1915 where, despite heavy casualties to the battalion, it was reported that "he deserved great credit for his coolness during the battle."[12] In June 1915 he was promoted to captain and given command of a squadron. With his position as an officer assured, Page could now pay formal court to Rose Whitehouse. Not surprisingly, her parents approved, and on 17 September they were married in Swanage, Dorset.

Their first child, Patricia Kathleen, was born on 23 November 1916. A year later, in anticipation of their baby's first birthday, Page wrote to her from the battlefront. He had three wishes for his daughter: that she would have "many, many happy" birthdays; that she would make "as dear and loving a wife to some poor devil as your Mother has to me"; his final wish was for "love, health & happiness."[13] A month earlier, in October, Page had a brush with death when he was gassed at the battle of Valenciennes. Perhaps fearing that he might not make it through the war, he began to jot a series of admonitory verses for his daughter:

> When things are bad, when life is black,
> Be sure a LOVE you never lack;
> For it will make your life quite bright,
> So hold it just as tight as tight.[14]

He sent a number of these verses to Rose, who transcribed them on rag paper and illustrated them with watercolours; she then sewed the pages together as a little book. The Whitehouse family explained Rose's gift for drawing by saying that Sir John Tenniel, the original illustrator of *Alice in Wonderland*, was a distant relative.[15]

Rose and Lionel Page called the book "Wisdom from Nonsense Land," suggesting an *Alice in Wonderland* connection, but the little book could just as easily have been called "Wisdom from No-Man's Land." Perhaps ensuring against the possibility that he might not return, Lionel wrote verses that embodied a Victorian code of behaviour for his daughter, spelling out the "beasts" that she should avoid ("The Greed," "The Measle," "The Temper") and the virtues that she should seek ("The Joy," "The Smile," and "The Love"). "The Joy" was illustrated with a smiling sun, under which was a gamboling, rosy-cheeked little girl. The child's round face, curly hair, and billowing white frock is similar to early photographs of their daughter.[16] Each night, as Rose put Patty to bed, she read from this book. The toddler soon began to pick up rhymes and, before she could speak clearly, would insist upon taking her little book to bed at night instead of a doll or teddy bear.[17]

⚏

Lionel Page returned from the Great War as a hero. Late in 1916 he had been appointed commanding officer of the 50th Battalion, and on 1 January 1917 he was awarded the Distinguished Service Order. His later outstanding service, while in command of a battalion, was recognized with two bars to his DSO, which meant that he had been awarded this high honour on three separate occasions. He was also mentioned in dispatches five times for valour.

In May 1919 Page and his family sailed from Liverpool to Halifax on a troopship, the *Empress of Britain*. Rose was the only woman on board and Patty the only child. A photograph, since lost, showed the girl scribbling on the ship with chalk, with a sign around her neck saying, PLEASE DO NOT FEED THIS CHILD. Many of the men, starved for family life, had wanted to share their chocolate with the toddler, and Rose, who had watched her daughter becoming plump, had taken decisive action.[18] The voyage, the complicated process of demobilization at Halifax, and the final journey by train to Alberta – Page travelled with his men – took almost two months. As their train drew into Red Deer on 11 July, the station was emblazoned with a large banner reading "PAGE'S HEROES." City officials gave the returning men and their leader a hero's welcome. "Red Deer turned out en masse on Friday afternoon … to welcome home Lt. Col. L.F. Page D.S.O. … commander of the 50th Battalion."[19] The mayor presented bouquets of roses to Page's mother, to his wife, and to "Miss Patricia Page, the charming little two-year old daughter of Col. & Mrs. Page."

The following weeks and months were difficult. Lionel Page had made a fortune in Canada – $25,000 on his homestead – but had invested his money in ventures that failed. He was now forced to drive a cab.[20] After five years serving with conspicuous gallantry at the front, Page had a wife and daughter but no job. On one occasion the family was so destitute that Page looked for a cow near the road and milked it to get milk for his daughter.[21] The realities of life on the Canadian prairies must have been a rude shock to the hitherto protected Rose.

The family stayed in Red Deer for nearly a year, but as their position did not improve Page decided to join Canada's permanent forces. He signed up with Lord Strathcona's Horse in Calgary on 1 April 1920. The

"Straths," as they were known, had a long tradition of fine horseman-ship and bravery. The regiment was divided into two squadrons, A and B, and because Page joined in Calgary, rather than in Winnipeg, he became a member of B Squadron.

⚌

When the Page family arrived in Calgary, it was still a frontier town, but already it was developing as a centre of commerce. Wheat fields stretched to the east, large ranches to the south and west, and still farther west, the oil wells of the Turner Valley. With a south wind, the child could smell oil. In twenty years, Calgary had grown from a little cow town of 4,000 to a city of 63,000. Many of the farmers and ranchers who now lived on the land were newcomers, "their imaginations caught by a world of lim-itless grassland wrapped in a light as clear as cellophane."[22]

The Pages were of course among the newcomers. When Lionel Page came "on strength" with Lord Strathcona's Horse in June 1920, he did so with the nominal rank of lieutenant-colonel, the rank that he had won during the war. But his actual rank was now major, and he received a major's wages of two to three dollars a day. As there was no regimental housing available, the family first moved into a boarding house called The Maverick, at 310 – 6th Avenue West. A "maverick" was a steer that wouldn't run with the herd, literally an outsider – as were most people staying at the boarding house. There were several expatriate English peo-ple, including Katherine Shaw, a war widow who had come to Canada to be near her sister May Bates and her husband William. As "Auntie Kit" and "Auntie May" they soon became close to the Page family. Another guest was Chief Buffalo Long Lance (Sylvester Clarke, who was part American, part Cree). He had come to Canada in 1916 and was now working as a reporter for the *Calgary Herald*.[23] The child was delighted with Long Lance and with the baskets he brought home: "Little sweet grass baskets woven by the Indians which I can smell to this day – the ecstasy of putting my nose into one of those little baskets!"[24]

P.K. Page's strongest memories of her childhood were of the Sarcee Camp. Each summer the men of Lord Strathcona's Horse joined the other army regiments in military exercises near the Sarcee Reserve and the foothills, just south of Calgary. There the men lived in tents, under-taking manoeuvres and training horses purchased from the Sarcee Band. Unlike the other military wives who stayed comfortably at home with the children, Rose Page packed up her daughter, her leather travelling case with its beautifully fitted silver brushes, and joined her husband under canvas for several weeks each year. P.K. remembered being lifted onto a horse. This moment was caught in a photograph "of my mother in a big hat, looking very elegant, and my father in uniform, and me as brown as a nut, and a whole string of people ... at Sarcee Camp."[25] A small child's perception of a horse is expressed in a late autobiographical poem, "The First Part":

> Horse. High as a house. Smooth as a nut.
> Its flaring nostrils snorted dragon's breath
> or snuffled, tickling. Its velvet lips
> lifted the accurate white sugar lump
> exactly from my flat extended palm.
> And crunch. The curving yellowish ivory teeth.[26]

On one such trip Patty contracted dysentery from eating the Saskatoon berries she had picked off the bushes. She became delirious with a fever and she was taken to hospital. Just after her return, she made a drawing with two shaky figures, which her mother later included in a second little book. Below the drawing, in her mother's handwriting, are the words "DONE 1/2 AN HOUR AFTER COMING OUT OF HOSPTIAL STILL SO SHAKY!"[27]

Patty was now helping to make her own books. Her parents read her nursery rhymes, such as "Higglety-Pigglety My Black Hen," which the child then drew. One morning, when her mother was out and her father was looking after her, he seems to have explained that the garden was beautiful because everyone worked to make it so. Patty drew a picture of a house and a garden in which four people – a mother, a father, and two children – all stand around, each holding a gardening tool. Again, her mother gathered the drawings and some verses into a booklet. She also traced some of Patty's drawings – highly precocious for a child of her age – and used them as the pattern for an embroidered sampler, where one of the captions said, echoing the father's moral, "And the reason they had such a *beautiful* garden was because they all worked so VERY hard in it."[28] This needlework is dated 1920 when Patty was four. The father's lesson and the mother's illustration instilled in their daughter's mind a strong sense of responsibility and may have encouraged her vocation as a writer and artist. On another occasion her mother said, "Patty, you can do anything you set your mind to do."[29]

During the winter evenings around the fire, Lionel Page read fairy tales to his daughter from the Brothers Grimm and Hans Christian Andersen.[30] Patty's imagination quickened early. Auntie Kit gave her a wonderful French doll with an embroidered face: she was dressed in satins with a marzipan cherry tucked into her belt. "I loved it – reservedly at first – but as time went on, I grew uneasy with it, frightened even … until I began to think it was alive, and mischievous, if not evil." Eventually, the highly imaginative child refused to have anything to do with the doll. Her mother suggested that she eat the marzipan cherry, but she had never tasted almond paste and it was "bitter made to seem sweet … One bite and I was sure I was poisoned."[31] Aside from echoes of Snow White and the poisoned apple, the evil doll remained a resonant theme, and P.K. Page later wrote of it in a short story.

Through Auntie Kit the Page family came to know the extended Bates family. Auntie May's husband, William Bates, an architect who was to help shape the development of Calgary, had come from Bedford, England, at the invitation of the Calgarian Gilbert Hodgson, with whom Bates set up the firm Hodgson and Bates.[32] They were part of a sophisticated group of English immigrants who brought with them a way of life that Lionel and Rose Page understood. The Bates and Pages visited often, and on some nights Patty was taken over to the Bates's house and put to bed upstairs. Sometimes the adults played mah-jong, but more often they spent the evening carving oak furniture, a hobby they all enjoyed. The Pages were furnishing their house, making stools and chests from quarter-cut oak, and the designs they carved were often *art nouveau* from the pages of *The Studio*. Rose, "claiming that she was too stupid to copy – ('all my brain is my fingers') – drew her own [designs], and attacked her oak with a bravado and flourish none of the others ever matched. They were all good carvers, but her style was different – more impressionistic, freer."[33]

After several months at The Maverick, the Pages moved into the upper floor of a duplex on the other side of town. Patty loved this flat because her parents kept chickens and she was allowed to feed them. Soon she was drawing pictures of chickens in a row. Then, in the fall of 1922, the family rented a small bungalow, one of three in a row, owned by "Uncle Bill" Bates, at 1411 – 7th Street West. Like many children without siblings, Patty had an imaginary playmate. Her mother's later stories about her childhood led her to wonder if perhaps she had pre-birth experiences. "Psychologists [would] say, 'Oh lonely child, just inventing something herself.' But we don't know that … I may actually have had an imaginative playmate. Mother said that I lifted her up on to chairs and strained – she could see my muscles straining to lift this creature; it quite frightened Mother … the realness of that imaginary creature. She felt that she ought to be able to see her if I had to strain to lift her."[34]

Rose was always alert to the psychic. She also loved jokes, had a good singing voice, and made life amusing for the family.[35] She had an incredible memory for words and rhythms and she could recite anything – from nonsense verses to Shakespeare – and frequently did. Elizabeth Wordsworth's "Good and Clever," with its wry observation about the way clever people treat good people, is typical of the quotations she sometimes declaimed:[36]

> But somehow, 'tis seldom or never
>   The two hit it off as they should,
> The good are so harsh to the clever,
>   The clever, so rude to the good![37]

Rose may have had some personal sense of the harshness of "the good," for the Pages were not part of the Anglican churchgoing English society that dominated the military base; and Rose, who loved parties, was considered "very social" – meaning she was thought to drink a little too much on social occasions. At the same time, she was very athletic and played badminton well enough to be an exhibition player in Calgary.

In 1923 Rose's sister Bibbi, a qualified nurse, came from England to help out, for Rose was expecting a second child. Michael was born on 22 July. His birth changed the dynamics of the family. Patty was now a big sister who was expected to help look after the baby. A year later, the family celebrated Michael's first birthday on the beach at Willow Point, on Kootenay Lake, in the southeastern interior of British Columbia near Nelson. They were visiting Uncle Frank Whitehouse, who had a vacation home there. To Patty it seemed like heaven because Calgary in the summer was so hot – everything burnt dry. There were fields of grass and an orchard of apple trees as well as the lake. "It was lovely. My mother lost … a gold watch that my father had given her and she was desolate. We all looked and she offered a prize for anyone who got it. I remember finding it."[38] During this visit, Patty also found several beautiful pieces of coloured quartz, but she had to surrender them to one of her cousins, her uncle believing that her cousins owned the quartz because it was found on their property.

This painful story is told in "The First Part," in which the watch becomes a ring. It recurs in a late short story called "Crayons," where a mother and daughter visit the mother's sister at a lake. The child narrator finds several pieces of beautiful quartz – one green, another white streaked with red – which one of her cousins claims, screaming, "Mine,

mine!" The girl's uncle pronounces judgment: "They are ours. If you found them here, they are ours … give them to Beth."[39] The girl's reaction is revealing. She is at first furiously angry but learns to transmute the experience. She picks up a black crayon and covers a sheet of paper until not one spot of white shows. Then she takes a piece of coloured paper and her white crayon and draws a white stone. "By mixing the blue and the green crayons she got nearly the right blue – almost exactly right. Then she made the stone with the green. She was beginning to work on the red when her mother joined her." In effect, the child in the story re-possesses the quartz through her art. The mother in the story looks at the drawings for a long time: "They're beautiful, darling … they are a work of art. Perhaps one day you will be an artist."[40]

When Patty was nearly seven, in September 1923, she was enrolled at St Hilda's, an Anglican school for girls on 12th Avenue South West. The school was named for Hilda, the seventh-century English abbess of Whitby, whose work was associated with education for young women. The Pages sent their daughter there because St Hilda's offered sports and drama programs, and the Calgary public schools did not. But they also continued to educate their children at home. When Michael was old enough to understand, the parents read to both children – "the Dr. Dolittle books … and the *Just So Stories* of Kipling. Or we played the old wind-up gramophone and listened to Irish songs: 'Cockles and Mussels,' or 'She is far from the land where her young hero sleeps.'" And they all sang. In the winter months, when theatrical companies from England performed *Peter Pan* or *Charley's Aunt*, the whole family went downtown by streetcar to attend the theatre with family friends and other children.[41]

In October 1924 Lionel was promoted and transferred to Winnipeg. Major Lionel Page was now second-in-command of Lord Strathcona's Horse. Pat was nearly eight when the family arrived in Winnipeg on 3 November, and they were stationed there for almost four years. The landscape of Winnipeg was largely flat when compared with that of Calgary and the foothills, and the city itself was highly industrialized. The Pages were in residence at Fort Osborne, 14 Tuxedo Barracks, and family life was much the same as it had been in Calgary, except that their flat now smelled of shoe polish, Brasso, and cigars, thanks to Lionel's batman who polished his boots and buttons and cleaned his Sam Browne belt. But the barracks, constructed during the First World War, were so shoddily built that cigar smoke wafted between the flats and, on one occasion, a tenant's leg went through the floor into the ceiling of the flat below. P.K. Page wrote a story about this, "The Neighbour," changing the characters from middle to lower class for, as she reasoned, who could believe that army officers lived in such conditions?[42]

Patty loved the barracks. In wintertime, she and her friends could jump out the kitchen window onto a flat roof and slide down to the snow below. Just across were the stables. To get to school – River Heights Elementary, where she was in grade 2 – she had to take a streetcar. The barracks were at the end of the line, where the streetcar made a loop and then went back again. On the way to the school she had to pass an orphanage: going, it was on the left; returning, it was on the right. Patsy, as she was known at school, always sat on the opposite side from the orphanage, trying not to think of children without parents.[43] Perhaps because of Lionel Page's storytelling, Patsy could not bear the Grimm brothers' "Hansel and Gretel" and screamed when her father attempted to read it – she agonized over the thought of brother and sister orphaned and alone in the forest. She also worried about Hans Andersen's "Ugly Duckling," who was ridiculed and ignored, and she was chilled by Andersen's story "The Snow Queen," which told of little Kay with a splinter of ice in his heart and of the enduring love of Gerda, who saved him. On the other hand, *Alice in Wonderland* attracted the whole family, partly because of the reputed family connection with Tenniel but also because of the wonderful absurdity of the tale: the nonsense, the humour, and – as Alice's story continued in *Through the Looking Glass* – the punning verse that Rose Page loved to quote.

The Pages managed to maintain a welcoming home, even in a ramshackle military barracks, and on the children's birthdays Lionel and Rose gave wonderful parties. There was "Pin the Tail on the Donkey" – a donkey that Rose had painted. And Lionel performed magic tricks. "One consisted of his slow, patient, filling of a glass with cigarette smoke until it was dense enough to pour like lazy cream into another glass. And, most wonderful of all, performed on the bravest of us, the 'operation,' that made us into babies again."[44] The adult P.K. Page did not explain this curious game, apparently a birthing ritual, but it reverberates in her late fiction.[45]

Patty's mother provided a home that was aesthetically appealing; her father introduced her to the larger world and her responsibility in it. At age eight or nine she walked through a puddle in her new shoes, a natural thing for a child to do. But the family had little extra money and she had ruined a good pair of shoes. Her father sat down with her, not crossly but seriously, and spoke to her at length about "selfishness" – the repercussions of her action would be less money for the family to buy things that

Patty the tomboy with her father Lionel and brother Michael.

were badly needed.[46] Fathers, then as now, did not usually talk to their children in this fashion. But this was Lionel Page's manner, and Patty responded by becoming more and more responsible.

It may have been during the winter of 1925 that a terrible fire occurred in the stables just across the street from the barracks where the family lived. It broke out in the middle of the night, and Rose woke her daughter to get dressed and join the bucket brigade helping the wives hand up water to the men who were fighting the fire. Patty never forgot that night: she was trembling with excitement as well as terror. The roof of their flat was tarpaper, and despite the snowy weather there were large sparks overhead. Perhaps the barracks would catch fire! "At the end you could hear the horses whinnying, the most terrible, terrible sound as horses in the fire rushed back into flames."[47] Fire was traumatic in her prairie childhood: "You'd see a prairie fire coming across – at night you would see the whole horizon – red, and you could see it coming closer and closer, and this was a very, very scary thing to me."[48] She was born under a fire sign, Sagittarius, and attributed to this the fact that she was subject to high fevers when young. If she was delirious and had a fever, she couldn't distinguish between dreams and reality. "I would tell people things that had happened in my dreams and they would think I was a liar."[49]

She began to learn to ride in Winnipeg around 1925–26 and was put through the riding-school drill by Olive Brown, the wife of one of the officers in Strathcona Horse, who was an accomplished rider.[50] Patty became a reasonably good horsewoman. At about this time Lionel decided to teach his wife to ride. Early in March 1926, however, Rose fell off her horse, striking her head. Michael, at the riding track with his parents and only three, still remembers looking into his mother's riding helmet and seeing it filled with blood.[51] Patty was at home, and she witnessed her father's panic as he banged on the front door of their apartment, attempting to get to the telephone to call the doctor. Rose had suffered a severe concussion, and Lionel took time off work (then practically unheard of) to nurse his wife. His response to the accident was a revelation to his daughter. "I think he loved Mother more than he loved us ... And when she fell on her head, the one thing that was important was that she be looked after."[52]

It is curious how family dynamics become established. For the Whitehouse family, Rose was the "baby." Bibbi, eight years older, always took responsibility for her, and indeed felt this way up to the moment of Rose's death. Rose herself escaped some of the responsibilities of adulthood because when Lionel married her he assumed the Whitehouse family attitude, which he passed on to his daughter. Entirely selfless himself, he didn't want selfish children, so he expected a great deal of his oldest child. And because Patty was big for her age, even more was expected of her. She was given the task of looking after her younger brother. But Michael was quicksilver, an active three-year-old continually wanting to explore. Unfortunately, his mother's accident came just as he was learning to talk. Because he had a speech defect and couldn't say consonants, he spoke in a series of vowels – e-a-a-e-o – and since Rose was an invalid, she didn't learn his early language. Only her daughter could translate: "Patty dear, what did he say?" Patty was expected to keep the boy quiet so that he didn't disturb his mother – a difficult task in a small apartment.[53]

As Rose slowly began to recover from her concussion, it was decided that she and the children should return to England to stay with her family until she was totally well again. The regimental records indicate that Lionel Page was granted a separation allowance for absence from his family between 31 May and 4 October 1926, which suggests that Rose and the children were away from Canada a little over four months. The ocean voyage was hair-raising because Patty was terrified that Michael, climbing everywhere, would fall overboard and drown. She also experienced several serious asthmatic attacks when she had to struggle for air. By the time the family reached Southampton, she was at breaking-point.

She found an oasis with her mother's Whitehouse family. They lived in the village of Romsey, near Southampton, and the house was almost in the country, near a river. Shortly after the Pages arrived, someone brought a newspaper into the house that smelled strongly of printer's ink, setting off Patsy's asthma and leading to hysterics when she couldn't breathe.[54] The family quickly recognized that it was too much responsibility (not just newspaper ink) that bothered the child. They cosseted her. The grandmother fed her calf's-foot jelly and put her to bed, and the grandfather spent a great deal of time reading with her. Most importantly, with Michael tended by others, Patty could relax and become a child again.

She now spent time with her grandparents, both then eighty-two. Their house in Romsey, Hampshire, was filled with Robert Whitehouse's collection of fine books and paintings, and with the dark carved-oak furniture that he had inherited from his father. A painting that Patty particularly loved was "one of those old Dutch Masters of flowers where the dew on the petals of the rose is so exquisitely done, a great enormous painting."[55] At this time of his life, her grandfather was mostly bald and rather stooped, often wearing a smoking jacket. He and Patty spent much time together in the library at a big table that was covered in green velour. They would lay on it the book that interested them and go through it together. Often the book was from his collection on natural history – a work of art in itself, with gold-embossed cover and gilt edges, and printed on India paper. Everything in the house fascinated Patty and helped shape her aesthetic sensibility.

Her grandmother was something of a mystery: "taller than her children, blond and blue-eyed and aristocratic looking. She was clearly powerful – and darling. She encouraged me. If I drew anything she'd always look at it and say, 'It's sweetly pretty dear, it's sweetly pretty.'" According to her birth certificate, the grandmother, Rosina Spriss, was the daughter of a shipwright, or ship's carpenter. This suggests a working-class family. Their granddaughter believed that Robert had been "knocked sideways" by Rosina's beauty.[56]

By September 1926, Rose was feeling a great deal better and the family was ready to go back to Canada, which they did in early October. They stayed in Winnipeg for three months until, in late December, Lionel learned that he had been selected to take additional officers' training at Sheerness, Kent, indicating that he was in line for a large promotion. It was decided that the whole family would return to England, with Rose and the children going to Romsey.

The family moved out of the officers' quarters at Fort Osborne on the day before Christmas in 1927 and sailed from Halifax early in the New Year. On the ship, Patty's anxiety about her identity was activated – the fear that she was adopted. She was on deck, walking with her father, when a fellow passenger exclaimed, "My God, that child looks like you." Patty found the comment strange. Wasn't it reasonable for a child to look like her father? "The fact that this is so extraordinary," she thought, "must mean I'm adopted." When she told her mother, Rose attempted to dissuade her: "Darling you weren't adopted, you came right out of my tummy"; but she added, "Even if you had been adopted, it would have meant we had chosen you specially." This reassurance was no comfort, and throughout her childhood Patty was haunted by doubts.[57]

Everything was fuel to her obsession. "And it wasn't that I wanted to be adopted, as some children, you know, think they must be a changeling because they can't belong to these parents. That wasn't the reason. It was a dread that those weren't my real parents." It may have been about this time that she was reading a children's book that she later recalled as her all-time favourite: *A Little Princess; or What Happened at Miss Minchin's* – a story about an orphan. Patty had one strong point of reference with the story. "Sara's father, Captain Crewe, was a soldier, whom I loved extravagantly. My father, too, was a soldier, whom I loved extravagantly." When Sara's father lost his fortune and she became a charity child, "My heart broke." But when her garret was "magically transformed into a haven of warmth and plenty, my heart was healed again."[58]

The question of identity continued to plague Patty during this second visit to Romsey. She recalls growing up half-believing she was Jewish: "Certainly you could imagine that my mother and my aunt were both Jewish, it's not impossible, with the dark eyes … And my grandfather had that same look – dark eyes, long nose, and when he was an old man he used to wear a skull cap."[59] When her mother said this was not the case, she was greatly disappointed. Her explanation as an adult was that she had been "in love with the exotic" as a child. She had seen a gypsy encampment when the family first arrived in England, and she was enormously attracted. "Mother used to think she'd have to chain me up or I'd run away to join the gypsies. So whatever foreign flavour was in the air captivated me."[60]

On this visit to England, Patty was sent to a school called the Parents National Educational Union, or PNEU. It had been started by a group of Englishmen who either sent their children home from overseas or wanted a curriculum for study when abroad. These schools were progressive. There was no classroom by grade, and children were placed in a room according to their age so that their social development was among their peers. If a student was bright, he or she advanced to new work but still stayed in the same classroom. It was also an egalitarian school. The teacher had no desk but circulated among the students, who received individual attention. There were no restrictions on talking, but whispering was considered "not friendly," because it excluded others. There was no homework until students became desperate to learn, as Patty did. Only then would the teacher say, "Why don't you look up such-and-such book in the library?"[61]

Students were encouraged to explore the community, and Patty became particularly interested in the river near their house in Romsey. There she first learned how a water plant has an immense structure to keep it afloat – either endless filaments, which spread out and make a kind of carpet underneath it, or little bladders. When she found a plant or flower, she would bring it to her grandfather, and they would look it up in a reference book. He would tell her the Latin name and she would paint a sketch of the plant.[62] A sketchbook Patty kept dated 1927 includes botanical sketches of a rose, purple clover, and a thistle, each captioned with its Latin name.

PNEU was a wonderful experience, the only school Patty ever really loved.[63] For the first time she was learning how to gain knowledge. The school was both a system and a philosophy of education, with the credo "Children are born persons. They are not born either good or bad, but with possibilities for good and for evil." The chief responsibility of the students as persons was "the acceptance or rejection of ideas."[64] It is tempting to speculate on the degree to which this early training fostered the mature P.K. Page's great independence of mind and her capacity to research a subject. More importantly, her childhood experiences fostered the development of her literary and artistic imagination.

Shortly after the Pages returned to Canada in late summer 1928, Lionel was promoted to the rank of colonel of Lord Strathcona's Horse and was stationed at Calgary, in charge of both A and B Companies. He had been an honorary, or brevet, colonel since he joined the Straths. But now, after formal officers' training at Sheerness and the approval of his new appointment, this rank became official in 1929.

CHAPTER 2

Calgary
Intimations, 1928–1934

Backdrop: the cordillera of the Rockies.
Infinity – slowly spinning in the air –
invisibly entered through the holes of gophers,
visibly, in wigwam's amethyst smoke.

Eternity implicit on the prairie.
One's self the centre of a boundless dome …
P.K. Page, "The First Part"[1]

The Pages returned to Calgary early in September 1928, in time to establish themselves again at 7th Street West and for Patsy (as she was called at school) to enrol again at St Hilda's. England had broadened her aesthetic sense, and her English school, PNEU, had both stimulated her and shown her how she might acquire knowledge on her own. During the next five years in Calgary she glimpsed a larger world beyond the family and began to feel the pull of the artistic life.

Her first sense of the widening world was provided by the Bates family, at 13th Avenue S.W., where the living-room floor was covered with a beautiful peacock-blue carpet. Tea was always served to the women in the bow window, while the children read magazines or played the piano. There were four Bates offspring, including Max, who was in his early twenties and became an artist, and Cynthia, who became Patsy's friend. There was a scene at the Bates's house that imprinted itself on Patsy's memory – the garden casting a green light through the living-room window while, sitting among the cups and saucers, were her mother, Auntie May (Bates), and Auntie Kit, whose shingled hair, bright lipstick, and cigarettes made them look like flappers. Patsy always focused on her mother, with her lovely aquiline face, light-brown eyes, and chestnut hair.[2] The house had been designed by Uncle Bill, and the Page family thought it had been built with special attention to the Bates's physical shortness. When Patsy had been younger, the proportions seemed just right, but now she had outgrown the rooms: "[A]s I sprang up tall in my teens, in their living room I felt like Tenniel's drawing of Alice after she had drunk from the bottle labelled 'Drink Me.'"[3]

About 1929, when Patsy was thirteen, Max Bates visited the Pages for a week or two at Sarcee Camp, where the regiment went each summer. The bush clearing where the family camped was on the edge of the Sarcee Reserve and overlooked a deep gully that led down to a narrow fast-running river, the only break in a landscape of dun-coloured foothills leading to the Rockies. Before the snow was off the ground, the Pages had already been picnicking there taking home prairie crocuses, and once school was over in June they moved into the bush and pitched their tents.[4] In previous years, they had lived under canvas, but now Lionel proposed that they build a wooden shack with tarpaper and shingles so that they could have a permanent extra room. Patsy helped, nailing in the shingles that she could reach. The family swam in the muddy river at the foot of the steep embankment. They sang around a bonfire at night, and during the day they searched for puffballs and explored a nearby dump.

Max was short, stocky, and sandy-haired; Patsy associated his voice with an "angry bee." Under Rose's direction they were soon undertaking mosaics. At the dump, Rose, Max, and Patsy collected coloured glass: "gorgeous colours – rich peaty brown, 'eye-glass' blue, deep amber yellow, blood-red, green; and the opaque white or patterned bits of broken pottery."[5] They made their mosaics by imbedding the glass on leftover shingles spread with clay from the riverbed. Max made bizarre figures prefiguring the Beggar Kings featured in his later oil paintings. Years later, when Maxwell Bates was a well-known artist, he spoke of Rose Page's influence on his early artistic development.[6]

As days of unending blue skies followed one another, the family rode for miles across unfenced prairie. Occasionally the Native people came to visit, brown under their black sombreros, asking about lost horses or bringing a cayuse to sell. Most of the children rode cayuses, and Patsy's was called Zena. One of her most poignant early experiences had come a few years earlier when she and her father were riding across the open prairie. "I remember on one of those rides seeing a small box on a hillside and dismounting, finding the skeleton of what must have been an Indian papoose, tiny bead bracelets around its wrists, a string of wampum brilliant against the bleached bones of its ribs and small scraps of discoloured cloth."[7]

In her poem "The First Part," P.K. Page describes a child riding with her father, the wind and rain, the gleam of spurs, and the jingle of bridles:

the grave-box, lidless, open
where we rode:
string figure in bangles and rags.
Small corpse picked to the bone.

The child of the poem feels a death within herself: "Dusk fell. / In all my cells dusk fell. / My shroud or winding sheet." What she longs for is protection against "this prairie eye / that stares and stares." She wants to be hidden, to be held, to be comforted by her father, who rides alongside:

O hide me safe
in cleft or coulee
fold me
in leaves or blowing
grasses.
Hold me.
Hold me.[8]

It was less than a decade since Lionel Page had fought on the battlefields of Europe, and an older P.K. Page believed that he had intended her to recognize the hard realities of life, including death.[9] Furthermore, Lionel expected Patsy, rather than her mother, to shoulder some basic family duties when he was called away. He taught her how to light the gas furnace in their house with long spills of paper, being careful to turn the gas up (but not so far up as to cause an explosion). Little by little she was encouraged to take on more responsibility, possibly because he believed that Rose could not do so.

Not long after Patsy was enrolled once again at St Hilda's, she was hospitalized with scarlet fever and placed in isolation for about six weeks. Around this time, she was beginning to write for the school magazine, essays such as "A Day's Fishing" (which seems to have taken place in Halifax on their return from England): "ah! at last you see the fish skimming through the water."[10] At the end of 1929 Patsy won the prize for her grade and was seen to be scholarship material; but finances were tight, and her parents wondered if they could afford to let her stay in a private school. But St Hilda's wanted to keep students of high academic standing, and Patsy was offered a special scholarship. In grade 8, which ended in 1931, she is listed as sharing a scholarship for first place; and in grade 9, ending in 1932, she won the Governor's Prize.

During her first year back at St Hilda's she admired the headmistress, Miss Dorothy Cleveland, who had studied at Cambridge like Aunt Bibbi. The following year, 1930–31, was less pleasant. Patsy was bored. There was now a new headmistress, a Miss Sara MacDonald, whom Patsy disliked. Her grades dropped considerably, and she barely scraped through. Rebellion is not surprising for a girl who has been taught at PNEU that the first task of any individual is to think for herself. But her rebellion may have been intensified by continual criticism: "They [her teachers] told me that my power was good, was very great, but I was not using it." Her natural independence asserted itself, and this in turn brought retaliation. She began to be known as a "difficult" student and seems to have rejected much of the academic program.

In fact, Patsy found theatre, sports, and writing much more interesting. She was an active member of the MicMac Basketball Team, took part in a number of school plays, beginning with J.M. Barrie's *Quality Street*, and was president of the Junior Club. She was showing great facility with language. An early essay, "The Autobiography of an Alarm Clock," is written in dialogue ("This 'ere blessed clock 'as stopped again") and was published in the school magazine.[11] But she had become a "smart Alec": a schoolfriend, the former Mary Gravely, remembers that Patsy sometimes answered questions in rhyme.[12] Her reading had broadened and included Gene Stratton-Porter's *A Girl of the Limberlost* (1909), about young Elnora, who was determined to pay for her education by capturing rare moths and butterflies in the Limberlost swamp of Indiana.[13] And she became an avid reader of Zane Grey's romances of the American prairies, with their chivalrous cowboys. All fed into an adolescent romanticism.

Yet she was brave and perceptive. When she was in her early teens and babysitting Michael, Patsy saw a man in the lane outside their house, beckoning her. She was frightened and wanted to run for help, but knew that she couldn't leave Michael. "I went out onto the front porch and screamed bloody murder, as loud as I could for help. And nobody came. But he went. That scared him."[14] On another occasion she and Cynthia Bates were coming home from the Carnegie Public Library. It was winter, there was a small path in the snow, and suddenly a large man pushed by them, shoving Patsy into a nearby hedge while speaking in a threatening manner. Recognizing that he was dangerous, she simply begged his pardon – he allowed them to pass.

The next year Patsy had a strange experience, which she later believed made her receptive to the supranormal. She and her mother were alone in the house with Michael, and her mother called her to look at the neighbour's dining-room window. "And I went in and looked. And I saw this face in the window that was smaller than life size ... the skin tones were greenish where the shadows were – if you'd been painting you'd have had to paint green shadows." The creature had enormous, expressionless dark eyes and very fine hair and was looking straight at them. Patsy was fourteen at that time, almost as big as her mother, but she flung herself into her mother's arms as if she were a child of five: "Oh mummy, I'm frightened, I'm frightened." Rose comforted her, but the next morning they talked about the experience and decided to draw the face they had seen, independently. When they compared drawings they saw that each had drawn "the same creature – these same enormous eyes and this same strange face, and this sort of wispy hair – it was the same creature we saw. We both saw it, whatever it was. And it scared me more than any other thing that has ever happened to me."[15]

Little by little, the sense of a larger world beyond the physical affected Patsy's mind – as it had her mother's. "Mother always used to say ... that my father and she and I had lived together in previous lives, over and over and over again."[16] Rose could see "auras" around people. She was intuitive and possessed the gift of precognition, accurately forecasting events before they happened. This characteristic drove Lionel Page mad. "'No' he would say. 'Old Thing!' – which is what he called her when he was really impatient – 'I don't want to hear that one more time.' And then the damn thing [the event she forecast] did happen right before his eyes, and she'd be proved right.'"[17]

In 1932 the Pages moved to 3802 – 6th Avenue in Calgary. Now that Lionel was colonel of his regiment, the family had a larger house, in a newer residential district near the Elbow River. In mid-November 1932, when she was nearly sixteen, Patsy was woken one night by the sound of her father groaning. Lionel Page never groaned, he never complained, so she knew that something terrible had happened. In fact, he had suffered a major heart attack – totally unexpected. He was taken by ambulance to hospital, and for almost a month the family feared that he would not live. But gradually he improved, and Patsy witnessed a conversation between her mother and father: "What did you think, Lionel, when you thought you were dying?" "All I could think was I couldn't bear to leave you and the children."[18] Early in the New Year of 1933 the couple decided that Lionel would go to Victoria to recuperate; Rose and Michael would accompany him, but she would stay behind as a boarder at St Hilda's for the spring term.

The shock of her father's heart attack was overwhelming, and the separation from her parents seems to have added to her sense of insecurity, making Patsy even more rebellious. She was lonely. To be sure, there were teachers whom she liked, including the vice-principal, Jessie Carter, an Irish woman who taught French. But as a boarder at St Hilda's, Patsy had a nagging sense of being right under the headmistress's critical eye. "And I can remember Mother phoning me from Victoria and asking me if everything was alright. And I said, 'Mother I can't talk now because Miss MacDonald is listening in.'"[19] Patsy was bright enough to take her teacher's measure and angry enough to let her know that she knew – a response that prevailed as she grew older: "Those are the sorts of things I have done all my life that have never done me any good."[20]

When the spring term was over, Patsy was reunited with her parents and brother. She had not been made a prefect – a sure sign of displeasure. It was partly that she continued to go her own way, refusing to obey school strictures. She and her friend Mary Mawer occasionally walked home from school together, up over the hill, stopping at the corner store on 17th Avenue and 8th Street, where for ten cents they could buy a package of Buckingham cigarettes. Pat had begun to smoke, with her father's knowledge, when she was fifteen. But the two girls were seen smoking on the street corner – rebels in the St Hilda's school uniform of tunic and black stockings – and were soon reported to the headmistress.[21]

In the following months, indeed throughout the next year and a half, Patsy seems to have turned to writing – especially verse – to express her feelings. In the next school term she wrote a poem, "On Being Ill," in which she was imaginatively entering into her father's experience of illness (with echoes of Keats): "My feelings are numbed. / Intense drowsiness overcomes me.

My head reels;
Again I fall,
Down, down,
Into that fathomless pit."[22]

She also wrote a long essay in which she took on the character of William Gladstone, the great English liberal prime minister who sponsored Irish Home Rule in the nineteenth century. This essay, which appeared in the school magazine, ended with a flourish when Gladstone gave up his career to be reunited with his family – now "together and happy, and we were"; both the Gladstone family and the Page family are implied in her words.²³ The essay was authored under a new name: Pat Page.

During this time she seems to have acquired a literary mentor in Shelagh Gianelli, the wife of Norman Gianelli, second-in-command of Lord Strathcona's Horse. Mrs Gianelli was kind, witty, and very intelligent. She had a BA from the University of Manitoba, was fluent in French, and loved to quote poetry. She had been a secretary, or "stenographer," and was great fun – a further recommendation to the young Pat. Mrs Gianelli once remarked that "the great key to a woman being able to succeed as a secretary was to be able to type 150 words per minute, look out the window, chew gum, and carry on a coherent conversation." Pat went to the Gianelli house regularly to talk about her writing; at fifteen, she was honorary godmother to Shelagh's daughter, Juliana; still later, she took typing lessons.²⁴

Throughout 1933, as Lionel regained his strength, he read a number of quirky books on time, life, and death: J.W. Dunne's *An Experiment with Time*, which presents time as infinitely flexible, blending the future with the present, and March Cost's *A Man Called Luke*, in which the physician/protagonist is a reincarnated soul.²⁵ Pat read both as soon as her father finished them. Lionel also read a popular war novel of the period, Charles Morgan's *The Fountain* (1932), as did Pat. This book questions the meaning of life and death. The narrator, Lewis Alison, is an airman captured in Holland, who is writing a history of the contemplative life. A "traveller" through life, he affirms that the only way to achieve inner peace – to be "invulnerable" – is to cultivate the spiritual or mystical life. At one point the young airman muses, "Is ... the body an instrument of the soul[?] ... I would say that human love is sometimes of [this] kind."²⁶ Ultimately, in the working out of his destiny, love triumphs. His meditation on spirit and flesh fascinated the adolescent Pat, but what she later recalled of the book was the idea of invulnerability (which suggests that the girl had reason to feel vulnerable): "[T]he only way one could be invulnerable was if you were like water ... [then] no knife could harm you, you healed immediately. A knife entered you, you kept going."²⁷ Many of the concepts that Dunne, Cost, and Morgan articulate – the flexibility of time, reincarnation, the view of man as a traveller, the importance of the spiritual life, the possibility of parallel worlds, and the final affirmation of love – would resonate in Page's later life and poetry. Underlying all was her internalization of *Alice in Won-*

derland and her sense of the parallel worlds to be found down the rabbit hole and through the looking glass.

Pat Page was developing a will and mind of her own. She was now very pretty, with dark hair and creamy skin. She was not keen on parties and although there was one Calgary boy who turned her knees to water, she did not let him know this. She continued to be bored with school, especially grammar classes, in which she read Zane Grey under her desk. Invariably caught and expelled from the class, she spent much of her last year at school underneath the stairs, outside the classroom, still reading. By 1933 she had convinced herself that, like her mother, she was "no scholar" and that she did not care about academic matters. In fact, she cared passionately about knowledge, and did so all her life; it was simply that the knowledge she now sought was not to be found at St Hilda's.

Fortunately, in her last two years in Calgary she found a friend who shared her real interests. Elizabeth Carlile, better known as "Fuzz," had been a student at St Hilda's in 1929 but completed high school at a private school in London, returning in 1933 to Calgary, where her father was an investment banker. Fuzz had made some important artistic contacts in London when visiting a classmate, Merula Salaman. The girl's father, Michel Salaman, was a well-placed impresario who kept an open house, overflowing with paintings and artistic people. Augustus John was a friend, and Merula later married the actor Alec Guinness.[28] Through Merula's parents, Fuzz was introduced to ballet, theatre, and art. She was particularly interested in cubism and pointillism.

Fuzz wanted to become an artist, and when she returned to Calgary she was just as bored and impatient with the city as Pat was. Both girls knew they wanted something more profound, and the Calgary library became their mecca. Together they discovered books introducing "the strange world of Cubist painting, pointillism, Dostoevsky."[29] They read Freud on dreams and books on the artistic life, such as Frances Winwar's *Poor Splendid Wings: The Rossettis and Their Circle* (1934), and they borrowed books illustrating Jacob Epstein's sculptures. Epstein's *Genesis* (1931), that monolithic earth goddess, had just appeared, and Fuzz later studied sculpture at the Slade School of Art in London. But Pat was more interested in the Rossetti book, because it talked about the artistic life: it was "wonderful to read about creative people … to read more about them is the next best thing to knowing them."[30]

The Pages and the Carliles lived on opposite sides of the Elbow River in an area of Calgary called Elbow Park, situated near the open prairie.

During the winter, when the river was frozen, Pat could walk across the ice to the Carliles' house.[31] She particularly loved the chinook, that warm wind that suddenly sweeps over the prairie, turning winter to spring – a "midwinter miracle." "At night, you toss off your bedclothes, suddenly hot. Your ears are filled with the rush of that great embracing wind, for it *is* a great embrace as it fills the night, and you want to run out naked to greet it. The icicles drip from the eaves. By morning, there will be nothing of winter left."[32]

During the late spring and summer, the two girls rode on the prairie and sometimes camped with a group of friends. On one occasion, the group camped on Highwood Ranch in the foothills of the Rockies, a property owned by G.W. Pocaterra, a colourful Italian who was trying to make a success of a dude ranch.[33] He came to their campfire, played his guitar, and told them stories of the Stoney people. They had such a good time that they went to camp a second time, now with Rose Page and Michael. That summer, around 1933, "Pokey" – as Pocaterra was known – wore an old-fashioned bathing suit that came down to his knees, and because the moths had eaten the crotch out of the suit, he wore a pair of canvas drawers over it. Pat, now sixteen, was disillusioned: "I've never seen such a sight in all my life. I was slightly in love with Pokey until then and that put me off him."[34] The two girls swam in the river, rode their horses, and went for walks discussing the meaning of life. "We slept under the stars," Elizabeth Carlile recalled, "and philosophized. We sun bathed in the nude, on the sun-baked big rocks in the river ... It was bliss."[35]

The family still spent part of their summer at Sarcee Camp. Pat now had new responsibilities when her father taught her to take the string of polo ponies from Sarcee Camp back into Calgary to the polo grounds. As she had to ford a stream with the horses, this was a long and tricky ride. Lionel was attempting to train his daughter to be as independent as possible, perhaps because his heart attack had made him aware of his own mortality. He was also teaching her to drive and to read a map. He regularly took her and the dog out to the prairie, indicating a "point on the map" where they were to meet: "He would walk with the dog to ... wherever the devil [the point] was, and I'd have to follow the map, and see the concession lines, and drive the car to 'that point on the map.'"[36] The map was to become an important metaphor in her later poems.

The young Pat was beginning to think about the life of an artist for herself. When studying for her dreaded final chemistry exam, she put on her "coolie coat," a quilted silk jacket with brilliant colours of appliqué and embroidery made for her by Auntie Kit. "In it ... I imagined myself an artist, although what kind of an artist, I didn't know."[37] She wrote some lines about the final exams, expressing her predicament:

> Those who are made of sterner stuff
> Can concentrate.
> Those who are made of sterner stuff
> Can sit up late;
> Can drill equations in their brains
> And bear up under all the strain …[38]

It was during this time that Pat and Fuzz built what they called their "studio": a small, rather shakily constructed cubbyhole in the rough basement of the Carlile house. There Pat wrote and Fuzz painted. In "The Hidden Room" (title poem in her later collected poems) Page alludes to this space as the place where art begins: "… you will see only / a lumber room / a child's bolt-hole …" But as she reminds us in the poem, the importance of this space is its transforming power, a force that is hidden. It may look like "a child's bolt-hole," but in fact it is a "prism / a magic square / the number nine."[39]

This year – 1933, Pat's seventeenth – saw a kind of literary outpouring: she wrote more than fifty poems, carefully transcribed in a poetry notebook titled "Seventeen." Pat alludes to her friendship with Fuzz in one of the verses:

> Do you remember how we rode together?
> With the wind in our face & our hair
> And swam whatever the weather
> And laughed at our bodies bare?[40]

Many of these verses include illness, despair, and death, interspersed with emotional upheavals: "tempests in and tempests out."[41]

What is most original in her poetry notebook is young Pat's strong sense of nature, especially the Rocky Mountain foothills and the prairie. She writes of the landscape that she and Fuzz experienced when they rode out on their ponies:

> I love the leafy stillnesses,
> The swishing of the wind,
> The swirling of the river,
> The rushing of the river
> And the town left miles behind.[42]

A beginning writer, Pat was in love with words which, as she recognized later, is simply sound leading to the thing-in-itself: "The pattern of vowels in a poem, / the clicking of consonants, cadence, and stress – / were magic and music. What matter the meaning?"[43] Although the young Pat believed she had experienced the depths of emotion, her commonplace diction and conventional metre tell us otherwise, as in this attempt at sophistication in "The Woods Are Full of Them":

> You ask me if I love you,
> You say it means your life.
> But others have before you,
> And they have each a wife ...
>
> I'm not your inspiration.
> Don't wince, it is a fact.
> It's merely empty passion
> That drives you to this act.[44]

The language and the suggestion of attempted seduction point to the influence of Edna St. Vincent Millay. In the early thirties, Rose Page gave Pat a small volume of poems by Millay, which Pat loved, especially "First Fig": "My candle burns at both ends; / It will not last the night; / But ah, my foes, and oh, my friends – / It gives a lovely light!"[45] In the 1920s and 1930s the poetry of Millay was admired by young women who wanted more freedom to burn *their* candles. Millay struck just the right note for Pat: "She was a passionate nature lover (which I was), she was cynical about human love, which I thought was very 'in.'"[46]

In her last year at St Hilda's, Pat's literary ability was recognized. She was allowed to edit the school magazine and was finally made a prefect. The biographical entry under her name states: "Next year she hopes to study journalism in England, and we know she will do well in this sphere of life."[47] St Hilda's had taught Pat to work in groups, take part in sports, and enjoy acting in school plays. More importantly, she had been given an opportunity to see her essays and verses in print. It was a good foundation. Unfortunately, in her last three years she had come to believe that she lacked academic ability – though it was more likely that her father's illness had put her off her stride. When her parents gave her a choice of attending university in Canada or going to live with Aunt Bibbi in England for a year, she unhesitatingly chose England.

Although missing a university education with her peers, Pat Page had the great advantage of being thrown back on her own interests and resources. She became an autodidact and, as a result, highly educated. Because her education was self-determined, her path was narrowed but deepened, perhaps helping her evolve into the artist she became. She later asserted that she was never ambitious, but in one of her early notebook verses she acknowledged "Ambition" as the spark that led her on:

It was you who gave me the courage
To look people straight in the face,
And strange, it was you who induced me
To step up & sit in your place.
Oh! creature elusive and lovely
You ran from my grasp and up higher ...[48]

In July 1934 Pat began her first solo journey to England by taking the train to Halifax where, on boarding the ship, she found a letter from her father sent from Sarcee Camp. It is a remarkable testament, not only to his love for his daughter but to Lionel Page's character and insight. He explains that he is inclined to become "withdrawn" when he attempts to speak of things he feels most deeply, and since advice is unpleasant to give "and a still harder thing to accept," he thinks that both he and Pat might be able to best express their feelings on paper.

He acknowledges the sterling qualities of his Dearest Pat: "You have always been faithful, always been a worker & have been little or no trouble to us in any way." But he is concerned about some of her other characteristics, particularly her primary quality, truthfulness: "You are so keen on the truth that you will adhere to it no matter how much you hurt others." He advises her to temper her honesty with kindliness, mercy, and tact. Another characteristic he cautions her against is her tendency to be self-opinionated. In a firm paternal tone, though with evident admiration for his daughter, he advises: "Be big enough & true enough to be willing to change your opinion."

He also speaks of Pat's ambition and approves of it, but warns her that it can become a "headstrong hardmouthed horse if given his way." Heading straight for one's goal is one way of proceeding, but it brings with it "many a scratch & bruise." He recommends taking a more level, if longer, path, keeping in mind the goal she is aiming for. Finally, he urges her not to be extravagant with money, for if she runs short the family and Aunt Bibbi will have to make sacrifices that they can ill afford. His last words wish her good luck and happiness for her journey: "Have a good time but stick to your ideals. Life is a great adventure – a great game – but stick to the rules."[49] Lionel Page was above all a military man. In his youth he had read Kipling's *Kim* (1901), in which the "Great Game" signifies the continuing conflict between Great Britain and Russia. He sees Pat's future life as a series of possible skirmishes and offers strategic advice. Now it is up to her to find her way.

CHAPTER 3

England
Discovering Modernism, 1934–1935

In July 1934 Pat Page took passage for England. There she "affront[ed] her destiny," as Henry James once said of another young North American, Isabel Archer, who was bound for Europe. The journeys of such young women, James tells us, "insist on mattering," because they embody what is best in our culture.[1] Tall and dark-haired, Pat was an attractive figure in a smart grey coat with a thin black stripe, wearing big silver earrings and bright red lipstick. On her arrival in Liverpool, she took the train to London. Sitting opposite her on the train was an elderly, aristocratic-looking Englishman, who leaned over and asked, "Are you thirty?"

"No," she said, "I'm seventeen."

"Never mind," he replied, "when you're thirty, you'll look seventeen."[2] It seemed that he could not quite place her.

She was a new type – not a suffragette, not a twenties flapper, but a modern woman in embryo. While she may have hoped to become a wife and mother, she expected more. She wanted also to become a writer, a journalist. That her ambitions were realistic was demonstrated five months later, on 2 December 1934, when the *London Observer* published one of her poems, "The Moth":

> I caught a moth,
> A silver moth
> That fluttered in my hair;
> And when I peeped within my hand
> I found but star-dust there.[3]

It was signed "P.K. Page," which became her professional name. Though the verse was romantic and the imagery conventional, she had enough self-confidence to submit her poem to a distinguished newspaper.

London itself excited her senses and fired her imagination. She later said that she wasn't entirely aware that she wanted to be an artist, "but seeing and looking made me spill over into trying to write and trying to draw."[4] The Whitehouse family now lived in Purley near Croydon, on the outskirts of London, and her aunt – who was very modern and had a car – met Pat at Windsor Station. Since her own academic ambitions had been thwarted by Cambridge's refusal to grant degrees to women, Aunt Bibbi was determined to give her bright niece every advantage to fulfill her ambitions.

She started by obtaining for Pat a special membership in Boots Book-lovers Library, which enabled her to request any book she wanted. Aunt Bibbi also purchased a season's pass on the Southern Railway for the trip from Purley to London. In effect, Pat was now engaged in her own Cook's Tour of London, by underground and bus. London lay before her, enormously exciting. In response to modern buildings such as the Battersea Power Station, her "whole being would arise … with such joy."[5] Almost every day she wandered around the city by herself: "I took in an enormous amount of elegant architecture, of beautiful paintings, of superb music, theatre. I wasn't a rich young woman in London, but all my money went to 'sitting in the Gods,' that is, queuing up to get cheap tickets to the theatre and sitting up high in the back."[6] Because she left Purley early in the morning and sometimes didn't return until late at night, her aunt soon took out a membership for her at the English-Speaking Union, a formal London club. There the male members read their newspapers and drank whisky, while the occasional woman, such as Pat, took tea or ate steak-and-kidney pie until it was time to meet friends or go to the theatre. (Aunt Bibbi footed the bill.) After the theatre, which didn't get out until 10 or 11 PM, the train ride to Purley took half an hour. There was a long dark walk home from the station, but this did not seem to bother her or Aunt Bibbi. London was a safe place then. Utterly independent, Pat was greatly excited by everything she was seeing and doing.

Pat saw Bernard Shaw's *Major Barbara* – and promptly began to read Shaw's other plays. She also saw the young John Gielgud in *Hamlet*, and was greatly impressed. The stage setting was monochromatic: everything was in shades of muted blue, but different shades of blue with the exception of Hamlet himself, who wore black. The visual effects were powerful, and with this performance Pat realized that colour could be used to create an effect and a mood.[7]

Early on, her aunt suggested that she ought to have some directed activity, and she asked Pat what she was interested in. "Well, I really want to write." Journalism was then a recognized path to becoming a writer, so Aunt Bibbi took Pat to a London journalism school run by Sir Philip Gibbs, a journalist and novelist knighted for his frontline letters during the First World War. Gibbs was a charming older man, who enrolled Pat in a correspondence course that may have concentrated on the mechanics of writing and publishing – she completed only three or four of the sessions. It was then, however, that she submitted "The Moth" to the *Observer*, which published the poem next to Rainer Maria Rilke's "Autumn Day" and gave her a pound. The poem was subsequently picked up by a little publisher in England who reprinted it with some poems by Edith Sitwell.[8]

Pat was equipped to write. At Aunt Bibbi's house she already had a room of her own, with a desk and chair and access to her aunt's large library. Although the Whitehouse grandparents had died since her last visit, the new house contained the old dark oak furniture and the green velour table-covering that she remembered from her childhood. She now read modern poetry at that table. In her room she worked on her correspondence courses, read critically, and jotted down comments on technique.

Journalism school gave way to personal exploration. Pat began to visit London's art galleries, especially the Blake room and the paintings of the Pre-Raphaelite Brotherhood in the Tate Gallery. She had become acquainted with the Pre-Raphaelites when from reading *Poor Splendid Wings* in Calgary and was now particularly moved by Dante Gabriel Rossetti's painting *How They Met Themselves*, which depicts a medieval couple in a wood, startled to meet their exact doubles, who glow with a strange light. In Aunt Bibbi's library Pat found a collection of Rossetti's poems that included "Sudden Light":

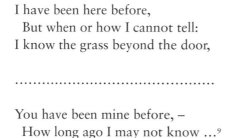

I have been here before,
    But when or how I cannot tell:
I know the grass beyond the door,

    ....

You have been mine before, –
    How long ago I may not know ...[9]

Like the painting, the poem suggests reincarnation – the continuation of life and love through centuries. (Years later, when Pat came across the Sufi writer Idries Shah's statement that man was multiple, Rossetti's painting flashed into her mind as part of a pattern.)[10]

The Tate displayed the best in English modern art, but Pat was also finding her way to some of the smaller avant-garde galleries, advised by Max Bates, who like her was a student in London. They met once in the underground, where he had stored many of his paintings in a locker. He propped them against a wall for her to see his brilliant and bizarre primary colours, while travellers scurried back and forth around them. Max also took her to the Werthein Gallery, where he was exhibiting, and gave her a list of the best painters in London. Many of the sculptors and painters were members of the London Group: Jacob Epstein, Paul and John Nash, Ben Nicholson, Stanley Spencer. The paintings that appear to have interested Pat most were either visionary or very modern – sometimes a combination of both. She particularly liked Paul Nash's surrealistic landscape paintings, which were influenced by Blake, and Spencer's elongated, El Greco-like *Saint Francis*.

One visit to the Leicester Galleries took place in the spring of 1935. An older woman, a friend of one of her former teachers in Calgary, had taken her to lunch in Soho. Pat found her conversation astonishing and radical: the woman spoke about polygamy, then about Rima, the bird-like woman in W.H. Hudson's novel *Green Mansions,* of whom Epstein had made a sculpture. After lunch she suggested that they see Epstein's new work, *Ecce Homo*. It was a *cause célèbre* in London at the time because of Epstein's rendering of Christ – a squared, roughly chiselled sculpture, eleven feet high, primitive and savage, revealing the power of the Old Testament Jehovah.[11] It was an intellectual awakening, as she wrote five years later in "Ecce Homo":

We entered the gallery
but what I remember most
was my unexpected entry
into the door of my mind
....
Never dreaming a swift awakening was what I needed.[12]

She was still reading visionary novels by Charles Morgan, along with critics such as James Agate[13] and the romantic verse of Humbert Wolfe. Pat was also acquainting herself with the modernist writers, notably Virginia Woolf, Vera Brittain, Winifred Holtby, Katherine Mansfield, and D.H. Lawrence. Woolf had the greatest impact on her evolving literary consciousness. When visiting the Boots library in Purley and "just browsing on the shelves," Pat came across *The Waves* (1931), "my hand went up and picked it off the shelf, and I opened it up and started reading it, and I burst into tears. It was such a relief to me to find that people wrote that way." She found the opening monologues of *The Waves* fascinating, unrealistic: it was as if the characters existed in another dimension. "And it seemed to me that she opened a whole new world that was ... magical to me, and then I started to read her with great enthusiasm."[14] Pat knew that she had to have the book, and although she had little money, she bought it.

The Waves seems to have led her directly to Woolf's *A Room of One's Own* (1929), which emphasized the fact that women were excluded from elitist English universities ("Oxbridge"). But if a woman was to become a writer, financial support and a room of one's own were essential. Not only was this the first modern attempt to set out the social, educational, and economic restraints on any woman who wanted to be an artist, but it also suggested how a young woman might see herself as an artist and go about the process of writing.

It is not at all clear whether Pat Page initially absorbed Woolf's argument. More likely, she responded to it over a period of six decades, celebrating Woolf's epiphany when she called her collected poems *The Hidden Room* (1997) – the title referring to a passage near the end of *A Room of One's Own* where Woolf situates the place of artistic creation in a woman's consciousness. Woolf describes a small room where the curtains are "close drawn," a private place in the mind where the marriage of the opposites in the self, male and female, is consummated. "I suppose I was reacting [to Woolf's encouragement of the woman artist]. But I don't remember that. I just remember the hidden room. I just remember the relief of it ... I was devastated when I learned she had committed suicide."[15]

Perhaps the relief that Page felt was the realization that it is this interior space (not Oxford or Cambridge) that enables a modern young woman to become a writer. She recalled that in the 1930s she was getting "food" from Woolf – "food" being a word Woolf uses twice in *A Room of One's Own* as shorthand for the "knowledge, adventure, art," the nourishment required by a woman who wants to become an artist. The critic Carolyn Heilbrun has suggested that the chief difference between a woman and a man who aspires to become an artist is that the woman must first "create a self"; that is, conceive of herself as an artist (in order to defy society's expectation that she spend her time in nurturing roles), and create time and space for her art: a "woman's selfhood, the right to her own story, depends upon her 'ability to act in the public domain.'"[16] Pat was moving to the point where she was ready to make changes in her life to accommodate her creativity.

In 1935, when Pat was reading Woolf, she came across a book by one of Woolf's younger admirers, Marion Milner, a psychologist, who wrote under the pseudonym Joanna Field. In *A Room of One's Own*, Woolf had asked, "[W]here shall I find that elaborate study of the psychology of women by a woman?"[17] I see Milner's *A Life of One's Own* (1934) as systematically developing a number of Woolf's ideas. Milner was later recognized as a distinguished English psychologist, so Pat was absorbing not only the latest in modern psychology but also techniques to encourage her art.

In *A Life of One's Own* Milner states that she was unhappy as a young woman until she discovered how to take control of her life and creativity. To do so, she mapped out a program for developing perception that moves the centre of awareness from the head into the body. In one exercise, for example, she tried putting herself into one of the chairs in the room – "at once the chair seemed to take on a new reality, I 'felt' its proportions and could say at once whether I liked its shape."[18] Woolf had talked about escaping from the common sitting room and seeing human beings "in relation to reality; and the sky, too, and the trees ... our relation is to the world of reality."[19] Milner, too, spoke about reaching out to the larger reality of nature and trees: "I remember to spread the arms of my awareness towards the trees, letting myself flow round them and feed on the delicacy of their patterns till their intricacies became part of my being."[20] In effect, Milner was extending Woolf's observations while offering some practical exercises for developing consciousness, with the aim of putting young women in touch with themselves. The importance of this book is that it provided Pat with a framework for self-discovery. Pat brought home to Canada copies of Woolf's and Milner's books. She also tried some of Milner's exercises; several references appear in her early poems and in her first novella, *The Sun and the Moon*.

At the same time, Pat was educating herself about modern poetry, aided by one of Aunt Bibbi's Cambridge friends, Fanny Poyser. On her first visit to Poyser's home in the fall of 1934, Pat discovered that she had a copy of Harold Monro's *Twentieth Century Poetry* (1929), which she borrowed. The next time she visited, she borrowed the book again. This happened so often that in June 1935, to judge from the inscription on the book, Fanny said, "I think you think that book is yours and you'd better have it."[21]

It was a kind gesture. Pat was reaching out, and Monro's anthology was a particularly good place to start, for it included poems by H.D.,

Hopkins, Lawrence, Pound, Sitwell, and Yeats – as well as a short poem called "The Moth" by Walter de la Mare which (together with several scenes from *Girl of the Limberlost*) may have suggested the title of her own early poem. Monro's introduction was informative. It gave a context to the modern period, stating that it was characterized by "short poems, and ... impatient readers," and identified T.S. Eliot as a major figure.[22] Pat's pencilled notes in the margins clearly show that she liked best the romantic lyrics by Yeats and Lawrence, and Pound's mythical poem "A Girl," which enacts the Daphne myth – a young woman's metamorphosis into a tree.

She was learning from poetry anthologies that a "strict realism" was not essential for contemporary writing. This discovery was heralded by Maurice Wollman's introduction to *Modern Poetry, 1922–1934,* on the flyleaf of which she wrote "Christmas 1934" and underlined a section expressing the editor's view that poetry need not be intelligible to everyone. He wrote: "[The poet] seeks ... to bring to the surface his underlying impulses, and then to record them by strange means of association [synesthesia] – impressions of one sense are expressed in terms of another, colours suggest sounds, and flavour suggests texture."[23] Pat was particularly attracted to the language of Edith Sitwell's "Aubade":

> Jane, Jane,
> Tall as a crane,
> The morning light creaks down again![24]

Synesthesia, the giving of the qualities of one modality to another, became a chief characteristic of Pat's own early poetry.

Her London experience evoked some light verse. One poem was titled "On Discussing Canada with the English":

> You say you hate the prairies, the long stretches
> of wheat & corn & tousled, wind-blown flowers ...
>
> You tell me that the prairies are depressing
> and that you find such solitude a bore;
> you say – but no I say it's too distressing,
> I've listened to these monologues before ...[25]

On another occasion, probably in spring 1935 at a flower show, she suddenly recognized a prairie crocus among all the flowers of England:

> Did you say crocuses?
> Soft & fiery crocuses?
> Did you? Oh tell me
> for the answer means so much ...[26]

The sight of the crocus made her homesick. She also watched (or imagined she had watched) a parade in which Mackenzie King passed in a carriage; the sight of his dumpy little figure, clothed in black, filled her with a longing for home. King stood for Canada.[27] Pat made the same emotional discovery that her father had made at the turn of the century. She had been brought up to think that England was home, but now she knew that Canada was home.

Meanwhile, she was widening her understanding of the English beyond her own superficial line of verse: "Grey London, grey cars, grey faces."[28] Many of the people Pat met were friends either of Aunt Bibbi or of her parents. Raymond and Marigold Patterson, whom her parents had met in Calgary[29] invited her to stay and took her to the beautifully costumed play *Lady Precious Stream*. One of Aunt Bibbi's friends, Ethel Warwick, took her to see a Cochran Review, *Streamline*, which included "Perseverance," a parody of Gilbert and Sullivan with lyrics by A.P. Herbert: "Fifty fisher-girls are we / Selling fishes from the sea."[30] The two performances were later fused in a short story by Page called "The Middleman."[31] To some degree the story is about perception. We enter into the consciousness of the young woman who is narrating and is spending two days in London with the Maxwells (the Pattersons). She takes in not only a London revue, which she attends with three other young people, but also the strained relationship between one couple, Sally and Derek. The story was preserved because Pat sent it, along with a few poems, to Fuzz Carlile in Calgary in the late thirties.

Although solitary most of the time, Pat made a number of friends in England, including a girl called Barbara, a kindred spirit she met on the train. With Barbara and a few others – including Barbara's brother, who was a boyfriend for a short time – Pat took a walking tour in southern England. She went farther afield, probably in the winter or spring of 1935, when Aunt Bibbi treated her to a Mediterranean cruise. They went to Spain, Portugal, Majorca, and North Africa. She was intrigued by a nightclub in Barcelona, where the girls stripped to the waist, and she recognized at once the implications when a man in a closed box summoned one of the girls. But it was in Morocco that her fascination with the exotic reached its peak. She had got off the ship at Tangier or Casablanca and was taken to a kasbah, where something in the air attracted her.

When she stopped at a school to watch some young children reciting the Koran, she became separated from her group and was lost. Suddenly she was "surrounded by beggars showing me their terrible sores ... I was anxious but I was still terribly, terribly drawn to it and to the hand of Fatima, which I saw on the doors" – prefiguring her later interest in Sufism.[32]

That year, 1935, widened her horizons and broadened her aesthetic sensibility. The Mediterranean trip was a watershed because Pat, who had always been shy, realized for the first time that she was considered attractive. Two young men whom she met on the cruise became something of a nuisance: one turned up to see her in Purley, and the other was sufficiently smitten to follow her to Canada, where he stayed with the Pages in Rothesay. He intended to go to South Africa and wanted Pat to marry him. Her father Lionel Page, rarely nonplussed, was rattled and quite literally took to his bed until the young man left.

Pat sailed for home in early summer 1935, and the trip was uneventful. Passengers dressed for dinner. She wore an evening gown and smoked, sporting a long cigarette holder from Piccadilly Circus because smoke irritated her eyes. To her surprise, the ship's engineer developed a crush on her. He was an older and very silent Scot, short and red-faced, who asked her for drinks before dinner every night. He bought the drinks – she had sherry and he had whisky – but he never spoke. As she later recalled half-humorously, "He wasn't exactly a burden, but he wasn't a treat either."[33]

CHAPTER 4

Saint John
Apprenticeship, 1935–1941

When Pat Page disembarked from the ship at Halifax, she found herself in a long queue of immigrants, including women in babushkas and their children. She was plucked from the line by a port official who said, "You're not Lionel Page's daughter, are you? Come this way!"[1] He had good reason to recognize her name because her father, now a brigadier, was second-in-command of the military district at Halifax.

Founded in 1749, Halifax was an old grey city dominated by the sea, a world apart from the clear wide skies of the prairies. Pat hardly had time to unpack when, in late September 1935, her father was appointed commanding officer of Military District No. 7, Saint John, New Brunswick. The family moved to Rothesay, a small close-knit town just north of Saint John, overlooking the Kennebecasis River. Old Loyalist families lived in Rothesay, and many of Saint John's professional class chose to live there and commute to the city. The Page family now took over a house rented by their army predecessor, a large gabled building on a corner lot, now 38 Gondola Point Road. During the summer months they rented accommodation farther south, towards the coast, at New River Beach on the Bay of Fundy.

Their new house overlooked the water and the Yacht Club, and Pat could walk down to the river in a few minutes. In one of the gables of the house, the upper-right bedroom on the second floor, she set herself up for creative work with a writing desk and a shelf of books. Like Mrs Gianelli, she took a secretarial course and received a certificate of graduation for filing and shorthand in 1936–37. Later, in 1939, her parents gave her a typewriter and she took typing lessons. Her library was quite small at first: the few books she had brought back from England, plus borrowings from the Saint John Public Library, but she soon added others, including some by Katherine Mansfield's. Pat admired Mansfield and thought of her as a contemporary, a young woman still writing. But

Pat Page and Phil Golding at a "Baby Party" (in bonnets). Rothesay, New Brunswick.

one afternoon, when returning on the tram from typing class, she was devastated to read – in Middleton Murry's preface to Mansfield's *Journals* – that the writer had died in 1923, sixteen years earlier.

The family was settling down to domestic life in Rothesay. War was already in the air, Saint John was a port city, and many large ships passed through the dry docks for refitting. As Lionel Page was the senior military commander, he was obliged to entertain the ships' captains and other officials, and his wife was responsible for innumerable luncheons, teas, dinners, and receptions. When he had been with Lord Strathcona's Horse, entertaining had been done in the regimental mess, but now Rose Page had to undertake it at home, which meant dipping into their scant financial resources. Rose loved company but hated "duty entertaining."[2]

Pat, who would rather be reading – or writing – found the official receptions dreary and the parties worse. On one occasion she rebelled and refused to attend. Her father took her aside. "I fully understand your feelings," he said. "I wouldn't like to go myself actually, but I have to do it, I have no option." He went on to say, "If you think about it, you will realize that maybe *you* have no option. If you're living in this house, if I'm feeding you, housing you, clothing you, giving you all the privileges of this household ... I think you have to assume responsibility. If you can't do that, I wouldn't blame you, but you must go." And then he said:

"If you go, I'll help you."[3] Pat liked living at home, she appreciated the logic of her father's argument, and decided that it was not too much extra effort to put on some lipstick and go downstairs to help with the entertaining.

Aside from the army's official entertainments, the town itself was highly social, with a yacht club, a country club, and a golf club. For Pat, social life in Rothesay was defined by a large group of well-to-do young men and women who called each other by nicknames (Pat, slightly plump, was known as "Podge," while the daughter of the Crosby molasses family was called "Sticky"). Many of the young men had not yet entered a profession, and the young women were filling in time before marriage – none were expected to take a job, and very few did. The young men had sailboats; there were weekly dances at the Yacht Club and the Country Club, and frequent house parties in large Rothesay homes. The group enjoyed charades, theatricals, and dressing up for theme parties. At a "Baby Party" attended by nearly fifty young people, Pat wore a frilled white nightdress and a baby bonnet, and sucked on a pacifier – there was a little of Rose's madcap in Pat. She went to the party with a young man dressed in a white nightgown and cap – Phil Golding, a budding playwright and sometime boyfriend.

Pat was high-spirited and liked having fun, but she disliked the superficial social round, and her attitude was apparent. Rothesay was an established community, and the Pages were newcomers, the cynosure of many eyes. No longer the inexperienced girl who had left Calgary for England, Pat had cosmopolitan interests, and her British accent seemed affected to prickly Maritime ears. She no longer called her parents "Mother" and "Daddy" but referred to both in a theatrical way as "Daaarling" – and waved her long cigarette holder for emphasis, like an ingenue in a Noël Coward play. But much simmered under this veneer of sophistication. Her year in England had sharpened her aesthetic sensibilities. She had seen fine art, had frequented the theatre, and met intelligent people. When she was deposited into provincial Saint John, and even more provincial Rothesay, she was a fish out of water, bored and unhappy.

In 1936, acknowledging her twentieth birthday on 23 November, she wrote in her poetry notebook a half-humorous verse called "Depression":

Twenty years & what to show?
Two red lips, a faithless beau;
massive girth; a case of books;
little in the way of looks;

a lot of hope & some despair;
a longing for real raven hair;
a published poem; one love-letter;
a pair of shoulders which are better
for weeping on than wearing dresses;
an English voice which over-stresses
superlatives & ejaculations;
little interest in the nations'
arguments & threats of fighting;
two large hands forever lighting
cigarettes with ceaseless motion;
a crazy longing for the ocean.
A hatred for tight shoulder straps –
and worst of all – I'm death in *caps!*
When twenty years have gone again
Will I have something more by then?[4]

She wants all the things that any modern artistic young woman wants – to be beautiful, to be loved – *and* to publish her poetry. She longs to be slim with raven hair, graceful in a *soigné* ball gown with thin straps – the contemporary stage image from Noël Coward's plays. But the reality of her situation is "little in the way of looks," "a case of books" and an "English voice." Only superlatives will do. It is DEATH. Pat's language echoes that of Coward's characters, who had established a new conversational tone for fashionable society, sprinkled with "daarlings," "divines," and other superlatives.

Pat had returned from England "stage-struck and unfocussed. Did I want to write or act?"[5] In fact, in the next few years she was to do both – and often with the same people. Among the few congenial young people interested in the arts in Saint John were Peggy Pickersgill (later MacDonald), Kay Smith, a high-school drama teacher, and Priscilla Hazen (later Prichard), who became a reporter for the *Montreal Star*. Peggy, a good friend, introduced Pat to the potters Kjeld and Erica Deichmann, and they, in turn introduced her to a group of Saint John painters that included Jack Humphrey, Miller Brittain, and Ted Campbell. And through Peggy, Pat met Toby de Bouvier Holly, a Saint John radio announcer with whom she wrote duologues (narratives for two people) and produced them for the local radio station. Every two weeks Pat met with Kay Smith and Jean Sweet, a newspaperwoman, to write poetry. Little by little she was moving closer to a group of people who were interested in art and the theatre.

"Tommy" Ross was one of the women who helped Pat make the transition. As Gertrude Tomalin, she had been a successful monologist on the English stage during the First World War and had arrived in Saint John in 1920 when she was in her late thirties. There she married Frank Ross, a dashing young businessman (and future lieutenant-governor of British Columbia), whom she had just divorced when Pat met her. Divorce was considered beyond the pale at the time, and Tommy was therefore set apart. Nonetheless, she was a respected figure, producing plays for the Theatre Guild of Saint John. The younger social set regularly visited her home on Ashburn Lake for swimming parties.

Larger than life, Tommy was to play an important role in Pat's life. A woman with great presence, then in her mid-fifties, directing plays in which Pat acted, she was tall, about Pat's height, striking, with pretty grey hair, casually waved. She was funny, quick with her tongue, and known for her witty repartee. Their relationship, somewhat like that of star and ingenue, turned into a close friendship. Tommy expanded Pat's vision: she introduced her to the poetry of C. Day Lewis, gave her Proust's *Swann's Way* and a book of Irish love lyrics. Most importantly, Tommy understood Pat's ambitions and tried to help her with whatever she needed at the time, including clothes and hats – she had fabulous hats, all of which she lent freely. "She somehow provided what life didn't," an older Pat recalled. "I loved her."[6]

In October 1936 Pat drove to Boston with Tommy and two of her friends – "Auntie Min," a society columnist for the Saint John *Times-Globe*, and Kit Schofield, a former nursing sister who distributed birth-control devices, then illegal. They went to see Gertrude Lawrence and Noël Coward perform in a group of Coward's plays that were trying out at the Colonial Theatre in preparation for his highly successful first American tour. Over the course of several nights, Pat, Tommy, and Kit saw *Shadow Play*, *Fumed Oak*, and *Still Life* – later filmed as *Brief Encounter*, about a man and woman, both married, who fall in love but lose each other because they lack the courage to act on their love.

From 1936 until well beyond the Second World War Coward's plays occupied a special place in the English theatre, and a number of them were also staged in Saint John. Among them was the popular *Blithe Spirit* (first produced in 1941 to entertain wartime Londoners) in which the protagonist's dead wife returns. The plays were witty and sophisticated and seemed to express the temper of the times. Pat loved Coward's songs, such as "Wild about the Boy" from *Brief Encounter*. There was a modern bravado to his frivolity which was described by one critic as "a sense of people gallantly waving sparklers in a newly darkened world."[7] When serving in England during the war, Lionel Page met Noël Coward and secured his autograph for Pat: "He sent you his love and told me to tell you that the next time you went to Boston ... to be sure and go back stage and see him. So there. Wasn't I a good daddy?"[8]

Maritimers were interested in all things British. A year after her return to Saint John, Pat was watching a movie when the action stopped for the surprise announcement of Edward VIII's abdication on 11 December 1936. It was an overwhelming moment for most of the audience. But Pat was adamant in her belief that Edward should have been able to marry Wallis Simpson, "the woman I love."[9] In the spring of 1939, when King George VI and Queen Elizabeth toured Canada, Pat refused to take part in the celebrations although her father, a senior military commander, was in charge of arrangements for the royal visit.

She was now gleaning feminist and socialist thought from the plays of Henrik Ibsen. She read not only *A Doll's House* but also *An Enemy of the People* and *Pillars of Society*, plays that indicted a selfish upper-class community. Pat was soon applying their principles to Rothesay. When the municipal water supply was discovered to be contaminated with E. coli, Pat raised the matter at a cocktail party given by Fred Crosby, chairman of the Rothesay Village Council. To the mayor's excuse, "Everybody has wells," Pat replied fiercely, "Everybody hasn't got wells!"[10] This was a highly conservative society and Pat was radical in her opinions, but her family did not seem embarrassed by her views, nor did they try to stop her, though her father sometimes told her that her points might be taken better if she did not antagonize her adversary.[11]

On another occasion she confronted one of her mother's acquaintances, wife of the lawyer who had handled Tommy Ross's divorce case. This was in 1937, when A.P. Herbert's proposal to reform the divorce laws had just been passed by the British Parliament. Pat had been reading Herbert's *Holy Deadlock* (1934), his novel indicting the British divorce laws, and she told the woman how delighted she was with the reform.[12] This elicited the furious reply that Pat, a mere chit of a girl, knew nothing about marriage or divorce.[13] But the divorce bill, like the emancipation of women, was of enormous interest to Pat because she understood that such issues affected her generation directly.

On 23 November 1937 Pat had celebrated a milestone – her twenty-first birthday. Her father, away on duty, wrote to her again admonishing her and saying that happiness does not depend on having an easy life. He did not suggest that she forgo experience in life, but that she try to think through the results of her actions: "The main thing is to live your life so that you have as little as possible to be sorry for."[14] In celebration of her birthday, a trip to the West Indies was planned for the New Year. Pat and her parents took a freighter in Halifax and began what was termed a "vagabond" cruise, sailing to the Caribbean and British Guiana, now Guyana. The ship carried cargo and a small group of passengers, stopping off at various islands, including Barbados and Trinidad, before reaching Georgetown, the capital of British Guiana. The food was wonderful, the air balmy, and Pat sometimes slept outside on deck. She met a girl her own age, Eleanor Bone, nicknamed Nell, whom she liked, and they spent time together. During the voyage Pat wrote some verse, including "Sleeping on Deck" and "Barbados Sights." While the family visited picturesque locations, her mother sketched the scenes before

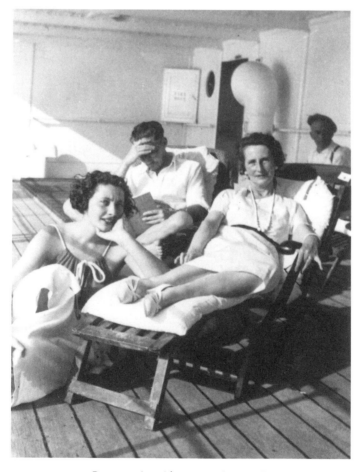

Pat on cruise with parents, circa 1938.

them. Once again – and for the last time – she combined Pat's poems and her own drawings in a booklet.

After the warmth of the Caribbean, the family returned to winter in Rothesay. Pat was now writing seriously. She had a group of intimates with whom she could talk about art and writing, chief among them Kjeld and Erica Deichmann. Pat learned that Kjeld, a grandnephew of the Danish philosopher Søren Kierkegaard, was something of a philosopher himself. He had come to New Brunswick with his wife intending to start a chicken farm, but everything went wrong. When attempting to mend some broken water pipes, a disgusted Kjeld found clay on their property and decided to try potting rather than farming. He and Erica went back to Denmark, where he studied pottery and she weaving. By 1935 they had set up their kiln on the Kingston Peninsula in New Brunswick, eventually called the Dykelands Pottery, which became known across Canada. Although their house was only a few miles from Saint John – and just across the water from Rothesay – their peninsula was cut off by the Kennebecasis and Saint John rivers. Ferries ran in summer and ice bridges connected them to the mainland in winter.

Both Deichmanns were interested in the arts in the widest sense. They joined the Theatre Guild of Saint John, then affiliated with the Dominion Drama Festival, and soon gathered a circle of literary and artistic folk around them, including the Saint John painters Jack Humphrey, Miller Brittain, and Ted and Rosamond Campbell. By 1936–37 Pat had joined the Deichmanns' circle. During the summer the group met at the Dykelands Pottery; during the winter they gathered in the Campbells' studio at 103 Prince William Street in Saint John. Pat found a confidante in Erica Deichmann, who was just three years older and shared her strong aesthetic sense. "Rica," as Pat called her, was then developing new glazes for their pottery and a series of fantastic animal shapes. The Deichmanns had two small children, Henrik and Elizabeth, better known as Skippy and Beth (who became the novelist Elizabeth Harvor). In 1938 a third child, Anneke, was born.

The Deichmanns were the first practising artists Pat had observed at close hand. She loved to be present when Kjeld fired up the kiln and then opened it to reveal the vivid glistening colours. During the summers she travelled to the peninsula by ferry; in the winters she skated over the ice (sometimes dragging a sled and firewood for a picnic on the ice with Erica). Occasionally she took a perilous journey in her father's car, driving over ice that sometimes reared up beneath her. She frequently stayed overnight – Kjeld made a little niche in the wall with a curtain to give her a place to sleep. In the long winter evenings when Anneke was a baby, Kjeld would sit turning his wheel (and looking as if he were listening to something far off) while Erica and Pat chatted. Pat later recalled asking him what he was thinking. "And he would reply, 'I was just wondering how many light years it is to Jupiter,' or some such planet. I've always thought of Kjeld since in terms of big generous concepts – seeming like a kind of giant among us, a kind of Gulliver among Lilliputians."[15]

While Erica and Kjeld worked in the evenings after the children had quietened down, Pat read to their parents her own short stories, or sometimes contemporary fiction and poetry. She wrote nearly a dozen short stories at Rothesay – one of them, "The Christmas Present," focused on a small piece of Deichmann pottery, a whimsical match holder. She also wrote some character studies, including "The Harp," about a labourer who played harp music in his head. These stories, usually around 1,000 words, were intended for magazine publication. A more ambitious and ironic 2,000-word story, "Easter Pie," is a poignant account of a child whose pet rabbit ends up in a pie. Attached to the text is a brief rejection from *Saturday Night*: "The Editor thanks you for submitting this contribution, and regrets that he is unable to make use of it." But in 1940–41 she won a prize for a story titled "This Happiness," which she had submitted to the *Atlantic* Short Story Contest. It is about the effect of divorce on a young girl, Julia, who adores her exquisite mother so much that she forces herself to condone her mother's actions in taking a lover – because in "cutting off her love for her mother she was cutting the stalk of her own happiness."[16] This recognition may have owed something to Pat's sense of loyalty to her own exquisite mother. She had learned not to resent her mother's avoidance of family responsibilities that consequently fell to her.

It also owed much to Katherine Mansfield's stories. Pat had been reading Mansfield seriously ever since her year in London. In 1937 she was given both volumes of *The Letters of Katherine Mansfield* as a birthday gift, and in the following years she acquired Mansfield's *Stories* and *Journals* and the *Scrapbook*, a collection of miscellaneous works. Erica Deichmann thought that "Pat Page used to feel that she looked like Katherine Mansfield – *was* her."[17] Pat felt an affinity with Mansfield's revelation that she did not see life whole: "Don't I live *in glimpses* only?"[18] As a young woman, Pat Page annotated this comment: "'Tis this very minuteness that fascinates in her stories." An older Page elaborated: "I can only see [life] in little, bright, intense glimpses. And I remember thinking to myself, that's where I am, I don't seem to see very big canvases, they're very intense and contained."[19] Enthralled with

Mansfield, Pat began to read more about her and her circle, especially *The Letters of D.H. Lawrence*.

Between 1936 and 1941 Pat's work broadened and deepened. She had been publishing regularly since the *Canadian Bookman* had accepted a poem, "The Chinese Rug," in June 1935. Every two weeks she met with her poetry-writing group – Pat, Kay Smith, and Jean Sweet – to discuss their poems. Her affection for Kay Smith is expressed in an unpublished verse from 1937, in which she remarks that their close friendship had grown from their common experience of attempting to create art, which she likens to sculpture:

We both have seen the edifice of stone
& in our hands we've held the common tool,
the finely tempered chisel & our use
has been – though miles apart, identical –
wielding it clumsily at first. Abuse
of steel on stone has hurt our mutual ear.
But later we have heard a harmony,
the harmony we always longed to hear ...[20]

In 1937 Pat received public recognition when one of her poems, "The Moon-Child," received an honourable mention in *Canadian Poems*, a chapbook publication of the Calgary branch of the Canadian Authors Association. The same competition lists a fellow Maritimer, John Sutherland, as a prizewinner. (Page later recalled that she and Sutherland also won prizes in a New York poetry contest sponsored by Henry Harrison.) She discovered Sutherland's address and went to visit him at his house in the neighbouring village of Hampton, New Brunswick.

Sutherland – three years younger – had greenish eyes and fair hair. Suffering from TB, he was lying on the verandah in a white bed with a white counterpane when she first met him. Pat's early images of the young man were white and green: "the white of the sheets, his pyjamas and his pallor were almost reflecting the enormous lawns and green trees of the garden. So the green was picked up in all this whiteness."[21] Although Sutherland was frail, his will was immense. Before the visit was over, he had convinced Pat to read aloud Francis Thompson's "The Hound of Heaven." While she read this complicated poem of God's love and man's terror, Sutherland's siblings – including his half-brother Donald, the future actor – were playing nearby. During the next three years John Sutherland became a friend. He continued to encourage her to read to him, especially from Nietzsche's *Thus Spake Zarathustra*; they showed each other new poems and talked. Sutherland knew of Pat's admiration for Virginia Woolf, and in 1938 he gave her a copy of *Three Guineas,* just published (which reminds us of how recently the belief in university education for women became current). Although Pat was not a feminist as we would understand the term today, she claimed to be a suffragette in that she believed that women had an equal right to the vote. Soon after her return from England she had written an essay on the suffragettes (now lost).

In the years 1936 to 1941 she became active in the Theatre Guild of Saint John and began a rigorous program of self-education. In 1938 she began to help Kay Smith and Jean Sweet with the plays they were writing for children's theatre. Pat was soon writing plays of her own, a series of one-act plays for children, including "Silver Pennies or The Land of Honesty," directed by Jean Sweet and performed in June 1939; and "The Magic Wool," performed in December 1940. Both are moralistic fables, akin to nursery stories. In April 1939 Pat had collaborated with Phil Golding to stage a popular play, *George and Margaret* by Gerald Savory, to raise funds to send a Theatre Guild production to the Dominion Drama Festival.

In the late 1930s, Pat reread Woolf's *A Room of One's Own* and Joanna Field's *A Life of One's Own,* underlining key passages. If Woolf helped her to see herself as a potential artist, and Field stimulated her interest in states of consciousness, Katherine Mansfield seems to have been the writer with whom Pat most identified. Above all she wanted to know more about the life of the artist and later remembered herself as "inquiring into, yearning to be a part of this life, but not quite sure how."[22] What Mansfield offered was both insight and intellectual company: "I felt I was feeling what she was feeling, yearning to write, to create."[23]

The passages in Mansfield's *Letters* that Pat marked, or commented on in the margins, are largely descriptions of the artistic life. She marked, for example, the following passage in Mansfield's letter of 3 February 1921 to her husband John Middleton Murry: "I believe the only way to live as artists under these new conditions in art and life is to put everything to the test for ourselves. We've got, in the long run, to be our own teachers."[24] What is striking is that Pat was becoming her own teacher: carrying on a critical dialogue with Mansfield, just as Mansfield, when learning her craft, had carried on an imaginary dialogue with Chekhov. Pat wrote a poem, "To Katherine Mansfield," alluding to this:

Are you bound to the earth again in some new shape?
Are you perhaps encased in form less frail,

or has your flesh at last earned banishment
& your pure spirit found its peace elsewhere?...
I like to think you mingle in a world
[with] Checkhov, whom you loved, but never knew.[25]

Pat responded especially to the descriptions of nature found in Woolf and Mansfield. Next to a paragraph in which Mansfield speaks of a wharf where sand barges unload, Pat wrote in the margin, "The wetness, the saltiness, the tang in this paragraph!," admiring Mansfield's technique and diction.[26] She also adopted (in a soon-to-be novella, *The Sun and the Moon*) one of Mansfield's primary images, the tree – which for Mansfield symbolized life and creativity in the short stories "Bliss" and "At the Bay."

Pat found freedom and time for writing during the long summers, when the family went to New River Beach. It was an idyllic spot on the Bay of Fundy, between Saint John and St Andrews, with a long sandy beach, wonderful for walking on and lying in the sun, or just for looking. Activity in the bay included tugs pulling log booms – lumber was brought down the New River to the sea. Although the water was freezing, the family swam. They usually rented a fisherman's cabin near the water but sometimes stayed in an old grey farmhouse, the main building owned and managed by two sisters, Nora and Kit Knight. Pat was especially fond of the younger sister, Kit.

One of the stories she wrote at New River Beach gives a sense of place – and also a sense of the apprentice writer. Like Mansfield's "At the Bay," Pat's untitled story describes a summer day experienced by several families who are vacationing "at the bay," a term common to both stories. Additional references in Pat's story to "Miss Cathie" and "Miss Ev" suggest the Knight sisters and their property: "A few white minnow clouds flicked their tails in the west above the line of evergreens. The morning was pale still, the sea flat and grey-pink in the bay between the two points of land. Far out a small fishing boat was returning home, skimming like a gull across the water ... The tide was out, the sand firm as young flesh, unpocked by footsteps."

The narrator's eye in both stories is focused on an inexperienced young woman surveying her world. In Mansfield's story, the protagonist Beryl Fairfield longs for male company ("It is lonely living by oneself ... She wants a lover"), but she bolts when confronted by a would-be seducer.[27] Pat's young woman, Elizabeth, shares Beryl's views. She had not wanted to come to the bay and she is cross with her mother: "If she insists on dragging me down to this godforsaken place what can she expect? Doesn't she know that a girl of eighteen wants men?"[28] There are no eligible men at the bay, but Elizabeth surveys an interesting older woman, Chris Mallory, a divorcée, longing to be her friend. Generous to the young woman, Chris provides coffee and a late breakfast. Aside from the tomboyish masculine name – so popular with Coward's thirties women – and her forthright speech, some of Chris's mentoring qualities suggest Tommy Ross. ("What's the matter?" she inquires of Elizabeth. "Every bloody thing's the matter.")

This story, probably written in 1938–39, reflects Pat's last two golden summers. War was in the air, but few of the Saint John group were aware of it. During the lazy prewar summers the younger set in Rothesay spent a lot of time on the river, sometimes sleeping overnight on their boats. Pat was a puzzle to her friends because she would never sleep with her current boyfriend. They would say, sometimes with annoyance, "Pat's coming. You have to have an extra bed for Pat." To Pat it was perfectly simple: she was not in love with any of the young men she was dating, so she could not sleep with them.

Now in her early twenties, thoughts of what she should do with her life must have weighed on her. Many of her friends were finding husbands; some of them were marrying artists. Should she? Or could she become an artist herself? These questions emerge in *The Sun and the Moon*, the novella she began to write a year later. There were many young men about, but none particularly attracted her. She had briefly been engaged to a young man who lived across the street, but the romance floundered. They had been walking from Pat's house to the Yacht Club along a path that bordered a vegetable garden when Pat picked a handful of peas and started to eat them. Her fiancé looked at her with horror and said, "You have no right to those peas. They're not your peas." She replied with a fine alliteration that may have ended the romance: "That's the penalty you pay for planting your peas on a public path."[29]

Pat and Phil Golding were good friends and would "jaw" until three in the morning, but she felt no "vibrations" from him – which was probably why her parents later allowed her to travel with him to New York without a chaperone to see the Rogers and Hart musical *Pal Joey*. Another good friend was the radio announcer Toby de Bouvier Holly, later known as de B. Holly, with whom she prepared duologues for the local branch of the CBC; but there were no vibrations from him either.[30] From 18 July to 18 August 1939, Pat took a drama course with Charles Rittenhouse, a dynamic Winnipegger who represented the Canadian Little Theatre movement and had been brought to the city by the Theatre Guild of Saint John.[31] Pat had a serious crush on Rittenhouse in the summer of 1939, and she gave him the manuscript of *The Sun and the Moon* to read. It seems that this crush did not go anywhere either, though she grieved when he left and recalls that in the next few months she slimmed down considerably, losing almost forty pounds[32] – and perhaps her nickname Podge. The plot of *The Sun and the Moon* may represent a high degree of wish fulfillment, with its slim young protagonist and older artist lover.

The outbreak of war caught Pat, and many of her Rothesay circle, by surprise. She was sailing with Phil Golding and a group of friends on the river when a radio program was interrupted to announce the outbreak of war. Everyone was sobered, suddenly aware that the world they knew was gone forever.[33] Some of the group immediately enlisted, others began to do what they could for the war effort. To make money for the English Spitfire fund, the theatre group toured a play written by Phil Golding around New Brunswick. Pat played the main character, an older woman whose life is destroyed when her husband betrays her with a younger woman. As the play combined a highly topical theme – divorce – and was directed by Tommy Ross, there would have been knowing remarks in the Saint John audience.

In early December 1939, Pat wrote to Erica Deichmann: "Phil's play went well, it's very funny; but they played it so hard for comedy that it was almost a burlesque show, which I consider a pity, because the pathos in it could have been brought out to a great advantage … Life is hectic here – so many parties. I am at the stage where I am disgusted with everyone and feel inclined to lead the life of a recluse. There is too much drinking and talk of women and drunks for my liking. I've seen enough of it now for even the novelty to be gone." Worse still, her stories were not being published. She had sent one to *Maclean's* and the editor returned it because the heroine told a lie: "Sanctimonious old so and so's!"[34]

The war now commanded everyone's energies. In 1939 Lionel Page was sent to Iceland, where he was in command of the Canadian troops who helped organize defences there in late 1939–40. Shortly afterwards, Aunt Bibbi Whitehouse, who was visiting Canada, decided to stay on for the duration of the war. With Lionel away, Rose gave up the expense of the house in Rothesay and the family moved to the residential La Tour Hotel in Saint John.

It was about this time that Pat had a strange experience. Tommy Ross had taken ill just before Christmas. It did not seem to be a serious illness, and it was a great shock to her friends when she died suddenly on 23 January 1940. Many people in Saint John were desolated, especially Pat, who later recalled that soon afterwards, or early in the spring, she saw in the darkness of her room one night "a whole lot of little specks of light dancing, like a little molecular dance, like a lot of illuminated gnats. And they danced and danced and they coagulated and got bigger and bigger, and it became an outline of a human being, all in this molecular light. Then, it filled out and it was Tommy" – a Tommy who was bright, shining, and beautiful, just as she had been in life. Pat and Tommy had sometimes argued about immortality: Pat believed there was life after death, but Tommy did not. "So when I saw her alive in the room, I said, 'So I was right after all.' And she said, 'Yes, that's what I came back to tell you.' And I said, 'Then tell me, tell me about it. I want to know.' And she said, 'I can't. Every death is personal, if you were to know about my death it would do you no good for your own. It's something we do individually.' And she said, 'I must go. But I just wanted you to know that.' And she put her fingertips on my arms to sort of lean forward and give me a farewell kiss, and I put my fingertips on her arms and underneath my fingers, the solid flesh began to turn into the texture of dry rice."[35]

The experience could have lasted only seconds, but it was vivid and totally convincing to Pat. It changed her. She had come to believe that "the impossible was possible; that the boundaries were not what I'd always thought they were, that there was a great deal more going on than I was capable of seeing. And that we were immortal."[36] Her helpless grief for Tommy, expressed in the following sonnet –

They have put people in her house already –
& filled her bowls with flowers & touched her books
& played her gramophone & nothing looks
the same. My lips will not stay steady ...[37]

now changed to affirmation.

Tommy's desire to help the British war effort may have encouraged Pat to take some practical action herself. In March 1940 she began a course in motor mechanics with Peggy Pickersgill and wrote to Erica: "Peg and I start our motor mechanics course on Friday. If only that will put me in a position to get over to England I shall be a happy girl. I am terribly eager to get over."[38] But in June 1940 Lionel was transferred to England to be in charge of the Canadian base camps. Now that he had received his marching orders, he worried about the family at home, especially Rose. He wrote to Pat from Ottawa saying, "You should not have to bear the responsibility but things seem to be turning out that way ... I hate to say it but I do feel your duty at the moment is to stay by Mummie & not go hare-ing off much as I am sure you want to ...

there are lots of people who can drive cars etc but very few of us who can help Mummie."[39] Lionel clearly thought that Rose could not manage on her own and urged Pat to reconsider the situation. Pat decided to stay with the family.

That winter she obtained her first paid position as a sales clerk in the book section of a Saint John department store, Manchester, Robertson and Allison.[40] It was a natural place for her to choose, especially as she had been writing seriously for over four years now, ever since her return from England. A series of notebooks titled "Eighteen," "Nineteen & Twenty," in which she wrote her poems each year, reveal a serious, independent apprenticeship. During this period she wrote more than two hundred poems, many personal, but some with wider reference. In a poem titled "For V.W." she refers to Virginia Woolf's suicide on 28 March 1941:

> Unable to shutter the eye,
> unable to pull the blind
> on the fine, bright embroidery of the mind
> she chose to die.[41]

Meanwhile, her small poetry-writing group, had now become interested in the Canadian Authors Association. In July 1940 Eric Gaskell, the secretary of the CAA, had been invited to visit Saint John to help organize a local chapter and, that August, Pat had driven to Quebec with Kay Smith and Jean Sweet to attend the annual meeting of the CAA at Ste-Anne-de-Bellevue. Some of the Canadian authors she met there, including Arthur Bourinot, Kathleen Strange, and Madge MacBeth, seemed "so self important ... appalling."[42] But there was one bright spot at the conference – her meeting with Anne Marriott (1913–1997), whose long narrative poem "The Wind Our Enemy" Pat admired. Anne told her that Alan Crawley in British Columbia was starting a new magazine called *Contemporary Verse*.

Crawley was a former Winnipeg lawyer who, in London in 1917, had become friends with the English poet Harold Monro and through Monro had come to love the Georgians and the younger war poets. In 1933, when back home in Winnipeg, Crawley had developed chorditis and became blind, so could no longer practise law. In the fall of 1934 the family moved to Victoria, where he met the poets Doris Ferne, Floris McLaren, Anne Marriott, and Dorothy Livesay, who convinced him to found a new poetry magazine dedicated to publishing good verse. What he visualized was a magazine based on *Poetry* (Chicago), then edited by

Harriet Monroe, and he wanted to emphasize good *modern* writing. *Contemporary Verse* came into being in June 1941. Crawley managed as editor, despite his disability, because sound in poetry was of crucial importance to him, and his wife Jean would read each submission aloud.

Pat was still meeting with the group of artists, poets, and playwrights who gathered regularly in Ted Campbell's studio on the second floor of a corner building on Prince William Street overlooking the water. The painters Brittain, Campbell, and Humphrey had been joined by Jack Bishop and also by Vi Gillet, who taught painting. Occasionally the painter Kathleen Shackleton – called "Shackie," sister to the famous Antarctic explorer Sir Ernest Shackleton – spent time with the group. The poets were still Kay Smith, Jean Sweet, and Pat and the writers Phil Golding and de B. Holly of the CBC. Occasionally they had parties, with Humphrey playing the violin and Campbell the large piano which dominated the studio.

Miller Brittain's studio was farther down Prince William Street and was much smaller than Campbell's. It was rather bare – just a couple of chairs, a couch, and a gallon bottle of Catawaba wine. Because he needed a model, Brittain asked Pat to sit for him. He spent much time on the preparation of the canvas, mixing egg tempera and oil glazes while talking about the technique of the Old Masters. Pat found the process "terribly exciting" and wrote about the portrait to Erica Deichmann, noting, "I am completely blind to whether it looks like me or not but it is beautiful work."[43] It is a striking portrait of the young Pat, with short dark hair, high spots of colour in her cheeks, and an arresting gaze – angry or unhappy. This is a portrait of a passionate woman. Her large eyes and full mouth, with her trademark bright red lipstick thickly applied, are the focus of the portrait. Brittain's handling of colour is superb: the mauve of the flimsy scarf blends into a deeper mulberry and then into the muted teal-blue of the girl's sweater. He painted a small white horse in the right background, and when Pat asked him why, he said it represented her "idealism."[44] There was apparently no discussion of the large prickly bush in the left foreground.

In a letter to Erica, Pat wrote, "I do like Miller. He has grand ideas about life. 'Don't get yourself low in your philosophizing, Miss. There is little to be gay about now – so don't, *don't* think too much.'"[45] She had much to be unhappy about – the war, Tommy's death, the fact that she had to stay home and "look after Mummie," rather than going to England to help with the war effort. There was also the general philistinism of Rothesay; only the artist contributed to society – or so she was beginning to think. The painting, finished in March 1940, seems to have taken

Ted Campbell's studio, Saint John, c. 1940. *From left to right*: Mr Nason, Philip
Golding, Pat Page, Miller Brittain, Vi Gillet, and Kathleen Shackleton.

three months.[46] Brittain may have hoped that Pat's parents would buy
it, but they did not.[47] Later, in the early fifties, International Business
Machines bought the portrait for an exhibition that toured North America, and it was later purchased for a private collection.[48] Artist David
Blackwood has remarked that in his opinion the three greatest modernist
portraits at the Art Gallery of Ontario are Augustus John's *Marhesa
Casati*, Miller Brittain's *Lillian Schaefer*, and Lawren Harris's *Rev. Mr.
Bland*. Equal in aesthetic accomplishment, Blackwood remarks, is Miller
Brittain's portrait of P.K. Page.[49]

On their return to Saint John in September after the CAA meeting,
Jean Sweet and Pat decided to establish a poetry contest, for which the
first prize would be five dollars. Pat was one of the judges. They received
a great many poems imitating the Confederation Poets, especially Bliss
Carman and Sir Charles G.D. Roberts. One poem, however, "Flirtation
in Silver," caught Pat's eye, with its fresh and original language. The
judges decided to give it an honourable mention, and when Pat discovered that the poet was another young woman, Elizabeth Brewster, she
wrote to her. In April 1941 Elizabeth (Betty) was invited to come to a
meeting of the group of painters and writers in Ted Campbell's studio.

When the young Betty Brewster came in April 1941, she saw at once
paintings of nudes on display. All of the group – unlike Betty – drank and

smoked. She was a little overwhelmed but took everything in. Much later, in the 1970s, Page wrote a short story called "Victoria" in which she describes Betty and her camera gaze: "short, self-contained, self-centered; hair cut straight and square above those bright eyes."[50] Brewster responded with the short story "Essence of Marigold," describing the handsome "Marguerite," a tall young woman in her twenties, who glowed like a crimson gladiolus as she blew smoke rings and flirted, observed by a much younger girl. "I thought that Marguerite was terribly sophisticated,"[51] she said.

The relationship between writer and mentor is sometimes a mixed one: Pat had been a little unkind in her depiction of the young Brewster in "Victoria," and the latter had responded with "Essence of Marigold." But the two were longtime friends. Pat had taken a real interest in the young Betty Brewster's poetry in the early 1940s and had helped her to understand the moderns. As she explained to her protégé, "The annoying part about poetry is that it really doesn't depend on inspiration entirely as is so commonly believed – it's a long hard grind to turn out a finished work, as I know only too well."[52] She also lent Betty her annotated copy of Harold Monro's *Twentieth Century Poetry* and encouraged her to give the moderns a fair reading: "[T]hey are the people who have been brave enough to experiment. Personally I *do* like some of them and *all* interest me. As to their search for ugliness I believe ugliness has as much place in poetry as anything else. Poetry is the expression of mankind and heaven knows the world is not only composed of beauty; if the poet is big enough he can endow that very ugliness with a grandeur that is in itself beautiful. And again I think poetry should be allowed to scream if it wants to – birth and death, the two inescapables – are screaming matters.[53]

In the late spring of 1941, Pat and her mother, aunt, and brother went as usual to the fisherman's house at New River Beach. The two-storey house was just across the highway from the beach. There was a simple living room with a wooden floor, of which every two boards were painted orange and the next two painted blue. The effect was beautiful, as if sunlight was coming in through the shutters. Despite the worry of having Lionel away at the war, the family seemed happy at the beach. Pat had a small bedroom upstairs, where she worked on her writing every morning.[54] She wrote to Betty Brewster that New River Beach was heaven: "I, at last, have a room to myself again. It is almost a year since I had a place of my own where I could work – so I'm hoping for an industrious six months. At the moment I have to work bundled up like an old crone for it is cold and our only source of heat is a fire downstairs which does little for my garret room."[55] During that summer Pat wrote several short stories, a novel, a three-act play, and "scads" of poetry.

Much of Pat's early reading also came together that summer. In the thirties, as we have seen, she had read deeply in such novels as *A Man Named Luke* and *The Fountain*, and had been attracted to Joanna Field's *A Life of One's Own*. Also in the 1930s she had come across a novel by John Cowper Powys called *Wolf Solent* (1929), in which the main character experiences changes in consciousness by identifying – and even projecting himself into – external objects: "He was a leaf among leaves ... He had fallen back into the womb of his real mother."[56] Pat had a similarly intense experience with the atoms of a chair.[57]

She had been very much taken by one of Ezra Pound's poems, "A Girl," which she had found in the Monro anthology:

> The tree has entered my hands,
> The sap has ascended my arms,
> The tree has grown in my breast –
> Downward,
> The branches grow out of me, like arms.[58]

In the margin, Pat had pencilled (probably when in London in 1935): "Since my tree experience, E.P. vaguely makes sense to me." This suggests that she has been trying some of Field's tree exercises when walking in the large beech forest close to Aunt Bibbi's house in Purley. The experience funnelled into one of her own poems called "Reflection," published in *Canadian Poetry Magazine* (July 1939), which expresses a similar girl-into-tree state[59] to that described in the Pound poem:

> In the noon of yesterday I saw a tree
> pretending it was a woman,
> bending over a stream, ...
> And I bent over the water beside it, ...
> and I was a tree ...
> In the reflection I saw
> a tree and a woman bending,
> merged in the water
> and knew not whether I was the woman or tree.[60]

By 1939 much of this early work and reading had found its way into a short story that is now lost (but which many years later her friend Kay Smith recalled she had encouraged Pat to develop into a novel).[61] This became *The Sun and the Moon* (1944) the story of a young woman, Kristin, whose birth coincided with an eclipse of the moon, giving her supernatural powers. Like the subject of Pat's mid-1930s poem "The Moon-Child," Kristin, too, is a "moon child" but is the victim of her ability to project her consciousness into material objects so that she becomes one with inanimate objects, for instance, a chair or the rocks on the beach.

Kristin is seventeen – Page's age when she began her own voyage of discovery – and a passive observer of the world when Carl, an established painter and an older man, falls in love with her. The two become engaged to marry, but Kristin is devastated when she discovers that she – associated with the moon – has the power to "eclipse" Carl's "sun," his talent as an artist. Ultimately, Kristin allows herself to be metamorphosed into a tree during a climactic storm, losing human consciousness and her power to harm the man she loves.

As Margaret Atwood pointed out in her introduction to a 1973 reprint, this tale is a "Romance" in structure, with psychological and mythic metamorphosis.[62] The male and female figures are associated with sun and moon, respectively, but the book also explores some prevailing contemporary stereotypes about the social roles of men and women in relation to art. Carl's painting, *The Boy*, "looked strong and virile and masculine against the pale femininity of her bedroom. Here we have it, [Kristin] said to herself, the sun and the moon together, and she looked from the painting and felt secure. Carl will predominate, she thought, as he does here."[63]

Pat was clearly intrigued by the modernist debate about the nature of the creative consciousness (although she may not have described it as such) and its relation to gender. Kristin's statement carries overtones of some of the twenties' and thirties' debates on gender and its relationship to art. In *A Room of One's Own*, Virginia Woolf had suggested that the truly creative mind is fertilized by both male and female, but D.H. Lawrence reflected, in his letters and novels, on the fearful possession of the male by the female, which he saw as a form of death. The modernist gender debate seems to be played out through the symbols of *The Sun and the Moon,* where there is finally an eclipse of one force (the male sun) by the female moon.

Although Kristin gives up her mind rather than sapping her lover's creativity – thus upholding the conventional mores of the period – the woman, possibly an embryo artist, sacrifices herself for the male's art. But Page's text allows for an alternative reading at the point where the climactic metamorphosis takes place:

[Kristin] could hear the wind again, pulling at the trees ... And she felt part of it, like a branch torn off and carried by the wind ... She knew only an instinctive desire to stay standing ... to dig her roots into the earth ... Graceful, swaying slightly, she faced the calm of the day and drank from the rich, wet earth – steady in the security of her fibre and bark; content in the sweet uprising form of her growth, holding her branches up to the sky in the simple, generous gesture of the victor who knows victory to be within.[64]

This final metaphor of woman-as-tree, ultimately the feminine life force, is strong and self-assured. After exploring in fiction the situation of a woman who sacrifices herself for her husband's art, in real life Pat determined to take up the role of the woman artist. To some degree the tale is a medium through which the young Pat began to explore, both consciously and unconsciously, some of the issues faced by the woman artist.

As she completed *The Sun and the Moon* in the summer of 1941, Pat received a letter from editor Alan Crawley asking if she had any poems to submit to *Contemporary Verse*. She sent him several, including "Ecce Homo," the poem describing her 1936 visit to a gallery to see Epstein's sculpture and linking the experience of viewing and talking about modern art with the evolution of her own aesthetic consciousness. This experience, so different from Pat's conventional verse of the mid-1930s, is incorporated into a free-flowing but discontinuous narrative, characterized by synesthesia and elliptical statement. It acknowledges an "unexpected entry / into the door of my mind":

I looked and the little room was filled with might,
with the might of fear in stone,
immense and shackled ...
the God of Death,
in a little room in a gallery in Leicester Square,
silently standing there.

"There is much we do not know,"
you turned to me.
(Behold the Man, Rima, polygamy!)
"I think we should find somewhere nice and quiet for tea.
To think," you said.
I nodded my head. "To think," I said.
And like a young tree I put out a timid shoot

and prayed for the day, the wonderful day when it bore its fruit.
And suddenly we were out in the air again.[65]

Shortly after this poem was submitted to *Contemporary Verse*, Pat left
Rothesay with the intention of becoming a writer. Her father, who had
read the manuscript of *The Sun and the Moon* when home on leave,
recognized that his daughter had talent. He offered her sufficient funds
to live on – eighty-five dollars a month – so that she could move to Montreal, rent a room of her own, and practise her craft.

CHAPTER 5

Montreal
Art and Life, 1941–1944

Love. There's another word for you. All but perished.
A concept with an inadequate label. *Love* won't do.
As many kinds as the Inuit's words for snow.
What is it you feel for your mother?
For your dog?

I once was caught in its slipstream
and like dust
in a ray of sunlight
everything shone.
P.K. Page, "Alphabetical"[1]

The young woman's skin was like velvet under the shade of her large hat. Tawny skin, huge grey eyes – her face was a portrait framed by a wide black brim. Or so thought Jori Smith, a Montreal painter. It was spring 1942 and Jori was lunching with her sister-in-law Constance Garneau at a new restaurant popular with artists. "Constance, look at that girl over there. Hasn't she a face like a pansy? You know, those dark-faced pansies with white inside and that special velvety quality." A week later Kit Shaw, the photo librarian at the *Montreal Standard*, telephoned her: "I've met this absolutely delightful girl, Jori, you'll love her. Can I bring her for tea?" When Jori opened the door to her studio on rue Ste-Famille, she recognized the younger woman instantly. "My God, you're the girl I saw in The Salad Bar."[2]

The young woman was Pat Page. She had been in Montreal for five months, and Jori had seen her having lunch with Eric Gaskell of the Canadian Authors Association. Many years later, reflecting on her life-long friendship with Jori Smith, Page said, "I think that people anticipate each other ... I don't think you meet for the first time ... Either you have opened the same door ... or something has anticipated the immediate physical encounter."[3] The doorway that opened to the friendship between the two women was their creative vocation; as Pat later wrote to Jori: "I know no one who paints more accurately as I would like to write."[4] Throughout the Montreal years she was to move between two groups of people – literary and artistic – but the boundaries were porous and the personal connections very close.

Pat Page had left Saint John in October 1941 with a suitcase, a hat box, and her typewriter. The box was large enough to hold, among other things, an aluminum kettle, essential for boarding-house living but impossible to buy during wartime. After a brief stay with the Jacquays, friends of her parents, she found a room at a boarding house called the Epicurean Club at 1484 Sherbrooke Street. An early 1940s story, "Looking for Lodgings," a combination of realism and surrealism, describes a young woman, much like herself, searching for a place to stay in wartime Montreal and encountering a series of landladies who fall back on the same refrain: "Ain't got no room. Ain't got none." When the young woman finally obtains a room of her own, her sense of possession is so expansive that it takes in the whole city: "She leaned on a curve of air, on the wide gradual slope of a foothill; she spread out like water, unconfined. Time shrank. She filled the room, became too large for it ... She went down the steps into the night. She spread over the city. She was the city – spreading out and out. She floated high and horizontal."[5]

Pat's room was small but high up – on the third floor of the Epicurean Club – with big windows that flooded the room with light; later, she moved down to the second floor, where her room was larger and there was a balcony where she grew pink petunias in the summer.[6] Here she kept regular office hours. She wrote and typed her stories, plays, and poems during the morning, had a quick lunch at the corner drugstore, and worked again during the afternoon. In the late afternoon or evening she would meet friends and sometimes invite one of them for dinner at her boarding house.

She was highly self-disciplined. From October to December 1941 Pat worked mostly on her own, sending out the manuscript of *The Sun and the Moon* and various short stories to editors and publishers. In effect, she adopted a regime that nurtured her creativity, and by setting herself up as a professional writer she evolved into one. It was an enormous encouragement when the novella was accepted by Macmillan, probably in early 1942. During this period she also wrote a half-dozen short stories and retyped her earlier work.

During Pat's first five months in Montreal, her most important literary contact was the blind Alan Crawley, the editor of *Contemporary
Verse* in British Columbia. Crawley was closer in spirit to the Georgians
and to the Imagists than to the later moderns, but he knew good poetry.
He accepted some new poems by Pat in a letter that arrived after she
had settled in Montreal; in the letter he acknowledged the high quality
of her work and offered to critique it. Replying in early December, Pat
said that she did not shrink from criticism; indeed, she welcomed it: "At
the moment I am on my own in Montreal knowing practically no one
who writes and having no critical eyes scan what I am writing and
should welcome anything you have to say. More than anything else in
this world I would like to be a good poet – which remark sounds so ab-
surdly young that I almost blush at having written it; I say it simply that
you may know that I am working in earnest."[7] Crawley was a careful
and sympathetic editor. An older Page recalled that he encouraged her to
rethink some poems and pointed out occasional weaknesses in diction
and structure. In the first issue of *Contemporary Verse* (September 1941),
Crawley included two poems by Pat, "Ecce Homo" and an imagist
poem, "The Crow":

By the wave rising, by the wave breaking
high to low;
by the wave riding the air, sweeping the high air low
in a white foam, in a suds,
there
like a churchwarden, like a stiff
turn-the-eye-inward old man
in a cutaway, in the mist
stands
the crow.[8]

In December Crawley published another of her poems, "Blackout,"
which expressed war fears.

In Montreal, Pat saw her old friend John Sutherland, who had left
New Brunswick and was taking courses in English at McGill University.
He had fallen in love with Pat, and before she left Rothesay he had written her long, importuning letters: "I wish you could love me ... love between us would make an anchor position from which I might launch
into new ventures." He later proposed: "We would have a new, rich, life
ahead of us ... of Montreal I know that everything here can be perfect."[9]
Sutherland was only three years younger than Page, but she found him

a little "wet behind the ears."[10] Their friendship was strictly literary, and he may have encouraged her to think of Montreal as a city where she might begin her literary career.

Sutherland was attending McGill in defiance of his father's wishes (he had not yet recovered from tuberculosis) and was badly in need of money. On several occasions Pat gave part of her living allowance to John, but instead of buying food he spent the money on chocolates and huge bouquets of roses – for Pat. This infuriated her. *She* couldn't afford flowers, and she saw her hard-won allowance being frittered away. In response, she wrote a poem called "Desiring Only" that contained the line "pass me nothing of love done up in chocolates."[11] Sutherland, who came across the poem in the April 1942 issue of *Preview*, misread it. Not recognizing his own actions, he believed it to be a poem about a lover.

After slightly more than two months in Montreal, Pat went to Truro by troop train to join the family for Christmas. Her father was now major-general in command of the Fourth Canadian Division stationed at Debert, Nova Scotia. She was the only civilian on board the train, which was continually delayed, stopping and starting as winter storms sent huge drifts of snow across the tracks. The soldiers were restless, knowing they would be embarking at Halifax for Europe and the war. At one stop Pat bought a pack of cards and started a game of poker with a group of soldiers. On a winning streak she won most of the hands, which made her feel guilty, since they were playing for money. At the next station she bought chocolate bars with her winnings and shared them with the men – a curious reversal of her childhood experience after the First World War, when the soldiers on the troopship returning to Canada had shared their chocolate with her.[12]

From 1939 to 1944 the emotional climate in eastern Canada, and especially in Atlantic port cities, was clouded by war fears. On this visit, Pat had a sense of impending disaster; indeed, this was to be her last Christmas with all the family. Immediately after the holidays, Lionel left for Newfoundland, and Rose joined him soon afterwards. He had been reassigned as general officer, commander-in-chief of the First Canadian Division and the Newfoundland forces, and Pat's brother Michael was preparing to go to sea with the Royal Canadian Navy. Many of her Montreal friends had brothers and lovers overseas or in the services, and like everyone else she was now scanning the newspapers for the "Missing" or "Lost in Action" columns.

It was strange to be living in a city from which most young men had disappeared. Pat was very much aware of the legions of women waiting for their men to return. Some were Englishwomen (including the artist Gertrude Hermes, who sculpted a head of Page) who had packed up their belongings and moved from England to Montreal for the duration of the war. Women especially experienced a great feeling of emotional need. There were also changes in daily life. Butter, sugar, tea, and coffee were rationed, and meat was available only once a week. Wine and liquor were not available. People who wanted a drink in Montreal and did not have access to bootlegged whisky were reduced to an unrefined *alcool* from the Quebec liquor board. Pat saved her coupons for cigarettes and other necessities to send overseas to her father and brother.

Men not in the armed forces were employed in factories, producing armaments and essential items, so there was no manpower for the usual services, such as road crews. During heavy winter snowstorms Pat made the first tracks along her street when she went out early. The city plowed only the main streets, leaving enormous banks of snow with arched tunnels at the corners for people to pass under. Sometimes old-fashioned *calèches* went by, their bells jingling. She was reading Tolstoy, Dostoevsky, and Gogol at the time, and it sometimes seemed that she was not in Canada but in Russia.[13]

The war and the war effort brought people together. Everyone in Montreal knew, or knew of, everyone else in the arts; eventually they connected in person. Pat's acquaintances included another Saint John friend, Priscilla Hazen, who had found a position as a columnist on the *Montreal Standard*. Through her she met Kit Shaw, the photo librarian at the newspaper, whose husband, Neufville, was a schoolmaster and was interested in poetry. Also at the *Standard* was Philip Surrey, the art director (and later a full-time painter) who in 1943 hired Mavis Gallant – in the thirties and forties, journalism was the first step for women who wanted to be writers. The *Standard*'s editor was Arnold Davidson Dunton, better known as Davey, an attractive man-about-town who dated Pat fairly regularly until mid-1942, when he was called to Ottawa by the Wartime Standards Board. (He was later chairman of the board of the CBC and co-chairman of the Royal Commission on Bilingualism and Biculturalism.)

Another acquaintance was a young Maritimer, Jack Cram, who Priscilla Hazen had introduced to Pat in late 1941. It was at a gathering at Jack's flat to listen to the new music of Prokofiev and Shostakovich that Pat met Patrick Anderson, a sleek young Englishman with an impish grin who wore his hair brushed back severely from his forehead in T.S. Eliot fashion. Page later described him as "weedy and extremely thin, he looked like one of those Englishman who'd grown up under a rock. No colour in his cheeks ... just very pallid ... he looked as if he drank nothing but tea."[14] Patrick had been active in the Oxford Student Union and in 1938 had been awarded a two-year Commonwealth Fellowship, a kind of reverse Rhodes Scholarship, to Columbia University in New York. There he and his American-born wife Peggy, an artist, had published a little magazine called *The Andersons*.

The couple had moved to Canada in 1940, and Anderson was now teaching at a Montreal private school, Selwyn House, with Neufville Shaw, Kit's husband. There he prodded Shaw into action with the remark, "Of course, if this were England, we would be founding a poetry magazine instead of grousing about schoolmasters' salaries."[15] Stung by this suggestion of colonial inferiority, Shaw made a series of phone calls that brought into being the first meeting of the *Preview* group.

Preview was to be a poetry magazine to "preview" writers' work, and was first published in approximately ten pages, 8½ by 11 inches., mimeographed. The first issue appeared in March 1942, and the editors were F.R. Scott, Margaret Day (who married the painter Philip Surrey), Bruce Ruddick (who was studying medicine and later became a prominent New York psychiatrist), Neufville Shaw, and Patrick Anderson, who became its most influential editor and the driving force behind the magazine. The first issue was assembled in the Andersons' tiny apartment above a garage on a lane near Dorchester Street. Working in the kitchen, the only room with a table, the group stapled and rolled the few pages of the magazine and affixed a one-cent stamp to an addressed wrapper. Several members made a list of people who might subscribe for a dollar a year, while others piled first issues on the stove because there wasn't anywhere else to put them. When Patrick said to his wife, "Peggy, I think we should have some tea," she lit the gas and burned half the first issue of *Preview*.

When Anderson first met Pat at Jack Cram's flat, he already knew her poetry from *Contemporary Verse*. He told her about *Preview* and asked if she would like to come to the next meeting of the group, to be held at Frank and Marian Scott's house at 451 Clarke Avenue in Westmount. Pat arrived at the second meeting of *Preview* in April 1942. She was frightened out of her wits and intimidated by Scott, a published poet whose work she had admired in the anthology *New Provinces* (1936). He was not only a law professor at McGill but a social activist to boot. Scott was older (b. 1899) than most of the group, but was witty and pleasant. Page later recalled that he struck her as very tall, thin, with an aquiline nose. He blinked a lot and tossed his head, so that it was sometimes difficult to focus on him. He was also a conjuror, fond of sleight

of hand, "and there was something of a conjuror in his manner and behaviour. Conjurors distract you with words or hand movements, so that
you never look at the thing they wish to conceal." It occurred to her
later that Scott may have developed some of these physical mannerisms
to draw attention away from his false left eye, lost in an attempt at a
fireworks display during World War I.[16]

Pat had brought several of her own poems to the meeting, including
"The Bones' Voice," which began "Who says the bone is mute / lies in
his throat."[17] Another was "Desiring Only," the poem written about
Sutherland:

> Desiring only the lean sides of the stomach
> sagging towards each other, unupholstered ...
> pass me nothing of love done up in chocolates ...
>
> Desiring only the bone on the Mount of Venus
> and the death rattle caught in the musical powder box ...
>
> Desiring only the bare soles of the feet
> pacing triumphantly the ultimate basement ...
> pass me no thick-carpeted personal contact,
> nor little slippers of pity and understanding.[18]

Like Sutherland, the *Preview* members may well have misread the poem.
Pat, annoyed by Sutherland's chocolates and flowers, wanted to get
down to basics in life as in art – "the ultimate basement" – and follow
her own destiny. To express this desire, she used a term from palmistry,
the Mount of Venus, which is located between the thumb and forefinger.
But to *Preview*-ites (as perhaps to us also), this may have seemed like a
much bolder – and more sexual – poem than she had intended.

The poems were passed around and all read them. After Pat had distributed hers to the group, nobody said a word. Pat was nervous and did-
n't know what to do. The long silence continued, which she interpreted
as a total dismissal; she began to think about how to get out of there.
"And then all of a sudden Frank, in a characteristic gesture, slapped his
thigh and said, 'Bones. Great God! Nobody writes about bones anymore.'
And instead of that falling on my ears like the kiss of death, it was the
most enormous relief just to have somebody say something."[19]

Suddenly everything was fine; everyone began to talk. The conversation turned to Eliot and his Anglo-Catholicism, about which Pat knew
little. She had heard of Eliot but she certainly didn't know what Anglo-

Catholicism was. Then they talked politics and Russia, about which she knew nothing. Anderson was a staunch Marxist, Scott a socialist (he was a staunch supporter of the Co-operative Commonwealth Federation, CCF), and the rest of the group were varying degrees of pink. Shaw was a keen intellectual, very interested in Carl Jung and Eliot's critical essays. But as Page recalled, "almost everything they talked about I knew nothing about. There was no way I could participate in the conversation and I sat there with my mouth open, looking stunned."

As the group rose to leave, Anderson said, very formally, "Miss Page, if you would like to come to the next *Preview* meeting, it will be held in the Samovar." This was a little restaurant in the basement of a boarding house, east of Main Street. To Pat's amazement, she was now a member of *Preview*. What she did not realize was that the long silence that had followed the first reading of her poems did not mean rejection but astonishment. This unaffected young woman possessed an assured contemporary voice. There was a polished turn in the last two lines of "The Bones' Voice" with its reference to "laughter / clinking about in the osseous cloister." And her poems were surprisingly sophisticated. "Desiring Only" was judged good enough for publication in the forthcoming issue of *Preview* (April 1942).[20]

Pat clearly had an original voice. She went on to become a better poet than either Anderson or Scott, which both may have sensed from the start. Convinced, however, that she knew nothing, she scrambled to read books the others had read, and she wrote continually. In typical female fashion she functioned as a helper to the *Preview* group, assembling issues, offering to type the poems selected for publication, and later cutting stencils for successive editions.[21]

Preview was the only "little magazine" in Canada east of the Rockies. Its first editorial said that the members rejected isolation: "As anti-fascists, we feel that the existence of a war between democratic culture and the paralyzing forces of dictatorship only intensifies the writer's obligation to work."[22] They clearly saw themselves as helping with the war effort. *Preview* encouraged creativity because the members wrote new poems to be read aloud at each meeting. And they learned from one another. Anderson's poetry, for example, was very fluent, characterized by Audenesque flights of metaphor, and Pat was soon experimenting with similar metaphors in her own poems.

On 9 May she wrote Alan Crawley saying, "I'd love to know your ideas on the *Preview* crowd. It is a strange group to be [in] association with – especially as I am the only non-political member." Despite her disclaimer, Pat was becoming more of a political writer herself. Her early

Montreal poems and stories deal with topics like bank strikes, ship-building offices, typists, conscription, bombs, and Guernica. In fact, by the seventh issue – in which, for the first time, the Page name led the list of *Preview* members – the whole group was actively reporting on contemporary events for about eighty subscribers.

Meanwhile, Pat's reading was broadening widely as she strove to keep up with *Preview* members. Shaw introduced her to Jung's *Modern Man in Search of a Soul,* which she found fascinating and continued to read over the next decade. Philip Surrey, the painter, talked about Eliot's critical essays. One of the unpublished verses in Pat's notebook, dated February 1942, suggests that she was already reading Eliot's poetry:

I should have brought my Eliot to breakfast
and read of out-worn disillusionment ...
I should have swallowed Wastelands with my porridge
and Mr. Sweeney with my egg and bacon;
the mood is definitely nineteen-twenty ...[23]

Her self-conscious lack of knowledge about contemporary poetry is echoed in the rueful line "I should have swallowed Wastelands with my porridge."

The acknowledged catalyst of the *Preview* group was Anderson, who spoke eloquently of the new 1930s poets, their concerns and their techniques, and referred often to "Holy Mother Russia." He was, as the other members of the group agreed, "a professional" poet who thought poets should wear capes and grow their hair, read the Communist Manifesto, and speak out for a second front for Russia. To Pat he seemed a kind of giant cuckoo, force-feeding his fledglings with poetry and Communism.[24] Although much of his political advice fell on deaf ears, Anderson's messianic sense of the poet's role was contagious.

Soon after Pat joined *Preview,* she proposed Sutherland for membership. But Patrick Anderson, Sutherland's friend, blackballed him. Sutherland did not know this and blamed others in the group. After this rejection, he started his own periodical, *First Statement,* subtitled *A Magazine for Young Canadian Writers,*[25] and reinvented himself as a critic, an editor, and a staunch supporter of Canadian literature.[26] *First Statement,* too, was typewritten and mimeographed, short (8–10 pages), and had a circulation of about seventy-five.

In September/October 1942, Sutherland published a somewhat dismissive article about Page's work in *First Statement,* saying that her poetry had been developing in the direction of Auden and Spender and that under *Preview*'s influence she had taken a large step forward. However, he disapproved of her wartime internationalism and chided her for a perceptive critical essay, "Canadian Poetry 1942" – one of Page's first forays into criticism – which had been published in *Preview*.[27] "P.K. Page advises young Canadian poets to 'hitch-hike to the towns and forget the country of your own head,'" Sutherland wrote, and he argued that she, like most Canadian modernists, had come to regard Canada as insignificant.[28] This was twisting Page's statement: she was not anti-Canadian. But Sutherland now wanted to find fault, and in the next few years he wrote essays that attacked both Page and Anderson.

His argument that most modernists and, by implication, *Preview* members were anti-Canadian and internationalists is not accurate, although many of them read and appreciated Eliot, Auden, Spender, and Day-Lewis. Pat's early verse often refers to Canadian subjects, as do her *Preview* poems. And Scott was strongly pro-Canadian. He had written a number of poems with Canadian subjects, including "Laurentian," as early as 1927. Other *Preview* members later wrote poems that were specifically Canadian, including Anderson's "Poem on Canada" in *The White Centre* (1946). But the clearest indication of the *Preview* group's interest is a discussion on the qualities of Canadian art at a meeting on 13 March 1944 in which Anderson, A.M. Klein, Page, Ruddick, Scott, and Shaw offered comments. Klein had asked whether the group may have been "too nationalist," in which Scott replied, "Not at all ... All we were concerned with was the development of art in Canada." The group later attempted to identify what Scott called "the real mooseness" of the moose (that is, the real Canadian-ness of Canadian life), which he thought had not yet fully appeared in poetry.[29]

Abraham Klein, a Montreal lawyer and poet, had been invited to join *Preview* at its inception, but he did not start attending meetings regularly until March 1944. Page recalls him reading his poem "Montreal" – "O city Metropole, isle riverain!" – in a robust baritone at a gathering in Patrick Anderson's kitchen. It was summer, and hot in the flat above the garage in the lane off Dorchester Street. The windows were wide open to let out the stifling heat while "Abe," as he was known, continued to read his bilingual poem:

> Where English vocable and roll Ecossic,
> Mollified by the parle of French
> Bilinguefact your air![30]

The *Preview* group. Margaret (Day) Surrey and Pat are at the centre of the photo and around them, in clockwise order, are Kit Shaw, Neufville Shaw, Bruce Ruddick, and F.R. Scott. Patrick Anderson is lying in the foreground.

Klein was the first Jewish person Pat knew. In an essay on him that she wrote much later, she recalled that he was wearing a dark suit when she first met him. But it was summer. "Summer dresses and open shirts. So Abe would not have been in the dark suit, which is how I see him in memory's eye. Memory, so faithless to fact, so eager to please and quick to invent."[31] There was an element of culture shock in her relationship with him. Nonetheless, as she once recalled, "love him I did" – platonically. They joked, read poems together, and occasionally after *Preview* meetings got together in the bar of the Ritz-Carlton Hotel. Once, in the Mount Royal Hotel bar, Klein declaimed the first lines of Rilke's *Duino Elegies* so that Page could hear them in the original German – so loudly and enthusiastically that he made the starched waiters nervous. Reflecting on her friendship with him (which, in terms of *Preview* meetings, would not have lasted more than three months), Page recognized how his poetry reached beyond surfaces to a larger reality, and credited him with helping to lay the groundwork that lead her to the Sufi poet Rumi.[32]

One evening, early in the formation of the group, they celebrated a windfall in subscriptions with a clowning picture-taking session.[33] But generally Page recalled Montreal as a sophisticated world, "polarized around Jung and Marx,"[34] and it was there that she first glimpsed the possibility of social solidarity through both poetry and politics. She thought Marx was preferable to Freud or Jung because Marx was bigger than the self. His work looked towards the future of humanity and society, whereas the psychologists were concentrating on the self and changing the self. Although she thought Marx's way was the better (because looking out was healthier than continually looking in), she remained unaffiliated with any political party. She did, however, do some work for both the CCF and the Communists.[35] Miriam Chapin, a well-known Montreal Communist, attempted unsuccessfully to recruit Page for the party.

By June 1942, recognizing that if she wanted to become a writer she should be self-supporting, Pat took a job as a clerk typist at Allied War Supplies. Her principal task was filing papers in the company vault, but it had the advantage that she could arrive early for work and cut *Preview* stencils on the heavy-duty office typewriter. She became aware of the unequal position of women in offices during wartime and wrote an essay for *Preview* describing this. She wrote several office poems including "Typists," "Offices," "The Stenographers," and "Shipbuilding Office" – all drawing on her experience there. When the typists at Allied War Supplies felt especially harassed, they sheltered in the vault and wept –

as she probably did. Her most vivid depiction of office life during wartime is in "The Stenographers," published in the July 1942 issue of *Preview*. Anderson, on holiday with Peggy at Baie-St-Paul, commiserated in a letter to Page: "It must be hell in the office and I can imagine that poems come slowly." Her boss was notoriously unpleasant to the staff, and Anderson's letter implies that he had fired Pat.[36]

But Pat distanced her experience by changing the feminine and personal voice of her earlier poems to a more detached narrator,[37] who observes rather than participates. She had discovered a new way to express emotion – through T.S. Eliot's conception of metaphor rather than through statement. Discussion by members of the *Preview* group of Eliot's "objective correlative" affected her deeply. Eliot argued that "the only way of expressing emotion in the form of art is by finding an 'objective correlative'; in other words, a set of objects, a situation, a chain of events which shall be the formula of that particular emotion."[38] As Page later concluded when discussing her poetry of this period, it was essential to connect the individual experience with something larger than oneself: "For your own experience to be valuable, you have to find an objective correlative for that experience, and by so doing, you can get yourself into larger realms than you would if you [continued] telling your own experience through your poetry."[39]

Certainly, "The Stenographers" expresses the universal:

After the brief bivouac of Sunday,
their eyes, in the forced march of Monday to Saturday,
hoist the white flag, flutter in the snowstorm of paper,
haul it down and crack in the midsun of temper.

Her images express the powerlessness and entrapment experienced by women workers during wartime, the sense of life first as a forced march and then as a frenetic race. Page's metaphors are military: the stenographers "bivouac" or rest from marching on the weekends, but their weeks are a "forced march" of continuous labour. They jump when the boss shouts dictation, rushing to keep up with his voice, unable to type fast enough. Between the first draft of a letter (when he reads and corrects it) and the finished letter and carbon copy, there is a pause when they think of happier days when they were children at the seaside. Their present "boy-friends of blood" – suggesting both that they are soldiers and that the connection is merely sexual – bring no love or respite. At night "Their beds are their oceans – salt water of weeping / the waves that

they know – the tide before sleep." The next day, the whole process begins again as the young women, crisp in their starched blouses and
dresses, arrive at the office:

> efficient and sure as their adding machines;
> yet they weep in the vault, they are taut as net curtains
> stretched upon frames. In their eyes I have seen
> the pin men of madness in marathon trim ...[40]

Through this narrowest of apertures, the iris and pupil of the eye, the
drama of their lives is enacted and speeded up. The iris is a stadium
where stick men run a frantic and endless race – like the typists. At the
conclusion, our attention is brought back to war with the reference to
"marathon," and the battle it signifies. In the lives of the typists on the
home front Pat sees intolerable stress and incipient madness beyond
tears. Her voice is crisp, assured, like those of Eliot and Auden, and deep
feeling is contained and distanced through metaphor. The poem is certainly one of the best written in Canada in the forties. But beneath the
objective lines, there is the perceptive and vulnerable subjective sensibility of the young woman herself. Scott, then visiting Harvard, wrote to
Page saying how very much he liked "The Stenographers."

In July 1942, when Pat left Allied War Supplies, her poem "The
Mole" was published in the prestigious American magazine *Poetry*. She
spent the next four months working on poetry and prose, and typing a
number of short stories. That fall she received a telegram from Ellen Elliott, an editor at Macmillan – which had postponed publicaation of *The
Sun and the Moon* owing to wartime paper shortages – saying they were
ready to go to press. Pat panicked. She thought that she and her writing
had changed and the novel represented juvenilia. But as Scott remarked,
she had written the manuscript in good faith; changing her mind about
its value did not invalidate it, so why not use a pseudonym?

Pat spent the Christmas of 1942 in Montreal. On this New Year's –
or the following year – she was walking with a group of people when she
saw the artist Miller Brittain, now in uniform, stepping off a tram. Im-
pulsively she ran to meet him, throwing her arms around him: "These
were my people. They didn't have money, they didn't dress well, but they
were interested in live things."[41] During the 1942 holidays, she met the
poet and critic A.J.M. Smith, better known as "Art," who was now
teaching at Michigan State University but had briefly returned to Canada
to socialize with his Montreal friends. On New Year's Day, Pat wrote
to thank him for his comments on her work. At the same time, she re-

sponded vehemently to Smith's remark that her poetry was becoming much like Anderson's: "What you said about me becoming Patrick has haunted me. It isn't so, is it? Say, 'no.' I'm terrified of anyone who influences me. I simply had to cut Hopkins out of my life."[42] But she was grateful to Smith for offering to read *The Sun and the Moon*: "The damn thing is still part of me even though I know how bad it is. Is one always sentimental about a first novel? I would sooner not be. Use your sharpest scalpel and I shall thank you."[43] We do not know what changes Smith made to the manuscript. Because of the wartime paper scarcity, Macmillan pulped Pat's original manuscript, recycling the paper for new publications. But I suspect that Page herself had made some changes and may have given the male artist figure some physical characteristics based on Frank Scott.

By November, Pat had found a new job through a fellow boarder at the Epicurean Club, Dorothy Dee, secretary to H.R. MacMillan, then head of Wartime Merchant Shipping, a government agency. Pat was hired to research and write the stories of historic forts after which commissioned ships would be named. She also charted the progress of the ships as they were being built. While at this firm she met Maggie Davies, an Englishwoman with two children who had moved to Montreal for the war years and worked in drafting. The two women became close friends, and shortly after meeting they decided to take an apartment together on Victoria Street, where they stayed from May to September 1943. The apartment, near McGill, was modest but pretty, with a tiny kitchen, one bedroom, a dining room, and a living room. They took turns sleeping in the bedroom and in the dining room. Maggie's children volunteered to help Pat find a pseudonym for *The Sun and the Moon*. Elizabeth, the youngest, scrambled letters in Page's name and announced: "You should be K.P. Gape." But Page, who had always loved the name Judith, decided to become Judith Cape.[44]

It was a hot summer, but there were trees outside the open windows. A nickelodeon could be heard from a store across the street endlessly playing "There's a Star Spangled Banner Flying Somewhere." One afternoon Maggie did a quick sketch of Pat, just home from work, with her hair piled on top of her head and her blouse open because of the heat. In September 1943 they sublet an apartment belonging to Hugh Mac-Lennan, the author of *Barometer Rising* (1941), who had been awarded a Guggenheim Fellowship in New York. Pat and Maggie used this apartment until May 1944, and Maggie's children, attending boarding school, visited occasionally; it was during this time that Page wrote "The Bands and the Beautiful Children" – about Maggie's children running outside to hear a band going by: "And always attendant on bands, the beautiful children, / white with running and innocence."[45]

.::

The avant-garde in Montreal during the war years were a free-floating, inter-connected group of writers, artists, and political figures. When Pat met Jori Smith, she became part of a group interested in all forms of art. And they socialized together. On a beautiful spring day in 1942 the *Preview* group trailed up to the Théâtre de l'Ermitage for an exhibition of Paul-Émile Borduas's surrealist paintings – forty-five in number. Most were gouaches, a medium Pat herself later favoured, and brilliantly coloured, like the crimson and maroon *No. 6*, the abstracted head of a rooster (later called *Chantecler*), or *No. 12* (later *The Bottled Condor*), a surreal head of a bird in a bottle in splashes of grey, black, and yellow. A number of these paintings appear somewhat cubist in their attempt to show different aspects of a figure. However, all were abstract or surreal. A Quebec art critic wrote that Borduas's visions developed on the canvas before the "dazzled eyes of the artist, not on the stage of his inner theatre." That is, they developed on the canvas in the process of the painting, just as Page's poems were beginning to develop as one image generated another.[46]

Jori and her French Canadian husband Jean Palardy – an authority on early Quebec furniture – had an enormous studio in an old Montreal house on rue Ste-Famille. It was one big room, forty to fifty feet square, with a tiny kitchen and a bathroom, and slanted studio windows up one wall, which flooded the room with clear northern light. During the long Quebec winter, people – many of them artists – congregated there: Philip and Margaret Surrey; Patrick and Peggy Anderson; the distinguished painter Goodridge Roberts, better known as "Goodie"; Frank and Marian Scott, an artist; Bruce Ruddick; Neufville and Kit Shaw; Hugh and Dorothy MacLennan, both writers; John Humphrey and his wife Jeanne, also an artist, and Myron Galloway, later a Montreal art critic; also the communists Louis and Irene Kon, and Miriam Chapin. Sometimes a man from the Russian embassy sang Russian folk songs; Jori, in a high vibrating voice like a Portugese fado singer, passionately sang "Brave Wolfe" and old Quebec folksongs collected by Marius Barbeau.

Pat loved the studio, "the boldness of it" – the antique French Canadian furniture and weavings and the old Portneuf china. Guests sat on daybeds covered with handcrafted fabrics and drank wine and talked and laughed. "It was beautiful to my eye – absolutely beautiful." Jean Palardy was an amusing storyteller, and Jori was fond of charades and party games. One night she asked all the women to close their eyes and draw a man, frontal, naked, and all the men to close their eyes and draw a women, frontal, naked. The results induced great screams of laughter at their creations.[47] One of Pat's late poems echoes this experience.

As a painter, Jori Smith shunned the merely pretty or decorative – even her nudes had character. Nudity was a marker of 1940s bohemianism. On one occasion Pat greatly embarrassed Bruce Ruddick by insisting that he help her carry one of Jori's nudes on a streetcar; later, Pat herself posed in the nude for Peggy Anderson and once had to be hidden under a rug when Patrick Anderson's Selwyn House students came to visit. Although Peggy had given her subject blonde hair, Pat was conscious of knowledgeable, assessing eyes when the painting was first exhibited: she was known to be the model. Jori, who flaunted her bohemianism a little, proved a lifelong friend to Pat. She was transparently honest, genuinely concerned about her friends, and devoted to her art. She carried the joy of creating and her love of life into old age. When she was nearly ninety, she told Page that she had just gone out to the park and shouted for joy.[48]

As a couple, the Palardys had a strong interest in French Canadian life and spent summers in their old farmhouse on the lower St Lawrence River. It was probably in early August 1943 that Jori sent a brief note to Page confirming a visit to the Palardys' house at Petite-Rivière-Saint-François: "Won't it be wonderful! We'll all be rude & unrefined again – unrestrained, I've been in such excellent well-bred society that it might take me sometime to get used to you all again."[49] Kit and Neufville Shaw and their son Michael visited at the same time.

The house sat on a hilltop looking towards the river and had a long verandah with a glorious view. Jori remembered Pat sitting there on the verandah writing a poem. "We all understood each other and loved the same things."[50] Every morning the group sat on a little rocky beach, sunning. It was an idyllic setting, and the Montrealers had planned to stay two weeks, but Kit Shaw took offence at some remark and returned to Montreal in a huff.[51] Pat's poem "Photograph," written around this time, was based loosely on Kit and Neufville. It begins:

They are all beneath the sea in this photograph –
not dead surely – merely a little muted:
those two lovers lying apart and stiff ...[52]

We understand, though we are not told explicitly, that something has gone awry with Kit's and Neufville's relationship. The surrealist beginning and conclusion of the poem is shocking, as we recognize that the normal seaside activity described is all imaged under water. (This technique is pushed a little further, and given a first-person narrator, in Margaret Atwood's poem "This Is a Photograph of Me," which in subject and treatment is a clear descendant of Page's "Photograph.")[53]

The last part of 1943 and the first few months of 1944 were very difficult for Pat. In February she published a fine poem in *Preview* called "Paradox":

> let us stand here close,
> for death is common as grass beyond an ocean
> and, with all Europe pricking in our eyes,
> suddenly remember Guernica
> and be gone.

It is a sombre poem. The outcome of the war in Europe was uncertain; her father was now general officer, commander-in-chief, Atlantic Command, and was subject to the enormous stress of protecting Halifax and the North Atlantic; her brother was at sea and at the mercy of enemy submarines and Frank Scott had fallen in love with her and she with him.

Their love affair had started with a joke about wartime shortages. In the summer of 1942, when Scott was teaching at Harvard, Patrick Anderson had mentioned that the group should contact Scott about *Preview* business, and Page volunteered to send the letter. In his reply, Scott praised "The Stenographers," which had recently been published.[54] In her poem Page had signalled deep pain and vulnerability – Scott may have responded on an emotional level as his own personal life was vitiated. At the next *Preview* meeting, Pat had joked that if a man wanted to show his love for her he didn't need to send roses or chocolates; what she really needed was typing paper for her poems. The next day – to her astonishment – Scott sent her a case of expensive paper.[55]

Their love had at first been a source of great joy to Pat, perhaps expressed in the Rilke-inspired "Landscape of Love," published in *First Statement* shortly before they became lovers:[56]

> Where the bog ends, there, where the ground lips, lovely
> is love, not lonely.
>   Land is

love, round with it, where the hand is;
wide with love, cleared scrubland, grain
on a coin,
Oh, the wheatfield, the rock-bound rubble;
the untouched hills
                    as a thigh smooth ...[57]

Pat had never been wholly in love before, or sexually engaged. And she recognized a great affinity with Scott. She admired his poetry, loved his ready wit, and respected his strong sense of social purpose. Their respective English family backgrounds and values were a bond; even their voices were somewhat similar. But beyond all these compatibilities, Page felt the presence of a mutual sense of the spirit, convinced as she was that their love had a spiritual dimension – that they had somehow known each other before.[58] The affair was passionate and engaged them completely.

Pat Page and F.R. Scott.

When Scott first met Page at the *Preview* meeting in 1942, he was one of the most active social reformers in the country. During the thirties and forties he had worked energetically for the CCF and protested against the illegal deportation of Communists who were Canadian citizens. As a result, he was branded a Communist. Like J.S. Woodsworth, founder of the CCF, Scott was convinced that Canada ought not to take part in a European war. These political beliefs cast him as an outsider. In June 1942 he had published the article "Why Québec Voted No," explaining why Quebecers rejected conscription. Some commentators interpreted the essay as condoning the French position, and two influential editors – J.W. Dafoe of the *Winnipeg Free Press* and B.K. Sandwell of *Saturday Night* – called Scott a traitor.[59] In Montreal he felt like a social pariah, a feeling that was not fully dissipated until his public courtroom victories in the 1950s against the autocratic rule of Quebec Premier Maurice Duplessis in the Roncarelli and Padlock cases. Scott had successfully argued that Duplessis had deprived a popular restaurant owner, Roncarelli, of his liquor licence because he had given bail to members of the Jehovah's Witnesses; in *Switzman vs. Elbing* Scott had provided the legal basis for a successful case against an oppressive Quebec law intended to padlock the homes of Communists.

These large public issues had been exacerbated by an emotional disruption in Scott's private life. In 1928 he had married Marian Dale, a young Montreal artist. But shortly after the birth of their son Peter in 1929 their marriage had gone wrong. It seems that when Marian became a mother,[60] Scott became impotent and could no longer approach his wife sexually. Some years later, in 1950, he wrote in his diary that he and Marian had not been intimate for eighteen years, which suggests the break took place in 1932.[61] But Frank and Marian Scott were progressives, and Marian had been strongly influenced by Dora Russell's book *The Right to Be Happy* (1927), which argued that sexuality and parenthood were separate issues.[62] The couple seem to have agreed at that time to seek "emotional nourishment" where it could be found. In Bertrand Russell's terminology, their relationship became a "companionate marriage," an early form of open marriage.[63]

Marian became a distinguished artist in her own right. And both Scotts appear to have had several intimate friends in the thirties.[64] Marian's 1930s and 1940s diaries (which she abridged in the mid-to-late 1980s, removing some looseleaf pages and recopying others) record her deep friendship with social activists King Gordon and Norman Bethune, and writer Hugh MacLennan without indicating sexual involvement.[65] Scott's papers and other sources suggest that he had a number of lovers:

poet Anne Wilkinson, artist Pegi Nicol, New York photographer Lois Lord, and others. However, his significant love poems were written to Marian and to Pat. But his situation was at best uneasy because Montrealers were unaware of the nature of the Scott marriage. Frank, who conducted his life in public, was considered a womanizer, while Marian, whose friendships were private, was considered the wronged party.

In 1940–41, as a visiting professor at Harvard when London was being blitzed, Scott recognized that England could fall and with it Western democracy. He came to see that his pacifist position (based on the belief that the Second World War was primarily a European war rather than a North American concern) rested on a false premise. The recognition of this fact brought him close to a nervous breakdown in September. But in November 1941 he was inspired by Rilke's *Duino Elegies* (in the Leishman and Spender translation):

Who, if I cried, would hear me among the angelic
orders? And even if one of them suddenly
pressed me against his heart, I should fade in the strength of his
stronger existence. For Beauty's nothing
but the beginning of Terror we're still just able to bear ...[66]

(He later gave his copy of this book to Pat. Rilke's poetry affected her profoundly and is reflected in "Personal Landscape.") Earlier, Scott had read in the *New Statesman and Nation*, an article called "Digging for Mrs. Miller" by John Strachey, and it gave him heart. Strachey had described the search for survivors during the London blitz and the discovery in the bombed wreckage of two bodies wrapped together, one of which had a disc on her wrist saying "Mrs. Miller."[67]

When Scott first met Pat Page, he had recently published – in the first issue of *Preview* – a poem called "Recovery" ("Is she alive after this shock, does she yet breathe?").[68] In Scott's poem, Strachey's Mrs Miller becomes "the lovely body of faith" associated with hope and love, as in the trilogy of faith, hope, and love found in I Corinthians. Whenever Scott was most deeply moved, his metaphors were religious. Here, his depression is clearly lifting. Some of his new poems from 1942 to 1950, including "Signature," "Message" ("He would lose / In choosing, what he did not choose")[69] and "Departure," express the emotional and ethical dilemma of their love affair.[70]

They became lovers in the fall of 1942. I once asked Mavis Gallant, who had known both in Montreal in the forties, why the attraction? Gallant said that Pat was young and lovely: "She was so beautiful all the men were in love with her, dark hair and creamy skin like a camellia. It was her big eyes. She had large eyes, grey, clear, thickly fringed dark lashes. Liked her voice. Loved her poetry." Of course Scott was attracted. And what about him? "Well, he was older, it was his work, he knew how to talk to a woman. And then there is the *mystère de couple* – he was a womanizer; it was the young-old thing, young women going through their married-man phase: but with them it lasted a long time."[71] In addition, character, background, and serendipity came into play. Scott, because of his lifelong emphasis on reason and "the rule of law," was a highly repressed individual who kept powerful emotions securely in check. He may have learned to seek out uncomplicated sexual situations. It will be remembered that Pat had shown "Desiring Only" at her first *Preview* meeting – a poem that erroneously suggested she was a liberated young woman. More importantly, in "The Stenographers" Scott's intuitive poet's eye may have seen pain, a longing for love, and great vulnerability – all securely controlled by a third-person narrator and a tight poetic form. The lives of the stenographers – and by implication Pat's life – reflected aspects of Scott's own constrained emotional life.

But despite her London sojourn and the apparent freedom of her poetry, Pat was far more innocent than her twenty-five years would indicate. To be sure, she had travelled abroad and dated others, but she had no sexual experience. Pat believed, from her readings in the 1930s about A.P. Herbert[72] and the new English divorce bill, that "it is love that makes marriage holy and not marriage that makes love holy."[73] Her family experience was that love was followed by marriage; she may have reasoned that if she and Frank loved each other, they would marry.

Shortly after reading "The Stenographers" and sending the typing paper, Scott had offered to give Pat a ride to what she thought was a *Preview* meeting. In fact they were heading to the Laurentians, where Scott apparently planned to seduce her, but she told him bluntly that she did not want to become involved with a married man. For the first time the two began to speak honestly, getting to know each other. A couple of years later, Pat wrote to Frank: "Do you remember that wonderful day in the autumn hills. That is a strange sort of a milestone for me. We knew practically nothing about each other then. You said 'tell me about yourself briefly – born?' And we both filled in both questionnaires."[74]

After this encounter, Pat's emotions were so overpowering that she thought she should get out of town. But there were difficulties. "I'd only just got to Montreal. I wouldn't have known where to go. I had just found people who were writing ... I was prepared to tell myself that, oh well, we'll get around it some time, some way."[75] But the attraction to

Scott was irresistible – partly because they were the same personality type, with a reserved surface and bottled-up feelings, partly because he had tapped her deepest emotions.

She had been greatly drawn to Scott when she first met him: "I saw this very interesting mind, that was what I saw. The vitality of it, electricity of it, quickness of it, the depth of it … And that's what I fell in love with."[76] To some degree he represented poetry and what she hoped to become. And she respected his work with the CCF for social justice. They also had much in common in terms of social class and their assumptions about their place in society. Scott was not unlike Lionel Page: both were tall, lean, angular men, with south-of-England British accents. And their respective family rituals – reflecting English middle-class aspirations – were not dissimilar: the "Page crest" that Lionel Page gave to his son Michael on his twenty-first birthday was of recent coinage, as was the "Scott family ring," which Frank's father, Canon F.G. Scott, presented to each of his sons on their twenty-first birthdays.

Far more important than family or class similarities was Pat's conviction that theirs was a special and unique union that could not be explained: "You can't know why … I have an immense sense of God and the Spirit, and I know this kind of relationship exists within the realm of the Spirit – it's the soul that's engaged. It isn't the heart and the genitals and the mind only, it is the soul that is engaged. And you cannot analyze that. Where does it come from? Did we know each other in a previous existence?"[77]

But for a young woman of Pat's character and upbringing, it was a strain to carry on a clandestine affair. A number of her short stories and poems from 1943–44 show signs of stress. She began to feel extraordinarily pressured, had nightmares, did not sleep well, and experienced bouts of weeping. She thought she was losing her sanity. At the same time, in the spring of 1944 there was hope that the war was drawing to a close. Her good friend Maggie Davies decided to return to England, and Pat resolved to leave Montreal and Scott at the end of May to rejoin her family in Halifax for the summer.

Scott shared her pain and recognized the implications of her decision. As her train pulled out of Windsor Station, he saw her as a lone tree on the shore of Lake Superior (Scott loved the art of the Group of Seven). Later, in an attempt to come to terms with her leaving and what it meant to him, he wrote "Departure":

Always I shall remember you, as my car moved
Away from the station and left you alone at the gate

Utterly and forever frozen in time and solitude
Like a tree on the north shore of Lake Superior.
It was a moment only, and you were gone,
And I was gone, and we and it were gone,
And the two parts of the enormous whole we had known
Melted and swirled away in their separate streams
Down the smooth granite slope of our watershed.[78]

CHAPTER 6

Halifax and Victoria
Loss, 1944–1946

Pat left Montreal because she knew she had to get away for a time. In late May she took the train to Halifax, where her father was now commander-in-chief of Atlantic Command; he and Rose had rented a furnished flat at 48 Cambridge Street. When Pat eventually arrived in Halifax after a day and a night on the train, she was completely exhausted. She went to bed and stayed there for several days, sleeping, drinking hot milk, trying to forget the world she had left behind. In the last troubled months in Montreal she had tried to keep awake at night because whenever she slept she had terrible nightmares – and they haunted her days.

She wondered if a whole summer away from Montreal – and Frank – would be bearable. Sending letters through the mail, as they did, was risky. Scott's letters at McGill were routinely opened by wartime censors, and Pat's family were unaware of the depth of their relationship. She arranged with a friend for Scott to send his letters to her and asked that he include a photograph as she couldn't remember what he looked like at the station. As she told him in a letter soon after her arrival in Halifax, "I felt so ill and used all my strength in refraining from flinging myself at you, with the result that I remember only a strong light and heat and our shaking hands ... Altogether whichever way I look I know you're the biggest thing that ever happened to me."[1]

Although she went through the motions of visiting old friends and even made some new ones, at the end of June she wrote to him saying that there was "no road back to the old life:" "Do I cut you out of me with a scalpel & pretend you never existed? I begin to think love is a bad thing. It doesn't make you strong. I seem to be going through some dreadful crisis that is worse than anything yet."[2] Ten days later she wrote: "Somehow I must learn the dreadful lesson of independence. But once learned then what? Is it possible for any relationship to exist between two complete independent people?"[3]

Pat Page, photo portrait. Terese Studios

Her spirits took a lift in late June when she received a first draft of Scott's poem "Windfall," telling her that he, too, was suffering:

Until this poem is over, I shall not leave
This leaf, held like the heartache in my hand ...

This small complete and perfect thing
Cut off from wholeness is my heart's suffering.[4]

Scott was grieving, but he had the great advantage of a political career that allowed him to throw himself into external activities. In June 1944 the CCF had just won an enormous victory in Saskatchewan and, as one of Premier Tommy Douglas's advisers, Scott was much involved in the installation of the new government. The CCF was ranking high in popular polls, and it seemed to have a good chance of forming the next national government.

Pat did not have this kind of release. Her father and brother were caught up in the war, in the struggle to hold the North Atlantic. But for the women at home – Pat, her mother, and Aunt Bibbi – the sphere was domestic. And Halifax society was just as stifling as she remembered. In mid-July she wrote to Jori Smith saying that her summer had been unproductive and that she felt like a "veteran limpet searching for a rock with no success." It seemed to her that Halifax life was a kind of society circus with "highly trained seals … dogs & fleas." She was desperate. "What possible solution is there for the 'likes of us'? One dreams of a place as you say where people live honestly & freely but I can't *really* believe in it. The only true reality is work but at the moment the ink becomes rusted in my pen."[5]

She had almost given up the idea of visiting New River Beach during the summer, but her mother encouraged her to contact the Knight sisters to see if they could find a place for her to stay. Kit Knight offered to share her room, and on 14 July Pat left her parents' apartment in Halifax for an upstairs room in the old Knight farmhouse. Once there, she found the landscape wonderful, as it had always been: miles and miles of sand reflecting the sky, fields of daisies and buttercups, great promontories of rock and evergreens. She swam happily, sunned, and visited with friends. Everything would be perfect if Frank were there to share this with her. She wrote to him saying that one morning she had run across the sands shouting his name: "Wish you were here, wish you were here, wish you were here."[6]

Nonetheless, she worked steadily. During three brief weeks she seems to have sent off a series of poems to *Poetry* in Chicago and turned back to the novel she had begun in 1943 at Jori Smith's summer house at Petite Rivière. It was a story narrated by a young woman, speaking of her feelings about the war and those of her husband Lukas, an army officer on embarkation leave in a small Quebec village. Pat found the relationship between husband and wife difficult to portray, perhaps because she identified with the wife, who sympathizes with the hardscrabble life of the Québécois. The husband, who has enlisted, has no sympathy for young men who will not fight.[7]

After about three weeks Pat received a telegram on Saturday night, 5 August, telling her to come home at once. Lionel had become seriously ill. She had realized earlier that something was wrong with her father. He acted strangely at the dinner table, freezing "as if he'd turned into a statue; and went bright red in the face and then came back. It was a temporary thing, but he wasn't there at all." Nobody said anything; but later, when she and her mother discussed the incident, Rose explained that this had been happening frequently, but that Lionel had refused to see a doctor.[8] He had always believed in the power of mind over matter, but even the strongest will could not have prevailed in his present condition.

As commander-in-chief of Atlantic Command, Lionel was responsible for artillery placement and the defence of all of the East Coast, including Newfoundland, Labrador, Prince Edward Island, and New Brunswick. He also had an administrative responsibility for the navy, although not operational responsibility. This was an extraordinarily bleak and difficult time. Ships were routinely torpedoed just outside Halifax harbour, and Michael was now on duty at sea in the St Lawrence River, which had become a killing ground by German submarines.[9] Then, on 6 June 1944, D-Day, the Allied forces landed on the beaches of Normandy, with enormous Canadian casualties. As one of the Canadian generals who liaised with the American generals, Lionel Page would have known just how badly the invasion had gone in terms of loss of life for Canadian soldiers. All these events undoubtedly contributed to his stress and his subsequent heart attack.

Pat pulled rank for the first time in her life and asked for a lift to Halifax in a staff car. She got home early Sunday morning and found her father in hospital suffering from his second major heart attack. Mentally he was quite alert, but wildly excitable and talkative. The family began to prepare for the worst when he was placed in an oxygen tent. Pat began to draft a poem, "For My Father":

> Your torso camping in the tent
> of cellophane and air
> alone and lonelier
> upon that northern spit of snow
> in that white unfamiliar continent
> where nurses come and go.[10]

In the midst of all this confusion, Frank Scott came to visit Pat in Halifax. For some time he had been planning to attend a conference that was to be held in Sackville, New Brunswick, in the third week of August, and he now wrote to Pat proposing that he come to Halifax on Sunday, 20 August. She consulted with her mother and Aunt Bibbi and they agreed that he could stay with them at Cambridge Street. Pat offered to meet him when the train came in. It was a long walk to the station – she could not get a taxi, and streetcars were not running. When she saw a car, she thumbed it. Unfortunately, the occupants were two policemen, who pointed out that thumbing was illegal. She promised not to do it again and carried on walking, but she thumbed the next car that came along. It was the same police car. When the warning was repeated, she said that she was trying to get to the station to meet a boyfriend. One of the policemen took pity on her and allowed her to crouch in the back of the car, where she couldn't be seen. When she finally arrived at the station, she announced triumphantly, "I'm here!" Scott replied, "Well, you said you'd be here."[11]

To some degree this was the pattern of their relationship. Frank could not recognize the sacrifices Pat was making for him. In the midst of her father's serious illness, she had worked herself up to make the large admission to her mother and Aunt Bibbi that she was in love with a married man and wanted them to receive him at home. During the visit, Rose and Bibbi took stock of Scott's character. They acknowledged his sincerity, intelligence, and charm, but they also thought him something of a "cad" a damning term for their generation. He had taken advantage of an innocent girl, but there was no sign that he was planning to do the honourable thing – Rose was heard to remark that even D.H. Lawrence married Frieda.[12] Scott stayed with the family for two days, visiting some of the local sights, such as Herring Cove, with Pat. But aware of the seriousness of Lionel's illness, he took the early train back to Montreal on Tuesday morning.

On that very day Lionel had another – and fatal – heart attack. The end came quickly. On 26 August 1944, at fifty-nine years of age, he died of what was termed "a complete heart block." Because Rose was totally devastated, Pat now had to take responsibility in the home – the role for which her father had trained her. There were undertakers to be called, a military funeral to be endured, and a reception to be planned. The funeral, at All Saints Anglican Cathedral, of Major-General Lionel Page, DSO, General Officer, Commander-and-Chief, Atlantic Command, was one of the biggest Halifax had ever seen. Lionel's horse was led riderless, his boots reversed in the stirrups. Michael, the chief mourner, had been flown back to Halifax, and he followed the hearse in naval uniform, carrying a pillow with Lionel's medals on it. Pat and

Rose were at the funeral, but Rose felt unable to attend the burial.[13] Even so, Pat was amazed at her mother's strength during the period of Lionel's illness and death.

When it was all over and Pat and her mother were at last alone, they sat together in the sitting room, answering innumerable cards of condolence. For Pat this was the start of the bleakest two years of her life because she felt entirely alone. And family finances were not easy, for although Lionel had died a general – and had probably died because of the stresses of a general's command – he received the pension of a colonel, which was substantially less. The military authorities argued that his heart problems had preceded his present position. Yet he had somehow managed to save eight thousand dollars during his lifetime. The Pages now agreed to pool their resources and leave Halifax – where Rose found the eastern winters so bitterly cold – for comparatively balmy Vancouver, where her brother Frank Whitehouse was a successful banker. They took a month to remove their belongings from Halifax and Saint John.[14] Although Pat loved Montreal and did not want to be separated from Scott, she decided that she must go with her mother and Aunt Bibbi to help get them settled in British Columbia.

The three women took the train to Montreal, where they stayed a few days to see friends – Pat and Frank found a brief time together – before continuing their journey. When Pat, Rose, and Bibbi took their places on the train leaving from Windsor Station in Montreal, Scott came to say good-bye. He had brought a novel for Pat to read on the trip, Gwethalyn Graham's *Earth and High Heaven*, a book that had just won the Governor General's Award for fiction. It depicted a love affair between a Montreal gentile and a Jew (then an impossible divide) that nonetheless reached a happy ending.[15]

When the Page family arrived in Vancouver, the end of the line, it was almost October, the rainy season. Pat was not impressed by the city, which did not compare with Montreal: "It all seems to me ... a bit ducky. Rows & rows of ducky little houses."[16] Her Uncle Frank lived comfortably in the West End, at 1109 Burnaby Street, and the three women stayed there, but they were anxious to get settled on their own. Day after day, Pat set out with the housing ads and the bus and streetcar schedules. She traipsed all over Vancouver looking for a place for the family to stay (and came back each night with her umbrella and raincoat soaked); it was wartime and there were no vacant rooms for civilians.

In early November, Alan and Jean Crawley took Pat to a party at the poet Dorothy Livesay's house. Apparently, Livesay was not one of Jean's favourites – Pat enjoyed Jean's "very funny, very tart" Scottish tongue.[17] At the party she discovered some interesting people but a low level of poetry appreciation. Many of the guests had heard nothing of *Preview* or of eastern poets. And Livesay's husband, Duncan McNair, spoke glowingly of that toothless old lion Sir Charles G.D. Roberts, the Confederation Poet. Pat found herself watching Alan Crawley, who did not appear to be a blind man in this crowd of people. His hearing was so acute that he moved to listen to the person who was talking.[18] Alan and Pat became immediate friends, and it was not long before she took the bus from her uncle's house in the West End, across the Lion's Gate Bridge, to West Vancouver and Caulfeild, where the Crawleys lived.

After several weeks the Pages decided against Vancouver, and they left for Victoria on 10 November. They had already visited old friends in Victoria – including "Dick" Francis, a woman who had lived next door to them in Calgary. Victoria was smaller and more manageable, and the sun was shining. They discovered there was less rainfall and, to clinch matters Pat found a hairdresser where she could get a good haircut. They took lodgings at 908 Heywood Avenue, just across from Beacon Hill Park and within walking distance of the centre of town. Housing was rationed, and three women living together were allowed only two rooms: Rose and Aunt Bibbi shared a room, and Pat had a room to herself.

There she worked on her poetry and continued freelancing for the Park Steamship Company, which had employed her in Halifax to research Canadian parks and find appropriate names for newly built Canadian naval vessels. She was lonely and increasingly depressed. Scott wrote rarely and briefly. But when Pat was still in Vancouver he had written replying to a long and honest letter from her asking if there was any hope for their future. Scott drafted a response speaking eloquently of love: "How can one be in love and not love? Love is an affirmation of belief, a sweeping and conclusive proof that right and beautiful things do exist and can be attained. Once you have really loved you *know*. Even if the whole world crumbles the next day that belief can never be destroyed, nor the experience obliterated. Every moment that love continues to exist it validates itself." Nonetheless – and this is the part of the letter that she perhaps should have later taken to heart – he replied that there was no hope: "[H]onesty compels us to say no, insofar as the future is controllable by ourselves. This I suppose is my decision, though I think you know enough of my situation to understand and even to approve my making it. While loving you, I care for all the things that depend on me." Despite this, he added, "I hope you will come back.

Whatever is needed to be done we shall do. One thing we should not do is to allow a great and genuine thing to become destructive."[19] It was a very mixed message.

Whenever Pat went out in Victoria she rushed back home, hoping to find a letter – or Scott. When neither materialized she sank into a deep depression. As a way of getting through each day she forced herself to follow an arbitrary schedule. She would breakfast, go to the park and feed the ducks, and then go to the library. And she began to write steadily, for she was achieving recognition as a writer. Within two months of her arrival in Victoria, *The Sun and the Moon* was published, and she appeared prominently in an anthology of new poets. On 10 November *Poetry* (Chicago) awarded her the Oscar Blumenthal Award for five poems that had appeared in its August 1944 issue. This was a great honour, because the magazine was recognized as an arbiter of literary taste. Among the group were two clearly subjective poems: "The Sick," evoking her father's illness, and "Element," a poem that translates her love affair into metaphor. The female narrator is a fish under water (there is a strong sense of victimization and lack of control); the male, the invisible wielder of a fishing rod, holds all the power. It begins, "Feeling my face has the terrible shine of fish / caught and swung on a line under the sun," and it ends with a fish hook:

> Ah, in daylight the shine is single
> as dime flipped or gull on fire or fish
> silently hurt – its mouth alive with metal.[20]

This is another powerful poem from which Margaret Atwood clearly drew inspiration.[21] Page was beginning to influence younger poets. Phyllis Webb recalls that in 1945–46 she was reading Dorothy Livesay, Earle Birney, E.J. Pratt, F.R. Scott, and A.J.M. Smith in the latter's anthology, *The Book of Canadian Poetry* (1943), "but the one who entranced me the most and made me feel I wanted to be a poet was P.K. Page. And I got a lot of courage from her poetry to think about being a poet."[22]

The Sun and the Moon came out later in November/early December 1944. But the novella failed to satisfy the critics, one of whom remarked that the author "has made us wish for Kristin's happiness, but has not convinced us that the tragedy was inevitable."[23] The tale gives us a would-be artist recording changes in consciousness, recognizing the artis-

tic journey, and perhaps even writing her own psychic plot in advance –
Pat's later poems and novels all deal with changes in consciousness and
with moving from one psychic state to another. Up to this point, she had
looked to other writers' stories and placed herself within a borrowed
plot – as, for example, when she saw herself as the orphan Sara, the
daughter of an army officer in *A Little Princess*. But she was now writing
her own plot, one in which she stars as the nymph-like Kristin, beloved
of an older painter, Carl, to whom she has added some characteristics of
actor-director Charles Rittenhouse and some that are suggestive of F.R.
Scott. Like Scott, Carl is described as "tall and thin"[24] and is also given
one of Scott's typical walking movements: "His shoulder up-pointing,
the tenseness of his whole body concentrated in that shoulder."[25] The
heroine, Pat/Kristin, is idealized as well. In 1939 when Pat wrote the
novella, she was still known by her friends as "Podge" Page and getting
much of her life from books.

By Christmas 1944, Pat was able to promise Jori Smith a copy of the
poetry anthology *Unit of Five*, which featured a group of young modern
poets – Louis Dudek, Ronald Hambleton, Raymond Souster, P.K. Page,
and James Wreford Watson – and was edited by Hambleton. Pat is quoted
(in the book itself) as saying that she had lived in various places from
Calgary to Halifax, acted for the CBC, and "sold books where laws for
minimum wages and maximum hours are unknown. Later worked as a
filing clerk in a vault."[26] What is most striking about the Page poems in
this collection is the social satire. She describes the young women of
"Summer Resort" – "They lie on beaches and are proud to tan" – who,
with a periscope, "scan the scene for love."[27] The waitress/prostitute of
"Snapshot" is "dime-dead … coveted by private fingers, / fumbled for,
clutched, caught and spent / in a second."[28]

Most autobiographical is the long poem "Cullen." Although Pat has
chosen to speak through a male narrator in the poem, many of her own
experiences come into it: her early dissatisfaction at St Hilda's school
("He didn't understand why they were taught / life was good by faces
that said it was not"). When Cullen tours stores in the city and sees rats
behind the counters, Pat's time as a salesgirl at Manchester, Robertson
and Allison in Saint John is brought to mind. Cullen goes to the theatre,
as Pat did in London, and sits in a high balcony. He seeks out the city but
finds it a failure. The newspapers are treacherous, and good poetry does
not come his way.

Tried out the seasons then, found April cruel –
there had been no Eliot in his books at school –
discovered that stitch of knowledge on his own
remembering all the springs he had never known.

Cullen finds Christmas thoroughly commercialized. In disgust, he now
renounces the city for the country (as Pat did) and sees the huge Maritime
fishermen as Vikings, returning to "women malleable as rising bread."
In this simple pastoral context, his future appears secure. But even here,
chaos invades and he is overrun:

Cullen evacuated overnight,
he knew no other region to explore;
discovered it was nineteen thirty-nine
and volunteered at once and went to war
wondering what on earth he was fighting for.
He knew there was a reason but couldn't find it
and marched to battle half an inch behind it.[29]

The reviews of *Unit of Five* emphasized the social satire informing
Pat's early work. B.K. Sandwell characterized the whole group as "Four
Angry Poets." He found Wreford obscure, Dudek unintelligible, Hambleton the angriest; but there was "some brilliance" in the twelve poems
of P.K. Page. He thought that one of the most successful was "No Flowers," which dealt with "the vivid anticipation of the death by drowning
of a bored rich lady on a luxury cruise who will ultimately become food
for the fishes":[30] "Octopus arms will hold you and sea snails / will stud
the lobes of your ears."[31]

The reality of Pat's life in Victoria, especially her first Christmas, was
strange and bleak; there was no snow, and "grey rain" fell. Yet from this
experience emerged the splendid "Stories of Snow," one of a handful of
poems by Page that demonstrate her mastery of the craft of poetry.
Lionel's aunt, her son Jim Burchett and wife Betsy, who lived in Victoria,
made Christmas as happy as they could for the bereaved family. There
was a traditional Christmas dinner with all the trimmings, and carols
afterwards. Among the guests was a Dutchman, Pierre Timp, well known
in the city as a horticulturalist. He began to tell stories about Holland
that Pat found "very very fascinating, very beautiful. He said that on

Christmas day in Holland, they used to go out swan hunting on ice boats. And the images of ice boats – swan hunting ... It seemed extraordinary to me."[32]

The images stayed with her. "Stories of Snow" is a long poem (by her standards) of fifty-one lines. Such poems came to her only in bits and pieces. Occasionally, they began as images, sometimes as lines: "Very often it's a rhythm I hear that doesn't have words at all, and I have to fit words to the rhythm. Sometimes it's an image, also that doesn't have words at all, and sometimes it will be a few words ... out of which can grow ... the poem."[33] "Stories of Snow" begins with a narrator speaking of those in milder latitudes who dream of snow as imaged in crystal globes that "hold their snowstorms circular, complete." Here, in Victoria, "where the leaves are large as hands / ... one will waken / to think the glowing linen of his pillow / a northern drift." The story shifts to Holland, where

> hunters arise and part the flakes and go
> forth to the frozen lakes in search of swans –
> the snow light falling white along their guns,
> their breath in plumes.

The hunters sink their fingers in the down of the dead swan's feathers and experience "that warm metamorphosis of snow."

> And stories of this kind are often told
> in countries where great flowers bar the roads
> with reds and blues which seal the route to snow –
> as if, in telling, raconteurs unlock
> the colour with its complement and go
> through to the area behind the eyes
> where silent, unrefractive whiteness lies.[34]

The power of the poem is focused in this last image of inner vision.

Scott had been a poor correspondent, writing infrequently and twice telephoning. But in March 1945 his first book of poems, *Overture*, was published, and he sent Pat a copy with a dedication saying that she had been present to see it all happening. The book contained several love poems, including the poignant "Windfall," already mentioned, and the sharp "Advice": "Beware the casual need / By which the heart is bound."[35] It also contained "Villanelle for Our Time," commenting on the 1940s generation and perhaps their mutual love: "From bitter searching of the heart, / Quickened with passion and with pain / We rise to play a greater part."[36]

In May, Pat told Jori that she still suffered from long, black depressions: "The worst is the inability to work. I get up each morning and sit with paper in front of me and I swear I go through psychic labour pains which leave me exhausted and which produce NOTHING."[37] Although Jori was still her chief confidante, Pat was beginning to make new friends in Victoria, most importantly, Floris McLaren, the business manager of *Contemporary Verse*. Alan Crawley had told Pat to look up Floris, and they hit it off at once. Floris was a poet, had a good critical mind, and was passionate about poetry. Older than Pat, she was prematurely grey and lived with her husband and two rambunctious sons in an Oak Bay bungalow. Mac, the husband, was a raw-boned Scot who had lost a leg in the war and walked with a wild gait, which got wilder as he got drunker. Pat had few literary friends, but she thoroughly enjoyed her time with Floris and Mac – their talks and their parties. Pat and Floris would discuss their poems and tell each other what was worth reading and why.

Another good friend who Pat made in 1945 was Myfanwy Spencer, whose family owned Spencer's department store in Victoria. Myfanwy was a visual artist. Describing her to Jori Smith, Pat reported: "She's the first person I've met who has any idea of anything & as yet with her – it's only an idea"[38] – meaning, perhaps, that Myfanwy had a sense of art that Pat could identify with. A gifted painter who married Nikola Pavelic in 1948, Myfanwy later studied painting in New York under Borielli, and in the 1970s painted a celebrated portrait of Prime Minister Pierre Trudeau in a long cape with a rose. The two young women, each working hard on her own art, took a break to drive to California and back in September.[39]

Soon afterwards, the Pages moved into a fairly large boarding house on Transit Road near Oak Bay. Set in a pleasant garden, it was run by an elderly English couple. He had been a surgeon in the Royal Navy but was too old to take part in the Second World War. There was a Scottie dog, and the house seemed "almost human" compared with other boarding houses the Pages had known. Nonetheless, in the fall of 1945, soon after the end of the war, Rose bought a small bungalow at 1626 Wilmot Place, also near Oak Bay, and they moved there in early November. She also bought a Morris car, which Pat drove.

That November Pat went to see the Canadians troops from Hong Kong who had been captured by the Japanese during the war and were just now being repatriated to Canada. They were living in Quonset huts, where the University of Victoria is now. Pat was conscious that they hadn't learned how to adjust to the world: they were emaciated, culture-shocked. The army authorities asked for young women to help sew insignia on the new uniforms the men were given, and Pat had volunteered.[40] Later, writing to Jori Smith, Pat described her contact with the veterans as very depressing, partly because she found the enlisted men "fearfully reactionary ... I'd have expected it from officers. All staunch Churchill men. It may be because they've been so out of touch, but Jesus! The men coming back from Europe depress me equally. No understanding or sympathy with the European peoples, insular as ever they were before they left. It seems so strange and depressing to find the bulk of the people who have been fighting for this so-called freedom know less about it than those who have been at home."[41]

With the 1945 general election on 25 October, she had recognized once again that she was an outsider in Victoria. This was the first federal election since the victory of the CCF in the Saskatchewan provincial election and many, especially Scott, had predicted a national breakthrough for the party. The Liberals, however, waged a nasty campaign, arguing that the CCF was Bolshevik or Communist. Page wrote a splendid poem, "Election Day." It begins when she leaves the boarding house in the morning to cast her ballot for the CCF:

and in the polling station I shall meet
the smiling, rather gentle overlords
propped by their dames and almost twins in tweeds,
and mark my X against them and observe
my ballot slip, a bounder, in the box.

The national results were close. In British Columbia the CCF received 29.4 per cent of the vote, the Progressive Conservatives 30 per cent, the Liberals 27.5 per cent. Nonetheless, the Liberals carried the country. Thus the pointed concluding lines of Pat's poem, addressed to the Conservatives of Victoria: "Gentlemen, for the moment, you may sleep."[42]

Since the summer of 1945 Pat had officially been "unemployed." There were no more battleships to be christened now that the war was over,

and some temporary work with the Park Steamship Company had come
to an end. It was then, when lying on the grass in Floris's garden while
smelling the fresh scent of sweet peas, that Pat had first realized, "I'm
going to have to get out of here."[43] She saw Victoria as a kind of lotus
land, filled with greenery and would-be Englishmen, an artificial setting
for someone like herself. With the New Year in 1946, Rose precipitated
matters. She said that she wanted to see some applications for positions for
Pat on the hall table. Pat sent out three letters: one to the CBC International Service, which would have brought her back to Montreal; another
to the Ryerson Press, Toronto, for a clerical position; and a third to the
National Film Commission, Ottawa, for a position as a scriptwriter –
she knew that her friend, the poet Anne Marriott, was working there. As
it happened, the Film Commission replied first and she accepted its offer.

During the early spring she sent a short story called "The Glass Box"
to poet Ralph Gustafson, for a book of Canadian prose called *Canadian
Accent II*. Penguin did not publish the collection but the story appeared
in one of Page's late collections of fiction in which she dates the story as
1943, presumably referring to the event which it describes. The story reflects a Montreal winter and her love affair with Scott: it shows how
fragile she felt and is remarkable for its pain and psychological insight.
It also reveals that Pat's much-anthologized poem "Landlady" (published
in the *Canadian Forum* in May 1944) is rooted in personal experience. In
"The Glass Box" a young woman, living in a boarding house, attempts
to sneak her lover into her room – past the eye of a vigilant landlady –
for a few brief moments of love. There was no other place to go. Hotels
were impossible because a young woman could not be seen in such
places with a married man without losing her reputation. Of course the
lovers are interrupted. The telephone rings, and the landlady advances
towards the girl's room while she frantically attempts to hide the man in
a closet. When the danger passes, he clowns a little. She becomes infuriated and lashes out: "I just can't take it any longer ... For months and
months I've done nothing that's spontaneous. Every move mapped out;
everyone a spy or a potential spy. Oh Christ! can't you see? Every door-
bell, every telephone, every voice in the hall."[44] The story continues with
the nerve-rending attempt to get him safely out of the boarding house.
Finally they sit in his car, invisible because the car has become a glass box
coated with frost – "Pitiful security – frost on panes of glass."[45] This
story has the ring of personal experience. When Pat was living on Sherbrooke Street in 1943, Scott had once been concealed in the closet of her
next-door neighbour, Dorothy Dee. Pat had been living a lie in Montreal

and she hated the deception it entailed. By early April 1946 in Victoria, however, she felt sufficiently free to send the story to Ralph Gustafson for publication.

Later in April, Pat took the train from Vancouver to Ottawa. A new phase of her life was about to begin.

CHAPTER 7

Ottawa
Recovery, 1946–1953

Pat found Ottawa to be completely different from Montreal – the whole city circled around Parliament and the government buildings, and French was rarely spoken. Then, when she got on the streetcar to go to work, she had the impression that even the lowest government clerk aspired to look like a cabinet minister, wearing a suit and a homburg and carrying a briefcase (for his lunch!).[1] She had been assigned to the Film Strips division of the National Film Commission at 196 Sparks Street, above a Metropolitan store.

The commission, which was scattered over five Ottawa locations, had come into being to oversee the use of film during wartime, and it drew on the work of the celebrated British filmmaker John Grierson. He was the first commissioner of the Canadian National Film Commission, appointed in 1939. He was so successful with propaganda documentaries, such as *Canada Carries On*, that after the war, in 1945–46, there was a feeling that the Film Commission (later the National Film Board) should move into features.[2] Pat was hired as a scriptwriter as part of this expansion.

Pat soon discovered that members of the Film Commission did not look or act like typical government employees, nor did they follow the usual Ottawa norms.[3] The men bicycled to work in shorts and sandals, and Pat herself wore slacks to work. She later called them "a ragtail, bobtail lot."[4] But Jay Macpherson – whose mother also worked at the Film Commission – remembers Pat as looking "free-flowing, glowing … attractive. She wore a lot of black, she held her head very high, and she was tall."[5] The usual civil service female with a responsible position took pains to look dowdy.

The head of Film Strips was Forbes Helem, and his staff included Lionel Reid and Fred Anders, artists, Joe LaCastro, who did line drawings, and his cousin Mike LaCastro, who ran the dry mounting and the letterpress. The whole group was highly creative and full of fun, though

Pat Page during her time at the National Film Commission

capable of working flat-out when necessary.[6] A close-knit unit, they socialized together. Pat thought Helem was like Groucho Marx in his mannerisms. Once, at a stuffy Film Commission party to celebrate his birthday, he blew out all the candles on the cake, picked it up, and put his face in the icing – breaking both the icing and the ice.[7] The group frequently swam in the pool at the Château Laurier during lunchtime, held parties in their flats during the winters, and spent the occasional summer weekend at "Norah's Ark," a cottage rented by Norah Helli-well, Helem's secretary. She sometimes typed Pat's scripts and the two women became friends.[8] There were very few rooms available in post-war Ottawa, but with Norah's help Page found a small bedroom with kitchen privileges at 71 Marlboro Street in Sandy Hill. She stayed there from April to October 1946 and then moved to a series of apartments on Daly Street, all close to Rideau Street, where the streetcars ran.

Page started writing for film strips but later progressed to writing commentary for films and the occasional movie. She discovered that the scriptwriter was central in getting each project going. The process entailed attending an initial meeting with the director and a representative of the government department that had requested the film strip in order to determine what was wanted for the proposed topic and how it should be treated. Should it be done photographically? Or by cartoon? In colour or in black and white? Then came the hardest part. Once the scriptwriter had understood what was required and had undertaken the research for the subject, she had to determine how a script should be supported by visuals. Only then could she write a draft of the script.

The visual images were the most important part of a film strip. When Page first began work, she was surprised to learn that initially they had to be created in her own head: "I had fondly believed some mysterious 'they' would present me with a series of pictures and I could simply dash off some kind of continuity. That is by no means the case." In fact, the scriptwriter had to dig for research material and then, keeping in mind the audience, set about organizing the material in terms of visuals. "This is the part of the work that has the trick in it – and strangely enough it seems a trick that no dog, young or old, can learn. It's something to do with having a visual imagination."[9] As the script not only showed off the visuals but integrated them, it unified a collection of apparently unrelated elements. Page instinctively knew that there had to be a marriage between words and vision,[10] and Helem soon decided she was "brilliant."[11]

The people she saw most frequently in Ottawa were her co-workers. Grant Munro, an animator and filmmaker, was in the next office. He soon became a good friend, and through him Page met the star animators Norman McLaren (honoured for his work at the 2006 Cannes Film Festival and for his influence on filmmakers such as George Lucas and François Truffaut)[12] and McLaren's co-workers Guy Glover and Colin Low. Grant Munro recalls, "I idolized her ... she was so intelligent and classy and considerate ... it just seemed strange that this exotic, talented creature was in this milieu. She was also a great friend and very amusing."[13]

Pat sometimes held parties and teas at the apartment she now shared with newspaperwoman Maudie Ferguson at 309 Daly Street. It was a pleasant room, with bright cushions and Deichmann pottery. One warm summer afternoon, Munro remembered, "the sun was shining and it was late afternoon, and we were all in a great mood and we got into martinis. And I remember we were all jumping over something – jumping over sofas and chairs – singing and whatnot. And I remember P.K. saying ...

she'd like to live long enough to have this impossible idea that one day man might get on to the moon. But of course, if she lived to be a thousand, he'd never get on the moon."[14]

One day, Munro – whose office was separated from Page's by a thin partition – overheard Page laughing uproariously. The crew, who liked to tease her, wanted to know why she was laughing. Munro listened and remembered her explanation. She told the crew she had worked all day and all night on a script. But when she came to work that morning, she couldn't stop laughing:

> These leeches goaded her: "What's so funny?" "No, I can't tell you." "What's so funny?" "Alright," she said, "I was drinking coffee non-stop, trying to keep awake and I had the radio on. And I had a station on from the southern States. And it was a guessing contest ... And they chose this young woman to answer the top question. They said, 'Before we ask this question, are you married?' And she said, 'Yes.' And they said, 'Is your husband here in the audience?' And she said, 'No he's posted at such and such – he's in the army.' So everybody applauded. And then the MC said, 'If you had one wish to be granted when you awaken tomorrow morning, what would that wish be?' And this poor little soul said, 'I would like to waken tomorrow morning and find my husband standing beside the bed with his discharge in his hand.' And the whole audience cracked up."[15]

The *double entendre*'s striking Pat as so very, very funny suggests that at some level she too would like to live a normal married life.

Pat had begun to see Frank Scott again. She had been in Ottawa only a few days when she pulled on a black sweater and a Black Watch tartan skirt and walked to Murray's restaurant on Rideau Street to meet Scott. They saw each other intermittently for the next five years. Pat had become a highly attractive woman, with dark glossy hair, huge grey eyes, and a generous mouth. Alan Crawley's daughter-in-law Lois, then living in Ottawa, caught a glimpse of her at an evening party: "Two simple hoops of silver hung from her ears, gypsy fashion, swinging against the curve of her cheek. Except for her eyes, you might say her hair was the most striking thing about her. It was very dark – almost black – neither wavy nor curly but tousled in shiny flicks that grew up and down and around her slender neck. As she turned her face more fully into the light, her eyes lost the shadows and shone a lovely, pale green beneath dark brows."[16] Pat had begun to wear distinctive silver jewelry, including a brooch adapted from her father's military insignia.

Life was exciting when she first came to the city because she enjoyed her work and Ottawa people. She was still seeing Jori Smith and her husband Jean Palardy, who was also working for the Film Commission. She met Dorothy Macpherson in the Displays department in the next building and discovered that her daughter Jay, only fifteen, was writing astonishingly good poetry. Pat became friends with Jay and put her in touch with Alan Crawley, who published her poems in *Contemporary Verse*. (In 1957 Jay Macpherson won a Governor General's Award for *The Boatman*.)

Through Maudie Ferguson she met Florence Bird (better known under her newspaper *nom de plume*, Anne Francis) and her husband John Bird, an Ottawa newspaperman. In Pat's eyes Florence looked so vibrant and healthy: "Every hair looked burnished – her eyes sparkled like lake water in the summer: blue sparkling eyes, and ... beautiful skin. And she seemed so energetic."[17]

Occasionally old friends from Montreal came to Ottawa on university business. One was David Thomson, the McGill biochemist who was dean of the Faculty of Graduate Studies. Thomson was tall, thin, and frail, with long tapering fingers. He was a Scottish intellectual, highly sophisticated, and he loved poetry. Pat enjoyed his visits – his pleasant wit had "a touch of malice."[18] A.J.M. Smith came in 1944 and read the manuscript for a new book of poems, helping her to elucidate the title, *As Ten, As Twenty*. Another visitor from Montreal was Bruce Ruddick, "a great raw-boned, bright-cheeked medical student,"[19] from *Preview*, training to be a psychiatrist. He was still a little in love with Pat. Norah (the secretary at Film Strips) recalls that Bruce came with Pat to visit at her summer cottage. Earlier, at a *Preview* gathering in Montreal, Mavis Gallant had seen Ruddick, a huge teddy bear, passionately attempting to kiss Pat while she struggled to get away.[20] Page did not care for Ruddick or for any other of the young men she met in Ottawa: her emotions were already engaged and her life structured around letters and visits from Frank Scott. Nonetheless, she did not allow him to interfere with getting her poems to publication.

In September 1946 the Ryerson Press published Pat's first book of poems, *As Ten, As Twenty*. A record of the war generation, it was very different from anything published previously in Canada in its unflinching combination of the realistic, the psychological, and the surreal. It includes a number of modern poems that rank among the best written in Canada: "Stories of Snow," "Adolescence," "If It Were You," "Landlady," "The Stenographers," and the semi-autobiographical "Cullen." Page had made the modern idiom her own, a fact noted by a reviewer of *As Ten, As Twenty* in the prestigious *Poetry* magazine, who also singled out "Stories of Snow": "[I]t would be impertinent to say anything about promise in this first book. Miss Page is, like modern poetry, way beyond showing promise."[21] The delight of "Stories of Snow," already discussed, is not only the story within a story but the prism-like way in which Page's imagery changed from the vivid, colourful flowers of Victoria to the imagined whiteness of the swan hunt in Holland.

Page wrote as a modern, part of the war generation, saying in a poem with that title: "Tragically, Spain was our spade." It was the Spanish Civil War, epitomized in Pablo Picasso's *Guernica* – with its images of broken and distorted human and animal bodies – that forced the 1930s poets, especially W.H. Auden, to articulate the cruelty of war and the necessity of love. Like her British contemporaries, Pat saw "eyes like our own / studding the map like cities" ("Generation").[22] "Love Poem," from which the title of the book is drawn, was written for Frank Scott and echoes Auden's famous line, "We must love one another or die" ("September 1, 1939"). In the latter poem, Auden recognizes that man and his state are intimately connected, as do both Scott and Page.[23] In Page's images, the two lovers contain multitudes of others – as does the socialism that both embraced:

> As ten, as twenty, now,
> we break from single thought
> and rid of being two,
> receive them and walk out.[24]

But the interconnection of body and landscape, found in this poem and others, also flowed naturally from her own experience of the Canadian prairies and the Laurentians. A mapping poem, "If It Were You," speaks of the way in which the boundaries of the young woman's "personal map" have been encroached by her lover – smudged like a child's painting after rain.

> If it were you, the person you call "I,"
> the one you loved and worked for,
> the most high

now become Ishmael,
might you not
grow phobias about calendars and clocks ...[25]

She had considered calling the book "The Untouched Hills," and this
may be why she placed a poem called "Personal Landscape" (originally
called "Landscape of Love") at the beginning of the book: "Where the
bog ends, there, where the ground lips, lovely / is love, not lonely." The
poem's surprising last image refers to "the valvular heart's / field glasses"
and is metaphysical in its fusion of feeling and seeing.[26]

Reviewers of the book, including A.J.M. Smith, singled out the au-
dacity of her imagery and diction. In "Waking," she wrote: "I lie in the
long parenthesis of arms / dreaming of love / and the crying cities of Europe."[27] Smith, who disapproved of political poetry, ignored Page's socialist writings and focused on her subjective work: "In the inner life of
reverie, of self-analysis, and of dreams she finds a mirror-like stage for
the re-enactment of the hesitations and struggles of the outer world of
objective experience."[28] He recognized that she had created a particular
landscape, half psychological, half mythological, but that she was still
searching for a myth and a language. Smith was also the first to note a
significant motif in her work, which he identified as the journey by train
and the "mysterious traveller": both are combined in the "ambitious"
poem "Round Trip."[29] A traveller, equipped for "the incredible journey"
with sword, binoculars, compass, food, topee, letters of introduction,
and even a mask, sets out for an exotic destination. But he discovers, to
his sorrow, at the end of the track "that nothing's changed, that everything's the same ... / Forever, everywhere, for him, the same."[30] Smith
does not identify the "ambitious" aspect of this poem, but it may be
found partly in the traveller's "inner girl" (perhaps a version of Jung's
anima) who comments on the journey, in some aspects the life journey.
At one point, she calls out, "Betrayed, Betrayed," perhaps reflecting
some of Page's own strong emotions on the long journey from Halifax
to Victoria in 1944. She and Scott were parting, not just because her
family needed her but also because he had not claimed her. In this poem,
as in "Cullen," the male narrator carries autobiographical freight.

When Page first received her copies of As Ten, As Twenty, she sent one
to Alan and Jean Crawley with a note expressing her heartfelt thanks.
"Whether you like it or not, I feel this is partly your book. Alan's criticism, help & encouragement since cv's [Contemporary Verse's] beginning have contributed more [than] any other thing to what progress I
may have made in the last few years – & I only hope to God that one day

I may do something half worthy of his faith in me. It's a terrific thing to have someone believe in you – but utterly humbling."[31] Page did not forget her debts.

And she was overjoyed to receive praise from "Art" Smith. In the late fall of 1946 he sent her a note saying, "It is 2:00 a.m. and I am a trifle drunk but I don't think I sh[oul]d go to bed without writing a brief note just to say how much I (and the guys who were here) admire your book." The guys included some of the major figures in the literary establishment: critic Northrop Frye, novelist Morley Callaghan, and professors Ernest Sirluck and Marshall McLuhan. Smith told Page that towards the end of the evening, "I read some of your poems. And to say that everyone listened with respect & awe is something of an understatement. I don't know from what depths you have dragged up your knowledge, but I think we all want to offer you our homage. You are a real poet."[32] This supreme accolade was "one hell of an encouraging letter," as Pat wrote the Crawleys.[33]

There was a postwar flurry of interest in Canadian writing in the latter part of the 1940s and P.K. Page was pronounced a "Canadian poet" in a CBC Radio broadcast by A.J.M. Smith and Northrop Frye – meaning perhaps that she was a good younger poet whose style and subjects were recognizably Canadian rather than English. A few months earlier, in mid-August 1946, Earle Birney had acknowledged her poetic ability when he wrote to Page asking her to join him as the associate editor for the *Canadian Poetry Magazine*, house organ of the Canadian Authors Association, which he hoped to reorganize. He knew that she thought that "*CPM* is the lousiest verse mag. in existence." But if she accepted she would be working with good writers such as Anne Marriott, Charles Bruce, Floris McLaren, Patrick Waddington, Philip Child, and F.J. "Ned" Pratt – the latter, Birney said, as a figurehead.[34] Page did not accept his invitation. (Later in the fifties, Birney wrote to Al Purdy saying that he feared Page might be a better poet than he[35] – not an uncommon reaction, Scott had earlier expressed a similar view.)

In October 1946 Birney proposed to Alan Crawley that *Contemporary Verse* merge with *Canadian Poetry Magazine* under his (Birney's) direction. Page was distrustful. She could not accept the idea of a two-time Governor General's Award winner allying himself, for the sake of Canadian literature, with what she considered the most reactionary magazine in the country. She wrote to Crawley: "We have too many Pratts & [E.K.] Browns already ... It's a damn sight harder to pull a thing up than to start from scratch. Also I *personally* like to feel C.V. is there – small & compact, reflecting you ... Mark you, *if* Birney does take this on

I will back him because I feel if the c.a.a. has enough wits to appoint him Editor they deserve whatever help we can give. But surely he can take it alone. Why is he coercing you?"[36]

Evidence of a new, though slight, interest in Canadian writing was shown by the Canadian Poetry "Saying" tour undertaken by Alan Crawley in the late fall of 1946. He recited poems, primarily Canadian, from memory. In ten weeks he spoke to fifty large and enthusiastic audiences from Vancouver to Montreal. He had an excellent speaking voice and retained a broad repertoire of contemporary writing in his memory. But the pace of the tour was hectic, with "three weeks of one-night stands, five days a week in Ontario."[37] Nonetheless, the Crawleys spent a week in Ottawa with Pat in November.

Pat was writing intensely and rapidly. In late 1946 she submitted seven poems to *Poetry* (Chicago), five of which were published in the December 1946 edition: "Young Girls," "Election Day," "Freak," "Blowing Boy," and "Sisters." This may have precipitated a sharp critical review of her work as a whole in January 1947 by her old beau John Sutherland, now editor of the little magazine *Northern Review*. He acknowledged that Page's work with *Preview* had led her to write a more original and vivid modern poetry, but he vigorously argued that her thinking – and her metaphors – were confused. He also categorized her as a Freudian rather than a Marxian (indeed, Pat at this time was most interested in the psychological make-up of the characters in her poems) and suggested that the vitality of her poetry was generated by her recognition of the conflict between the individual and society.[38] Undergirding some of the critical judgments of this essay is Sutherland's sense of personal rejection by Page.[39]

Sutherland's article may have caused her to consider the qualities essential to a good critic. She wrote to Jori Smith in mid-January 1947 commenting on the shallowness of Canadian critics: "They use words much as they would shovel snow. It's damnable. I wish I had a critical facility myself that was more acute, more founded in knowledge. Our critics praise too much or damn too much ... they don't approach the work with any *real sympathy*."[40]

Later in 1947, Sutherland wrote a dismissive review of Robert Finch's new book of poetry, *Poems*, which had just been awarded a Governor General's Award.[41] Pat, who had not protested about his review of her own work, felt that Sutherland's treatment of Finch was cruel. She wrote to him on 23 August 1947 pointing out that her name was still on the masthead of *Northern Review* but that she was resigning as a regional editor. In the next edition of the magazine, Sutherland acknowledged that P.K. Page had had no knowledge of the review.

There were other irritants. Pat's work left her constantly tired and stressed. She was "busy as hell in the office" because film strips on subjects as diverse as "geology, citizenship, labour-management, feet, family allowance, Newfoundland, French tapestries" kept her running. She wrote Jean Crawley to say that she had been working at the French Embassy, reading magnificent magazines in French while researching a documentary on tapestries.[42] There, she discovered Dom Robert, a Benedictine monk influenced by Sufism. Robert's designs of peacocks, gardens, and stylized trees had been adapted by the Aubusson tapestry industry, and his images appear in some of Pat's later poems. When not working, she often stayed at home, hoping against hope that Scott would come to visit – she didn't have a telephone until late in the decade. When her mother and Aunt Bibbi moved to Montreal at the end of the decade, she tried to see them on weekends.

Pat liked her co-workers at the National Film Commission, but after two years she knew the job was not for her. She wrote to Elizabeth Brewster in December 1947 saying, "I do the research and writing of all Film Strips. It is a good job in many ways, but I simply don't want to work for a living. I'd like to sit on a cushion and write a fine poem."[43] At the turn of the New Year, in January 1948, Pat wrote to her dearest friend: "Jori, I think the world will perhaps die of Earnestness. It's a quality I grow to *despise*. The Film Board is full of Ernest Earnest young men all wanting to tell you the story of a book they've just read because they think it has a message & which [they have] not the wits to know what detail is irrelevant & not worth the telling. We have lost somehow the quality of magic. In most of our writing there is none, in most of our painting. Our music. And Jesus in our relationships. It's the one thing that makes the work of art transcend our knowledge – as in Blake."[44]

A few months later, in March, Pat met someone who did not fit this mould, Khushwant Singh, a Muslim born in India who had joined India's diplomatic service and was cultural attaché at the Indian Embassy in Ottawa. It was his job to contact writers and artists. As Singh later wrote, "The year in Canada proved to be a turning point in my career." Singh met Pat Page at a Film Board gathering and later telephoned her, asking for her help in meeting creative writers. She invited him to a party, where he met Frank Scott and Abe Klein. Singh was fun, he regularly brought champagne to literary gatherings, and he and his wife befriended Pat with hampers of food when she was incapacitated with back problems.

Subsequently, as he tells us in his biography: "I cultivated a lot of Canadian writers and poets. After reading their works, I invited them over to my home. Amongst them were the poets ... Page and Abe Klein."⁴⁵ This proved to be a turning point in Singh's career because from then onwards he became a writer rather than a diplomat. Not only did he find Pat Page to be the "best looking, the nicest and the most gifted" person he met in Canada, but the early stories he published in *Saturday Night* and elsewhere got him started on his career.⁴⁶

In Ottawa, Pat saw a fair amount of Florence Bird. She liked Florence for her honesty and directness but thought she did not have a "feeling for poetry"; she had more of a journalistic and political bent. In later life she thought Florence "half a hippy," with a crazy sense of humour, though she was not so fond of Florence's bossy side, likening her to a ship in full sail, dragging all in her wake.⁴⁷ Florence suggested in 1948 that Pat drive her to Rhode Island, where her family had a summer home. Pat now had a car because her mother had sent to Ottawa the little car she had in Victoria. Setting out in August, they had a leisurely drive and Pat stayed a week with Florence's family.

Pat had arranged to rendezvous in Boston with Jori Smith, who travelled there by bus. The two old friends set out along the Cape Cod Peninsula. It is a long cape and Provincetown, their destination, was at the very end. The journey seemed interminable, the car sputtered, and the weather was so hot they thought they would expire. The sea was on their right, but they couldn't swim because in the United States the foreshore was private property. Jori suggested that they stop at one of the houses and that Pat should do the talking because "Americans are so susceptible to English accents."⁴⁸ They selected a likely house and a pleasant young woman answered the door. She gave them permission to use their bathhouse and swim at the beach. When Pat and Jori eventually reached Provincetown, they rented a studio apartment on the pier. They had a great week, meeting the fishboats at night and getting fresh fish, sitting in the sun drinking cheap wine, and listening to a New York Symphony violinist practising; he was on holiday and staying nearby. "So we would eat fresh, fresh fish and Jori painted and I sat about and wrote 'Portrait of Marina,' I guess. That was a lovely week."⁴⁹

"Portrait of Marina" is one of Page's outstanding poems. Although it was generated by the visit to New England, many of the details came from Pat's imagination, as if she were developing a film script to fit the visuals. The poem begins with an artifact – a seascape of a lost four-masted ship embroidered on canvas by an old skipper – which hangs in the sunny parlour of one of his descendants, a young woman. Nobody remembers now that the stitches were made with the skipper's oaths and curses, or of their effect on Marina, his "one pale spinster daughter." The skipper had hoped that her name would make his daughter a water woman; but for Marina herself – who fears the sea – her name is synonymous with her father's roar, summoning her to thread his tapestry needle.

The poem shifts back to the present, with his great-great-granddaughter recalling the captain's advanced age and infirm docility; her Aunt Marina is described as "warped / without a smack of salt" – a wonderful line in context because it is not the sea that has warped her but the bullying skipper himself. The physical effects of his constant harassment is demonstrated in the next stanza (four), where our focus shifts again to the embroidered picture: "Each wave is capped / with broken mirrors," the waves being equated with Marina's continual waves of pain:

> She walked forever antlered with migraines
> her pain forever putting forth new shoots
> until her strange unlovely head became
> a kind of candelabra – delicate –
> where all her tears were perilously hung ...

In the ironic conclusion of the poem, our focus turns back to the fabulous sea and all that it represents: but to Marina, even the warm and beautiful shallows have become threatening: for her, the sea was "Father's Fearful Sea / harsh with sea serpents / winds and drowning men."[50] Two years later, Pat submitted the poem to Alan Crawley for publication in *Contemporary Verse*.

Pat knew some of the likely forebears for this poem. She had been reading T.S. Eliot's "Marina," and she also recognized the great power of the unconscious – Jungian or Freudian – which the poet taps but does not always understand.[51] But the older Page could not remember anything of the house they visited briefly on the way down or their hostess's manner to suggest the themes of "A Portrait of Marina"[52] – the spinster daughter, the dominant father, and the transformation of pain into art. Pat was now thirty-one – almost a spinster daughter herself – with residual memories of a dominant father[53] that may have been activated by her closest "bossy" friends, Florence and Jori.[54] Furthermore, she had been in considerable pain for the last five years with a disc problem. She also had a lover who made her head ache. Like her mother Rose, Pat knew the blinding agonies of a migraine headache. She once told a friend, "They're in the blood."[55]

120 OTTAWA

On the return journey from New England, Pat wrote to Alan Crawley telling him about her holiday: "A lazy and lovely time with waves and sun and the rich, much loved land of New England flowing by. I ... spent a beautiful night and early morning walking about Boston's Beacon Hill – and – oh bliss – I returned to my own crazy little apt. What a difference this place has made to my general peace of mind."[56] This apartment, 173 Daly Street, where she lived for her last two years in Ottawa, allowed her peace and quiet for her own creative work, and she could invite Frank Scott to visit without considering the sensibilities of roommates.

☰

Nonetheless, she felt that the deception involved in her love affair with Scott was destroying something integral to her sense of self – and to her poetry. As early as 1947 she had decided that she needed help and had approached an Ottawa psychiatrist. She told him that she thought she must be totally neurotic, but he said that she was not and he would do his best to help her sort herself out. The psychiatrist lived at the other end of Ottawa, so twice a week for several months Pat boarded two street-cars to get there. When she took what was then called a "truth drug" to determine if there was anything further in her psyche than what she had consciously revealed, she became hysterically giggly, but nothing further surfaced. The whole experience, however, eased her mind, and she began to think seriously about making changes in her life.[57] Later in the decade she again sought professional help.

In 1947, as she told Jean Crawley, she found "a magnificent letter" which in the twelfth century the beautiful and intelligent Héloïse had sent to the monk Abelard.[58] The letter moved Page so deeply that she sought out Helen Waddell's book *Peter Abelard* and Scott Montcrieff's translation of their letters. Héloïse, the niece of the canon of Notre Dame, was tutored by Abelard, a French philosopher and teacher, commonly thought to be the founder of the University of Paris. According to Abelard's account, he made his way into her family home: "our books lying open before us, more words of love rose to our lips than of literature ..."[59] Héloïse attempted to run away, fearing that their love would ruin Abelard's life as a scholar-priest. But she was drawn back to the man she loved and their tragedy unfolds inevitably. As Héloïse says, "Were there ever two great lovers, but they ended in sorrow?"[60]

Page read of these star-crossed lovers during an unhappy phase of her relationship with Scott. It was an enormous strain to keep their relationship secret. Only once, in Montreal in the late fall of 1948, had she expressed her emotions in public. She had come to Montreal as a guest of David and Marie Thomson, who had obtained tickets for the Royal Ballet's *Swan Lake* starring Margot Fonteyn. To Pat, the ballet had enormous personal resonance. It told the story of Prince Siegfried torn between two women – symbolized by a white and black swan. The white swan is his true love, the enchanted Princess Odette, but the black swan is Odile, the daughter of an evil magician determined to destroy the two lovers. When pressed, Fonteyn once indicated that she saw the central core of the ballet as "Love, a rock around which swirl all the forces of destruction."[61] The young prince, blinded by the magician, chooses the wrong swan (Odile disguised as Odette), thus condemning his beloved to death. But, in the transcendent conclusion of the ballet, Prince Siegfried and Odette rise beyond their evil fate by choosing to die together.

Pat was so affected by Fonteyn's performance (she danced both swans) that she began to weep and then to sob loudly. She may have seen her own story in the ballet – seeing Frank as Siegfried, torn between her and his wife Marian, possibly in danger of making the wrong choice. The Thomsons, Page's companions, were greatly embarrassed by her weeping.[62] When Scott, who attended the performance with Marian, encountered Pat in the foyer, he took her by the arm to drive her to the after-theatre dinner party at the Thomsons' house. At the dinner, when Marian suggested that she and Frank could drive her home, Pat bolted from the house.[63] She believed passionately that she and Scott belonged together and had done so since time immemorial. But it would work only if Scott wanted it.[64] She didn't want to pressure him; she hoped he would make a free choice and marry her. But she was now near her mid-thirties, and may have felt that life was passing her by while she waited for Scott to decide.

⚌

The previous year she had attempted to renounce Scott and had gone west to visit her family for six weeks. But like Héloïse, she had eventually returned to the man she loved, a "return" described by Scott in his 1948 poem of the same name.

> One time you heard upon the outer air
> Your freedom calling, and you turned and fled
> Up the long pathway of your own descent
> To the lip of the world, your hand upon the door,
> But stopped too soon, looked round the way you went –
> Eurydice, drawn back by the deeper blood.[65]

Later, in August 1949, Pat again attempted to break with Scott. Again she went west, this time spending a week in Caulfeild, West Vancouver, visiting the Crawleys, who reported to Anne Wilkinson: "P.K. Page was staying with us for 168 hours and in each of the 24 we talked endlessly and with much floor pacing, on the terrace in the sun and before the fire for a good eighteen hours. Everything was covered, from the heights of Ezra Pound to some ribald stories and the best methods of preparing crab for food. It was a very good seven days."[66] Pat may have discussed Scott with the Crawleys, because she was seriously considering a life without him. Whenever she left Ottawa she recognized the truth of her situation – she was living in a fantasy and she could not write. She began to stiffen her resolve to live her life without Scott if she had to.

After leaving Vancouver, Pat went to Victoria. There she was interviewed by a newspaper reporter and offered her dues to the province's literary establishment. "I don't know why I wrote so much when I was in British Columbia three years ago," she is quoted as saying. "There is something mysterious about this province which makes people write poetry, and a large part of the important verse of Canada is produced here ... It may be because of the encouragement of men like Earle Birney, editor of *Canadian Poetry* magazine, or Alan Crawley of *Contemporary Verse*, or Ira Dilworth."[67] Dilworth, a long-time B.C. educator, was then the British Columbia regional director for CBC Radio and was the host of a well-regarded radio program on poetry.

That winter, in December 1949, Pat went to Toronto when undertaking research for a film strip about factories for the Department of Labour. She had read Anne Wilkinson's poetry in *Contemporary Verse* and sent her a note asking if she would be free to meet. Wilkinson invited her for tea and then suggested that she stay to dinner. Page accepted and Wilkinson said to her husband, "We'd better get out a bottle of wine to celebrate."[68] As women poets, Page and Wilkinson were isolated in so many ways. Each must have recognized a kindred spirit, because they talked all evening. In her journal for 28 December 1948, Wilkinson wrote: "P.K. Page came to see us. The most beautiful creature. She is what you imagine a poet to be."[69]

The two poets carried on their friendship by correspondence. In mid-August, circa 1949, Page wrote to Wilkinson saying that she had just returned from a summer trip to the Gaspé Peninsula. She was in despair about her poetry – couldn't write but had an urgent desire to write. "I understand too well the dilemma of the Eunuch! Have just been reading Coleridge's 'Ode to Dejection.' Do you know it? I had not read it before. It seems a most unresolved poem but perhaps is better for that reason –

it gives the impression that it was written actually when the death of the soul was upon him. Even its beginning, so arbitrarily wrought from lines from the 'Ballad of Sir Patrick Spens[e],' starts one off with the ashes of a fatal discipline in one's mouth."[70]

Pat felt she understood the death of a soul. She may also have guessed, from Marian Scott's kindness at the *Swan Lake* ballet, that Marian not only knew of her relationship with Frank but condoned it. Pat had been wracked by guilt, not for herself but for the effect of their relationship on Marian; she saw herself as "the other woman" (the black swan?) breaking up the Scott marriage. It appears that Scott, always reticent with regard to personal matters, had not fully explained the nature of his marriage, which was simply that he and Marian had agreed that each was free to seek emotional nourishment elsewhere.[71]

No past relationship appears to have threatened the marriage (although Marian and Frank did recall, with great amusement, that Scott had punched Norman Bethune in the nose when the two men encountered each other on a ship returning from Europe in 1935).[72] But Pat Page was beautiful, emotionally honest, and highly gifted in the area where Scott was most vulnerable. He seems to have recognized Pat as a genuinely serious poet, one who cultivated her talent, while he had let his own fall by the wayside. Throughout the twenties and thirties he often felt guilty when the urge to write poetry – "the little voice," as he called it – overtook him, because he frequently suppressed it in order to get on with the immediate business of earning a living or fighting for CCF politics. His dilemma was that, at heart, he felt himself to be a poet and knew he was betraying his gift when he allowed other activities to claim his attention. Not only did Scott see in Page the better poet who would surpass him, but her desire for marriage and a child may have enlivened disturbingly the ambiguities of his marriage.

Although Frank and Marian Scott had reached a rational solution to the problems of their marriage, the reality of a "companionable marriage" was more painful in fact than in theory. Marian had earlier recorded in her diary her anger and dismay about the relationship between her husband and P.K.: "I wait. I know he is with another. My rational mind says why not, why not live richly. Live to the full each experience. Why should I hold him back. It says all men are polygamous. A certain kind of love passes away but another kind can keep holding ... It says I would rather suffer than be deceived. But the rest of my mind moulded by the conventions, the taboos of many generations

intensified by literature cries out. I cry, I bleed. It says you wrong me …
It says you are cruel and immoral."[73] Later in the same entry, referring
to the lack of a conjugal relationship with Frank, Marian adds that their
situation is both unnatural and unbearable. The pressure was removed
when Pat left Montreal for Halifax and then moved to Vancouver
Island. However, it returned when Pat came to Ottawa in 1946 and she
and Frank resumed their relationship.

By 1948, both Pat and Marian had become aware that their respective situations were intolerable – Marian, because she sensed that Frank
was moving farther away; Pat, because she was living a lie, which she
found abhorrent. Her free time was spent waiting, hoping for the arrival
of a man who did not come. Initially, she had felt that Frank had nour-
ished her poetry, but now she could no longer write because she was so
unhappy. Ultimately, Marian was a catalyst in changing the situation.
Intuitive, soft-spoken, and reserved, she was intensely emotional. Myron
Galloway, a Montreal art critic, described her as "a very Virginia Woolf
type of person, you felt her world was just millions of atoms storming
around inside her."[74] Marian seems to have taken stock of their situation
in her diary between 1946 and 1950, reading psychologist Karen Hor-
ney for guidance, and reasoning that Frank was getting to the age when
such *bouleversements* as his love affair with Pat were not uncommon.
She thought he was a somewhat cold personality for whom romances
rekindled feeling. Most importantly, as Frank had told her, for him Pat
represented poetry, whereas she believed that their marriage represented
convention, which he always wanted to overthrow.[75] However, Marian
recognized that she provided her husband with the settled family life that
made all of his other activities possible. She decided to take the initiative
in changing matters.

It was clear to all three principals that Scott had to make a choice. But
from his perspective, any choice would produce a loss. He had somehow managed to compartmentalize his life into separate areas: the university and law, socialist politics, Marian and home, Pat and poetry. Each
contributed to his sense of a fulfilled life, and without any one he would
be deprived. Selfishly perhaps, he put off the fateful moment of choice.

Marian now proposed a trial year of separation – between July 1949
and July 1950 – during which time Pat could move into the family home
at 451 Clarke Avenue and she would move out. The younger woman
was wise enough to refuse, and Scott continued to visit Ottawa. Before
the year had ended, on 15 June 1950, Marian herself moved out of
Clarke Avenue and took a flat at 3425 Peel Street, her "cloister" as she

termed it. This greatly embarrassed Scott, as his university colleagues began to ask questions. The separate compartments of his life were not only merging but were subject to public speculation.

The events of the years between 1948 and 1951 were to affect Page's poetry, Scott's public life and his poetry, and Marian Scott's painting. At the same time, Pat began to make changes in her life that took her farther and farther from Scott's orbit. Although an older Page later looked upon it as a rejection by Scott, the decision about whether he would leave his marriage was a mutual one. Pat's unhappiness precipitated the question of choice, and Marian's action in leaving home forced Scott to recognize what he would lose. He was finally brought to the point where, by default, he offered a reluctant No to the prospect of leaving his marriage.

While her emotional life see-sawed violently, work had become very tense for Pat at the Film Commission because a continuing investigation by the RCMP concluded that it harboured Communists. In September 1945, Igor Gouzenko, a Russian cipher clerk in the Soviet Embassy in Ottawa, had defected, alleging that a Soviet spy ring operated in a number of Canadian government organizations, including the Film Commission. A woman who had briefly been one of Grierson's secretaries in 1944 was connected with the spy ring. Prime Minister King, who already considered Grierson sympathetic to Communists, confided to his diary that "the whole situation at the Film Board needs looking into as there is reason to believe there is quite a Communist nest there."[76] King probably considered the Film Commission especially vulnerable because it was administered by the Department of National Defence.

Unfortunately, when Grierson appeared before a royal commission, called in 1946 to investigate allegations of espionage in government service, he was not able to dispel suspicion. A typical intellectual, he was considered a "leftist" or Communist by the commissioners.[77] His successor as film commissioner, Ross McLean, was not judged to be capable of containing the damage. In the next two years, following the line of Cold War paranoia and McCarthyism in the United States, members of Parliament began to consider closing down the Film Commission. Finally, in 1950, Cabinet decided to reconstitute the institution as the National Film Board of Canada, and a search was begun for a new commissioner.

Lester Pearson, who was then Canada's secretary of state for external affairs, approached Arthur Irwin, a former newspaperman and editor of *Maclean's* magazine, to ask him to assume the job.[78] His appointment in

February 1950 was not popular at the Film Board; most employees were angered by Ross McLean's dismissal and considered Irwin a hatchet-man with no creative experience. Pat, too, was suspicious of the new commissioner. She wanted to resign when he was first appointed but felt she could not leave while an investigation was in progress. She was also dubious about the charge that hard-core Communists were among the employees, though one of her colleagues, Hazen Sise, was an avowed Communist and had gone to Spain with Norman Bethune in the 1930s. When Irwin was first appointed, Sise told Pat that he had some important official papers, clearly Communist, that were too dangerous for him to keep but too valuable to dispose of. He proposed that she keep them safe for him and became indignant when she refused.[79]

One weekend in late June 1950, when visiting her family in Montreal, Pat had tea with Jori Smith and Jean Palardy. As Jori recalls, Pat said, "I'm not at all happy with Ottawa, it's just not my world, the job's stale, I'm not happy there." The couple suggested that she return to Montreal, "where your friends are," and she said, "You're right ... I shall resign, Jori, I shall simply resign. The first thing I'll do Monday morning."[80] She appears to have given in her resignation to the new head of Film Strips, Lionel Reid, in early July, possibly on Monday, 3 July.

As Reid did not want to lose a good scriptwriter (one characterized by John Grierson as "a much gifted woman"),[81] he promptly contacted the new commissioner, because one of Page's film scripts, "Teeth Are to Keep," had just won an international award. The following Saturday morning – the office was open on Saturday mornings – Arthur Irwin telephoned Page asking her if he could take her out for a meal to discuss her resignation. He took her to dinner at a good restaurant, the Mountain Lodge in the Gatineau Hills. Although he did not drink himself, he ordered drinks for her, listened to her beefs, and made a few judicious comments. He began to talk intelligently about Canada and asked for her opinion. Page began to warm to him, recognizing that this short, balding, distinguished-looking man, the son of a Methodist clergyman, was "absolutely straight, that he couldn't be deviant, or do anything underhand or prevaricate."[82] Irwin, in turn, must have received a similar sense of Page's emotional honesty. In response to his offer of a better job, she responded that it was not her ambition to have a good job or be a writer for films. He was unable to persuade her to stay on indefinitely, but she does seem to have delayed her resignation. And he did persuade her to see him again.

Pat was now in the final stages of breaking with Frank Scott. In July 1950, the trial year that Marian Scott had stipulated had finished, and Frank came to Ottawa in mid-July to tell Pat that he could not leave Marian, perhaps for the reasons that he later explained in the poem "Message" (a poem perhaps meant for both Pat and Marian because his images contrast a wilderness lake with a settled home): "He would lose / In choosing, what he did not choose." Scott chose Marian and family because, as he said in the same poem, some paths "lead outward from the wood ... / Where houses stand whose quiet mood / Of love is seasoned."[83]

As Scott acknowledged in his diary on 16 July, "the dilemma has had to be resolved." He recognized that the resolution was inherent in his own character and speculated that perhaps he had the habits of the Classic and the character of the Romantic. "But I prefer to believe I have gone after the living, the creative, the stimulating in whatever form it has come. I did not try to see the end of any road that invited me ... It seemed almost as though I broke two hearts today, being late in returning, yet mine which should mark the strongest change, seemed least disturbed."[84]

But Scott was perhaps maintaining a stiff upper lip for the benefit of his diary (and posterity). Pat, whom he had visited in Ottawa, was heartbroken and weeping because he had chosen to remain in his marriage; and Marian, waiting anxiously in Montreal, was weeping when Frank telephoned home because he had been delayed by missing his train. As he put down the telephone in Ottawa, P.K. saw that Frank, who himself was given to tears in these days, also began to weep.[85] Despite Frank's decision, Marian continued to live in her apartment in Montreal and was determined to stay there until their relationship changed. He became increasingly uncomfortable with their separation, and on 13 August 1950 Marian recorded in her journal that Frank had asked her "what would he have to do for me to come back?"[86]

Two months later, in October 1950, Page telephoned Jori Smith with astonishing news. "She said, 'Jori, you'll never believe what I'll tell you.' And I said, 'Go on, what happened? And did you resign?' 'Oh yes, I resigned, and I'm going to marry Arthur Irwin.'" Jori's reply: "Who's he?"[87]

⚎

As P.K. had quickly discovered, Arthur Irwin was a widower in his early fifties with three children. He had solid credentials for his new post as commissioner and chairman of the National Film Board. He was a member of the Parliamentary Press Gallery, had spent twenty years

Canadianizing *Maclean's* magazine, and possessed remarkable moral courage. He had provided the information for an exposé by George Drew and an article in *Maclean's* revealing that the Canadian military had sent soldiers to war with Bren guns that jammed under fire. A man whose values were unquestioned, he began his work as commissioner by interviewing every employee and firing three whom he believed to be Communist. He then set about running the reorganized National Film Board – and courting Pat Page.

Pat had accepted an invitation from Arthur to visit his summer cottage at Belmont Lake, between Toronto and Montreal. She was chaperoned by Maudie Ferguson, and Arthur's grown children – Neal, Sheila, and Patricia – were also there. Pat impressed Arthur's family by doing flying cartwheels on the lawn. She was bitten by a blackfly and Arthur recalled that her arm swelled enormously: "Damn good-looking arm."[88] They had intended to go to a local dance, but Arthur said that he would like to show Pat a waterfall: "We got into the boat and went across the lake and came to a path, and by this time it was getting dark. He clearly knew his way absolutely, and he was very sure-footed ... I felt at that moment I could follow this man – I could trust this man anywhere he led me ... And he led me to a waterfall, and it was moonlight, and it was beautiful, utterly beautiful. I realized that he had a real aesthetic sense – a real feeling for beauty and nature."[89]

An extremely taciturn man, Irwin spoke only when he had something that needed to be said. His judgment was impeccable, and Pat found this quality admirable, especially when combined with a strong ethical sense and a practical knowledge of the world. Arthur also understood the writing process. As an editor, he had trained many journalists and writers, including Pierre Berton, Ralph Allen, Blair Fraser, June Callwood, and Peter Newman. Finally, he made Page aware that he appreciated her as a beautiful woman – "a corker," as he confided to one of his newspaper buddies.

They had met at a vulnerable time in their lives. Irwin was lonely after the death of his wife Jean – she had died suddenly in an asthma attack in the fall of 1948; and Pat was on the rebound from Scott. She told Irwin candidly that she had loved a married poet for some years. Although Irwin was concerned about a marriage on the rebound, he was willing to take his chances. Page did not reveal the name of the man in question. (Later, when Irwin had an occasion to phone Frank Scott in connection with the Film Board, he knew instantly, when he heard Scott's voice, that this must be the man she spoke of – he found their slightly English voices identical.)[90]

Much later in their lives, in the 1970s, I asked Arthur Irwin what he had liked most about Pat Page. "I liked everything about her," he replied: "everything except her god-damned Brit voice!"[91] Irwin had spent much of his life as a colonial struggling against the British – especially the British generals of the First World War when he had been a Canadian gunner at the front. Then, after the war, he had spent nearly twenty years as managing editor of *Maclean's*, attempting to modify the strongly pro-British attitudes of Colonel Maclean, the longtime owner of the magazine, and that of another Englishman, H. Napier Moore, who was parachuted into the job of editor-in-chief, a position Irwin considered rightfully his. Nonetheless, line by line, inch by inch, Irwin had converted *Maclean's* into the most popular and genuinely Canadian magazine of the period until, in 1945, he himself became editor-in-chief.

During the later summer of 1950, Neal Irwin, Arthur's son, came back from his summer job as a forest ranger and found Page visiting his father. Neal thought that his father was "attracted to the same things that I found very attractive in her: you know, this terrifically lively mind, and her interest in so many things, and the depth of her getting into them … and pursuing them."[92] On Pat's part, she must have appreciated Irwin's willingness to commit himself. Norah Helliwell, her confidante at the Film Board, believed that Arthur provided "understanding"; after Pat met Arthur, she changed and became happier, and more contented.[93] A year older than Scott, Irwin fitted the pattern of the dominant men in Pat's life: her father was born in 1886, Irwin in 1898, and Scott in 1899.

Arthur Irwin and Frank Scott were very much alike, although they appeared quite different. Frank was tall and lean – a witty and assured extrovert; Arthur was rather short and a little plump – an incisive, equally assured introvert. Beneath the veneer of personality, their characters and their formative backgrounds were similar. Both were the sons of clergymen who had been urged by their fathers to enter the ministry. When the Great War was declared, both tried to join up as soon as they could, but Arthur was accepted while Frank, who had lost his left eye, was rejected. Arthur joined the McGill battalion, the battalion of Frank's later university. Both recorded their disgust when they heard the same unctuous Montreal clergyman glorifying war to members of the battalion on the eve of their departure from Canada. While serving in the army, Arthur met Brooke Claxton, who became Frank's good friend. Later, Arthur's friends in the Parliamentary Press Gallery, especially Blair Fraser, were people whom Frank also considered friends.

Both men were branded by the war and its after-effects, especially by the Winnipeg General Strike of 1919 when J.S. Woodsworth and Canon

Scott, Frank's father, supported the strikers. Each man was shaped by the strong Canadian nationalism that prevailed in the twenties, and each sought independence for Canada from Great Britain – Frank in the legal, political, and literary fields, Arthur in the social and literary fields. Arthur had returned from Europe to a Canada where there was very little art or literature, which he regretted – both he and Frank had a strongly aesthetic side. Arthur attended the University of Toronto, where he wrote verse and a play, and he later became a Sunday painter; Frank, who studied history at Oxford and law at McGill, read literature and began to write poetry as a contributor to the *McGill Fortnightly Review* – Canada's first group of modern poets.

In their working careers, both put their jobs on the line for their principles. Arthur exposed illegal government and industry scandals. Frank opposed government oppression in his arguments for Communists in Toronto and for the Duplessis and Roncarelli cases in Quebec. On two occasions, Arthur lost his job for his principles; Frank would have been fired from McGill for what was considered his Bolshevik sympathies had he not been protected by his father's standing and his family name. In later life they had the same circle of friends, not only Brooke Claxton and Blair Fraser but Davidson Dunton, Wynne Plumptre, and Jack Pickersgill. As a result, both had privileged access to Ottawa mandarins and the Liberal establishment. Paradoxically, each man saw himself as an outsider – and to some degree each was.

Arthur Irwin had asked P.K. to marry him in late October, and on 30 October she sent a letter to Scott telling him that her engagement to Arthur would soon be announced. A day later, Scott wrote in his diary: "And now, my darling, you have chosen, as I must leave." By this, Scott seems to have meant that because he had to leave their relationship, Pat had chosen Arthur. But in the pages of his diary he continued to try to understand: "The thing I could never believe in or accept – the end – has come. I fought it like death, and for the same reason. But I was not willing to die and be born again."[94] Whenever deeply moved, Scott expressed himself through religious metaphors: unwilling to give everything up for Pat, he could not be redeemed.

Two weeks later he continued to worry the question, recognizing that the past year had been the most troubled of his life. A man who governed his life by reason, he had been unable to resolve this pressing crisis. "I said no, not because I believed in no, but because I could not make up my mind to say yes."[95] This was largely because he loved Marian and accepted responsibility for their problems: "Was it her fault that for the past 18 years I had not been intimate with her? Must she start living in some cramped apartment, with no one to look after her in order that my special problem should be solved? She was willing to do this; I knew that. How could I ask it of her?"[96] But there were other practical problems: the effect on his work at McGill, inadequacy of income, and the fact that a divorce would involve a break with many friends. It was not, he thought, a matter of courage but a lack of conviction. Whatever it was, by November 1950 he felt himself "absolutely zero, a nothing. I crave so much that inner peace and quiet that only a very dear and intimate relationship with a woman can give me. It is really such a small and simple thing. Perhaps it should not make so much difference, especially at my age [51], but it does. No mere casual connections can supply it."[97]

Yet to some degree both were still hesitant. A few weeks later, Pat telephoned Frank to see if he was free for lunch, and they met at the Windsor Hotel on 20 November. There the reason for the meeting came out: Pat had heard that Frank and Marian had separated. Was it true? He told her that they had been separated but were now together again. And Pat? Her feelings for Arthur Irwin were different from her feelings for Frank, but she had now made a commitment. And Frank? As he recognized, "I grew alive with the talk, I felt at ease inside, the naturalness of our understanding was sunshine that melted the thickened fibers of my sensibility, yet I went along with the assumption that the course was settled." As they prepared to leave, he put on his overshoes to go out into the snow and looked up: "I could see that in her eyes which she had to give in such abundance."[98] The awkwardness of Scott's syntax (and the avoidance of the real subject – the love he saw in her eyes) reveals the depth and complexity of unexpressed emotion.

All of their lives were to be changed by this decision. Frank and Marian separated for a time, and he then took a position as a United Nations representative to Burma, leaving Canada in 1951 but returning a few months later, desperately ill with an amoeba that was to plague him for the rest of his life. Several years later, in 1954, he published a collection of poems, *Events and Signals*, which contained "Departure" and "Message." The events in the first poem refer both to Pat at the Windsor Station in Montreal, as she was about to leave for Halifax in 1944, and a few lines from a letter she wrote Frank shortly after her arrival in Halifax: "I remember only a strong light and heat ... and the sensation of some great tidal wave rising in one which broke when I said goodbye."[99] Scott

transferred many of his religious beliefs to socialism, but in the concluding verse of "Departure" – a poem that was greatly to influence Pat's
last poems – he recognized a spiritual dimension to their parting: "We
shall find, each, the deep sea in the end ..."

> And we shall know, after the flow and ebb,
> Things central, absolute and whole.
> Brought clear of silt, into the open roads,
> Events shall pass like waves, and we shall stay.[100]

Pat's mother and aunt, who had felt extremely uncomfortable about her
relationship with Frank Scott, were delighted to announce her engagement to Arthur Irwin. Photographs of Pat and Arthur appeared prominently in most of the larger Canadian newspapers, for Arthur was a
distinguished editor, known across the country, and Pat was by now
known nationally for her poetry. Rose Page wanted Pat to have a proper
trousseau, with a wardrobe appropriate for Arthur's circle. Lillian Farrar
of Montreal, known for her classic elegance, was the designer the family
favoured. Pat had a photograph taken by a Montreal photographer in a
gauzy grey strapless gown – a photograph that thereafter stood on Arthur's
desk at home.

Their wedding on 16 December 1950 was very simple. Pat was willing to be married by a justice of the peace, but Arthur insisted on a proper
wedding in an Ottawa Anglican church – and he cut "obey" out of the
marriage vows. It was a small family wedding, and Pat wore a powder-
blue wool crepe dress and matching hat. The guests were her mother
and Aunt Bibbi and Arthur's children, Neal, Sheila, and Patricia and her
husband. Maudie Ferguson and Bob Farquarson also attended. Rose had
arranged for a reception at the Empress Hotel, and Pat and Arthur then
took the train to Montreal, where they planned to fly to New York.

However, the plane had engine trouble and turned back to Montreal
where all the passengers were put in a hangar and had to wait for hours
until the next flight. The plane was full of newlyweds – most of the brides
were dressed in frilly clothing and covered in confetti – whereas Pat and
Arthur were older and she wore black. Arthur talked only when he felt
like talking, and this was not a moment when he felt like it. Determined
not to start their marriage on this note, Pat persuaded him to play a game
in which he had to mentally change, one by one, all the men into women
and vice versa: "That man over there, what would he look like if he were
a woman? What clothes? What earrings?" They had a great many laughs

over the whole situation.[101] In New York, they stayed at the St Moritz Hotel. Arthur, who had the room filled with yellow roses, had arranged a big city honeymoon with visits to restaurants, shopping, and light theatre (including *Gentlemen Prefer Blondes* starring Carol Channing). It was a honeymoon arranged for Pat's pleasure; Arthur would probably have preferred being in the country.

Later they moved into a house just outside Gatineau Park, Quebec, near Mackenzie King's farmhouse. P.K. had left the Film Board. Arthur was opposed to nepotism and Pat was not unhappy to go ahead with her resignation because some of her friends at the Film Board were anti-Arthur and she felt caught in the middle. The couple's friends in Ottawa included some of her old ones (she and Arthur travelled in similar circles). They socialized with John and Florence Bird, Davidson and Kathleen Dunton, Blair and Jean Fraser, Gordon and Beatrice Robertson, Maudie Ferguson, who had married Bob Farquarson, managing editor of the Toronto *Globe and Mail*; also Nick Cavell, an Englishman who became head of Canadian Economic Development Abroad; Louis Rasminsky, later the third governor of the Bank of Canada, and his wife Lila; and Wynne and Beryl Plumptre, both economists, he with External Affairs.[102]

Arthur Irwin redeemed himself at the Film Board when he advocated the use of a new photographic stock for the state visit in 1951 of Princess Elizabeth and Prince Philip, Duke of Edinburgh. The weather was poor for conventional photographs, but fortunately Eastman colourstock produced fine photography of the tour. Before the end of its run in Canada, the completed film, *The Royal Journey*, had played in more than 1,200 theatres. As Irwin boasted, it "broke all records for attendance of any film produced in Canada up to that time. United Artists took it for the United States, General Films took it for the rest of the world ... I personally believe that in terms of the original job of restoring public confidence in the Film Board, that *Royal Journey* possibly contributed more than any other single factor."[103]

Irwin was also responsible for commissioning one of the most celebrated Film Board shorts, a film called *Neighbours*. The federal government had given him a large sum of money by for a film on an international theme. He consulted Norman McLaren, who was developing a new technique – which he called "fixalation," in which the filmmaker takes one picture after another in single-frame technique. McLaren had always wanted to do an anti-violence film strip because he had spent a year in China when the Communists took over: he had seen the full horror of executions and bodies floating in the streams. *Neighbours*, the new film strip that he created, has since become internationally recognized as a classic. It shows, frame by frame, how a disagreement between two neighbours – over a flower – could escalate into a full-fledged war.[104]

Irwin also gave a great boost to the film industry in Quebec. He was convinced that the Film Board would be better situated if it were not in Ottawa, underneath the nose of what he considered to be interfering bureaucrats.[105] He proposed that it be moved to Montreal, and it was in 1956. This event marked the beginning of the film industry in Quebec because outstanding filmmakers such as René Jodoin and Claude Jutra, who trained at the Film Board, began to make independent films.

Pat's new life as Arthur's wife meant that she had more time for herself, hours in which her whole being was given over to poetry. After the break with Frank, she had steeled herself to a new discipline, recognizing that her poetry must now be primary. She worked on her poems every day, kept house with the aid of a somewhat unreliable housekeeper, and began to bird-watch. And for the first time in many years, she had time to read and talk with friends. In early January 1952 she wrote to Jori Smith, saying that after reading the French writer Pierre Emmanuel she concluded that Jori was a "Tragic optimist ... The person who is so intensely aware of the tragedy of life that in a kind of self-defence he is gayer than most people" – though it was not just self-defence but "an intuitive balancing of the scales." She told Jori that she felt close to her because "I feel the same kind of blood flows in our veins ... I feel a kind of bond which owes more of its strength perhaps to the fact that we have not slogged about in each other's private wastelands too much. It is very debilitating to friendship I think. A time comes when only the wasteland exists."[106]

Pat and Arthur settled down to domestic life until one day, in the late fall of 1952, Arthur told Pat that he had been invited to join Canada's Diplomatic Service as high commissioner to Australia. If he accepted, this would mean a complete change in their lives. Relations between Canada and Australia were not close, and the Australian election in 1949 of Robert Menzies's Conservative anti-Communist coalition government threatened to make matters worse. The outbreak of the Korean War in 1951 accentuated differences, but it seems that Richard G. Casey, the new Australian minister of external affairs, had convinced Canada's secretary of state for external affairs, Lester Pearson, that there was a wide field for closer cooperation between Canada and Australia.[107]

Pearson had suggested Arthur Irwin as the high commissioner to help maintain harmony between the two countries. Pearson and Irwin shared a similar Methodist background, and both were members of the Canadian Institute for International Affairs. Irwin was a passionate Canadian, but he was also a staunch supporter of the Commonwealth; indeed, he felt that Canada had, to some degree, invented the Commonwealth. Nonetheless, he had reservations when first approached by Pearson. He had become progressively more interested in the National Film Board, and now that his really tough job was out of the way, he was looking forward to a more comfortable life. Furthermore, he and Pat were beginning to feel at home in Ottawa as a couple. But while Arthur hesitated, Prime Minister Louis St Laurent called him into his office and pointed out that Canada needed him.[108]

This was very flattering indeed. Arthur consulted with Pat at length. Both recognized that the post of high commissioner would entail far more social life than either of them enjoyed, but at the same time "it was a completely new experience and to say no would be a kind of denial."[109] Pat put her thoughts on paper in late November 1952: "The more I think about it the more I think that if Arthur wants to go – we should go. I feel perhaps this is what I need. I have gathered ghosts in Canada. They can perhaps be laid by going to a different country."[110] And so the couple agreed to go to Australia, where for the next decade their public lives were to be orchestrated by Canada's Department of External Affairs.

CHAPTER 8

Australia
The Journey Out, 1953–1956

On 18 June the Irwins left Canada for Arthur's posting as high commissioner to Australia, sailing on the *Empress of Amsterdam* bound for Liverpool. They passed Quebec City in the "early evening, lights on, the last of the sun making the water violet, from the Bridge. It looked beautiful & strange. The foam from Montmorency Falls picked out of the darkness by the Dom[inion] Textiles neon sign. As A.[rthur] said, looking like … spiral nebulae."[1] At first they were so exhausted from getting ready to go that they slept most of the time, but after several days Pat began to feel the excitement of being outward bound.

There had been a great deal of advance preparation. Pat had begun to read about Australia and also plowed her way through the Post Reports, thick documents prepared by External Affairs informing diplomats of conditions at their assigned posts. The couple stocked up on warm clothing – they would arrive in June, the middle of the Australian winter, and the houses had no central heating. There were goodbyes to be said and arrangements to be made for her mother and Aunt Bibbi, who had now moved to Ottawa. Pat was relieved when Jean Fraser, wife of Arthur's newspaperman friend Blair Fraser, said she would keep a friendly eye on Rose and Bibbi. Jean became surrogate daughter to both sisters, and it is largely through her correspondence with Pat that we learn about the couple's day-to-day life in Australia.

When the Irwins reached London, they stayed at the Dorchester Hotel, saw Noël Coward in Shaw's play *The Apple Cart*, and visited Pat's good friend Maggie Davies. On 2 July they left London on the ss *Strathnaver* of the P&O lines – which Arthur promptly dubbed "Perverse & Obnoxious." It was a rusty old ship that became a torture chamber as they passed through the Red Sea, where it heated up to over 90° F. There was no respite, because the temperature of the hot and cold water in the pipes was exactly the same. And there was little relief on shore: the captain was in a hurry to get to Australia, and he tried to dock only at night, which discouraged sightseeing – three hours was the usual stopover time.

The Irwins loved the exotic ports of Colombo and Bombay, but nothing had prepared Pat for Australia and its violent contrasts. When the ship stopped at Perth, she found the city "full of palm trees, bougainvillea, poinsettia trees, flame trees and great tree cacti." Adelaide and Melbourne had flowering almonds and great wattle trees, and Melbourne was beautifully laid out with broad streets. But the surrounding countryside provided a shock – "nature had no sense of form any longer. The ground looked as if it might grow barbed wire."[2] They saw very little of Sydney, where they disembarked, because an hour after their ship landed Arthur was due to speak at a noon lunch. The same afternoon, they boarded a plane to Canberra, the capital city. In arriving early, before the American ambassador Amos J. Peaslee and the Indian high commissioner General Kodandera Madappa Cariappa (who had set foot on Australian soil the same day as Arthur), the Irwins scored a diplomatic coup, because the first diplomat to present his credentials in Canberra achieved seniority.

Arthur's role was both political and commercial. He was expected to stay close to Prime Minister Menzies and External Affairs Minister Casey and make their views known to Canada's External Affairs – a task that was to become somewhat complicated at the time of the Suez Crisis in 1956. In addition, he was expected to facilitate commercial relations between Canada and Australia. He was successful in both tasks. After the visit of Canada's deputy prime minister C.D. Howe – whom Pat considered "a darling" – to the Snowy River in April 1955, a number of joint agricultural projects were initiated, including a large Massey-Harris-Ferguson enterprise. By the end of the decade, both countries had signed an agreement on nuclear cooperation, and Canadian trade with Australia had doubled.

Canberra was an artificially constructed city with Capital Hill as its centre. Parliament House and the other official buildings stood out on the hill, softened somewhat by parks and fast-growing suburbs connected by broad avenues. Because it was a very new and small city – with only eighteen thousand inhabitants in 1951 – there were few shops or amenities and only one hotel, where most members of Parliament stayed, having left their families at home. Pat's first sense of the city was that many houses were small and square "with so much gingerbread painted such odd colours that they looked for all the world like ornamented biscuit boxes."[3]

The Canadian Embassy was located at 32 Mugga Way, next to the Indian Embassy. It was a 1½-storey white bungalow. There was a small dining room, three bedrooms, and two servants' rooms – a chauffeur, gardener, housemaid, and cook were all provided – and a little study near the front door. Everything in the embassy seemed to be in a state of neglect and disrepair. The stove was almost useless, there were no curtain rods for the windows, and the kitchen looked rather dirty.[4] Diplomatic life required a great deal of entertaining, but this was difficult because parties were not easy to arrange. Fish could be bought only one day a week, and a roast had to be ordered a week ahead. The living room seated only ten, which limited the size of groups they could entertain. Worse, the electricity tended to shut off just before a dinner was cooked. Nonetheless, the house had a certain charm. Although the garden was rather bleak, they eventually found a younger gardener who transformed it.

Arthur's day was filled with commercial transactions and problems relating to Canadians abroad, but Pat's day was filled with the protocols of domestic life. She had been in Australia for only two weeks when she realized that she had never been so pressed for time and energy in all her life. She wrote home: "Certain things have to be done whether there's time for them or not – eg invitations, correspondence etc. I deliberately make time for some reading but mostly it's reading about Australia and I make time also for some kind of record but apart from that my time is anyone's but mine. Attractive but not highly efficient staff take a fair amount of attention. Just when you think things are fairly smooth, one of them comes in drunk and disorderly."[5]

The Irwins' days began with breakfast in bed, the newspapers, and the mail. Pat would then go downstairs to the kitchen to organize the day's menu. When she discovered that their cook, Mrs Clark, knew only basic outback cooking, she consulted cookbooks and began to teach her how to make a broader range of dishes. After consulting about the day's menu, Pat had some time in the garden, where she played with their newly acquired dog, watched the colourful flocks of Australian birds, and talked with the gardener – a brief interlude of free time.

Every day brought calls to be paid or received. Each new diplomat had to present his credentials to the head of state. Then his wife was expected to "sign the book" at Government House that registered arrivals; until it was signed, they had not formally arrived. Within a set time, the new diplomat's wife was expected to call on each of the resident diplomats' wives, presenting her card. Only then would they call on her or invite the couple to social functions. These initial calls had a set procedure and were usually very stiff, requiring formal attire.

There was a great deal of protocol to absorb. In September 1953 the Irwins attended a ball hosted by the governor general of Australia, Lord Slim. Dinner at Government House was formal, with tails for the men, long dresses and elbow-length gloves for the ladies. Pat wore her favourite long dress, a billowing dark green taffeta shot with copper that required a crinoline. On arrival, the guests assembled in the drawing-room, attended by aides. When the governor general and his wife arrived, the men bowed and their wives curtseyed. Drinks were served. "Then the G-G, His Excellency Field Marshall Sir William Slim of Burma fame, led the way into the dining-room … Five courses." When dinner ended Lady Slim, on a signal from her husband, rose. "Everyone rose with her but only the ladies left the room, curtseying once again to the G-G as we did so, leaving the men to their port and cigars."[6]

This was an opportunity for the ladies to visit the "loo" and powder their noses. As they were escorted back to the drawing room, Pat realized with horror that she was losing her crinoline; she held up the back of her skirt until an aide de camp found a safety pin. The story must have passed from embassy to embassy because before one of Lady Slim's new ladies-in-waiting called on the Irwins, she was told: "Oh you don't have to be nervous about her, she's the one who lost her petticoat."[7]

Later, near the end of their time in Australia, Pat wrote frankly to Jean Fraser: "I feel rather strange being the oldest in time and age of the Canadian wives [on the embassy staff]. And as for calling – I shall never feel it's anything but a kind of Let's-pretend and make-believe game." Pat found much of the protocol of embassy life "utterly absurd … I don't think I was ever meant to be a *lady*."[8] But however she thought of herself at the time, Pat, with her military background, was instinctively a lady, and with age her public persona acquired further distinction.

The official visits with Arthur were much more fun. In August they went to Yass, a small town about forty-five miles from Canberra, to open a lawn-bowling green. The greens were like velvet, and men in white, with navy-blue bands on their Panama hats, were already playing. On arrival, they were greeted by the mayor and lady mayoress and became part of an official party. Arthur and Pat were addressed by the presidents of the club as "Your Excellencies," and Arthur replied appropriately. The audience was friendly, laughed, and cried "'ere! 'ere!" at various parts in the speech. Pat was handed the "kitty" bowl to throw and she threw it off-limits. Arthur then threw a bowl that went "wobble-wobble" down the green. She later ruefully concluded, "What idiots we made of ourselves!"[9]

It was a friendly afternoon, but she found some of the Australian women disconcerting. This had to do "with their place on some ladder – the gender ladder, perhaps. They are not really included in social events – they go to the party, but just for the ride. They rarely speak within earshot of the men." Yet she recognized that this was not entirely true. "The wives of professional men whom I have met in Canberra appear to be strong – maybe quite strong."[10]

Early in their stay they began a series of official tours – to Sydney, Melbourne, and Adelaide – where receptions were held, officials greeted, and announcements of their visits reported in the newspaper. "Fantastic safaris these – busy from 9–midnight, going round factories, being entertained, seeing sights etc. Very Exhausting."[11] Their long trip to the Nullarbor Plain in December 1953 was their first real taste of the country at large. They went by train: "Quite an experience – 1000 miles and not one sign of water, only its ghastly mockery: the dry salt lakes and rivers that traced the lovely shapes and movements of water."[12]

The rush of diplomatic life, keeping a home for Arthur, and adjusting to life in the Antipodes – where everything was upside-down and winter came in the summer – took much of Pat's energy. Although they gradually began to make friends, she felt rather alone during the first few months in Australia. She no longer had the impetus of a close literary community, although she kept in close touch with her family and with Jean Fraser, writing frequently. Later, she began a correspondence with Floris McLaren. She told both Floris and Florence Bird that she had been reading a number of the nineteenth-century Australian novelists, especially Henry Handel Richardson (a pseudonym for Ethel Florence Lindesay Richardson). She already knew a little about Australian art. (While Pat was still at the Film Board she had met one of the officers at the Australian High Commission, who had a wonderful collection.) She liked the artists Donald Friend, William Dobell, Sidney Nolan, and Russell Drysdale. What she found most interesting about the early painters in Australia was that they, like the early painters in Canada, saw the landscape through European eyes.[13]

Pat became fascinated by Australia, by the extraordinary colours of the land – so often brown and sere but then suddenly green and flowering after "the wet" – and by the different light that filtered through the gum trees that held their leaves down, vertically rather than horizontally. And the endless sheep and the flies! (If she and Arthur ventured

out, they were instantly covered with small black flies.) She was astonished and delighted by the birds – the cockatoos, the rosellas and mag-
pies – and by their brilliant colours and raucous cries. They were so
tame, she felt like St Francis. "The laughing jackasses [kookaburras]
laugh like maniacs in the trees & the parrots screech."[14] Australia had a
flavour all it's own: "a combination of light and the smells and the
colours and the temperature which give it all a certain, very distinct taste
that couldn't be anywhere else."[15]

The Irwins met many people in Australia, largely through diplomatic
circles: the American ambassador Amos J. Peaslee, a Quaker and Republi-
can, and his wife Dorothy; the British high commissioner Sir Geoffrey
Holmes and his wife Lady Noreen Holmes; the French ambassador Louis
Roché, who had a sophisticated palate and a taste for opera (his wife
stayed mainly in Paris). The Indian high commissioner General Cariappa,
a widower, charged around Australia washing war memorials. Page later
wrote a poem, "Warlord in the Early Evening," about an aging military
man with a hose. Critics have identified him as her father, but the poem
was modelled on Cariappa. He lived next door to the Irwins with his
niece and daughter. Across the street lived the Wunderleys. He was a
medical doctor, knighted in 1954 for his service to the Anti-Tuberculosis
Association of New South Wales. Pat liked Alice Wunderley very much;
they seemed to talk the same language. Because Alice suffered from a bad
hip, Pat helped her hang out her washing. The Irwins also made friends
with two ministers in the Australian cabinet: a Greek, Dmitri Lambros –
Pat found him intelligent and amusing – and Richard Casey.

"Dick" and Maie Casey were one of the first couples the Irwins came
to know fairly well. As Australia's minister of external affairs, Casey was
the most important contact Arthur could make. He was also an amusing
and attractive man, with an aristocratic Irish face.[16] He had travelled in
distinguished circles, had been a member of Churchill's Cabinet during
the Second World War, and was later governor of Bengal. His wife Maie
– who was interested in art and architecture and poetry – later wrote
several books.

Pat's introduction to the Caseys had been a literary one. A week or
two after their arrival in Australia, Prime Minister Menzies called a
meeting in Canberra with the premiers from all the states. The chargé
d'affaires at the Canadian High Commission, Georges Charpentier, told
Arthur he should give a dinner, since this would be a fine opportunity to
meet all the premiers at once. Arthur asked Pat if she'd manage a dinner,
and she said she could.[17] The night of the dinner, she had hers on a tray
upstairs in the bedroom, just above the dining room where Arthur was

entertaining – among others – Prime Minister Menzies (and possibly Casey) at a stag dinner. It must have been her first experience of the Australian proclivity for separating the sexes at political and social gatherings. Coincidentally, she was reading a novel by Nevil Shute, *In the Wet*, set in Australia in the future, in which Menzies and Casey are mentioned as characters.[18]

When Pat telephoned to make her duty call on Maie Casey, who lived in Melbourne, Maie responded warmly on a first name basis and broke protocol by inviting both Pat and Arthur for tea. When they arrived, Maie told them about her enthusiasm for protecting the old houses in Melbourne that were then being torn down by builders. The two couples all piled into a car and went to look at some of them. Maie seems to have become quite fond of Pat because of her interest in art and poetry. She soon arranged for Pat to give a talk on Canada in Melbourne; and Dick Casey, when he "batched" in Canberra, liked to come to dinner with the Irwins.

By the New Year the diplomatic community was gearing up for a royal visit. Queen Elizabeth and Prince Philip arrived in Australia on 3 February 1954, and this time (unlike her early years in Halifax) Pat was obliged to attend a whirlwind of receptions, lunches, dinners, and other events – a hectic time, memorable only for the number of times a day she changed clothes and for the length of time she and Arthur spent waiting for a royal appearance, wedged between the high commissioner from India and the high commissioner from Pakistan. "What were memorable moments to most people were not for me. Not even the opening of Parliament when [the Queen] wore her coronation robe, a dress which was to most dresses as St Peter's is to the Unitarian Church in Ottawa."[19] Pat's strongest memory of the royal visit was an interlude between official activities when she and Maie Casey, dressed in their formal clothes, ran across the tarmac at the airfield to see Maie's new airplane – a present from Dick.

Before Pat had a chance to write her impressions of the royal visit, her mother and Aunt Bibbi came to Australia to stay at the embassy for several weeks. At a tea in the garden with Lady Slim, when someone pointed out a beautiful deodar tree, Rose burst into song: "Under the deodar, lit by the stars ..." and seems to have charmed her hostess.[20] When reporting to Jean Fraser on their Australian progress, Pat told her that she and Arthur, who was a talented amateur painter, had gone sketching with her mother and Aunt Bibbi. Pat had painted as a child, but this is the first time that we hear of her painting in the open air – an isolated tree, probably gum, in a pale wash of green. The sketch was never titled. "What

impossibly ghastly preconceived ideas one carries in one's paintbox,"
she commented. "How can one ever be newborn enough to paint?"[21]

Possibly, Pat took up painting and accompanied Arthur to his painting lessons because she was not writing poetry. But in fact she had little
uninterrupted time even for letter writing. "This life doesn't lend itself to
letter writing – I practically need a private secretary to keep up with all
the invitations & thank you notes etc. Dozens of letters from shut-ins requesting stamps, books of bad verse from poets, requests to speak."[22]
The Irwins were frequently missing a servant and Pat was obliged to do
the housework. She was still learning the ropes of diplomatic life, and the
official tours demanded all her attention. Furthermore, as she lamented to
Jean Fraser: "I seem to have mislaid whatever small talent I had. I really
need some dynamite to blast down the brick wall that seems to have
arisen between me and what I want to write." But the embassy garden
was now a joy: "Two trees heavily laden with apricots, one with peaches
the size of grapefruits."[23]

Despite the distractions of diplomatic life, in April 1954 Pat wrote the
poem "Arras." Northrop Frye, like many subsequent critics, singled out
"Arras," often considered P.K. Page's best (and most difficult) poem. He
described it as "a somewhat elliptical treatment of the Alice-through-
the-mirror theme"[24] and characterized it as a "fantasy," perhaps because
the abrupt juxtaposition of thought and image engender a surrealist
quality that requires the reader to work carefully from one image to the
next. A succession of surprising, beautiful (and sometimes private) images,
"Arras" is the work of a highly visual poet.

When in later life Page was asked what the poem meant, she replied,
perhaps too easily, that "a poem should not mean but be ... The poem
is a labyrinth of the self."[25] The first half of this statement (echoing
Archibald MacLeish's "Ars Poetica") implies that the meaning of the
poem is the artifact itself; the second implies that the poem reflects the
hidden depths of the creating self. I incline to the second interpretation
and would argue that "Arras" is a poem about Page's aesthetic, that it
describes her sense of the poetry-making process, and that it contains
submerged traces of her own poetic and emotional situation.

In the arresting first line of the poem, "Consider a new habit / classical," we are confronted with the arras – a tapestry – that evokes the art
of the classical tapestry for which the ancient French city of Arras was
known.[26] "Habit," also suggesting a monk's habit, reminds us that much
early art, especially image-making, was associated with religious orders

– tapestries often being associated with nunneries. In this stanza, the female narrator passes from what we consider "reality" to enter the arras – like Alice walking through the looking glass. There she takes her place on a green lawn, where "peaches hang" and trees are "espaliered on the wall like candelabra. / How still upon that lawn our sandaled feet."

> But a peacock rattling its rattan tail and screaming
> has found a point of entry. Through whose eye
> did it insinuate in furled disguise
> to shake its jewels and silk upon that grass?
>
> The peaches hang like lanterns. No one joins
> those figures on the arras.

In this poem P.K. Page describes both the creative process and her actual situation: "Who am I," she asks, "or, who am I become that walking here / I am observer, other, Gemini, / starred for a green garden of cinema?" This question (reflecting her early concerns with identity and her attempts to project herself into the landscape, reinforced by several years developing visuals for the Film Board) develops a series of metaphorical equations in which the tapestry becomes an introductory metaphor for both cinema and poem. The other part of this equation is the artist, or "I," who projects these images for the unworked fabric of the tapestry ("arras" in medieval use meant simply the fabric itself on which the scene was embroidered), the screen of the cinema, or the blank page of the poem.

In Page's aesthetic, the peacock is projected from the eye of the artist – "Voluptuous it came … strangely slim / to fit the retina" – in the same way that a film projector projects images.[27] But this action separates the observing artist from her projections – the screen now includes peacock and figured self. For any artist, but especially for Page as a woman artist, the creative process is fraught with anguish and self-doubt. The process of creating a work of art is done in isolation, part of the self is split off and projected outwards, and success is not guaranteed. "I ask, what did they deal me in this pack?" This allusion to playing cards and a royal suit suggests F.R. Scott, who Page associates elsewhere with the king of diamonds, but that card is no longer part of her "pack."[28] Although the narrator's plaint is personal, it is also generic in that it refers both to herself and to her art: "I want a hand to clutch, a heart to break."

The poem here reaches a climax as the narrator tries to bolt – "take to my springy heels" – but nothing moves, the world is stuck on its poles, and death threatens: "the stillness points a bone at me. I fear / the future on this arras."[29] The paradox is that the artist as narrator has made this tapestry, projected these images, and imagined this future. It is this acknowledgement that Page now makes: "I confess: / It was my eye" – through which the peacock emerged and, by inference, the tapestry of the poem.

The process of creating images is an enormous joy, sexual perhaps: "Voluptuous it came. / Its head the ferrule and its lovely tail / folded so sweetly …" (A.J.M. Smith, no mean poet himself, wrote to her in admiration and envy saying that this line "really lifted the hair on my head … Damn you, Pat.")[30] But although the genesis of art is sometimes spotted, "a peacock – living patina, / eye-bright – maculate!" (as opposed to "immaculate"), the joy of creating and producing the artifact might be considered ample reward. Not so. The poet still longs for human and loving acknowledgment: "Does no one care?" A hand from one of the figures on the arras, or even a bite from the peacock, would be better than nothing. But nothing happens, and despite her fears – or perhaps because of them – the obsessive creative process (or "habit") of making images continues as she brings yet another peacock into being: "another line has trolled the encircling air, / another bird assumes its furled disguise."[31]

Pat began the poem in the embassy garden. She later recalled writing it in one fell swoop, rushing indoors only to look up a word, "maculate." It is a signature poem, containing echoes in structure of her childhood love of *Alice in Wonderland*,[32] her discovery of Dom Roberts's jewel-like designs for Aubusson tapestries (often gardens adorned with peacocks, drawn from Persian Sufi manuscripts or medieval illuminations), and perhaps recollections of the Héloïse and Abelard story (Héloïse became a nun and Abelard was a monk), which she had read at the same time. The poem also reflects aspects of her present life – where large golden peaches (like grapefruit) "hang like lanterns" in their Australian garden.

Among many other things, "Arras" evokes the beauty, fascination, hypnotic quality, and sometimes overwhelmingly lonely task of creation. Shortly after the publication of the poem, Pat wrote to Jori Smith saying, "I don't think there is any satisfaction in being an artist except at the moment when one is working, when one is suffering the doing of it. Are all artists masochistic? Because it is a painful pleasure, isn't it." She goes on to say that she doesn't believe that the critical reception of a work, whether positive or negative, can ever please the artist, and concludes that "being a painter *is* a damn lonely life, so is being a writer."[33]

She felt that the artist was often an outsider. In October 1954 she had written to Jean Fraser about her sense of not quite belonging. Having spent periods of her youth thinking that she was adopted, she mused, "I wonder if any of us *ever* feel we really belong. I've almost always felt either a borrower or a borrowee – except for a few periods when I was lost ... And I can't see how my family can be blamed. We were a close family unit. I must wonder if all of us haven't, to some extent, flashes of almighty singleness."[34]

⚏

Some years earlier, in 1948, Pat had started to put together a manuscript for the Ryerson Press, which had accepted the book but wanted to postpone publication. She then submitted the manuscript to McClelland and Stewart. The publisher, Jack McClelland, and his readers were happy with it and ready to publish, but by then Page had developed cold feet. She refused publication three years in a row because she thought she had not been writing up to her usual level. But in 1952 she had received a request for poems from the respected American poet and critic Cid Corman, who wanted to feature her work in his avant-garde little magazine *Origin*. He told her that he greatly admired her work and wanted to publish her poems, "10 pages, 20 pages, 40 pages," however many she could give him.[35] Page told him that she had written nothing new and felt uneasy with the poems she had at hand. Corman responded bluntly: "Why are you writing so little?" For him, the best of Page's poems were those that were preoccupied with self-impelled "problems," that is, psychological poetry.[36] Corman's letters were helpful because they made Page look again at her poems, and she realized that they weren't as bad as she thought. In Australia, Arthur was eager (as she was) for her to get a new book of poetry underway.[37] She asked Corman what he knew of Australian writing. He replied that he found it less exciting than Canadian writing and predicted that hers would be "rather extraordinary avant-garde for them, apart from any intention on your part."[38]

This proved to be the case. She had read a number of modern anthologies and journals – including *The Anthology of Australian Verse* (1952), *A Book of Australian-New Zealand Verse* (1950), and issues of the journal *Australian Poetry* for 1951 and 1952 – but she found the work depressing. There was a great concern with the land, democracy, and mateship, but the language was frequently dated and prosaic. As A.D. Hope, one of the most articulate Australian moderns, once remarked, the long shadow of Wordsworth fell over the poetry. Pat read Hope's poems and those of David Campbell, but even Hope's witty classical allusions must have seemed very different from *Preview* and the Canadian poetry of the forties. She liked Campbell better and thought his poetry "full of a strange romantic concept about Australia and the beauty of the inarticulateness of the real Australian."[39] Even so, she sent one of Hope's books, *Wandering Islands*, to Floris McLaren.

Page was now corresponding again with Jack McClelland about the possible publication of her drafted manuscript. By September 1953 both had agreed on a title for the new book, the poems to be included, and their order. However, she was still unsure about her own work. No one but the readers at McClelland and Stewart had seen the manuscript, and as she later wrote to Anne Wilkinson, "From first to last the book has scared me stiff."[40] But by the following summer, 7 July 1954, Page felt assured enough to write to Jack McClelland with some real changes: "To start with the title. 'Images of Angels' is too soft and smudgy for a title and I am now of the opinion that THE METAL AND THE FLOWER is O.K. It is a phrase from a poem and seems to me to have some sympathy with the contents generally ... also I have three new poems I would like to include: "Intractable Between them Grows ..."; "Bright Fish Once Swimming Where We Lie ..."; "Arras." I like them and I hope you will."[41]

The title, she suggests, came from one of her recent poems, "Intractable Between Them Grows," which was duly retitled "The Metal and the Flower." It is a riveting depiction of a profound division between two lovers and refers to her relationship with F.R. Scott. In tone, it is darker than much of her early work and reflects her growing assimilation of Freud and Jung:

> Intractable between them grows
> a garden of barbed wire and roses.
> Burning briars like flames devour
> their too innocent attire.
> Dare they meet, the blackened wire
> tears the intervening air.

The lovers, who have laid out this garden, find "the metal and the flower / fatal underfoot," and even if they were to try to change the garden in daylight hours, there are within them Freudian subversive forces that grow powerful as they sleep, destroying rational intent:

> While they sleep the garden grows,
> deepest wish annuls the will:
> perfect still the wire and rose.[42]

As Pat had noted when she and Arthur drove up the coast from Melbourne on their arrival to Australia, the landscape was as metallic as barbed wire: "One minute impeccable Melbourne. The next drab spikey hostile country feeling for all the world like a barbed-wire entanglement."[43] The title poem of *The Metal and the Flower* filters Page's reflections on her past emotional experience through the hard and arid Australian landscape.

Another of Page's memorable poems, here reflecting her sense of social injustice, is "Photos of a Salt Mine." The first photos look like "a child's / dream of caves and winter" and "underfoot the snow of salt," in which angels could be made "in its drifts, / as children do in snow." Miners light up an "Aladdin's cave: / rubies and opals glitter from its walls ... / Except in the last picture," where "Like Dante's vision of the nether hell / men struggle with the bright cold fires of salt / locked in the black inferno of the rock: / the filter here, not innocence but guilt."[44]

Page had been very nervous when she returned the proofs of *The Metal and the Flower* to McClelland and Stewart in the summer of 1954. As she was far from Canada when the book came out in the fall, she had no idea of its reception, though she was greatly reassured by a brief note from Anne Wilkinson that said, "*The Metal and the Flower* is in my opinion the best book of poetry so far produced by a Canadian."[45] Page told Wilkinson how little reaction there had been in Australia – only one review in a newspaper, the *Telegraph,* by someone she had never heard of. "The antipodean days drag by; Orion stands on his head. I am engulfed by silence."[46]

Wilkinson's letter was the first of a series of congratulatory letters that arrived in spring 1955 – from Alan Crawley, Floris McLaren, A.J.M Smith, and David Thomson; there were also highly appreciative critiques from literary arbiters such as Northrop Frye and Ira Dilworth. In March 1955 Floris wrote to tell Pat about plans for a new literary magazine called *The Tamarack Review.* Floris also singled out a quality of Page's work that she found remarkable: "It seems to me it is more difficult for a woman than a man to make that communication of emotion successfully. Art Smith can do it; so can Scott ... [Alfred G.] Bailey; Klein (in a less personal field) ... [but] most of the women are either too tight and restrained (Anne W[ilkinson] and Jay [Macpherson]) or else too uncomfortably explicit ... Anne M[arriott], Miriam [Waddington], Dorothy [Livesay] sometimes (sometimes she pulls it off). You can do it. Your virtue is that you avoid always the deadly feminine approach."[47]

Frye's review of *The Metal and the Flower* in the *University of Toronto Quarterly* consolidated positive critical opinion about Page's poetry. He remarked, "If there is any such thing as 'pure poetry,' this must be it: a lively mind seizing on almost any experience and turning it into witty verse." He recognized that Page had a very broad sensibility but that she "looks for the human situations involved in what she sees ... She is also admirable in seeing a story within a scene, [as in] 'Man with One Small Hand,' 'Portrait of Marina' ... and 'Paranoid' ... More elaborate are the longer fantasies, 'Images of Angels' and 'Arras,' both very beautiful." Frye concluded with high praise, saying Page's book was as consistently successful in reaching its objectives as any book he had read since beginning to write his "Poetry" survey in *Letters in Canada*.[48]

Page later remarked that "Arras" was one of her first paintings.[49] By this she may have meant that she had begun to write poetry and prose rich in verbal description at a time when she had just begun to paint. She was certainly aware that her writing style was changing. A few months later, in September 1955, she wrote to a friend: "I become more and more hypnotized by the sounds of words. I remember reacting with amazement to the gall of Dylan Thomas when I first read his lines "until the one loved least / looms the last Samson of his Zodiac." She concluded the letter with the painterly observation that everything is blossoming now. "The trees are all like pink spun sugar – great torches of it lining the streets. The mountains in the background are very blue. It has the strange innocence that Van Gogh captured in his very early paintings."[50]

Page's *The Metal and the Flower*, Scott's *Events and Signals*, and A.J.M. Smith's *A Sort of Ecstasy* were all contenders for the Governor General's Award for poetry in 1955. She, a younger woman writer, was now pitted against two older and established male writers – both of whom had been her mentors. And of the eighteen previous awards, only three had been given to women poets, two to Dorothy Livesay and one to Anne Marriott. Nonetheless Pat won. She may have known in March, because her mother wrote at the end of the month: "We were so overjoyed – so very proud of my baby girl! ... I think so many will be pleased for you darling."[51]

In early April, Alan Crawley wrote to congratulate her, saying, "Damn it all it isn't just the award that counts or proves I did know,"[52] meaning that he had recognized the high quality of her poetry from the start. There was a telegram of congratulations on 5 April from External Affairs

Minister Lester Pearson. Shortly after, Page received an astute letter from David Thomson of McGill, himself a fine judge of modern poetry. He thought the choice pretty obvious, "yet I had a faint feeling of surprise that the jury would make the right choice."[53]

The superiority of a number of Page's poems to those of Scott and Smith stem not only from their originality of subject and treatment but also from their psychological honesty – whether her mode is complex or lean. Scott's love poetry is sometimes elliptical and romantic and Smith can be overly erudite and mythic. Page's poem "The Map" is a good example of her "lean" style. It depicts two lovers who believe they are completely alone in a world of their own – "a world away on Precambrian rock" – but later find, when consulting a map, that they are actually close to a public path and only a stone's throw from a farm. They try to dismiss this fact, but in the bleak and final stanza it reasserts itself.

> But we were wrong and the map was true
> and had we stood and looked about
> from our height of land, we'd have had a view
> which, since, we have had to learn by heart.[54]

As Floris McLaren wrote to Pat, this poem has an understated clarity that is deeply satisfying.[55]

The announcement that Pat had won a Governor General's Award aroused a certain amount of speculation in Australia's diplomatic community, and it may have generated some interest about her by Australian poets. She was gradually becoming a semi-public figure, both as Mrs Arthur Irwin and as poet P.K. Page.

In mid-June 1954 she gave an address to the American-Australian Association in Melbourne on the cities in Canada, arranged by Maie Casey. Page described for her Australian audience the Canadian cities in which she had lived: Calgary with its cowboys and "Indians" ("looking swarthy in black sombreros, asking about lost horses or bringing a stocky cayuse to sell");[56] Saint John, New Brunswick, where the air was salty and damp, where the foghorns droned and ships hooted; Montreal, focal-point where two cultures meet, a hooting and bustling port, surrounded by outlying villages – to her "the most Canadian city." In contrast was Victoria, "the most English city in Canada," where lonely expatriates gather and where flowers are everywhere. Finally there was

Ottawa, the capital of Canada, centred on Parliament Hill, a city of 300,000 people, two languages, archives, museums, art galleries, and soaring spires – above all, a city of government.[57]

On another occasion, Pat delivered an address on Canadian poetry, possibly at Australian National University, on 1 July 1955, Canada Day. Pat's talk depicted contemporary Canadian poetry as she saw it, beginning with E.J. Pratt, whose poems represented the first break with the older Romantics. But she did not consider him a modern.[58] The focus of her discussion was the modernist anthology *New Provinces* (which included the poets Robert Finch, Leo Kennedy, A.M. Klein, Pratt, F.R. Scott, and A.J.M. Smith) and she acknowledged Smith as the most influential of the modern poets.[59] But it was Klein whom she set above all of the others in the group: "He writes as a whole man ... his love of words runs away with him sometimes – but what a rich error – he weaves you an Oriental tapestry; and latterly, much influenced by Joyce, he coins words, invents elaborate puns."[60]

It would be interesting to know what the Australian poets thought of Pat's lecture, especially David Campbell and A.D. Hope, who were in the audience. She was later to discover that Hope, whom she had met briefly and casually in Canberra, had around this time written a poem entitled "Soledades of the Sun and The Moon" for P.K. Page:

Be Circe – or be my Queen of Sheba; come
Silent at nightfall to my silent palace
And read my heart, and rest ...[61]

His poem, dedicated to the wife of Canada's high commissioner, was more personal than might be expected – it was a great surprise to Pat. Some years later, in 1985, the Victoria poet Marilyn Bowering was visiting Australia and met Hope. He reminisced that he and David Campbell had announced that they "were going to fight a duel over PK – a beautiful woman and a poet." Arthur came looming up: "This woman is my wife!"[62]

Again and again, we are conscious of the fact that Pat was struggling against great odds. A letter to Anne Wilkinson explains how enormously difficult it was for her to submit her poetry manuscript to McClelland and Stewart.[63] And in a letter to Jean Fraser, she wrote, "I must gather my courage and send some poems to CBC. You've no idea how I hate doing it.

I feel so uncertain of them. I am working at the moment on some very simple poems about the gardener. I would very much like them to come off. And I do think the gods might have given me just a bit more talent when they were at it. To be given such a tiny drip is hard."[64]

Pat was continually nervy. She felt the usual woman's insecurity in the world of letters: poetry and publishing were still largely a man's world. She feared to send her manuscript out, yet was convinced that she must – and forced herself to do so. She was nervous about public performance but forced herself to appear. The imagery of "Arras" reflects a sense of being alone, a moment of overwhelming terror, of intense feeling. In this poem, as perhaps in the living of her life, she resolves isolation, fear, and uncertainty by focusing on her art and the process of creation. Her refusal to allow fear to dominate her raises the question of *why* she forced herself to do things she was so afraid to do. Her response was one of her father's sayings: "You're no daughter of mine if you won't try anything once."[65]

The Governor General's Award for *The Metal and the Flower* may have helped Pat's self-confidence. She dealt with her fear about submitting her new poems to journals by sending them to Floris McLaren to submit on her behalf. The new poems included "The Glass Air," "Frieze of Birds," "Photos of a Salt Mine," "After Rain," "When Bird-Like," "Portrait," "Nature Poem," and "Offering of the Heart." *Poetry* (Chicago) accepted several. At least one of these poems, "The Glass Air," may have been sparked by her talk on the cities of Canada, because there she refers to Calgary's transparent air: "this land of limitless grassland wrapped in light as clear as cellophane."[66]

In "After Rain" (as in "Arras"), a garden figures prominently:

The snails have made a garden of green lace:
broderie anglaise from the cabbages,
Chantilly from the choux-fleurs, tiny veils –
I see already that I lift the blind
upon a woman's wardrobe of the mind.

The garden – and the sight of a "gaunt delicate spidery mute" and "its infant, skeletal, diminutive, / now sagged with sequins, pulled ellipsoid, / glistening" – gives way to a gardener, Giovanni, "a broken man."

Giovanni was an Italian immigrant gardener, and the cook, Mrs Clark, would not give him a "cuppa" tea at break-time with the others in the embassy because he was a "foreigner."[67] "After Rain" addresses his dismay in the devastated embassy garden after attacks from rain and slugs.

As the poem develops, Page humanizes the young man and acknowl-edges his grief – a deeper response from her first feminized and somewhat whimsical imagery of the "broderie anglaise" made by snails on cabbage leaves. She wishes for him a wider perception that includes the beauty that she sees:

> O choir him, birds, and let him come to rest
> within this beauty as one rests in love,
> till pears upon the bough
> encrusted with
> small snails as pale as pearls
> hang golden in
> a heart that knows tears are a part of love.

But at the same time, in the last stanza, she reminds herself "to keep my heart a size / larger than seeing": that is, to recognize the whole situation which includes not only a perception of beauty but its human cost. In terms of her poems she wishes that "the whole may toll, / its meaning shine / clear of the myriad images that still – / do what I will – encum-ber its pure line."[68] When Pat sent this poem to Floris McLaren, Floris immediately recognized that the new poems were utterly different in idiom and image from Pat's previous work. Would she mind if they were submitted to the *New Yorker*?[69] If she did, nothing came of it, but *Poetry* (Chicago) accepted several poems, including "After Rain" and "Gio-vanni and the Indians" for its November 1956 issue.

Willy-nilly Pat was now being caught up in the 1950s new wave of Canadian writing, partly because of the success of her book, and partly because she herself was attempting a poem on a Canadian theme, Louis Riel. As early as April 1955 she knew that critics were discussing her work in a Canadian literary context. Alan Crawley, when congratulating her on the Governor General's Award, told her that he had recently heard a critical discussion on CBC Radio in which Morley Callaghan, A.J.M. Smith, and Malcolm Ross had taken part. Smith had argued that in Page's new book of poetry there was work as good as any to be found in contemporary British or American books of poetry. Callaghan retorted, "Well if that is so why did not Miss Page have her book published out-side of Canada? Why not in the USA?" Smith and Ross defended Canadian writers who publish in Canada, but Callaghan said, "I think the reason was that Miss Page was frightened to submit to American publishers."[70]

Up to the mid-1950s, Canadian writers habitually validated their work by publishing in Great Britain or the United States, although by the 1960s more Canadians were publishing in Canada. In late November 1955 Arthur Irwin ordered some new "Canadian" books, most of which had been published outside the country: Mordecai Richler's *Son of a Smaller Hero*, Brian Moore's *Judith Hearne*, Ethel Wilson's *Swamp Angel*, Mason Wade's *The French Canadians*, Bruce Hutchison's *The Struggle for the Border*, Ernest Buckler's *The Mountain and the Valley*, Irving Layton's *In the Midst of my Fever*, and Patrick Anderson's *Snake Wine*, a travel book about Singapore. Page was reading *Snake Wine* in May 1956 and was also reading Mason Wade and Bruce Hutchison about the same time, being much interested in Canadian history.[71]

Bruce Hutchison was one of Arthur's good friends. In 1952 Arthur and Pat had read aloud Hutchison's *The Incredible Canadian*, and now they were reading *The Struggle for the Border*. Hutchison's description of Louis Riel with his dark face – "bois-brulé" – brooding character, and mental illness in 1875–78 seems to have captured Pat's imagination. The fragments of her unpublished poem on Riel present Sir John A. Macdonald, a map, his making of Canada, and the manic-depressive Riel as an obstacle in the process. In attempting to write the poem she drew upon her memories of the clear prairie skies but incongruously added the metaphor of an iceberg to the flat plains when she suggested "the buffalo, moving like icebergs, huge a dirty white / over the snow."[72] She may have been influenced by her recent reading of Pratt's epic poems *The Titanic* (1935), with its iceberg, and *Towards the Last Spike* (1952), with its depiction of Macdonald, a map, and a railway connecting Canada from sea to sea. The subject fascinated Pat – she knew the prairie, the buffalo, and had strong memories of the Sarcee Reserve.

Nonetheless, she could not marry the content and form of her poem. "Is there no way to start this thing flowing? My head / is crammed with facts about Riel – the silver crucifix ... / his training for the priesthood, his strict face ..."[73] Riel's life was too fluid to be contained on her pages. The poem was never finished or published, although sections found their way into Page's semi-autobiographical poem of the 1970s, "The First Part."[74] But the fact that she began to write it after or while preparing her talk on Pratt and Canadian poets suggests that she was attempting a "Canadian poem." She was certainly writing some fine poetry in Australia and also travel journals and letters (on top of everything else). She was not, however, bringing many of the poems to publication, perhaps as Brian Trehearne suggests, because she was developing a new aesthetic.[75]

Pat was taking stock of her mode of expression. At the same time as she was working on the Riel poem, she was considering revisiting her old alter ego "Cullen" – "the perfect vehicle to blast the Tory mind. For Cullen must by now be, if he is alive, harboured in safety, cynical – who? Drinking a bit perhaps, but not reading."[76] In this poem, for many years unpublished, she depicts a middle-aged Cullen, all passion spent, in danger of sinking into a conventional life and mode: "Now forty years sit fat upon his thoughts, / fill him with platitudes fleshy as fruits."[77] (Pat was forty in 1956.) It was after this recognition that she began to change her poetic tone from the cooler, more impersonal T.S. Eliot mode of the forties into something closer to her own personal voice and gender.[78] The "I" of the observing poet now enters the poems, and the scenes are quite often domestic or identified as female. The new Giovanni poems, "After Rain" and "Giovanni and the Indians," have shown this change.

While a new poetry was taking shape for Pat, the work of the embassy carried on. Arthur, influenced by his newspaper training, was convinced that part of his task as high commissioner was to send back to External Affairs a first-hand account of actual conditions, so he undertook extensive travels across the country. Pat happily accompanied him. In their first year they went to Swan River and Kalgoorlie in West Australia; and in the second and third years they completed a rough geographical inventory of Australia, with trips to remote sheep stations, to Alice Springs – and a flight to New Zealand.

In July 1954 an official visit to Queensland was followed by a holiday – much needed by Arthur, who was tired, overworked, and plagued by headaches. By the time he returned to his post, the Canadian first secretary had left, the second secretary was on sick leave, and a new and inexperienced staff member arrived the following week, leaving Arthur carrying most of the responsibility for the embassy in the midst of the Petrov affair, a Russian spy story similar to Canada's Gouzenko affair.[79] Vladimir Petrov's defection took place just before the 1954 federal election and became a matter of partisan politics when a former justice of the High Court accused Prime Minister Menzies of arranging the defection to coincide with the elections for the benefit of the ruling Liberal Party. Pat wrote Jean Fraser: "Arthur is trying to balance the world on his nose." To add to their problems, it was extremely cold in the embassy in July, and the electricity kept going off during formal parties.[80] That year they took their holidays at the Great Barrier Reef, which they found exceptionally lovely. The corals and the fish and the shells were a delight, but the weather was unseasonably cold. Arthur was now having trouble with his stomach (prefiguring the return of an earlier ulcer – he had nearly died of a bleeding ulcer in an Ottawa hotel room in 1940 when working on the Bren gun scandal).

In October they travelled to Narooma and Bermagui. During these visits she saw not only the premiers and their wives, who were part of the diplomatic circle, but also the Aborigines ("Abos," as they were then called, from the Australian predilection to abbreviate everything – but this term carried derogatory overtones), who lived in the outback and were often servants in many of the "stations," or farms, the Irwins visited. Pat became fascinated by Aboriginal culture and art, which she first encountered in an early visit to the Melbourne Art Museum. Arthur found a wonderful book of Aboriginal drawings, published by UNESCO, and gave it to Pat in April 1955 to celebrate her Governor General's Award.[81] Also in 1955 he sought out an Aboriginal bark drawing and gave it to her as a Christmas present.[82]

In 1955 they celebrated New Year's Eve with some Australians, realizing that next year at this time they might be back in Canada. In January of the following year they took a brief trip to Tasmania and then to New Zealand, where Arthur took his annual leave. For some time Pat had wanted to talk with Irene Norman, wife of the high commissioner to New Zealand, Herbert Norman. They had visited the Normans in Ottawa – Norman's posting to New Zealand had concurred with Arthur's posting to Australia. Pat found Herbert a little petulant, but his wife Irene was open, friendly, frank – and she thoroughly understood the diplomatic world. Pat wanted to ask various questions of someone of her own rank. For example, as the wife of a colonial high commissioner, she was required to curtsy to the British high commissioner and his wife, and to the premiers of the various Australian states and their wives. But supposing the British high commissioner and his wife were staying in your house and you met them on your way to breakfast in your dressing gown – were you still required to curtsy?[83] Herbert Norman and Arthur Irwin got along well, possibly because of their common background as sons of Methodist ministers who had attended Victoria College. During this trip the Irwins took the time to observe Maori culture by visiting Waitomo, Rotorua, and Taupo.

Although they had been in Australia for three years, Pat had still not seen a corroboree, the Aboriginal ritual of music and dance. Scheduled for 9–23 June 1956 was a projected trip to the Northern Territory, which included Arnhem Land, where much Aboriginal art was to be found.

She and Arthur flew from Canberra to Sydney on 9 June and resumed their journey the following evening for Darwin, on the north coast. They arrived there on 11 June and began with a tour of the town. At one of the outlying settlements, at the Bagot Native Mission, they finally attended a corroboree, in which the Aborigines played the didgeridoo:

> Under a powerful sun, twelve or fifteen men danced fitfully. They had stripped down to what looked like rompers, and painted their bodies with the same polka dots, herring-bones, cross-hatchings they use in their bark paintings. One boy had put his head in the paint pot, so from the neck up, he was flour-white ... In the foreground a young "black fella" lay extended with a digiridoo – a long, wooden instrument made from the bough of a tree, its centre hollowed out ... which is played lying down, with one end in the mouth, the other supported by the big toe.[84]

Once the music started the dancers began to shuffle, making occasional singing or chanting noises. Finally they jumped, let out a yell, and the dance was over. Page was disappointed. She had been reading a book by Colin Simpson, *Adam in Ochre*, which had suggested that a corroboree was worth going half round the world to see. Later she wondered if her expectations had been too high: "I had imagined – what had I imagined? That they would dance as if we were not there? That I, a foreigner, through instant empathy, would understand? ... How could I have been so arrogant as to think myself capable of understanding?"[85]

Their travels in the outback took them through dirt roads, agricultural farms, official cemeteries, cattle stations, and innumerable mines. Most interesting to Pat were the visits to the School of the Air, where she observed operators instructing children isolated at remote stations, and the Flying Doctors' base, to which the sick of the outback were brought for medical attention. However, it was at Tennant Creek that they had their most personal experience of the outback. Arthur had been bitten high in the groin. At first they thought it was by a bull ant because it raised a white bump "about three inches in diameter with three scarlet spots." But the area around the bite became inflamed and his leg began to swell. A local nurse gave Arthur an injection, and he fell into a stupefied sleep; but at ten o'clock that evening, P.K. awoke, fearful for his safety. Everyone was asleep. She could not find the inspector they were travelling with, and when she knocked on his door, a stranger answered. She went downstairs, trying to find a public phone and found instead a man in a tweed jacket who was looking for the Canadian high commissioner – a doctor. The nurse had recognized the bite of a red-backed spider and had called for help. The spider's sting was not necessarily fatal, but it was serious. The doctor wanted to give Arthur morphine, but he would not have any. So all three trailed to the hospital for observation.[86] Fortunately, the Irwins were able to leave the next morning, but not before a surreal encounter with a golden lioness, presumably someone's pet, that entered their bedroom from the verandah and leapt onto their bed among the articles to be packed – "all with a swift inquisitive movement of muzzle and paw and settled down among my underwear – square shoulders and square paws perfectly synchronized – rhythmically pumping and purring."[87]

The highlight of the trip was to have been a visit to Ayers Rock, that great red pyramidal rock in the dead centre of Australia, a little way south of Alice Springs. But – "Oh bitterest blow!" – the rains, or "wet," came earlier than expected, their jalopy was stranded in the mud and the plane they had expected would take them to the Rock was lost in the bush. They were stranded for three days because it rained almost solidly from the moment they arrived in Alice Springs until the moment they left. Eventually, on 22 June, they left Alice Springs by plane for Adelaide, then back to Sydney and Canberra.

A couple of months later, in August 1956, the Irwins flew to Papua New Guinea, a protectorate of Australia. Looking down on the Great Barrier Reef during the flight, Pat likened it to "the back of some large turtle under the water, with waves breaking in its edges – its 'shell' a lovely green in the surrounding deep grey blue of the sea."[88]

Meanwhile, the gathering crisis over the Suez Canal had been hanging over Arthur's last year in Australia as Britain and France sparred with Egypt over ownership of the canal. Egyptian President Nasser's nationalization of the canal in July 1956 had escalated the crisis, leading to the invasion of Egypt by Israel, Britain, and France in October. By then, Arthur's term as high commissioner of Australia was over, but in the previous months he had been deeply involved in negotiations, transmitting the views of Australia's external affairs minister, Dick Casey, to Canada's external affairs minister, Lester Pearson. As is well known, it was Pearson who defused the situation by suggesting the creation of a United Nations Emergency Force to be sent to Suez "to keep the borders at peace while a political settlement is being worked out." Herbert Norman, recently appointed Canadian ambassador to Egypt, was credited with persuading Nasser to allow Canadian troops to enter his country for this purpose. In 1957 Pearson was awarded the Nobel Peace Prize for brokering the peace.

The Irwins left Australia on 22 September 1956. Pat's time there had changed her somewhat. Not only had she learned the ropes of diplomatic life, but the beauty and isolation of the country had caused her to turn inwards. She had begun to paint a little, and her poetic language had taken on a more personal, painterly idiom. Stored away in her aesthetic consciousness were the stipples and cross-hatching of Aboriginal art, which resurfaced in her own later art. She was genuinely sorry to say goodbye, despite the fact that she found many Australians ultraconservative. "On the whole those with taste are the most politically reactionary and those whose politics I am most sympathetic with have so little awareness of beauty or need for it in their lives that you can barely communicate." Nonetheless, Pat found in Australia "a kind of ingenuousness, something more child-like than we have in our make-up, and it's attractive." Australia, she concluded, was far more than the sum of its parts.[89]

On the first lap of their journey home, they went by of Sydney, Darwin, Jakarta, Singapore, and Egypt. When they arrived in Cairo, Arthur received a telephone message from Herbert Norman. Apparently, he had written to Arthur inviting the couple to stay on their way home, but their mail had been held up by the Suez Crisis, and Arthur could not now accept. They had arranged a rendezvous in London with Arthur's son Neal, who had taken special holidays to be with them. Norman was enormously upset that they could not see him, and Pat and Arthur did not understand why. In fact, Norman was being hounded by the CIA on the grounds that he had been a member of the Communist Party.

A year later Arthur said to Pat, "I have bad news."

"About whom?" she asked.

"Herbert Norman."

Her response: "He's committed suicide."

"How could you know?"

"I don't know how I knew."

Looking back, both realized that the cause of Norman's emotion on the telephone in 1956 had been that he badly needed to talk to Arthur, someone of his own rank in External Affairs whom he could trust for advice.[90]

From Cairo, the Irwins flew to Rome, where they had several hours to spare before their next plane. Arthur hailed a cab. He was insistent that

Pat see the Sistine Chapel (he had seen it during the First World War when he was with the Canadian infantry). The driver went at the speed of light, and they had a whirlwind tour of Michelangelo's marvellous frescoed ceiling. Rushed back to the airport, they took the plane to Canada, landing in Montreal on 2 October. In Ottawa, Rose Page had found a furnished apartment for them in her block, and there Pat and Arthur spent the next three months, winding down – and then up – in preparation for their next post.

CHAPTER 9

Brazil
Exotic Worlds, 1957–1959

I paint like a maniac and go through the most ghastly and torturing
times. I don't know what I think about anything anymore and barely
know what I'm trying to do, which I once did. Confusion absolute.
But now and then I produce a not bad painting. One very large oil of
my dressing table [*Woman's Room*] quite pleases me. But oh, God,
why did I have to start this half way through my life.
P.K. Page to Jean Fraser, 25 March [1959]

To the Irwin's great surprise, they were posted to Brazil – something of
a disappointment: they had hoped for a European embassy, where
Arthur's experience and interests would be more applicable. Yet Pat
found Brazil both "surrealist and seductive" – an environment that
fostered her emotional and artistic life.[1] On 4 January 1957 they left
Ottawa, going by train to New York on the first leg of their journey.
Blair and Jean Fraser came to the railway station to see them off. Many
years later Pat recorded the shock of encountering F.R. Scott, who
brushed against her but did not see her, since she was on his blind side
– Pat crumpled against Jean Fraser. She later wrote in an autobiographical poem, *Hand Luggage*: "I'd have fallen had not / a friend held
me up. There were ghosts in that town."[2]

In New York they embarked on the ss *Brasil*. Their first view of Rio
de Janeiro from the ship on 21 January was silvery-blue, monochromatic, "a flat, platinum city."[3] As the American poet Elizabeth Bishop
says of Rio, the mountains are so close to the ocean that water in the sea-
winds condenses quickly and clouds float low about them. This damp-
ness gives a softness to the atmosphere and a delicate pink or blueish light.[4]
Pat's first response was to this delicate beauty of Brazil. The Irwins' embassy residence in Rio was a bright pink building with a white trim set

in a formal garden containing a swimming pool. Opulent, but somewhat run-down, it had been built by a wealthy Portuguese named de Braga and modelled on his *palacete* in Portugal. It was fairly isolated, lying some distance to the west of the main part of Rio at the foot of two mountains known as Os Dios Irmãos, "the twin brothers." Just behind the embassy, in one of the deep mountain fissures that surround the city, was a large *favela*, or slum, from which the sounds of drums resonated as the evenings cooled.

The grounds were exceptionally beautiful. Burle Marx, a famous Brazilian landscape gardener, had planted the garden with three different shades of grasses to make a kind of abstract painting; there was always the sound of running water, for a stream had been dammed to make a little pool. The main entrance to the embassy residence was at the back of the lot, at the end of a circular driveway. It led into a large marbled hall with stairs leading up to the main bedrooms and down to the kitchens. Just off the hall was the main reception area – a huge white-walled room with a grand piano, chandeliers, and yellow satin drapes. The house had only recently been purchased by Canada and had not previously been an embassy. Although brilliant in architectural design, nothing worked in practice. The swimming pool couldn't hold water, the elevators didn't rise, the showers didn't shower, all the plumbing was defective – and these problems fell squarely on Pat's shoulders. Because she spoke no Portuguese, she was endlessly dealing with workmen with whom she couldn't communicate. But the greatest problem was finding the right staff to keep the residence in good order. Their German house-keeper spoke seven languages but not English; their food budget was astronomical; and small items regularly disappeared from the kitchen and from the Irwins' dressing tables. It took them almost a year to winnow out problem staff and hire replacements, but the problem of finding a senior servant continued.

Arthur was promptly installed as ambassador with great brio – he presented his credentials to Brazilian President Juscelino Kubitschek, attended by motorcycle troops in jungle-green uniforms. Thereafter, he left home each morning for the Canadian Embassy offices in downtown Rio, but Pat remained behind with a houseful of strangers. It was a big house with marble floors that echoed as she walked, and she was confined there for several months as their car had not travelled with them. She was alone and very depressed. Although language lessons had started immediately, her progress was slow. Beginning to learn a new language, she discovered, was like becoming an infant: "One is a toy at first, a doll. Then a child. Gradually, as vocabulary increases, an adult again. But a

Mrs Arthur Irwin at the Canadian Embassy in Brazil.

different adult. Who am I, then, that language can so change me? What is personality, identity?"[5]

Brazil was a watershed for Pat because she experienced three major changes in her life – all in 1957, her first year. Brazil "pelted" her with new and astonishingly beautiful images. For example, a few weeks after their arrival, she saw a yellow-bellied flycatcher flying from the yellow flowers of a cassia tree, which in turn was set in a flower bed of yellow day-lilies[6] – the subject of her late glosa "Ah, by the Golden Lilies." But by early April, after three months in Brazil, she was disoriented. "What to do about writing? Is it all dead?"[7] For Pat, writing meant writing poetry. It was as if she could not write poems because she no longer heard English spoken around her. She later wondered about the deeper changes of losing one's language and with it, one's identity: "the profounder understanding – partial, at least – of what man is, devoid of words."[8] In fact, she did find words for a number of short poems, mostly unfinished, and she began to record her impressions of life around her in her personal journal. These impressions she used as the basis for letters home to her mother and Aunt Bibbi, to Arthur's children, Pat, Neal, and Sheila (Sheila and Neal visited Brazil separately), and to Jean Fraser. This journal was to provide the basis for *Brazilian Journal* (1987).

In mid-June, after six months in residence, Pat registered another change. She had been attempting to fire Salvador, the embassy's handsome but woefully inadequate *mordomo*, or senior servant. Feeling that he should understand clearly why he was not being kept on, she spoke to him in halting Portuguese and, while doing so, doodled nervously on a pad of paper on the desk. Arthur, who came into the room after the interview, picked up the paper, looked at her sketch, and said, "You could draw."⁹ He then encouraged her by buying a roll of expensive drawing paper. It was just the push she needed. She couldn't bear to use this fine paper for her early sketches and found some bright wrapping paper in a Rio department store. On this she began to draw the world about her, with the bold marking pen that she had used to label their belongings for travel. As she later recorded, "the pen that had written was now, most surprisingly, drawing."¹⁰

Brazil itself, together with Pat's inability to find a creative outlet in poetry, made her very conscious of colour as she put the residence in order. She longed for some of artist Pegi Nicol's "jujube colours" to brighten up the great spaces of their reception rooms and envisioned a large glowing Goodridge Roberts still life from the National Gallery to replace the rather drab Roberts in the small *sala*.¹¹ She was also seeing a great deal of visual art in her formal capacity as the Canadian ambassador's wife. She and Arthur visited many Brazilian museums, galleries, and art exhibitions in their first year in the country, particularly the Museu de Arte Moderna, where Pat encountered the art of Brazilian painters Candido Portinari, Lasar Segall, and Maria da Silva. She especially loved Portinari's work, partly for his subtle colour and strange perspectives, and partly, it seems, for the content of his paintings, reflecting his youth in the small Brazilian town of Brodowski.

She was particularly attracted to a Portinari painting of children in a playing field: "Those little running kids in a vast space, scattered like grains, go through me like needles."¹² (Pat longed for a child and hoped that one day she and Arthur would have children.) In September the couple attended the São Paulo Biennial, an art exhibition that she found extraordinary. She loved the dreamlike canvases of the Canadian artist Harold Town, whose work was ranked first in the Biennial. She also saw the work of Ben Nicholson again and several new Chagalls and Pollocks. As a result, she began to read a series of books on art and artists, including Ortega y Gasset's *The Dehumanization of Art,* and books about Portinari (including Antonio Callado's *Retrato de Portinari*) and about Klee, Dufy, and Matisse.

Simultaneously, she was responding to subtropical Rio, not only to the brilliant colour but to the rainforest atmosphere. In *Brazilian Journal* she describes the effect of this exotic world on her sensibility as a kind of seduction, a love affair with Brazil. In early February, dazzled by a tree in the embassy garden that had four great sprays of brilliantly coloured tree-orchids growing from it, she lamented, "I wish I knew how to describe the vegetation, or indeed how to paint it."[13] With Arthur's encouragement, she attempted to recreate the shapes of leaves and the patterns of mosaic tiles in the embassy residence. "I think I might be able to draw if only I could ... what? If only I *could.*"[14] Over the next three years she became almost totally preoccupied with drawing – and recognized that she had never been happier than she was at that time, living "almost entirely through my eye."[15]

In March, with the residence now habitable, Pat made the first of her diplomatic calls, visiting the wife of a senior minister in the Brazilian government. So often such visits made her feel "that the whole thing is make-believe and that I am dressed up in my mother's clothes."[16] All the obligatory visits to the embassy wives brought her only two kindred spirits: Molly, the wife of Donald McKay, the Australian ambassador, and Lucy, the wife of the American ambassador, Ellis Briggs. Molly – who drew her white hair back over her temples – reminded Pat of Florence Bird, who had a similar hairstyle. Lucy had a fund of nursery rhymes at the tip of her tongue; she would say to Pat, "You bring out the Mother Goose in me."[17] She also made friends with Trixie, wife of the Panamanian ambassador, Julio Briçeno. Pat found Trixie amusing, and they later took painting lessons together.

Politics dominated Brazilian life. The recently elected President Kubitschek had promised, during his 1955 election campaign, "Fifty years of progress in five," and he had set about a series of ambitious plans, including major road construction, the creation of a Brazilian automobile industry, and the development of a new capital city, Brasília, in the geographic centre of the nation. To undertake this transformation he encouraged foreign investment, especially from Canada. One of the major Brazilian utilities – Brazilian Traction, Light and Power – was a Canadian company (known to many Brazilians as "the Light") and was not only Brazil's largest foreign-owned firm but supplied most of Brazil with vital utilities (electricity, gas, water) and telephone services. One of

Arthur's primary tasks was to encourage trade, and during his tenure Brazil purchased from Canada a number of locomotives, tractors, and even a cobalt bomb.

Pat had been advised by some members of the expatriate community in Rio that it was impossible to become friends with Brazilians. But others, notably the wife of the Swiss ambassador, said, "You can make friends with Brazilians easily if you let them know you like them."[18] Arthur's diplomatic position brought him in contact with a number of prominent Brazilians, not only the president and members of his Cabinet but various Brazilian cultural figures. The Irwin's made quite a coup when they became friends with Austregésilo de Athayde, a journalist and longtime president of the Brazilian Academy of Letters, and Assis Chateaubriand, the most important newspaper owner in Brazil, who was ambassador to Britain. The Irwins also met the architect Henrique Mindlin, who had originally designed their residence, and they regularly saw Joaquim Nabuco, president of the Museum of Modern Art in Rio and one-time ambassador to the United States. Maie Casey had given Pat a letter of introduction to Maria Martins, a sculptor who had a wonderful collection of paintings in her home, including Renoirs and a Picasso.[19]

In order to familiarize himself with Brazil and Brazilian industrialists, Arthur made a number of trips to the major cities and to the interior, and Pat accompanied him. She was delighted with their first visit to a Brazilian *fazenda*, or farm, which many years later inspired a poem of the same name:

On the wide veranda where birds in cages
sang among the bell flowers
I in a bridal hammock
white and tasselled
whistled ...[20]

Subsequently the couple took extended trips to São Paulo, Brasília, Ouro Prêto, Florianópolis, and Bahai. There was a pattern to these trips: officials were greeted, Canadian products were presented or inspected, local sites were viewed, and innumerable coffees, lunches, and dinners consumed. Occasionally, there was an interview, followed by a newspaper photograph of the Canadian ambassador and his wife. Typical of such gatherings – although more manic than usual – was the reception for six Canadian-made General Motors diesel locomotives at a railway station in Campinas, São Paulo, in early June 1957. When Pat arrived at the square where the locomotives were expected, she thought it looked exactly like a Portinari painting of Brodowski. A loud brass band was playing and rockets were fired as the locomotives, each covered with a Brazilian flag, pulled into the station. Arthur was asked to make a speech, and Pat was invited to unveil the diesels. "By lifting the flag in an ungainly upward throw, I unveiled the *Jânio Quadros* [a locomotive named after the governor of the province], a *bispo* blessed it and threw holy water on it, the band played the Brazilian national anthem. The women cried. Then a kind of madness took over and nothing would do but I unveil all the diesels, and so – in a dream that was not a dream – I continued to lift Brazilian flags and find diesel engines. Meanwhile, in an ever-milling mob, people greeted each other and shouted and embraced, and the band continued to play."[21] That night in her dreams she "lifted larger and larger Brazilian flags over [her] head."[22]

Although life in the small towns was spontaneous, both Pat and Arthur found certain aspects of Brazilian society extremely formal, several notches higher than in Australia, and male-dominated. Pat occasionally expresses astonishment at the strict division between men's and women's activities, and the lengths to which Brazilian women carried the process of beautification. Her Canadian self, accustomed simply to washing her face and cutting her hair, was taken aback by beauty regimes involving hair tinting and depilation that were customary for Brazilian women. And not only were tails routinely worn by the men at evening receptions, but the women were "perfectly groomed, extravagantly dressed."[23]

The first party for the Irwins was given in April by Antonio Gallotti, the Brazilian head of Brazilian Traction, Light and Power, and his wife Mimi, sleek and elegantly dressed in a designer gown. (Arthur privately thought she looked rather like a panther.[24]) Pat enjoyed some of the pageantry of diplomatic life but found many social relations superficial. Her closest friend, however – Doña Helena Borges, wife of Brazilian businessman Juan Borges – was direct, honest, and deeply spiritual. Doña Helena also had a strong aesthetic sense. In person she was short and rather stocky, always beautifully manicured and coiffed, with heavy eyelids and a distinguished air. She had married into the old, wealthy, and influential Borges family and regularly entertained any crowned heads who happened to be visiting Brazil. The two women met in July 1957, when Helena invited Pat to join a Brazilian charity called *As Pionerias*, and their friendship was cemented when they began to paint together.

Pat recognized that Helena Borges was part of "intellectual" Brazil (to which she felt she herself belonged), whereas the Gallottis embodied "social" Brazil. This recognition came in late July when the Irwins attended a special dinner at the Borges home where the guests included a leading woman novelist, a noted criminologist, and a former president of Brazil. Dinner was served in a living room whose walls were adorned with four beautiful eighteenth-century paintings, more like tapestries than paintings. Outside the house was the floodlit garden: "There, as if under a black dome, every conceivable kind of leaf – green with white stripes or white splotches ... pure red the colour of blood; of all shapes, all sizes; and anthuria – miniature white ones, large patent-leather pink ones, deep red ones, shining from the depths of Rousseau's green." A young man with a guitar sang a Brazilian folk song about *favela* life, how the sun shining through holes in the roof made stars on the floor, so that "my man walks careless among the stars at his feet."[25] The evening strongly appealed to Pat. It may have reminded her of past dinners, accompanied by art and folksongs, at the home of Jori Smith and Jean Palardy. Pat wrote in her journal: "And it is all [a] queer feeling – as if in some way I hardly know, I belong to this life."[26] Often she had experienced a strong sense of not belonging, of being separated from other people and becoming depressed. But now, slowly, she felt more closely connected to the country, and Doña Helena was an intermediary.

Back in May, she recorded this feeling of being connected to the country, writing in her journal: "Disturbed and excited by Brazil."[27] In mid-July, she wrote: "Something mad is happening to me. I seem to be falling in love with the world. And something in me is afraid. It is hard to know joy from pain."[28] Indeed, she later said that she felt as if she were "wired and someone (Someone?) had a finger on the buzzer all the time."[29] It was partly the wonderful sensual heat, the warm sun that Pat loved so much. But it was also the people themselves. "They are so warm, Brazilians – touch you, flatter you, kiss you, love you. Forget you next day, of course. But while they are with you they are whole-hearted."[30] For Pat, it was a blossoming time. Feeling at home, she began to respond to the world around her.

She became obsessed with painting, and thus connected with the landscape. The combination of the wonderful unexplored world she was in – especially the golden Baroque churches – and her newly found graphic skills focused her creative energies. She began to sketch the embassy and objects in it – the great hall, the stairs, her dressing table – in effect, recording her world through a new medium, perhaps a response to the culture shock of losing her language.[31] With Helena she began to sketch in the beautiful old churches. Helena, on her part, intuited a strong spiritual element in Pat and hoped that Pat would convert to Catholicism.

Helena wrote out a prayer to the Holy Ghost for her in Portuguese on a scrap of paper which Pat kept with her Brazilian papers.[32] Indeed, there was a sense in which Pat did encounter the Holy Ghost in Brazil.

The third major change in her life came in December 1957, some ten months after her arrival in Brazil. The facts of her experience are given in *Brazilian Journal* but in a coded manner. The reader is not told that the operation she underwent was a hysterectomy for an ovarian cyst, but Pat's later description of the operation alludes to a "child" who helped her recuperate. Nor are we told that before the operation, her gynecologist asked if he should make efforts to solve the problem and help her conceive. Pat was then forty-one and Arthur eighteen years older. The diplomatic life seemed to her to be inimical to everything she considered proper for the life of a child. Thinking of this, and recognizing that she would be in her mid-sixties when the child was twenty, the couple decided against it, but it was a hard decision.[33] Pat's recognition that she would now never have children may have contributed to her obsession with painting. Paradoxically, this brought recognitions of mortality when she feared that she did not have enough time left to learn to paint properly.[34] Nonetheless, she threw herself into her art – every day attempting to find time to sketch – and derived enormous happiness from it.

Shortly after the operation, in early 1958, Pat and Arthur took a month's vacation and went to visit a series of spas in Minas Gerais, where they relaxed and took the waters. In May that year Austregésilo Athayde invited Pat and two other wives of ambassadors to address the Brazilian Academy of Letters. As no Brazilian women had been invited, Pat accepted, thinking that the precedent might encourage the academy to invite them. Although she was nervous about speaking in public, she put off preparing the actual speech, reading a great deal of background material and then panicking as the time for delivery approached. Everything fell into place when she wrote two small nature poems in Portuguese, describing her discovery of Brazil. She constructed her talk around this and decided to conclude it by speaking to the academicians directly with a quotation from a Brazilian writer, Gonçlaves Dias: "Meninos, eu vi." ("Little boys, I've seen it myself.")

When the time came to speak she was so nervous that her hands were shaking, but fortunately there was a rostrum to hold her text and hide her hands. She realized she had to throw her voice to be heard and did so. When she looked up, Athayde "smiled so lovingly" that it gave her heart. She was overjoyed when the academicians laughed at her "little boys" climax. When she allowed herself to turn and look at Arthur, she saw that he was extraordinarily pleased. The next day there were front-page stories and photographs in the press. She received flowers, phone calls, and telegrams – and President Kubitschek complained that he hadn't been invited.[35] But in the end, Pat was deeply disappointed. Writing a few days later to Jean Fraser, she said that she had only been invited "because we were 'Ambassadresses' ... I had fondly hoped that it might be [Athayde's] way of getting women accepted by the Academy – to start with us, but when I tackled him on it his attitude was 'heaven forbid.'"[36]

Not all of Pat's Brazilian experience found its way into the published *Brazilian Journal*. A few months earlier, after their return from Minas Gerais, she had speculated in her diary: "I suppose what I really want to write about is drawing – or painting or whatever I'm doing. But I hardly know what I want to say." She was not interested in "the thing as it is" but was intrigued by "the literal in a context of phantasy."[37] In fact, Pat was moving towards what we now call "magic realism," but at first in the mode of visual art; later she was to infuse this sensibility into her prose. As she told Jean Fraser, "I want the solemnity of reality, that reality that goes right to the heart, but washed, transformed by the light that never was. It is for this that I so much like Dufy, Chagall, Klee, Matisse. But only occasionally Picasso and I can't think why."[38]

As Pat's drawing became more proficient she sought further instruction from Brazilian artists, first attempting to attend a series of art lessons at the Museum of Modern Art (her Portuguese was not up to it). She then contacted artist Ivan Serpa, whose paintings she admired, having seen them at an exhibition in Rio. He was a young man, small and gnome-like, who taught kindergarten. To take lessons from him, Pat had to come in at recess and sit in the small chairs like a child. Serpa forced her to think for herself by refusing to tell her what to do, but there was a note of warning. He told her that some of her paintings, had Dufy done them, would have been admired – her use of paint and pen led straight to Dufy. He suggested that she throw away her marking pen and dream a little more.[39] Pat complied, but throwing away her pen was like an amputation.[40]

Friends had suggested Frank Schaeffer as a teacher, and her reaction to him was more complicated. He had a program that he expected each student to follow, and Pat did not like "formula painting." But he was an excellent judge of art and helped her to begin working with oils. She grumbled but returned for painting lessons for over a year. By late February 1959 he praised one of her paintings, *Woman's Room*, which he considered worthy of exhibition. It depicts a scene from domestic life: a white sink with gold fixtures, surrounded by a three-way mirror. Gold, slate blue, and mauve are the dominant colours. There are some fine effects: the substantial white of the porcelain, a filmy curtain in the left mirror panel. What is curious is the artist's perspective: it is not at all easy to determine where she has positioned herself and where we should fix our eyes when viewing the painting. Like Alice walking through the looking glass, we seem to step into the mirror – the painting has a series of images within the picture, all refracted by the three-way mirror. The central mirror reflects a woman's dressing table with various lotions and perfumes and offers a glimpse only of a dressing room and bathroom, with clothes hanging over the tub. It is a domestic and wholly intimate scene. The left mirror panel gives us more of the bedroom – a small black table with a bottle of wine, a manuscript and possibly a chair in front of it, while the right panel, a partial reflection of the centre panel, also gives us a little more of the dressing table and the sink. The artist is clearly a beginner, learning to work in oils, but the painting is complex and has life.[41]

In spite of Pat's enthusiasm for painting, the thought that she was not writing poetry disturbed her. She occasionally refered to this in her journals and in July 1958 wrote a poem on this topic. It begins: "Could I write a poem now?" and speaks of her guilt because she is not writing poetry: "having believed (and pledged my troth) / art is the highest loyalty & to let / a talent lie about unused / is to break faith." But how, she wonders, "do you write a Chagall?"[42] That is, how do you capture the magic, the fantasy, the out-of-this-world flavour? Her imagination was focused on the visual.[43]

Now and then there was news from home. Pat had been horrified to hear from the young wife of a fellow diplomat that A.M. Klein had suffered a mental breakdown, which she attributed to anti-Semitism.[44] "But we all loved Klein!" Pat exclaimed, without knowing the buildup to his breakdown. Later in the year, in mid-November, friends informed her that the British poet Stephen Spender had said she was "Canada's best poet." This caused her to reflect in her journal: "Strange, too, how so many things come at the wrong time." Of Spender's remark, she wrote, "It's nonsense, but he said it, nevertheless … And the last *Tamarack Review* has an article that treats me, along with eight or ten others, as one of the serious and interesting poets. Would it have borne poetic fruit two years ago?"[45]

Subsequent literary critics have referred to Page's time abroad as her "decade of silence."[46] There is some truth in this comment as far as her poetry is concerned, yet during this period she was extraordinarily creative, especially in her diaries. Much of her creative energy was applied to visual art, which stands for strong communication, not silence. But why painting and not poetry? Is it largely, as Pat earlier speculated, because without being immersed in the English language, she found poetry more difficult to write? In her unpublished journal of 17 February 1959, she wrote that when an Australian friend "M" (probably Molly McKay)[47] asked why she no longer wrote poems, she replied with the phrase "a growing secrecy." Molly was horrified, claiming that secrecy was concealing and contrary to art. Pat disagreed. "I feel whatever this is it may be protective – part of the keeping whole and I feel too that I may have changed from writing to painting because one is freer to uncover oneself without in the same way being exposed."[48]

In late February, when Pat was still painting *Woman's Room*, she found some support for her belief when reading the journals of Albert Schweitzer, who stated that "no one should compel himself to show to others more of his inner life than he feels it natural to show. We can do no more than let others judge for themselves what we inwardly and really are, and do the same ourselves with them. The one essential thing is that we strive to have light in ourselves." Pat recognized this feeling: "One's own core forms, assumes weight, grows its lode. And where that points, one must go."[49] Pat was describing the growth of the self as the lodestone that provides further direction. Her own inner direction had changed, as indeed it was to change at several other points in her life.

The Israeli ambassador Arie Aroch – "a very fine painter" – helped her greatly. "Ever since he heard me say I had begun drawing he has been rude to me about it, telling me I am a good poet, why chuck overboard all the understanding of one art form in order to begin another about which I know nothing? Logically, he couldn't be more right." But when Aroch saw her painting for the first time, he phoned saying that he was impressed. He offered to help her with the handling of oils. He explained "how to mix the tempera of the Old Masters – egg, oil, and water – and how to use this as a surface to scratch through." He also showed her "how, in oils, to paint wet on wet" without smudging the colours.[50] Both techniques proved to be extremely useful.

During their last two years in Brazil the Irwins made a number of journeys, including two trips to Brasília, the projected capital designed by the celebrated architect Oscar Niemeyer and still under construction. The first visit, a complete surprise, was initiated by President Kubitschek at the last moment. Pat and Arthur departed under the impression that a Canadian-made airplane was to be tried out. In fact, as they later discovered, the real reason for the journey was to deliver a statue of Our

Lady, *Nossa Senhora*, to Brasília. The following November, they returned to Brasília with Sidney Smith, then Canadian secretary of state for
external affairs, and his wife.[51] The Irwins also went to Ouro Prêto, a
charming seventeenth-century town built on a steep hill, where they visited two entrancing Baroque churches in which the altars were covered
with gold. The couple stayed in a hotel designed by Niemeyer – a building that stressed form over function: the stairways were so narrow that
guests were forced to carry their suitcases sideways. They also visited
the province of Bahai. During their last year, 1959, they took a long-
anticipated trip to the Amazon. They went by way of Belém, visited the
legislative assembly and various gardens, and a museum, where Pat
found a shrunken head, lips sewn together. This was followed by excur-
sions to the cities of São Luis and Manaus, on the Rio Negro, a tributary
of the Amazon. The river was "tar black, hence the name. Yet a glassful
taken from it is a sparkling, crystalline, pale urine."[52] And they visited
the "golden-domed opera house, capacity 1,500, built at the turn of the
century [1896] at the height of the rubber boom – where Patti once
sang." At the time of their visit it was empty, its four galleries, governor's
box, marble, chandeliers, and elaborate paintings all moldering in the
steaming heat.

Pat was presented with a *macaco-leão* (lion monkey), which to her
eyes looked like a marmoset.[53] The little creature, first called Benjamin
(later called Benjamina when it turned out to be female) complained bitterly for some days – missing the company of her siblings in a small den.
Pat picked her up and instinctively held the monkey by her side, thinking that her warmth would comfort her: "I was wearing a dress with a
pocket and the moment she saw it, she dived into it and came up again,
head over its edge – her complaints changed to a song of joy ... We are
already good friends."[54] The lion-monkey often perched on Pat's shoulder, apparently defleaing her. Benjamina was a kind of child, much loved
– but ultimately lost. "I realize I have never reported the flight of Benjamina, or, in detail, her charming and tiny life with us. Or the small but
real tears I shed over her loss. How describe her delicious smell or record
her habits?"[55]

Theorists remind us that autobiographical writing, especially when
dealing with painful incidents from the past, tends to recreate the experience in a manner compatible to the individual's sense of self at the time
of writing. This is especially true of the reticent Pat, who reminds us in
the published *Brazilian Journal*: "Strange how I rarely write of things
that distress me. Why? Because I cannot bear it? Because I try to forget?
(I don't succeed.) 'A Refusal to Mourn the Death, by Fire, of a Child in

London' [a reference, added later, to Dylan Thomas's poem]? I don't even know why."[56]

Pat began to think about publishing her diary in 1963 and worked on it off and on for two decades. In 1982 she sent a version of the diary to a possible publisher. The earliest copy of this manuscript that I was able to find at the time of writing this chapter (successive copies had become "lost" in Page's literary manuscripts) is in two parts: the entries for 1957 up to 4 December have obviously been rewritten (and this includes the "falling in love" with Brazil metaphors), but the entries from December 1957 seem to be in their original unedited form. From a comparison of the two, we can see that Page's treatment of the hysterectomy is different from what it subsequently became (the special nurse who attended her was not helpful, Pat found the incision grotesque, and she was horrified by the nature of her illness, concluding that "the gods took every precaution to make sure I had no children!").[57]

When later editing the journal with Arthur, these references were removed. The encompassing metaphors for her Brazilian experience, emphasized by the older Page, are sexual and reproductive. The entries where she speaks of falling in love with Brazil may have been constructed after the event. "Something mad is happening to me. I seem to be falling in love with the world."[58] Then she asks, "*Can* one fall in love with a country?"[59] The implicit imagery is that of a sexual relationship, reinforced by several references to naked bodies,[60] by the discussion of the *figa* (a Brazilian charm to encourage conception),[61] and by the penis identified in exotic Brazilian flowers.[62] Much of this imagery is expressed in the published *Brazilian Journal* during a period of almost nine months, that is from April 1957 (and a remark by the Israeli ambassador's wife which equated nine months spent in Rio with a "pregnancy")[63] to Pat's "operation" in December 1957.[64] This palimpsest of imagery suggests that at some level Pat saw her paintings (and possibly the baby monkey, Benjamina) as children of her union with Brazil. The later process of editing *Brazilian Journal* may have ameliorated some of the pain of not having a child of her own.

On New Year's Eve in 1959 Pat and Arthur, on their return from a party, saw the enormous curve of Copacabana beach alight with a million candles. It was a *macumba* ritual in honour of *Iamanjá*, Queen of the Sea: women and men wear white clothing and dance on the beach. At midnight they wade into the ocean and pour drinks, cosmetics, and flowers into the waves for *Iamanjá*. At Ipanema beach Pat, in evening dress and borrowed slippers, walked among the groups – some men were smoking black cigars and others writhing on the sand, said to be possessed by a saint.[65] Pat later reflected that she felt very differently about Brazil after seeing *macumba*: much had come into focus. To some degree the carnival, the music, and much of Brazilian society (the "golden world" that she saluted when concluding *Brazilian Journal*) now seemed shallow. A couple of years earlier, when Molly McKay had learned that the Irwins would be staying in Brazil less than three years, she had said, "Good, I'm glad it's no longer. You may still love it when you go."

In July 1959 Pat learned from Arthur that in August they would be returning to Canada. Not long before their departure, Trixie Briçeno arranged for Pat to spend a day with her so that she could meet Trixie's old friend, Margot Fonteyn, and her ballet partner Michael Somes, a Brazilian. For Pat, Fonteyn was someone who had, "in the past, moved me so totally." She was referring to the time she had seen Fonteyn dance in *Swan Lake* in Montreal in the late 1940s, a performance that had left Pat with the feeling that she knew Fonteyn. But this feeling did not carry over into the reality of meeting her: "She is smaller than I had thought, and spare, almost taut, in the way she holds herself from the waist up – head, neck, back, too straight ... And there is another quality, hard to describe – a kind of total self-awareness, as if she is on guard for leaks." Yet when she saw them dance in Brazil on 1 August, she wrote: "Where does her tautness go? ... They are wonderful. Danced *Giselle*."[66]

⚏

Pat was sorry to leave her friends, especially Helena, and the servants, and Arara the parrot and Duque the dog. "Sorry, too, to leave my Brazilian self, so different from my Canadian self – freer, more demonstrative."[67] Earlier, in an unpublished section of her journal, she had recognized that "there is a side of me which will always react to this place, a sensuous side ... which loves all the tropical growth – the shapes and colours – which loves the baroque – and above all loves the sun. But even this brings out one's worst, I think. To sit in the sun becomes enough, becomes, almost, a way of living."[68]

Finally, on 14 August the Irwins left Brazil. On the ship, returning home, she reflected on Brazil and thought that she had changed. "Certainly as the years have passed, my sensitivity has lessened. And this of course is the real problem. To stay wet – a strike for lightning. This is the only thing that matters, for without it one cannot be an artist." The previous night, when trying to work on wet paper with inks, she had been unable to conjure an image. "Nothing. This will be my down fall of course, unless ... by that act of will? – I can strip once again"[69] – that is, shake herself free from her present depression and inhibitions and become open once again to a life-giving stimulus – the lightning strike that generates art. But for the moment she felt nothing, neither a pang at leaving Brazil nor a thrill at returning to Canada.

CHAPTER 10

Mexico
New Maps, 1960–1964

What I like about Jung is that he is a philosopher and a man with faith … He *is* difficult to read. Too true. However I just kept on reading; didn't stop when I found him difficult and finally discovered I had taken in more than I realized by some form of osmosis.
P.K. Page, 1963[1]

Some years after her Mexican experience, Pat wrote an essay titled "Traveller, Conjuror, Journeyman" in which she gave a retrospective account of her four years in Mexico in the early 1960s. In it she spoke of reading philosophical texts that led her on a psychic journey and concluded: "I am traveller. I have a destination but no maps. Others perhaps have reached that destination already, still others are on their way. But none has had to go from here before – nor will again."[2] Certainly, she had had no idea that Arthur's new posting to Mexico would precipitate an inner journey that would be reflected in much of her subsequent poetry and art.

The Irwins arrived in Mexico on 10 March 1960. Pat's first impression of Mexico City was that it was very grey compared to the bright sun and colours of Brazil, but she found it cosmopolitan and architecturally sophisticated, with broad boulevards and many skyscrapers and fountains. The Canadian Embassy residence was fifteen minutes from the city centre on Paseo de la Reforma, one of the main boulevards, down which on Sundays the local men rode their horses, their large felt sombreros tilted according to personality – "dour, cheerful," and sometimes "fierce."[3] The residence itself was ugly; the main entrance led into a great rotunda with two enormous pillars at one end that looked like elephant legs, and the dining room was quite dark with no windows.[4] The Irwins were not accustomed to the high altitude, and in their first days they puffed their way up two long flights of stairs to reach their bedroom. Pat had to go up a further flight to a room in the attic where she painted.

March in Mexico is like midsummer. Some mornings were hazy, and thick smog hid the mountains, but there were days when the air was so clear that the city was absolutely beautiful – and Pat could see the volcano, Popocatépetl – though there were also terrible days when dust and pollution hid the sun.[5] She thought Mexicans very different from Brazilians (a witty, warm, laughing people) whereas the Mexicans, of Spanish Indian ancestry, were more dark, and to some extent death-oriented.[6] Initially, Pat found her new environment depressing. She had not yet made friends, couldn't proceed with her art, and the residence was a mess. Everything was under reconstruction because Prime Minister John Diefenbaker had notified the Irwins that he would visit in April. Pat's first letter back to Canada was to Jori Smith: "This is some house! And some job, too, to get it ready in a little over a month for the P.M. and wife. It is full of Spanish speaking painters, plumbers, carpenters, slip-coverers, electricians, varnishers, cleaners, washers, window cleaners, hornets' nest removers and God knows what more!"[7] And she was having to learn a new language.

Diplomatic life in Mexico proceeded as in Australia and Brazil, with the difference that Pat now knew the ropes. The Diefenbaker visit turned out to be a great success. He and his party arrived in the late afternoon of 21 April 1960, and were greeted by such dignitaries as the president of Mexico, the British ambassador, the dean of the diplomatic corps, and in the rear, Arthur and Pat and the Canadian Embassy staff. A twenty-one-gun salute was fired at the airport. After innumerable speeches, everybody returned to the residence, which was festooned with flowers. Pat jotted down her recollections of Diefenbaker's remarks that evening: "The P.M. did not like the [Jean-Paul] Lemieux painting and made it quite plain. He was amusing to listen to – I say listen, advisedly. Regaled us with anecdotes about his early days as a book salesman."[8]

The next day there were various tours and in the evening a formal dinner at the president's palace, where women wore full evening dress and men wore dark suits (since the Mexican revolution, solidarity with the working class forbade the wearing of tuxedos). The following night the Irwins gave a formal dinner, attended by the president, prominent Mexicans, and various international diplomats. There "A.[rthur] worked like a snorter getting Ambassadors up to talk to the P.M."[9] They were later told that this had been the most elegant party of the season, and Pat realized that in Brazil she had learned a great deal about diplomatic entertaining. The next morning everything about the Diefenbakers' arrival reversed, complete with a final twenty-one-gun salute at the airport. As Pat recorded in her journal, "Now, of course, I have time to think of my show and am nearly dying of frustration."[10]

Pat's "show" was an exhibition of her art that opened on 23 April at the Picture Loan Society on Charles Street in Toronto. In early 1960, before leaving for Mexico, Pat had taken a portfolio of her drawings to Douglas Duncan, who had co-founded the Picture Loan Society in 1936 to encourage artists and collectors with regular showings and picture rentals. The sole agent of the distinguished painter David Milne, he was known as a fine collector whose judgment could be trusted. Pat, without an appointment, had gone to his office one morning – he was busy. She waited until late afternoon. Finally, just as he was leaving for home, she accosted him and said, "Mr Duncan, I've been waiting all day, and if you could give me a minute now I would be very grateful." Reluctantly he took her back to his office and examined her portfolio. He closed it, reopened it, and went through it again, slowly. Finally he said, "When can you have a show?" Pat was flabbergasted. She had wanted his opinion of her art and had the gumption to wait him out – she had not expected an exhibition; it was too soon. But after discussing the offer with Arthur, she decided to go ahead, and she exhibited under the name of P.K. Irwin.[11]

Her show, which continued until 6 May, was a great success, in the circumstances. It consisted of approximately two-dozen paintings in various mediums; many were oil pastels but there were also several etchings and works in gouache. The etchings included *Aladdin's Ship* (an early version of her later "Barco" series). The oil pastels made up the majority of the exhibition: *Labyrinth*, a red and purple womb-like form, *Bark*, a study in green and gold, and a grey two-humped landscape entitled *This Church My Dromedary*. There was also *Escaping Suns* and *Red Whirling Crayon Drawing* (possibly an early version *Dance*). One of P.K.'s better-known paintings, *Stone Fruit*, later reproduced in colour in a *Malahat Review* tribute, was first exhibited here. Pat was very pleased to hear that Frank Scott had bought two of her paintings. There were encouraging comments in the Toronto *Globe and Mail*, and her work was being seen and was collected for major institutions such as the National Gallery, which bought *Keyhole* and *Milkweed Forms*.

Although the Diefenbakers' visit had gone well, Pat was beginning to feel doubtful about the whole diplomatic endeavour. This was confirmed one evening at an official dinner when she sat next to the chief of the diplomatic corps, a Latin American. He admired Pat in her black lace dress, remarking that she was "an asset to the corps." She was a full twenty years younger than most diplomatic wives – and knew herself to be attractive – but she felt constrained to tell him that she did not take diplomatic life as seriously as perhaps she should. "Good, good," he said. "You see my wife. Thirty years ago she was the most beautiful, joyful girl you could possibly imagine. Now look at her." Pat looked at his wife, her hair dyed and her face painted, a brittle society woman. "And," the man added sadly, "she has done it all for me." Page believed him. Her comment: "This [diplomatic] life might have been possible for a woman raised to do nothing else, but today ... women want something more."[12]

It was not that Pat Page did not "do her job" or that she was not appreciated. Landon Pearson (now a retired senator), wife of Geoffrey Pearson (son of Lester B. Pearson), who was the second secretary at the embassy, recalls that Page was always helpful, always supportive and kind to younger wives.[13] There was never a whisper that she neglected her diplomatic duties to pursue art or poetry. It was simply that women's lives and expectations for their lives had changed. Wives now had more freedom to have careers of their own.

To some degree, Pat was caught between the old order and the new. As a young woman, she had expected to be "somebody's wife and somebody's mommy."[14] Arthur was a considerate, tender, loving husband (albeit somewhat taciturn), and she was happy as his wife. To be sure, they had not been blessed with children, but that gave her more time for her art, more time to reflect on the direction of her own life. But when the ten-year anniversary of her break with Frank Scott came on 20 November 1960, she wrote in her diary: "Disproportionate desolation. Grief's enclave. Dominion of despair."[15] She was now forty-four, an age when many thoughtful people re-evaluate their lives.

She did not overtly ask, "What am I doing with my life?" But she may have thought it, because much of her reading while in Mexico was self-directed towards the search for "a way," or a path, as described in the writings of the psychologist Carl Jung. She had read Jung's *Modern Man in Search of a Soul* in Montreal in the 1940s and had reread it during the next two decades. In this book Jung speaks about the malaise of modern life and the fact that many of his patients, when they reached forty, were conscious of a lack of meaning and of "getting stuck."[16] What was required was transformation, but not all were capable of it.

Jung often advised his patients to listen to the unconscious as revealed in dreams and, when possible, to paint their dreams. In the fifties and sixties, as Jung's *Collected Works* came out, Pat had volumes sent to her in Australia, Brazil, and Mexico.

In August 1960 Page was also reading Joseph Campbell's *The Hero with a Thousand Faces,* which argues that all myths and folktales "from little Red Riding Hood to the Crucifixion are nothing more than the quest for the Grail – the pilgrimage of the hero." The hero sets out on a lonely journey and faces enormous dangers. If he is brave – and lucky in his friends – he returns home transformed.

In early April 1961 Pat wrote in her journal that discovering one's own path "seems to take an eternity. What a journey with always the possibility that the Minotaur will get you in the end. I wonder if in earlier and simpler times the journey was shorter ... or whether it has always been equally difficult. Once I thought I knew the route, that I could even see the promised land; I had even stepped within its gates. But an earthquake demolished it and by some fluke left me alive. I had then to start a new map, and like Meaulnes [of Alain-Fournier's *The Wanderer,* a translation of *Le Grand Meaulnes*], I had almost no facts to put on it – nothing *known.*"[17] When Pat spoke of a journey she was referring to her life as a quest, a pilgrimage in search of meaning. She had always had problems with identity – Who am I? Where am I going? At one point in her life she imagined she could see the promised land – meaning, perhaps, a life with Scott. But an earthquake had demolished her old life. Now she had to establish a new map for her future.

She had already found in Arthur Irwin her most important guide: his love, good sense, and sure instinct for what she needed had provided a secure balance for her life and art. In Mexico she met a different kind of guide, the well-known English Mexican painter Leonora Carrington, at a dinner party given by the British chargé d'affaires: "The Carrington woman is a surrealist, and I believe, dotty. But I enjoy talking to her." At the dinner Pat described her childhood experience in Calgary of having seen a small face at the window next door, a face that frightened her and gave her a sense of evil (p. 28). Leonora responded immediately: "You're telling the truth; I recognize truth."[18] She believed that her creative genius – in Jung's terms, her *animus* – had threatening aspects, and she may have recognized in Pat (whose story sparked their friendship) another artist with the capacity to see beyond the mundane.

A little later Pat attended an exhibition of Leonora Carrington's paintings at the Museo Nacional de Arte Moderno. A schizophrenic, Carrington was inspired by her visions, giving her paintings titles such as *And Then We See the Daughter of the Minotaur* and *Litany of the Philosophers*. Pat found them powerful: "Her fantasy is quite extra-ordinary and I was tremendously impressed by about five of her works – one of a ghost of a heraldic beast with a luminous egg near him and a completely transparent bird."[19] The latter painting was probably *Who Art Thou, White Face?* (1959), a griffon-like creature with wings and a minotaur-like head poised above a luminous egg. Carrington often painted an egg, which she saw as the cosmic egg of creation (containing the macrocosm and microcosm, "as above, so below") associated with female power and the "alchemical vessel."[20] She had studied alchemy and frequently drew upon alchemical terms to indicate psychological transformation. Alchemy interested Carrington because, as André Breton observed, surrealism and alchemy had similar goals – "the transfor-mation of man in his quest for spiritual enlightenment."[21]

Pat found Leonora remarkably perceptive, informed, and practical: "We discussed matters, she had information about art that I didn't have. She never acted as a critic at all. She opened doors and I walked through."[22] Physically, Leonora didn't look like anyone else. "She was so narrow. You always felt as if she could slip through a crack in the door." She had dark curly hair and golden eyes – "like two suns in her face."[23] Her violent behaviour when gripped by her schizophrenia could make others uncomfortable; during bouts of madness she could be terrifying. Page was frightened of her only once, in July 1963, when Leonora had an extreme nervous breakdown.

Like Pat, Leonora was a seeker. Born in England in 1917, she had re-jected the privileges of an upper-class life in order to study art. When she was twenty she met the surrealist artist Max Ernst, who helped trans-form her life. When he returned to Paris, Carrington joined him, but she had a nervous breakdown when Ernst was interned as an enemy alien at the beginning of the Second World War. Her parents placed her in an asy-lum, but with the help of a Mexican diplomat she escaped from France and settled in Mexico, where she met the Spanish Mexican painter Reme-dios Varo. The two women became close friends and shared an interest in the occult and interpreting dreams. By the time Pat met Leonora, Car-rington and Varo were becoming ranked among Mexico's major painters.

When Pat first met Leonora, she wrote in her journal: "I would give anything if she would teach me how she handles paint." Not long after-wards she added, "I do have the most extraordinary luck, I am working with Carrington."[24] Page admired Leonora's "control over a medium, because if you're a painter you're seeing a hundred things that a non-painter doesn't see. You're seeing brush strokes ... you're seeing layering, you're seeing transparencies." Leonora taught Pat how to use tempera. "It is like working hand in hand with the Holy Ghost. It is so sublimely luminous. I could never have dreamed there was a medium so supremely well suited to my temperament. First its luminosity – for which I have always liked my crayons – second you can polish it – it dries in a matter of seconds and comes up to a lovely gloss like soap stone under your fingers ... Also it is the most perfect medium for scratching through. Layer upon layer of paint goes on transparent and lovely. It is the first time in my life that I have ever really enjoyed working with a brush."[25]

Leonora's art reflected her interest in philosophy and the occult. She was influenced by G.I. Gurdjieff, a Greek Armenian mystic and teacher, who taught that "the work on one's self" was the most important work one could do. Gurdjieff argued that most people live in an unconscious state and must continually exert themselves to evolve. But no work could be done without an enlightened teacher. Gurdjieff insisted that the teacher's progress depended on his student's progress, and Leonora appears to have mentored Pat.

Leonora told Pat about her schizophrenic episodes – "how the ego dissolved or explodes ... and one is completely at one with the universe and this is a kind of ecstasy which no sanity can approximate." Pat noted that Leonora "had read a lot of Zen and knows old [D.T.] Suzuki and claims to be an amateur cabbalist – whatever the hell that is. At any rate she has a very queer diagram which she calls the tree of life on which almost anything can be mapped."[26]

Pat had read D.T. Suzuki and knew about the Tree of Life, or Sephiroth, which maps the external and internal worlds. Individual Sephirah are emanations, channels through which divine powers manifest themselves; they are defined by their place on the Tree of Life, the chief being the kether, or crown, which symbolizes the divine plan. At the back of her copy of Jung's *Symbols of Transformation*, dated Mexico 1962, Pat sketched a diagram of the tree, reaching from the earth, a "lower level," to heaven and a "higher level."[27] Soon after meeting Leonora, she began to experiment with crayon and drew a very large egg, which she called *A Kind of Osmosis*, referring to Jung and his symbolism of the cosmic egg but also, perhaps, to Carrington's egg imagery. This painting of a large glowing egg was purchased by the Art Gallery of Ontario.

Through Leonora, Pat encountered a number of like-minded people, who influenced her thinking. Besides Remedios Varo, Pat met the potter Eleanor Lincoln, the poet Laura Villasenor, the painter Mimi Fogt, and an Englishwoman, Pam Duncan, who had studied with Maurice Nicoll, a British psychiatrist who was also a student of P.D. Ouspensky, who in turn was a student of Gurdjieff. Eleanor Lincoln, an American who had settled in Mexico, became a good friend, lending Pat books and sharing information. She had read deeply in Gurdjieff and Ouspensky, knew Mrs M.A. Atwood's influential nineteenth-century book on alchemy, *Hermetic Philosophy and Alchemy* (1850), and had discovered Subud, an Indonesian spiritual practice. Lincoln gave Pat a dog, Chico, who accompanied her back to Canada. She was also the subject of Page's later poem, "Phone Call from Mexico."[28]

Pat met a second Leonora, Leonora Cardiff, wife of Maurice Cardiff of the British Council. Both Cardiffs became close friends. In Paris, Maurice had befriended Peggy Guggenheim, the noted philanthropist and art connoisseur, and he also knew Carrington, Varo, and members of the surrealist circle. The Irwins occasionally travelled with the Cardiffs to Cuernavaca, where the Canadian government had a pleasant house in the mountains. This group of friends had many artistic connections. They supported one another, socialized regularly, and when Leonora Carrington had her serious breakdown, Maurice acted as a kind of intermediary.

They also offered practical help: Varo's husband, Walter Gruen, ran a record store where Juan Martín rented space to open an art gallery. Martín sponsored exhibitions by Varo and Carrington, and in June 1961, held an exhibition called "Dreams and Superstitions," which featured five of Pat's paintings and etchings, including an etching and aquatint, *Bright Fish*, now in the National Gallery, and *Noche Levantine* in oil tempera.[29]

The opening was attended by an enormous crowd. Pat considered that she was in good company – Carrington's paintings regularly hung with those of Max Ernst and Pablo Picasso. Varo, she noted, was "one of the finest technicians I have met ... [she] paints remarkably like Bosch; and ... Gunter Gerszo, an abstractionist ... is also an incredible technician."[30] The exhibition was viewed by Pat's Canadian friend Florence Bird, who thought it ridiculous that although the wife of a Canadian ambassador was taking part in a major art show, no one was reporting on it. She thereupon appealed to the magazine *Canadian Art*, asking the editors to commission an article – and they commissioned her. In Bird's piece, entitled "P.K.," she reported Pat's saying "that she never planned a painting before she began, 'I had always thought that the idea of the emotion comes first. But now I think the medium comes first. I think the artist draws in order to see not the other way around.'" Bird asked Pat why she had stopped writing poetry in Brazil, and Pat replied, "I didn't stop. It did. I could find no vocabulary for a Baroque world."[31]

Reflecting on the show later, Pat recognized that her own work was quite different from everybody else's (perhaps because much of her art-work seems to have emerged from her perceptions of the world about her and the medium itself, rather than from any particular school of painting). She saw that there were three schools of art in Mexico: "the surrealist of which Leonora and Remedios are the leaders and masters; the abstract of which Gerszo is by far the most subtle; and the neo-Aztec into which fit a group who paint Mexican figures as well as a group which do non-objective paintings."[32] Pat's work was reviewed favourably by the Mexican critic Carlos Valdés, who spoke of "the poetry of its symbols" and, while noting the affinities of her early work with Klee's, concluded that it was not imitation, "rather it is the artist who has the same plastic concept as Klee; the creation of poetic and mysterious sym-bols which represent the world of concrete reality." Shortly afterwards, in late September 1961, the Art Gallery of Ontario exhibited two of her oil pastels, *This Church My Dromedary* and *Stone Fruit*. A year later, in April 1962, she had an exhibition at the Galerie de Arte Mexicano, where she exhibited, among other paintings, *How Is the Gold Become so Dim*, an oil pastel in gold with undertones of brown and green, and *Sky Drawing*, a subtle version of the night sky in turquoise watercolour, oil pastel, and pen and ink.

Throughout her time in Mexico, Pat kept in touch with Jori Smith. When she first arrived she told Jori she was working with black scratchboard and described her delight in scratching through the black to make de-signs on the white surface beneath. She was also learning to use gold leaf as she described: one misplaced breath, and "the wide leaf of gold is fly-ing in fragments through the air. Grab one of the fragments ... & it evap-orates ... disappears completely. Yet treat it correctly & it is firm and strong and lasts centuries. Rather marvelous, isn't it?"[33] With Jori, she could express herself completely with the joy of one artist speaking to an-other in full confidence that she would be understood. She was eager to share new discoveries, like the recipe for tempera that she had just been given by Leonora Carrington: "Mix, in this order, in a tall bottle: 1 part linseed oil, 2 parts retouch varnish, and 5 parts turpentine. Shake well. Now boil a tall bottle & its top." After the bottle has cooled you "mix, in this order, 1 part of the above mixture, 1 egg yolk, 2 parts water that has been boiled and chilled. This you keep in the frigidaire, decanting small quantities as required."[34]

As Pat came to know Leonora Carrington better, she frequently went to her apartment in a house on Rosa Moreno. Inside, Leonora had one table in the dining area on which she piled everything – from the vice used to tighten painting frames to the frames themselves, from a chili bottle to a roll of toilet paper. There was no living room, only Leonora's studio and a bedroom. Her husband, a Hungarian photographer, Emerico Weisz (better known as Chiqui), worked at a newspaper, but at this time the couple had no chairs. So when visiting, Pat lay on Chiqui's bed and Leonora lay on hers, and their discussion of Jung and transformation floated in the air between them.[35] From 1961 until 1964, when the Irwins left Mexico, Leonora Carrington was Pat's closest friend.

Arthur's term as ambassador to Mexico was bracketed by postings to the United Nations. In mid-October 1959, after he had returned from Brazil on Canadian leave, he had been briefly posted to New York to represent Canada on the Fifth Committee (Administrative and Budgetary) of the General Assembly, and Pat accompanied him. He was particularly concerned about financial compensation for Canada's peacekeeping troops during the Suez Crisis. A year later, in September 1960, he left Mexico for another UN posting in the General Assembly, and Pat followed shortly after. At this meeting of the Second Committee, in October 1960, Arthur helped to put forward Canada's co-sponsored proposition concerning redistribution of surplus food to needy peoples, the first time the United Nations had considered sharing between the "haves" and "have-nots."

Dick Casey was now Australian representative to the United Nations, and Pat and Maie Casey resumed their friendship. Maie introduced her to people in her art circle, including Marian Willard (Johnston), who ran the Marian Willard Gallery. "Marian will guide you,"[36] Maie told Pat. Among Marian's friends were Nin Ryan, daughter of the late Otto Kahn, wealthy banker and patron of the arts who was an influential board member of the Metropolitan Opera; and the artist Charles Seliger, an abstract expressionist who had been influenced by surrealism. Nin took Pat to a Whistler exhibition at the Metropolitan Museum of Art and to rehearsals at the Metropolitan Opera, and invited both Pat and Arthur to her sophisticated society parties. Pat liked Nin, who had such a positive feeling for art and beautiful things, but was overwhelmed by the enormous wealth and influence of her social group, which included "Tony" (Anthony) Eden, former prime minister of Britain.

Pat did not take advantage of this entrée to high society, preferring Marian Willard's world of museums and art exhibitions. The work of one of her favourite artists, the American painter Mark Tobey, whom she had discovered at an exhibition in Brazil, was on show at the Willard Gallery. Tobey is best known for his creation of "white writing," in which he overlays an abstract, densely painted design with calligraphic symbols that are usually white. In Brazil, Page had written to Jean Fraser: "Reading about Mark Tobey the other day, the 'white writing' man whose work I am mad about, he is reported to have said he only learns by a kind of osmosis. It surprized me so much because the only other person I've ever known to say that is myself. Strangely some of my things are rather like his and I feel it can't be influence as I've only just stumbled across him in the last few months."[37]

Although Marian told Pat not to bother taking art lessons ("Follow your nose, you're alright – you know where you're going"), Pat protested that there were techniques she didn't know anything about.[38] Marian suggested that since Charles Seliger was also self-taught, he might take her on as a private student. Seliger – who worked on small panels of masonite, often with thick oil paint – agreed to teach Pat, so on Saturday mornings she and Arthur drove to his studio, just outside New York. Seliger taught her a technique using both oil-based and water-based paints, where the water repels the oil; he showed her how to build up several layers with tempera to create a wonderful stippled effect. Seliger also discussed balance and composition in painting, which gave Pat an opportunity to look at overall form.[39]

Pat had also hoped to learn etching while in New York and was directed to Harry Sternberg at the Art Students League. He was an avowed social realist and accepted Pat as a student. She worked in the league's studio on five mornings a week, and Sternberg taught on two of them. Etching is a complex process that involves incising the negative of an image into a metal plate coated with acid-resistant wax and then using acid to cut an image into the metal. Sternberg was a good teacher, but Pat's progress was slow and the class unfriendly. Most students at the school were young and poor, though committed to their art; they assumed that a middle-aged woman in a fur coat (Pat's uniform against the New York cold) was a wealthy housewife filling time. She floundered without help until she showed Sternberg some of the paintings she had exhibited in Toronto. He was surprised. "[Y]ou've done nothing to indicate that you can draw as sensitively as this."[40] When Pat began to produce several competent etchings, Sternberg became supportive.

Pat and Marian Willard remained friendly, and Marian showed Pat "whatever she had new that she thought interesting." Pat confided to her that she had been thinking about contributing to another exhibition in Toronto earlier that year and remembered Marion's advice not to show new work again too soon. Marian replied, "You're alright, you're alright. It's when artists feel content afterwards that they're done for."[41]

That fall New York was abuzz with election talk – John F. Kennedy was running for the Democrats and Richard Nixon for the Republicans. Kennedy pledged to "get America moving again." Arthur's friend Blair Fraser of *Maclean's* magazine had been hired as a freelance reporter by the CBC to cover the election, and on 12 November Jean and Blair Fraser arrived in New York – a welcome visit for both couples. While Arthur and Blair talked politics, Pat and Jean visited galleries. At the Museum of Modern Art, Pat became aware that a skinny man in a turban was following them from gallery to gallery. Every time she looked up he caught her eye, but she didn't know him and looked away. Later, in the cafeteria, the man came over to her and said, "Were you Pat Page?" With her "Yes!" she was grasped in a bearded hug. It was Kushwant Singh, the Indian cultural attaché from her Ottawa days.

He had aged: his hair and beard were grey and he had lost about forty pounds. He looked like a grizzled clerk and seemed colourless without the bright turbans he used to wear.[42] He was now a writer, novelist, and political correspondent. His first book, *Train to Pakistan*, 1956 (in translation), dealt powerfully with the partition of India. Subsequently, he had entered politics and become a political correspondent. In later years he settled in Delhi, where he became India's best-known political journalist.[43] Curiously, after this meeting with Singh, Pat had an important dream (discussed later in this chapter).

Arthur's UN session finished in December 1960. His incipient ulcer acted up one evening during a dinner party, and he became very ill in the night. Pat phoned the Canadian ambassador to the United Nations, Charles Ritchie, to ask him to find a doctor. In Manhattan that night there was a mammoth fire, and it took a long time for the doctor, with his patient, to get to the hospital, where Arthur was diagnosed with a gastric hemorrhage. He convalesced in Ottawa, but had another hemorrhage that kept him in hospital for about six days. After spending Christmas in Toronto, Arthur and Pat drove down to Mexico in January, but the trip took several weeks. Pat acquired a virus in New Orleans, and in Monterrey, Mexico, she was so ill that they flew the rest of the way. On their arrival at the embassy, they discovered that she had become anemic, symptoms that had become worse because of the high altitude of Mexico City. Consequently, she was treated to increase her red cell count.

⚏

Arthur's role as Canadian ambassador to Mexico changed when Kennedy's government came to power in January 1961. Cuba was a major concern of the new American administration, and much of Arthur's task was to keep the Canadian government informed about Mexican and South American views of Cuba. In February 1962, ten months after the Bay of Pigs fiasco, the United States launched an economic embargo against Cuba.

On 30 June 1962 President Kennedy and his wife Jacqueline visited Mexico. The visit was "a howling success." Mexicans, who were not overly fond of Americans, lined the route of the procession. There was confetti in the air, flags flying, "firemen, troops, members of a youth club, mariachis, police, rich, poor were in holiday mood and ready to wave at anyone." Pat thought that Jacqueline dressed like a teenager but that Americans, because of their passion for youth, probably liked the "coedness of their Presidential pair." The diplomatic staff did little for two days except turn up at events featuring the Kennedys: "airport, lunch, ballet, lunch, reception, airport."[44] Pat was struck by John Kennedy's personality. When she shook hands with him in the receiving line – looking elegant in a pale blue strapless dress of heavily embroidered peau de soie and a matching stole – she had a strong sense of Kennedy's assessing eye. At a lunch given by the Kennedys, she was also impressed by the appropriateness of a non-political speech, delivered in Spanish by Jacqueline, about the children of Mexico.[45]

In October, American-Cuban relations deteriorated when US reconnaissance photographs revealed missile bases being built by Russia in Cuba, apparently in response to the US bases built at the Turkish border with the Soviet Union. The American cabinet considered direct military invasion, but cooler heads prevailed,[46] and after protracted negotiations, the Soviets agreed to remove the missiles from Cuba, and the United States agreed to remove American missiles from Turkey. Pat wondered "how long the escaping continues possible … Leonora says she has felt the last few days just like one of these monkeys in a rocket flying through the stratosphere completely alone, surrounded by instruments she cannot understand. It's a good image."[47] (A year later, on a diplomatic tour in Mazatlan, Arthur and Pat learned of Kennedy's assassination on 22 November. "A symbol has gone and we all feel that much less. Almost everyone I know has been moved to tears as if a personal friend had died.")[48]

P.K. was continuing to paint. Surprisingly, Leonora and Arthur sometimes offered the same practical advice: "Leonora ... tells me what Arthur tells me: that I must get back to drawing from nature. He says I need outside stimulation. She says I need to draw force from the thing drawn, which is impossible when one deals in abstractions, as the thing drawn is non-existent. She says, 'See if you can draw its movement in space.'"[49] Leonora made Pat think, even when she didn't fully understand her: "For her it is all a question of evolving – mutating. She says this was the end purpose of the alchemists. Painting is a means ... She thinks writing less 'useful' as the 'other' does not enter it as it does with painting." This discussion made Page analyze why she painted. "Do I paint to be successful? No, although if I were successful and that success did not make me content or vain or empty, I would not mind it. Do I paint to pass the time? No. All too often the time has literally to be stolen. I think in some part of myself I paint in order to externalize something that seems to me beautiful."[50]

On 1 July 1961 the Irwins had celebrated Canada Day with an Open House. It was a huge event with many guests, and Pat was exhausted when it was over. That year, Carrington was restaging her play *Pénélope*[51] and suggested that Pat help construct the papier mâché figures, which Pat did in her spare moments: "Leonora is doing the designs for everything – sets, costumes, etc. She is also making the sets. Sundry of her friends are helping her with large papier mâché headpieces for ghosts, cows, birds, cats, god knows; plus the entire rocking horse. It is great fun."[52] The play was staged in early September: "I can't say I approve of the production – but I found it beautiful."[53]

A year later, Pat and Arthur attended a dinner party given by Leonora for Isaac Stern. Leonora had no idea that her guest was the famous violinist. (She had confused him with a local urologist named Stern.) During the dinner, Stern remarked that the artist performs in order to be heard by his audience; the main task is communication. Pat and Leonora were outraged and retorted that they created their art for a "higher power" – God perhaps. Stern opined that anyone who said that was a liar. Pat was so angered that she threw a glass of red wine over her shoul-

der – and it sailed out of the window to crash on the street below.[54] To
this point, Pat had been every inch the diplomat's wife – only now did
she let her passion as an artist express itself. To Jori Smith she exploded,
"He said the artist's only concern was with communication. I claimed it
was secondary. I paint in one of 2 states: anguished – & the work is healing; elated & the work is worship – a celebration. Only afterwards do I
feel the need to communicate."[55] The difference between a performing
art like Stern's, to which listeners respond immediately, and painting is
perhaps that the latter is at first the artist's private experience. For Page
and Carrington, art had profoundly spiritual dimensions and was connected more with self-development than with performance.

In fact, both women were now actively searching for spiritual knowledge, and Mexico was a particularly appropriate venue. After Aldous
Huxley published *The Doors of Perception* – on changing consciousness
based on his experiences with mescaline, the principal agent in peyote –
Mexico became associated with the psychedelic revolution. Carrington
knew Huxley, and many in her circle took peyote or "magic" mushrooms. Pat was tempted but refused, a little reluctantly, because Arthur
had asked her not to try the mushrooms: they might be dangerous. Later,
when followers of Timothy Leary set up a large and rather commercial
group in Mexico to experiment with LSD, both Pat and Leonora were
scornful because their real interests did not depend on hallucinogens but
were far more esoteric in nature.

Some of the impetus for Pat's spiritual journey goes back to the beginning of Arthur's Mexican posting and her readings at that time. It was
also evoked by a highly significant dream she had shortly after meeting
Khushwant Singh in New York on 14 November 1960. She had dreamed
that she was walking along the sand with a companion when she saw before her something "highly ceremonial and medieval" – a group of people, dressed in strange archaic clothing, forming dense circles on the
sand, in which those on the outside ring of the circle held instruments
that were a cross between a violin, a kite, and a bow and arrow:

> They were curious instruments with yards and yards of black
> string from which the bow (violin) or arrow (bow and arrow) was
> launched. As we approached I was vaguely aware that we were
> intruding into some secret rite and became uneasy. And I indeed
> learned of this quite directly the next moment by receiving exactly
> on the crown of my head, a bow? arrow? kite? – which hit with

such delicacy that I at once knew the immense skill of the man who
could so incredibly control his stroke – as well as the immense gen-
tleness of the man who "shot" me.

Pat recognized at once that this was one of Jung's numinous "transformation" dreams, because it was highly charged with emotion.

Because the protagonists in her dream wore old-fashioned Lapp costumes – which Jung would associate with the archaic – it suggests reaching down to the fundamental level of the psyche, which Jung had
discussed in *Memories, Dreams, Reflections.*[56] Recalling Jung's suggestion in *Psyche and Symbol* that dreamers should draw their dreams, Pat
began to do so, and she records that she felt compelled to put strings of
black cord on the arrows. The arrow suggests the homing arrow in
A.J.M. Smith's poem "The Archer" (a poem which Pat knew and liked),
but the implications are very different. For Smith, the homing arrow
symbolizes death and the grave; but for Page, the homing arrow suggests birth and transfiguration.[57] That in Page's dream the phallic arrow
hits the crown of the dreamer's head suggests some of the reading (and
talking) that she and Carrington had done together, especially with reference to Leonora's favourite symbol, the Tree of Life, which symbolizes
the universe and cosmos in macrocosm and man in microcosm. The
kether, or crown of the tree, also stands for the crown of the head of
man. This is the point at which man and the universe intersect – where
the infinite rays of light from the Ain Soph Aur, or the light of creation,
touches the kether and brings man and the universe into being.[58] In Jungian terms, Page has had an initiation dream; it seems to be associated
with mind and consciousness, and so connects the dreamer with the
larger spiritual universe.

Seen in this perspective, the dream seems to signal a change in Pat's
creative psyche. Indeed, a few days later she recorded this fact, noting
that she had been very depressed but her dream had changed this. "I have
been down a long way since being in New York this time ... Dead country – below everything. Kushwant's arrival seemed part of a stirring in
the black depths ... I felt and feel rather as a bulb must feel when it begins to sprout."[59] This dream clung to Pat's imagination, and some years
later it gave birth to one of her finest poems, "Another Space," which begins, "Those people in a circle on the sand / are dark against its gold,"[60]
demonstrating the power of imagination to project the dream-state into
a new energy described as "love" – literally, into "another space."

A few years later, in 1963 and 1964, a number of sequential avenues
coalesced as Page's readings in philosophic sources began to merge. Page

was now in her forties, and as we have seen, Jung had observed that people of her age sometimes become "stuck" until their psyches regenerate. Specifically, Pat was seeking "a way." Ouspensky, paraphrasing Gurdjieff, states that a guide to the way is essential: "The moment when the man who is looking for the way meets a man who knows the way, and is willing to help him is called the first threshold, or the first step." The seeker cannot go up the stairway by himself but only with the help of the man who is his guide. "*The way* begins only when *the stairway* ends."[61]

Ever since reading Campbell's book, *The Hero with a Thousand Faces*, Page had seen herself engaged in a quest for the way. After her dream in April 1961, she had reread Alain-Fournier's *Wanderer* and noted in her diary the need to "start a new map"; but like Alain-Fournier's protagonist, she had "almost no facts to put on it – nothing *known*."[62] During her four years in Mexico she set up a kind of self-directed reading course by working her way through Jung's *Archetypes of the Unconscious, Psychology and Alchemy* and his autobiography, *Memories, Dreams, and Reflections*. Leonora gave her a copy of M.A. Atwood's *Hermetic Philosophy and Alchemy*, which Pat read with "utter fascination." She also reread Suzuki's *Introduction to Zen Buddhism*,[63] which she had first read in New York in 1960, and some notes taken by a friend from a lecture given by the Indian guru Krishnamurti.

By June 1962 she was making her way through Ouspensky's *In Search of the Miraculous: Fragments of an Unknown Teaching* (1949), the record of his eight years as Gurdjieff's student, learning his practices of self-development. To a large degree Gurdjieff, Ouspensky, and Maurice Nicholl were all concerned with the development of consciousness, which Ouspensky terms "the Fourth Way." He posited three traditional ways of development: the Fakir (the Sufi tradition), the way of the Yogi (Hindi and Sikh traditions), and the way of the Monk (Christian and Buddhist traditions). Gurdjieff, by combining all three approaches, had evolved a Fourth Way.

Pat liked Ouspensky, but she still found Jung more interesting and returned to Jung's *Psychology and Alchemy* and *Archetypes of the Unconscious*. She added to her reading list Gerhard Adler's *The Living Symbol*, Maurice Nicholl's *The Mark*, Aldous Huxley's *The Perennial Philosophy*, and Gurdjieff's *All and Everything*, a supposedly autobiographical book. What she gleaned from much of this reading was a sense of a number of ways in which one could achieve higher consciousness. For example, in 1962, when reading Adler on Jung in *The Living Symbol* (1961), Pat wrote to Jean Fraser: "If I were rich and Adler available, I think I would go to him ... because I have been convinced that we are composed of autonomous parts which need to meet. And I'm damned *I* know how to bring them together."[64]

Pat learned that one of the Gurdjieff disciples, a man called Henri Tracole, would be visiting Mexico City. "For some time I have been looking for some kind of a way. One is always told if one wants a way, one will make itself available. *This* way has appeared. Whether or not it is mine I can only go and find out."[65] But the visit did not go well. Tracole tested Page and found her wanting. He said that Gurdjieff taught "'self-remembrance' – but mostly we don't remember ourselves at all. That one had to ask: 'Who am I?' but not mechanically, really trying to discover." Tracole tried pushing her a little. But Page resisted stoutly. He then suggested she was not ready for a guide. "I suggest you go on reading," he said. This is not an unusual response, but Pat was angry and upset at his rebuff. When she described what had happened, Leonora proposed she turn this experience into increasing her own strength and purpose, for no matter how much one might desire a certain goal, there is always a part of the personality that resists.[66]

In January 1963 Pat met Stella Kent, a friend of Eleanor Lincoln, who had been a former Harley Street physiotherapist – a sturdy little woman with white hair and bright blue eyes. Page liked her. "She has an aftertaste stronger than you would guess in the moment of being with her. She appears balanced & intellectual. Not that the latter is essential but she seems my kind of a person in a way ... She seems in no way to play upon one's emotions. Yet a whirlpool commences."[67] Stella knew Gurdjieff's work well and also practised Subud, the Indonesian mystical practice in which a spiritual exercise known as *lahitan kejiwaan* opens the practitioner to the power of God. Despite her reservations, Page attended several lahitans and at one experienced a sense of great peace, but ultimately the emotional and generally formless atmosphere of the lahitan made her feel uncomfortable.

In early April "Bapak," the Indonesian founder of Subud, Muhammad Subuh Sumohadiwidjojo, and his wife Ebu came to Mexico City to give a lahitan. The session schedule was disorganized, and the two practitioners acted somewhat capriciously by not turning up on schedule. Nonetheless, two weeks after their visit Pat experienced a significant "birthing" dream: "Dreamed last night that I – as I am today – was in a passage that was very crowded & narrow. (It was much as Alice would have felt when she grew too big for her surroundings.) I thought how queer it was that it should have been made so small. And then, in the dream, it occurred to me that I was being born."[68] An important dream, it is reflected in some of Page's later fiction, particularly the stories in *A Kind of Fiction* (2001). It also suggests that she was becoming aware of a change in her consciousness, perhaps generated by the reading and meditation she had been engaged in for the last three years.

It was about this time that Stella Kent shared with Pat a series of notes written by Idries Shah, an Afghan living in London who wrote on Sufi subjects and was beginning to be described as a new prophet of the Fourth Way. Shah was writing a book and had shared the first chapters with Stella. These described the inhabitants of an island, some of whom possessed higher knowledge and others who were unwilling to receive it. Pat found the concepts intriguing, and Shah wrote well: "He has an exactness that is like good poetry."[69] But although she was impressed, Sufi thought did not yet assume prominence in her life.

In December 1963, Arthur gave Pat, as a Christmas present, René Daumal's *Mount Analogue: An Authentic Narrative of Non-Euclidean Mountain Climbing* (1959, translation). Daumal was associated with Gurdjieff and surrealist circles. His book is an allegory in which he convinces us that the real ascent of the mountain is within us. Mount Analogue does not exist in the physical world, and the pilgrims who set out to find it, renouncing all else, succeed only when "the invisible doors of that invisible country had been opened for us by those who guard them."[70] The book's introduction is by Roger Shattuck, who remarks that Daumal understands that the basic act of consciousness is a disassociation of the "I," or the self, from the exterior world. The division of man and nature in *Mount Analogue* is meant to indicate this disassociation. However, Shattuck argues for a responding, contrary rhythm, one in which "the pure consciousness expands again into all things, experiences the world subjectively once more."[71] The two steps are essential but man must return to the universe.

Mount Analogue describes the trials of the journey of those who fall by the way and of those trusty souls who find their "peridams" (small crystals) – an indication that they are on the right track – and eventually arrive at the mountain to start their climb. But at this point the book ends abruptly. Daumal, who was writing in the final stages of tuberculosis, stopped in the middle of the penultimate chapter. Before his death, he described the ongoing plot to a friend, explicating the most important principle of the ascent: to reach the summit, travellers need to understand they must proceed from encampment to encampment. Before setting out for the next level, they must prepare for those coming after them, who will occupy the place they have left. This accords with Gurdjieff's injunctions. The last chapter, containing this information, was to be titled with Gurdjieff's requirement of self-knowledge: "And you, what do you seek?"

This book was influential. It inspired Remedios Varo to paint *Ascension to Mount Analogue* (1960), one of her more important paintings, which depicts an androgynous figure on a pilgrimage. In the foreground is the bare-headed pilgrim with the wind behind him/her. Using the robes as sails, he/she floats along the great curve of space and water towards the spiral-pathed Mount Analogue. Varo's biographer, Janet Kaplan, argues that the work, undertaken by the artist in the last decade of her life, was encapsulated in the "journey as metaphor." Among Varo's many surrealist paintings of characters on wheels undertaking journeys is *Vagabond* (1958), in which a male figure sets out on a journey in a kind of carapace, travelling on wheels. These paintings were exhibited while Pat and Arthur were in Mexico.

In the spring of 1963 they gave a dinner at the embassy residence for Kathleen Fenwick (1901–73), curator of prints and drawings at the National Gallery of Canada. Several artists were invited, including Carrington and Varo. At the last moment, the Irwins added recent visitors from Canada: Zena Cherry and her husband Westcott. Zena was a newspaper woman, later the writer of a society column in the *Globe and Mail*. That night she wore some wonderful Italian shoes with wheels on them, which Varo immediately claimed as her own in voluble and aggressive Spanish: "They're my shoes; you've got to give them to me." Despite Pat's entreaties, the astonished Cherry would not relinquish them.[72]

Whether or not Pat knew Varo's painting of Mount Analogue, she seems to have responded to the book itself. Daumal's closing question, "And you, what do you seek?" intrigued her. A painting from May 1961 bears this as its title (though it was probably applied later). It is a question that asks one to confront and understand one's own deepest desires and hopes. Pat also responded to some of Daumal's ideas about analogy, ideas that she had found in Jung and Gurdjieff. Later, in her essay "Traveller, Conjuror, Journeyman," she spoke of attempting to copy something "in a dimension where worldly senses are inadequate."[73] Before Pat left Mexico, Leonora gave her a small, smooth, oval stone – a "peridam," she called it, recognizing that Pat was beginning to climb her own Mount Analogue.

Earlier, in mid-January, Pat had seen a performance of the Fu-Shing Chinese opera, which she described as "one of the outstanding events of my life."[74] The performance, depicting the Han dynasty, had various levels of interpretation. The principal actor wore a headdress with two long antennae-like pheasant tail feathers that moved in the air with his movements. His "immensely intricate clothing" also moved, with every step "exactly calculated to set the maximum number of things in move-ment," which produced "a kind of whirr on the stage ... creat[ing] an extraordinary many-colored vibration." What made it so remarkable, Pat wrote, was the "impression that it was 'upstream' of the senses" for both the dancers and the audience. She was "seeing colours and hearing sounds and watching movements in another 'space' ... as if, by sudden alchemy, your senses have all gone up an octave." She felt she had en-tered a world at the molecular level and that the dancers, too, "move[d] as in a molecular world – as if they had no notion of our being able to see them. As if unobserved and intent upon a ritual."[75] Clearly, this perfor-mance resonated with Page's readings. Her references to "vibrations" and the "molecular" world echo the language of Ouspensky's inter-pretations of Gurdjieff on the Fourth Dimension.[76] This experience lies behind one of Pat's most striking paintings from this period, *The Dance*, with its vibrant movement and Chinese vermillion background.

During their three-year posting in Mexico the Irwins had received a num-ber of visits by prominent Canadians: Howard Green, a Conservative MP; Pierre and Janet Berton; Florence Bird; Earle and Esther Birney; Bruce Hutchison and his wife Dorothy – along with the English writer J.B. Priestley and his third wife, Jacquetta Hawkes. Rose and Aunt Bibbi also came for an extended visit in April 1962. Rose purchased one of Leonora's designs of a tapestry depicting a "big curious creature that looks like a horse and has two horns – on an orange background."[77] (In later years, it hung near the entrance staircase to the Irwins' house in Victoria.) When Lord Louis Mountbatten came in February 1964, near the end of their posting, he and Pat had an interesting, and surprising, discussion about the miracles of the New Testament.

In April 1964 Pat and Arthur left Mexico and set out to drive home to Canada, driving their own car. Arthur was now sixty-six. He had worked a year beyond his official retirement date, and there was no hope of a further government appointment. He had arranged to meet his old friend, the best-selling author Bruce Hutchison, in Washington on his way home. Arthur and Bruce had begun as young reporters together and on one occasion, when Bruce had lost a position at a crucial point in his life, Arthur had helped him to find another. Now Bruce returned the favour. He brought along to their Washington meeting Richard S. Malone, who owned two newspapers in Victoria, British Columbia. Malone was looking for a publisher for the Victoria *Daily Times* and the *Daily Colonist*. He offered the job to Arthur, who said that he and Pat would consider it.

CHAPTER 11

Victoria
Finding Oneself, 1964–1969

On 13 October 1964, Pat and Arthur climbed aboard "The Canadian" in Ottawa for the five-day journey on the Canadian Pacific Railway to Vancouver. After crossing the prairies, they experienced a snowstorm in Banff, viewed the Rockies through the dome, and did a loop-the-loop through the spiral tunnels beyond the Great Divide, which separates the watersheds of the Pacific Ocean from those of the Atlantic and Arctic oceans. The next morning they wakened in British Columbia "to a green world and wet. All the leaves and grasses soft and the whole rinsed in milk – mountain, forest, water and [sea]gull."[1] From the Vancouver station, they took a bus to the ferry that carried them through the Gulf Islands to Victoria, where they stayed a few days at the Empress Hotel to get their bearings.

It had been a long six months since the Irwins had left Mexico. After their leisurely drive back to Canada by way of Washington, they had gone to Ottawa for debriefing. They stayed in the East during the summer, visiting their respective families, while Arthur considered Richard Malone's offer to manage his Victoria newspapers. It was a tempting offer, a position in his area of expertise, but he hesitated before committing himself. Finally, the couple agreed to accept. Pat's chief regret was that it would mean leaving her mother and Aunt Bibbi, who were still living in Ottawa, and leaving a Gurdjieff group that she had begun to attend. But she took much pleasure in "the idea of a house of one's own," along with Chico – the little dog that Eleanor Lincoln had given her – and regular painting.[2]

By 18 October the couple were registering their impressions of Victoria. It was very English: a fact brought home to Pat by the expensive tweeds worn by women and to Arthur by the Union Jack and the British-inspired red ensign flying from many houses. He later remarked that he was viewed by some Victorians as a "rabid nationalist" and "an alien."[3] His managerial role with the two Victoria newspapers placed him at the cultural heart of the city, but his liberal and nationalist views stood out in a dominantly conservative community. Twenty years earlier, Pat had reached a similar conclusion about conservative Victoria when writing her poem "Election Day."[4]

But in October 1964 she did not feel this way immediately: "The people are so sweet – responsive & warm ... And it's so beautiful. We've got a house & move in the day after tomorrow. I am so grateful at the thought of a headquarters after all this trundling about."[5] Their new home was at 3260 Exeter Road in Oak Bay, a few blocks from the water. It was a pleasant one-storey house, with a living room full of light, a lovely old tree in front, and many Garry oaks in the back. There were three bedrooms on the main floor, one of which Arthur insisted Pat take for a study, and a large finished basement. But it was expensive, $38,000, and to pay for it Arthur sold some shares of MacLean Hunter stock which he had kept from his days as editor of *Maclean's*, and Pat contributed her savings of $10,000.

This was the first home of their own. The living room and dining area was L-shaped, with big windows facing east and west and a large natural-stone fireplace. To the right of the fireplace they built bookcases for their favourite poetry and art books. One of the first women friends Pat made in Victoria was Shushan Egoyan, of Ego Interiors, who supplied the material for curtains and slipcovers for their old furniture and helped them place some of their art work. Shushan, a painter, brought an artist's eyes to home furnishing. Pat picked a heavy white fabric for the sofa and armchairs and soft green for the drapes. In front of the fireplace there were matching chairs. It was a lively, welcoming room, with many boldly coloured artifacts from Mexico and Brazil. There were two big red bulls to the left of the fireplace and a black ceramic vase filled with large, vivid paper flowers. The cream walls were covered with paintings from their travels and from artists Pat had known in Montreal. Pat had a sense of having come to a resting place in her journey. When she was young and still living at home she used to think, "My life will start when I can make decisions on my own." Later on, when she became an adult, she thought, "My life will start when I get married." Now, in Victoria, she wrote in lipstick on the bathroom mirror, "This is it."[6]

Victoria was still a small city with little industry, but it had a theatre, an art gallery, and two or three interlocking artistic circles. Downtown consisted of three department stores: Eaton's (formerly Spencer's), Hudson's Bay, and Woodward's. There were few restaurants, and social life revolved mainly around visits, dinners, and parties in family homes. Victoria College had become the University of Victoria a year earlier and was the recognized centre of culture. The English Department was largely becoming staffed by British and American professors. A Canadian, Roger Bishop, head of English in the early sixties, had attempted to develop a department that was one-third Canadian, one-third English, and one-third American by hiring Canadians at the master's level and encouraging them to take further training. But later heads insisted on PHDs,[7] and unfortunately there were few qualified Canadians available. Canadian literature was still a wallflower and considered non-existent by many.[8]

Early in November, when Pat was checking out Munro's Books on Yates Street, she came across J.B. Priestley's *Man and Time* (1964). When she had met Priestley in Mexico, he told her about this book. Pat wanted to buy it, but she had no money with her. She asked the clerk if she could have it on credit, giving Alan Crawley's name as a reference. The young woman replied, "Oh, I know Alan Crawley, how do you know him?"

"I write," Pat said.

"Who are you?" the young woman asked.

"I write as P.K. Page." As she spoke she saw that the young woman, Alice Munro, went bright pink in the face. Pat learned that she wrote short stories but did not know how deeply Munro admired her work. Munro thought she might faint: "I had read her poetry and I could not believe that this person was flesh and blood ... in front of me."[9] Later, she recalled, "What was really important to me was just her existence as a good Canadian writer whom I read in the forties and fifties when Canadian writers were so rare. Her example, the sense that it was possible."[10]

In December 1964 Pat invited Alice and her first husband Jim Munro to their house to meet the publisher Jack McClelland. Well into Arthur's Scotch, McClelland warmed towards Munro and suggested she write a novel. When Pat later reminded McClelland in a letter that he had agreed to publish a new book of her selected poems in 1966 and a proposed Brazilian journal the next year, she added, "Have you thought again about Alice Munro to whom you throw out the possibility of a book? I mention it as I admire her very much and think you might find her a good investment."[11] It was a shrewd letter, especially the reference to possible profit, a perennial concern with McClelland. But Munro had already been approached by Ryerson.

When Pat and Arthur first came to Victoria, they were too busy getting settled to think very much about literary and artistic friendships, but Pat soon found that some of her old friends – Max Bates, Alan Crawley, Floris McLaren, and Myfanwy Spencer (now Spencer-Pavelic) – were either ill or unavailable. Alan was now old and frail, and Floris had suffered a severe stroke; Pat had known Myfanwy in the forties and thought she would be a friend, but the artist now spent the winters in New York and did not return to Victoria full time until 1969. Maxwell Bates, the expressionist artist her mother had encouraged as a boy, was settled in town, but his allegiances were elsewhere, with the existing Victoria artistic circle. This circle, as Pat learned, was dominated by an expatriate Englishman, Robin Skelton, a new English professor at the University of Victoria, hired in 1963.

Pat met Skelton in early November 1965 at the home of Tony Emery, another English professor. Her first impression was positive: Skelton was knowledgeable and keen about his discipline and wrote poetry himself. However, as time progressed, her opinion changed. A brash young Englishman, raised on T.S. Eliot and W.H. Auden, Skelton tended to dismiss Canadian poetry – and poets – out of hand. Then too, Pat had been out of Canada for a decade, and Skelton's first impression of her, a diplomat's wife in tweeds, may have been that she was a Sunday poet and painter – a judgment he would soon be forced to revise. Friends of both poets recall that Skelton was protective of his turf and was prepared to fight for it. He prided himself on his knowledge of poetry and art, and came to view her as a potential rival.[12]

Pat now realized she was back in small-town anglophile Victoria, where she had been so miserable during 1944–45. What was worse, she felt cut off from the creative life of the city. After so many years abroad, where she had functioned as an artist and a poet without even knowing the language of the countries in which she practised her art, she was ignored in Victoria. The sense of creative isolation was combined with a kind of reverse culture shock. After the cosseting of diplomatic life, she had to learn all over again how to keep house, cook, and shop for food – all the while living without a literary community. It was a double whammy. "Life *is* lonely," she confided to Jori Smith.[13] She couldn't shake off her unhappiness and became acutely depressed. An ink-on-rice-paper drawing from early in this period depicts skeletal bare trees, the remnants of a dead forest: *Is This Gray Ash All That Is Left?* the title asks the viewer.

Arthur was deeply worried. He thought that if Pat could see some of her good friends in Mexico, especially Leonora Carrington, it might cheer her up. In the summer of 1965 he was asked to go to Bogota, Colombia, to represent the Canadian government at a conference, and he encouraged Pat to accompany him as far as Mexico. She was eventually persuaded, and in Mexico she enjoyed Leonora Carrington, Eleanor Lincoln, Mimi Fogt, and Laura Villasenor, four good friends. They laughed and talked, took pleasure in being together – but Pat's depression remained. Then, at Eleanor's house, she met a woman who had studied with Ouspensky. Her face, Pat thought, was rather like Virginia Woolf's, and it had a kind of translucence (she was dying of liver cancer). They managed to find two hours to talk together before Pat left Mexico. Although the woman spoke very clearly and well about why she had joined Ouspensky and why she had left, something else was happening as she talked. As Pat later told Jean Fraser:

> It's very difficult to explain. She gave me a totally new concept of love as if I had never understood the definition before; she made me understand "waiting" – that nothing can happen outside its own time (and I mean understand emotionally – I had "understood" it intellectually before). And she made me understand that one aspect of the work is being happy – not apparently happy – but happy. That you cannot "work" from unhappiness. None of this was spoken, so I don't know how it was conveyed. She seemed to have the quality of "seeing" you and knowing who you were.[14]

It was one of the most profoundly moving encounters that Pat ever had. Her diary reference to "the work" is significant. Gurdjieff had taught, and Ouspensky had interpreted, that "the Work" – the development of one's own higher consciousness – was primary. Now her attention was to be directed to the same concerns in the work of Jung and Idries Shah – and in the company of a new friend in Victoria.

⚏

When Page returned to Victoria, her depression had lifted somewhat. She wrote to William Toye, editorial director of Oxford University Press: "We're just back from Mexico and I feel almost human again. God how one needs one's own kind of animal to cavort with."[15] Fortunately, another such person was at hand. On her return, in late summer or early September 1965, Page saw an exhibition of prints by Pat Martin Bates. On impulse, she phoned the artist to say that her name was Pat Irwin and she loved her work. Bates promptly responded, "You don't fool me at all P.K. Page." She invited her to come over to the Canadian army camp in Esquimalt where Bates lived.[16] An hour later Pat knocked on her door and Bates opened it to see an attractive dark-haired woman in a green tweed suit with a small dog at her side.

The two women sat around a kitchen table for an afternoon discovering multiple connections. Bates had worked in Ottawa for the magazine *Canadian Art* and had done the paste-ups for Florence Bird's 1963 article on P.K. Page's paintings, and Bird had told her, "This is the work of the poet P.K. Page who paints under the name of Pat Irwin."[17] Bates had gazed in wonder at "all these beautiful paintings." Her "eyes just glazed over because there was so much joy in them."[18] Like Page, Bates had grown up in Saint John, New Brunswick, and although Page was eleven years her senior, they might have met in the book section of the department store where Pat had once worked. Both were newcomers to Victoria and had not yet built up a circle of new friends. They soon discovered that each of them was "on a spiritual quest."[19]

Both women were interested in Carl Jung and Sufism. In 1965 Page and Bates were reading both Jung and R.A. Nicolson's translation of the Persian poet Rumi. For over two decades, Pat had been subscribing to the Bollingen editions of Jung's *Collected Works*. Now, in 1965, she was reading Jung's *Man and His Symbols*, from which she derived "great joy,"[20] and Idries Shah's newly published *The Sufis* (1964). She had underlined the introduction to Jung's thought in *Psyche and Symbol*, which discusses Jung's search for the essential self and its relation to dreams and symbols. Shah's book was not traditional Sufism, usually defined as an ascetic and mystic spiritual order associated with Islam: as we shall see, it was a little more free-spirited and directed towards raising consciousness. Shah claimed that Sufi thought had preceded Islam, and he was interested in the Sufi poets – whom he quoted at length – and the possibilities they offered for spiritual development. Now, with Pat Bates (as she had done with Leonora Carrington in Mexico), Pat talked daily on the phone, discussing not only art and painting techniques but also philosophical issues.

Shushan Egoyan's interests were similar to Pat's, and they too became close friends. Not only was Shushan a painter, but she was familiar with traditional Sufi practices from her childhood in Egypt. Dark haired, petite, and very intense, she saw in Pat an alert, intelligent woman, with a sense of humour: "She was ignited."[21] Shushan and her husband Joe were recent immigrants who had expected to teach painting in Canada, but a chance encounter with Don Adams, an early importer of Scandinavian furniture (who provided a meeting place for artists in his Victoria showroom), led them to become proprietors of a furniture and design business. The Egoyans had two children. Atom, who became a well-known film director, and Eve a concert pianist. Both credit Pat and Arthur Irwin for inspiration and help during their formative years.

Shushan and Pat often went to movies and art galleries together – Shushan was part of a group associated with the Nita Forrest Gallery. As Page later recalled, "She had this highly-evolved, developed, visual sense. She has a sense of my paintings, my drawings. She and Pat [Bates] are about the only two people here, I think, who know anything about my drawings."[22] Pat Bates and Shushan Egoyan were very important to Pat because they provided unconditional friendship and encouraged her painting, the only part of her artistic self that was functioning freely at the time.

Occasionally, Pat met Alice Munro in the Snug, a lounge in the Oak Bay Hotel, for a lunch or a drink, until Alice left Victoria in 1972. Alice sensed that Pat felt isolated, but at the time she did not know why. Years later, reflecting on Page's difficulties with Skelton, Munro marvelled at how remarkable she was: "She could have just let go and allowed her art to fall by the way. But, well, she couldn't, because her gift wouldn't let her. I didn't realize … that Skelton had it in for her … that must have been hurtful." Munro added that Skelton held "literary Thursdays" but "never paid any attention to us" – Munro and her husband Jim – although in the seventies Alice Munro was emerging as one of the most important Canadian writers.[23] Pat took being excluded from the creative world personally, but she was not alone in her resentment; Margaret Atwood has expressed similar views about this decade.[24] In many Canadian English departments, the British and American professors who, like Skelton, were for some time arbiters of taste, considered Canadian writing to be of little consequence.

Pat had turned back to art, perhaps because – as she had found when on the diplomatic circuit – it was easier for her to paint than to write poetry in a literary vacuum. In March and April 1964 two of her works were included in "Surrealism in Canadian Art," an exhibition that appeared in four Ontario venues, including the London Public Library and the Agnes Etherington Gallery, Kingston. They were *World Within World*, a black-and-brown ink study of what seems to be an embryonic egg-like form cradled in a tangle of bushes, and *Who in This Bowling Alley Bowl'd the Sun?*, an oil pastel of a huge golden ball dominating a darker green-blue background.

In the fall of 1965 Colin Graham, director of the Victoria Art Gallery, saw Pat's work in the Irwins' home, and he invited her to include some of it in a December exhibition at the gallery along with two other local artists – Herbert Siebner, then considered the strongest of the Victoria artists, and Michael Morris, a young up-and-comer. The show was opened with some pomp on 7 December by the lieutenant-governor, Major-General George Pearkes, Lionel Page's old classmate from Red Deer, who joked about knowing both Page and Morris as children. Later in the day, Graham phoned Page to say that she had a "hit on her hands."[25]

Pat had contributed nearly forty pieces to the show from her years in Brazil and Mexico. They were arresting. Many of the paintings were in bright colours – red, yellow, and green – and revealed the artist's familiarity with numerous media and techniques: watercolour, oil, oil pastel, gouache, gold leaf, and ink. In some paintings, the colours were richly applied; in others, the artist had scratched through gesso; and still others were delicate sketches in pencil. There were also several etchings. Her titles were miniature poems in themselves. *Who in This Bowling Alley Bowl'd the Sun?* was filled with a golden sun; *A Kind of Osmosis*, a luminous egg set into clouds of red and green, had been executed in oil pastel; *Shape of the Flower Is Yellow* was a deep verdant emerald with orange-yellow flowers; *And You, What Do You Seek?* was of a bird, never seen on land or sea, scratched into tempera.[26]

On Sunday afternoon, 12 December, Page went to the Victoria Art Gallery with her niece and nephew, Wendy and Tim Page, and learned she had "sold 10 out of the 28 [paintings] for sale. Siebner none. Michael Morris one." This may have been an unfortunate introduction of Pat Irwin (as she signed her paintings) to the resident artists of Victoria, for she may have done too well. After reading "a rather dirty review from the local critic," she reported in her diary: "He is the great Siebner admirer ... I can't say I liked it, but feel it's sufficiently unfair to be unimportant."[27]

Pat was also unable to sustain her old friendship with Myfanwy Spencer-Pavelic. A rift developed between the two women, despite goodwill on both sides. When Pat and Arthur first came to Victoria, Myfanwy had invited them to dinner to meet her husband, Niki Pavelic. The two men did not get on. Arthur, taciturn at the best of times, was positively silent during the evening and conversation dried up. Myfanwy, in turn, was a little in awe of Pat's intelligence. The friendship languished. Later, in 1969, when Myfanwy returned to Victoria permanently and was, with Skelton, one of the organizers in 1971 of a group of artists called the Limners, P.K. Page was not invited to join. This was a serious omission that Spencer-Pavelic later regretted. She said that her awkwardness in response to Page's intelligence had superseded her "best self." She came to realize there were "things I didn't do, that under other circumstances I know I would have done. I wasn't myself maybe with P.K."[28]

Robin Skelton was now a highly influential figure in Victoria, at the centre of the literary and artistic groups that Page would normally have expected to join. He launched a Thursday-evening "at home" for Victoria artists and writers; and in 1967, at the University of Victoria, he and a colleague, John Peter, started a literary magazine, the *Malahat Review*, subtitled *An International Magazine of Life & Letters*. Later, he became head of the university's Creative Writing Department, where he was in a position to invite writers to visit the city. Page recalled, with some pain, that she was never invited to Skelton's Thursday socials or proposed for the art group or asked to submit poems to the *Malahat Review* (but in 1971 Skelton did invite her to read at the university).

Skelton was the art critic for the Victoria *Daily Times*. In 1967 he reviewed *Hundreds and Thousands*, the journals of Emily Carr, when it was launched in Victoria. He did not like the book's lack of apparatus and damned the publisher, Clarke, Irwin. His review was titled "Emily Carr Book an Insult – Don't Buy It,"[29] the latter phrase taken from the body of the review.[30] As representatives of the publisher Clarke, Irwin were present for the launch and as Arthur Irwin published the newspaper in which the review had appeared, Pat and Arthur found themselves providing tea for a distressed Bill Clarke and a furious dowager, his mother Irene Clarke. Arthur managed to mollify both, but as publisher of the paper he had a word with Skelton. Relations deteriorated further, and Irwin eventually fired Skelton. Friends of both parties later speculated that Skelton had mistakenly believed that Arthur Irwin had some connection with Clarke, Irwin.[31]

Blocked by Skelton in Victoria, Page looked beyond the island's horizons to George Woodcock, the editor of *Canadian Literature*, a journal established in 1958 by Roy Daniells, head of English at the University of British Columbia. She had written to Woodcock on 22 February 1965, thanking him for a CBC program on T.S. Eliot that she had enjoyed "tremendously." Woodcock responded by asking if she had something for *Canadian Literature*. Although his primary interest had been British writing, he admired a number of Canadian writers, including A.J.M. Smith, F.R. Scott, Al Purdy, Margaret Atwood, and Page herself.[32] Page's correspondence with Woodcock was important to her. Their letters continued regularly for the next two decades, and after a formal beginning – Mrs W.A. Irwin to Mr George Woodcock – by the seventies they had become Pat and George. Woodcock provided encouragement, stimulus to write, a place to publish, advice on contracts, and the occasional admonition. Pat contributed fine poetry, interesting copy, and the occasional drawing for *Canadian Literature*. She also supplied paintings for Woodcock's Tibetan refugees project and wrote supportive letters to the Canada Council for his books and creative projects.

Arthur had no patience with Pat when she moped around and felt sorry for herself at being cut off from the artists and poets in Victoria. "Make work your friend," he said,[33] and urged her to go back to the poetry manuscript she had earlier discussed with Jack McClelland. After a long spate of writer's block, Pat began to write poetry again as she prepared her manuscript for McClelland. The reasons were twofold: putting the book together stimulated her, and she was reading new poems by Margaret Atwood and rereading Anne Wilkinson – she felt a kinship with both poets.

A.J.M. Smith had selected five of her poems for his *Modern Canadian Verse: In English and French* (published by Oxford in 1967): "Element," "Images of Angels," "Puppets," "Man with One Small Hand," and "Arras."[34] Two years earlier, he had written to her: "I wish I could persuade you, or goad you, into writing. It seems to me that you could paint *and* write, and indeed, write some poems to illustrate the paintings (not vice versa)."[35] This comment may have encouraged Pat to include her drawings in her new poetry collection. Smith had agreed, once again, to read her draft manuscript, and she felt that he had made some marvellously generous suggestions. On 15 March 1967 she sent her finished manuscript to McClelland and Stewart.

Cry Ararat! – P.K. Page's third poetry collection, beautifully produced – was published in November 1967. The book contains a half-dozen of her drawings – minutely complex extravaganzas – while the book's jacket reproduced in gold on a dark brown background the bird in her painting *And You, What Do You Seek?* This allusion to *Mount Analogue*, where Daumal poses the same question and asks us to confront and understand our deepest selves, points to the themes of many of the new poems that follow. Of the fifty-seven poems in the book, fourteen were new, and the rest were extracted from *Unit of Five*, and from P.K.'s solo collections, *As Ten, As Twenty* and *The Metal and the Flower*.

Part one of *Cry Ararat!* has two subsections, "Landscape with Serifs" – containing new poems (including "After Rain") from Pat's years abroad – and "Dreams of Caves and Winter," which represents her association with Canada in "white poems," including her fine early poems "Stories of Snow," "The Snowman," and "Photos of a Salt Mine." The two sections of part two include her poems of the 1940s about childhood, adolescence, and wartime – for example, "Generation," a pivotal poem about the transformation of herself and her peers by the Spanish Civil War and the Second World War; and two love poems to Scott, "As Ten, As Twenty" and "Love Poem." Part three – whose two sections are entitled "Permanent Tourists" and "Personal Landscape" – includes two of Page's most anthologized poems, "The Stenographers" and "The Permanent Tourists," along with "The Metal and the Flower" and "Arras."

Poetry, with its wonderful multiple resonance, can suggest so much more than what is being said at the level of word or line. Part four consists entirely of the long title poem, "Cry Ararat!," which I read (in part) as a response to Scott's "Lakeshore."[36] The latter was first published in *Northern Review* in 1950 when Scott and Pat were moving apart as lovers, and it was included in his collection *Events and Signals* (1954), which he sent to her with the dedication "To Pat, who saw it happen." *Events and Signals* included "Message," a poem meant as a message to Pat, whom he no longer saw. Indeed, as Scott recognized in his diary on 1 December 1956, even though Pat was then visiting in Montreal, "we can never communicate, unless an accident throws us together, or unless our poems speak."[37]

In "Lakeshore," Scott's narrator looks underwater "through windows" as he evolves from "a tall frond that waves / Its head below its rooted feet" until, with other swimmers, "we rise / Upon our undeveloped wings / Toward the prison of our ground / … This is our talent, to have grown / Upright in posture, false-erect, / A landed gentry, circumspect." The last stanza of the poem is evocative:

> Sometimes, upon a crowded street,
> I feel the sudden rain come down
> And in the old, magnetic sound
> I hear the opening of a gate
> That loosens all the seven seas.
> Watching the whole creation drown
> I muse, alone, on Ararat.[38]

Scott's imagery has multiple meanings: man is an animal who stands on his hind feet and thus is "false erect." But the latter term also has secondary sexual connotations – "false erect" is followed in context by "sudden rain." Some readers might also hear, in this last allusion, overtones of the anonymous medieval English lyric, "Oh Western Wind" ("Oh Western Wind, when wilt thou blow? / The small rain down can rain? / Christ, if my love were in my arms, / And I in my bed again").[39] When Scott first heard of the title and publication of Pat's book, all of these complex associations came to the surface in his diary entry of 20 April 1968, in which he speaks of a dream about sitting on a sofa with Pat, of a renewal of their sexual intimacy, and of the publication of *Cry Ararat!* He also notes the connection between the title of Pat's book and his poem "Lakeshore": "I have seen that her next book will be called *Cry Ararat!* – where I mused alone."[40]

Ararat is the traditional name for the mountain (actually, two mountains in present-day Turkey) where Noah's ark landed. Pat's "Cry Ararat!" – a dream poem, centring on water – takes up Scott's biblical image in the first lines: "In the dream the mountain near / but without sound. / A dream through binoculars / seen sharp and clear: / the leaves moving, turning / in a far wind / no ear can hear." This is a positive poem, in which the poet becomes one with nature:

So flies and blows the dream
embracing like a sea
all that in it swims
when dreaming, you desire
and ask for nothing more
than stillness to receive
the I-am animal,
the We-are leaf and flower,
the distant mountain near.

Pat remembered when Noah for the second time sent the dove out of the ark, "the dove came in to him in the evening; and, lo, in her mouth was an olive leaf ... so Noah knew the waters were abated from off the earth" (Genesis 8:11). Towards the end of the poem, she wrote: "Will the grey weather wake us, / toss us twice in the terrible night to tell us / the [dove's] flight is cancelled / and the mountain lost? O, then cry Ararat!"

The leaves that make the tree by day,
the green twig the dove saw fit

to lift across a world of water
break in a wave about our feet.[41]

The last lines of the poem are Blakean: "A single leaf can block a mountainside; / all Ararat be conjured by a leaf." It also evokes Tolkien's parable about art, "Leaf by Niggle," and the apprehension of all of nature through a single leaf.

Pat began the poem in Ottawa in the early 1950s, shortly after her break-up with Scott and her marriage to Arthur – but she could not complete it. It *was* eventually completed, however, in Victoria in the mid-1960s. After reading Daumal's *Mount Analogue*, a new understanding came to her. One can infer that the title of her jacket painting has been turned back on her reader: "And you, what do *you* seek?," with the emphasis on the second *you*. "Cry Ararat!" is, among other things, a response to Scott's godlike irony: she affirms (as does Tolkien) that only innocence, love, and faith can bring about rebirth, or (in Daumal's terms) the ascent of the elusive mountain. But Pat titled her book hesitatingly, asking Arthur Smith: "Do you think *Cry Ararat!* is really a possible title?"[42]

Completing and publishing a manuscript is a draining business. Pat wrote briefly to Jori Smith, "My book is out but But what? Just BUT."[43] It received excellent reviews from major critics, including A.J.M. Smith, who wrote to Pat thanking her for a book that was "doubly precious for the poems and the paintings." He considered her imagery new, exciting, and satisfying, and saw that she was achieving a new simplicity in fine poems such as "Cry Ararat!" which, with the exception of "Arras," he considered the most beautiful and deeply significant of all.[44] Floris McLaren, Pat's closest friend in Victoria in the mid-1940s (who had suffered a severe stroke and whose critical faculties were impaired) thanked her for a copy of *Cry Ararat!*, inscribed generously to Floris and her husband Mac.[45] Alan Crawley was now old and frail and spoke with great difficulty. Nonetheless Pat felt a huge debt of gratitude to these old friends who had helped her with her poems. The book was dedicated to Arthur, whose support was "unfailing," and to Alan Crawley.

Cry Ararat! had later ripples of influence. The filmmaker Atom Egoyan recalls seeing P.K. Page's book among his mother's collection. As a boy he was drawn to it because he hoped it might be some key to his national identity. Ararat figures strongly in Armenian cultural nationalism because in 1932, at Greater Ararat, a boundary was drawn displacing the Armenian tribes and favouring the Turks. When Egoyan was a student at Mount Douglas high school, Page came to read from *Cry Ararat!* This led him to an important discovery about the power of art. After a childhood of seeing Page in the world of books and art – "that wonderful atmosphere she created around her house ... it was so odd to see her juxtaposed in this banal ... fluorescent, nondescript space" of a cinder-block school building. The sight shocked him. Despite this, he said, "her poetry was able, in my imagination, to take me right back to the space that I connected her with ... She was able to transport herself ... with her art." He found Arthur, too, to be a powerful and compassionate interlocutor, "asking me to give my interpretation of things and how I felt ... There was such a sense of romance around his vision of Canada." This combination of Page's art and Arthur's political commitment may have had some influence on Egoyan's subsequent career as a filmmaker, especially of his films that are politically and nationalistically structured, such as *Ararat* and *Calendar*.[46]

The publication of *Cry Ararat!* in 1967 coincided with Canada's centenary. The year-long celebration of national identity inspired a wave of Canadian nationalism in both politics and literature. Even conservative Victoria was on the cusp of change; the hippie revolution was in full swing, and the women's movement was just getting off the ground. Prime Minister Pearson established the Royal Commission on the Status of Women to "inquire into the status of women in Canada ... to ensure for women equal opportunities with men in all aspects of Canadian society." Page's good friend Florence Bird was named chair of the new commission, and their letters chart Pat's growing interest in Canadian women writers and their lives as professional women. The naturalizing of Canadian culture, especially writing, was quickly becoming national policy. The Canada Council established a program to fund readings by Canadian poets and writers. And as more qualified Canadian candidates became available, university English departments slowly began to hire more Canadians and more women.

In Victoria, Robin Skelton began to profess an interest in Canadian writing, and in an article in 1967 he offered qualified praise for F.R. Scott, "a poet of the middle slopes." Scott's poetic techniques, Skelton wrote, were derivative of international poetry: "Nevertheless on the Canadian scene he is an important figure, he represents emotional discipline, intelligence, and craftsmanship, and must be reckoned one of our four or five finest living poets."[47] This was indeed an about-face and Pat promptly wrote to A.J.M. Smith: "I think Skelton is being forced now into trying to become a Canadian."[48]

She was probably right. The new nationalism generated by Canada's centenary had a transforming effect. By the end of the sixties, the old Victoria that Pat had experienced in the forties and early sixties was slipping away. Indeed, the old pro-British Canada began to change after the April 1968 election of the charismatic Pierre Elliott Trudeau. Trudeau, a protégé of Scott's, took as his mandate the repatriation of Canada's constitution from Britain. He was a keen observer of the arts, and the year after he became prime minister he told a reporter, "I used to enjoy *Tamarack [Review]* very much – in the time of P.K. Page and [A.M.] Klein."[49]

In the spring of 1969 Margaret Atwood was invited to read at the University of Victoria. Page was not invited to Skelton's reception for Atwood, but she attended the public reading. When she had read Atwood's *The Circle Game* (1966) in 1967, she had written to Smith: "I find the images so like mine and the poems are quite individual."[50] After the reading at UVic, Atwood phoned Page and visited her on Exeter Road. Atwood sat cross-legged on the living-room floor and read the tarot for Page. She later wrote Page acknowledging an affinity: "I greatly enjoyed seeing you, as you know, and had some sense of parts of one's mind being a shared area … with you [it is] images transformed to myths."[51] The two poets became friends and remained friends to the end of Page's life. As Atwood has remarked, "P.K.'s importance as poet, cultural figure, and inspiration to many younger poets (including me, way back when) cannot be overestimated."[52] Certainly, by the end of the sixties, Page was an important influence on many younger Canadian poets, writers, and filmmakers, including Atwood, Munro, Michael Ondaatje, and Eli Mandel. In the following decade, Marilyn Bowering, Atom and Eve Egoyan, Rosemary Sullivan, Jane Urquhart, and Patricia Young can be added to the list.

In 1969, for the celebration of the tenth anniversary of *Canadian Literature,* Woodcock asked Page to write specifically on her images and the relationship between her poetry and painting.[53] This led to an important article, "Questions and Images," one of the first statements of her emerging interest in Sufi and philosophical thought.[54] Page reviewed the last two decades of her life, spent in Australia, Brazil, Mexico, and Canada, and the relation of place to personality and identity. One of the dismaying effects of her time abroad had been the realization that she had stopped writing – but she had begun to draw. In Mexico especially, she had become aware of something beyond the tangible world; at that time her only access to poetry was through drawing and the dream. She began to think that "drawing and writing were not only ends in themselves ... but possibly the means to an end which I could barely imagine."[55]

≡
⋯

Years later, reflecting on her 1965 Mexico trip and her brief meeting with Eleanor Lincoln's friend who was dying of cancer, Page thought "it was about that point that the old business of Sufism quickened ... That was my life saver."[56] Earlier, when Pat was living in Mexico City, Stella Kent had told her about Idries Shah and given her three unpublished papers by Shah, which became the first chapter of his book on the Sufis. Now, in the late sixties, Pat was still in touch with Stella, who was living in Wiltshire, England. Their correspondence covered Sufi ideas, Idries Shah, and the Jungian psychotherapist Alan McGlashan's *The Savage and Beautiful Country* (1966), which Stella had sent her. This book raised more questions: "Who or what is the Dreamer within us? To whom is the Dreamer talking? ... Can projected images be manifested as dreams?" These again drew Pat's attention to Jung's focus on the life of the mind and especially the function of dreams in directing the psyche.[57]

Shah's book, *The Sufis* (1964), incorporated many of the ideas that Pat had absorbed from Jung and Gurdjieff, and had an introduction by Robert Graves, a poet she admired. Her copy is dated 1965 and is heavily annotated; however, the earliest notes on *The Sufis* in her journals and correspondence is in 1967, which suggests she was reading it seriously in that year. Graves describes the Sufis as "an ancient spiritual freemasonry" which has an "Oriental flavour." He points out that the devotee is offered a "secret garden" for the growth of his understanding, yet unlike the mystic does not withdraw from ordinary life but is enlightened by actual experience.[58] The dynamic force in Sufism is "love" rather than aestheticism or the intellect. Human love is one of the stages towards divine love. And Shah, when defining Sufism, points out that the word itself contains in "enciphered form, the concept of Love. Also encoded ... are the following words, which convey an abbreviated message – above; transcending; correcting ... Sufism, then, is a transcendental philosophy, which corrects, is handed down from the past, and is suitable to the contemporary community."[59]

Shah taught by parable, and his first chapter, "The Islanders: A Fable," is about an island populated by the El Ar people, most of whom are "asleep" and please themselves, but a small elite are entrusted with the secrets of swimming and shipbuilding to effect an escape from the island when danger threatens. At the end of this fable, the voice of Shah, the writer, intercedes, telling us that the story continues because there are still people on the island. He reminds us that Sufis use verbal ciphers to convey their meaning. If we rearrange the letters in El Ar, the name of the original community, we find it is an anagram for "real"; and "Please," the name adopted by those who opposed efforts to escape, is an anagram for "asleep." Like the teachings of Jung, Ouspensky, and Gurdjieff, Shah's message is that much of humanity is "asleep" in a "prison" they do not recognize, where people please themselves, where only a few look for escape, and still fewer actively work to make escape possible.

This story of the islanders, Pat felt on first reading, had a resonance "that was always just beyond my grasp."[60] She enjoyed Shah's writing and his quotations from the Sufi poets. But she did not claim, then or later, to be a Sufi herself: "Being interested in Sufism is not like saying that you're interested in Christianity. Or not like saying you're a Christian. I would never say I was a Sufi, because I'm not a Sufi. I don't even know who the Sufis are in the world. They never proclaim themselves with the exception, I think, of Shah."[61] Nonetheless, for Pat, Shah's book was the beginning of a spiritual odyssey that continued to the end of her life.

As early as 1966 she and her good friend Pat Martin Bates were meeting with a small Sufi-studies group. Shah had apparently told Stella Kent that if P.K. Page wanted to develop her interest in Sufism it was necessary for her to organize a group.[62] Bates recalls that it came into existence when P.K. advertised in the local newspaper for people of like-minded spirit who wanted to achieve a higher level of consciousness. Six or seven people replied, and the first meeting was held. There was no leader, but P.K. functioned then and later as the group's "deputy" – the person who was sent information, books, and cassettes by the Centre for Sufi Studies in London and received instructions on how to use them.[63] The group – which now included Shushan Egoyan, Dorothy Hodgetts, and Harley and Nancy Schwartz – discussed Sufi tales and undertook projects. It was thought that individuals could not learn alone, as true learning came only from instruction from the "wise" and from group interaction. During periods when the group was not actively learning, activities such as weaving or rug making were recommended to facilitate the group's development.

By 1968 the members of the group had found a place of their own at Signal Hill, in a derelict red brick building belonging to the Department of National Defence. They rented a small suite of two rooms for a nominal sum and they cleaned it up with the help of a number of volunteers. Romany Miller helped to find wooden benches and Shushan Egoyan made beautiful pillows from Persian material to make the hard benches more comfortable. P.K. helped with the painting of the walls, as did a Victoria artist, Robert DeCastro. The space became a kind of creative centre. There were two rooms; one served as a pottery and painting studio and was used by Pat Martin Bates among others, and the other was used for meetings. Shah provided printed material that gave directions for group meetings, and a steady stream of books from Octagon Press followed, many edited or written by Shah, including Shah's *Recollections, The Way of the Sufi, Tales of the Dervishes*, and *Thinkers of the East*. These books contained traditional Sufi tales, and some, such as *The Magic Monastery,* provided contemporary commentaries by Shah. One of the clearest statements of the Sufi quest is found in an article in *Thinkers of the East*: "Man ... originates from far away; so far, indeed, that ... such phrases as "beyond the stars" are frequently employed. Man is estranged from his origins ... [but] has the opportunity of returning ... He has forgotten this. He is, in fact, "asleep" to the reality. Sufism is designed as the means to help awaken man ... Those who waken are able to return, to start "the journey" while also living this present life.[64]

Pat's investigation into Sufism continued with a visit to England in 1969. On 10 April she caught an overnight flight to London. Stella Kent met her at the airport and they drove to Stella's cottage in Wilcot, Wiltshire. A few days later, on 14 April, the two women travelled to Langton Green, where Idries Shah lived on forty acres that had originally been the site of the local squire's house. The property enclosed the village green and a number of small cottages that were being converted to new ends, including an office and housing for Octagon Press, founded by Shah. They stayed there for several days.

Shah lived very comfortably – his estate had been initially purchased with gifts from his admirers. P.K. and Stella were invited for dinner with the Shahs and several others. Shah was then in his late forties, an elegant Afghan with an aquiline profile, dark hair and skin, and "splendid long fingers" that gestured as he spoke. Page found him attractive and very funny: he affirmed that God is in laughter. It was a merry evening. Shah "talked a blue streak" and took his guests on a tour of the grounds to see the various activities underway, including wine making. Page found the house and furnishings "very rich"; the rooms were hung with colourful paisley in tall panels, and there were piles of white sheepskins on the floor.[65] She and Stella took part in the daily life of the community, and a few days later Pat peered at the extraordinary octagonal building on the grounds that was used for sound research. Shah explained that it was an

exact replica of two ancient buildings, one in Spain and one in Afghanistan. At various points in the building, the acoustic properties changed,
and as they did so Page found that the sounds created a kind of scale.

Later she tried to reconstruct Shah's conversation and her responses.
He would sometimes talk for hours "in order to rest something, some
part of his listeners – to stop something happening in them." She was
conscious that something was happening within herself but didn't know
how to describe Shah. "He leaves you without words. You feel he knows
everything there is to know about *you* and that he knows you know he
knows – *yet* in some extraordinary suggestion of shame. You can look
at him feeling unjudged – but known. Shah spoke of one being unable to
control or change certain things, of human powerlessness. How one
could only say, 'I am oppressed. Help,' when there was nothing you
could do." In Shah's presence, Page found herself saying silently, "I am
oppressed. I am oppressed. Help," recognizing her need for emotional
release but not how to go about it.[66]

On leaving Langton Green, Pat went to London, where she met the
distinguished phonetician Dennis Butler Fry – associated with the sound
research in the octagonal building at Langton Green – who was teaching at University College London. Pat appreciated most his conversation
about the kind of work conducted by an organization he had established,
the Institute for Cultural Research, known as ICR. "He spoke of the
teaching as an organism – its outer skin related to the world around us
– ICR for example." Fry emphasized the importance of imparting some
Sufi concepts through ICR, and Pat was willing to take part in the
process. From her conversation with him she concluded, "It's a matter
of developing the intuitive part of me and trusting it."[67]

On 1 May Pat was on her way back to Victoria, assessing the whole
experience. One of the after-effects of the trip to Langton Green was that
she became much more conscious of coincidence, especially relating to
people around her. A striking example occurred while she was still in
London. She had contacted Gertrude Hermes, the sculptor whom she
had seen daily in Montreal several decades ago in the company of her old
friend Maggie Davies. Pat had agreed to have lunch with Hermes, and
as they drove together to the restaurant, Hermes stopped the car to allow
a woman to cross the street. Astonishingly, the pedestrian was Maggie
Davies, whom both had last seen in Montreal. A number of such coincidences reinforced Pat's sense of the necessity of being awake to the
larger significance of such patterning.

That year, for her birthday on 23 November, Arthur gave Pat a copy of Doris Lessing's novel *The Four-Gated City*, possibly at her suggestion. She would have learned at Langton Green that Lessing was an active follower of Idries Shah and indeed had reviewed *The Sufis* when it was first published. Lessing defines Sufism as "the inner secret teaching that is concealed within every religion."[68] She points out that Sufi thinking, or perceiving, can only be understood in terms of itself and that the form of Shah's book (teaching stories, aphorisms, ciphers) is meant to demonstrate this. At present, man is caught in his own thought patterns. But Sufi thinking sees man as evolving towards a certain destiny and developing new "organs" as they are required. Lessing reiterates Shah's arguments that major figures and ideas of the past – including alchemy, Chaucer, Dante, Jung's Collective Unconscious, and Freud's ideas about sexuality – were anticipated by Sufi thinkers. Even granted the great contribution of Arabic learning, Shah's claims – echoed by Lessing – are large. Nonetheless, Lessing's concluding remark is accurate: "[A]rtists will profit most by this book."[69]

Page already knew Lessing's work. Over Christmas 1965 she had read Lessing's *African Stories* with great pleasure, recognizing in them the same qualities she had admired in Katherine Mansfield: "How minutely she observes & how exactly she describes."[70] As Pat began to read *The Four-Gated City* in early December 1969, when the Irwins were travelling by air to Ottawa, she could not put the book down. It resonated with her own concerns. It was as if the writer was speaking to her in person about all the issues – political, social, sexual, the present state of the world – that concerned her. When she arrived in Ottawa, Pat did not phone the many old friends she had intended to contact because she was lost in the book and continued to read.

Lessing's book begins with Martha Quest, an independent young woman from the colonies who is much like the young Page herself, highly observant, seeking love, and above all a purpose in life. The working out of Martha's destiny draws upon ideas that Page already knew from *The Sufis*. In *The Four-Gated City*, as in Shah's parable of the islanders, most people are "drugged and asleep," but the locale is now specified as post–World War II England.[71] It is a world of growing violence where the traditional English values of democracy and freedom are threatened by naysayers, extreme conservatives who support oppressive government control. The "saving remnant" is initially associated with Mark Coldridge, a novelist, along with his "mad" wife Lynda, whose madness allows her to see into the truth of things, and Martha herself, who has an initial vision of a golden city. In this parochial Britain, misfits are persecuted by labelling them "Communist" and jailing them, or by diagnosing them as "mad" and placing them in hospitals. But Lynda has developed new evolutionary organs, the ability to hear others think.

When the inevitable catastrophe strikes and it is necessary to leave the British Isles, it is discovered that there are others, working underground in secrecy and silence (as in Shah's parable of "The Islanders"), who had "a kind of trust vested in them on behalf of mankind"[72] and all along have been planning to escape. Social realism characterizes the first part of the book, but by the end of *The Four-Gated City*, especially part four,[73] which is preceded by Sufi epigraphs from Rumi and Idries Shah stressing evolutionary changes in consciousness, we have moved into science fiction.

It is a disturbing novel because the personal journey of the protagonist, Martha Quest, is also a racial and cultural journey. Pat, who saw the author as a teacher, learned from Lessing's narrative that "we can't go much further than our race has already gone. Individuals can but the majority of individuals can't. We're in a train, this civilization we're in is a train and we're in one of those carriages, hurtling along. And unless we have some extraordinary extra powers, we can't get out of that train."[74] For her part, the great attraction of Sufi teaching was perhaps that it offered her the possibility of help for the human journey – extra powers, extraordinary ones.

After finishing *The Four-Gated City*, she wrote to Jori Smith: "Read Doris Lessing's 'The Four-Gated City' & see if you don't think it was written by a magician too. An absolutely INCREDIBLE book. I am still unable to walk straight from its impacts."[75] Initially, Page may have responded to the consciousness of the young Martha walking the streets of London – as she had once done – excited and savouring a rich culture. She also understood the life that the older Martha had to lead, nurturing others. Finally, Martha's descent into madness may have touched on Page's memories of her own bouts of extreme depression. Page thought that Lessing held nothing back in her modern treatment of sexuality, as in Martha's relationship with Jack or her affair with Mark. But for Page, the primary interest of the book was its Sufi message: the importance of the journey, the necessity of a saving remnant, the evolving of new powers, and the capacity to connect with a higher reality.

Pat's years in Victoria in the mid-1960s were rich and fruitful, though not always in ways she expected. She affirmed to herself, and to critics, that she was both a writer and a painter, and demonstrated that the two activities were interrelated. Although she was hurt and puzzled by her exclusion from the literary life of Victoria, this forced her to look outward to the larger Canadian literary scene. As the quality of the poems in *Cry Ararat!* solidified her reputation, both to established writers and to emerging poets, she reached outwards, over the heads of Victorians, and established a national reputation. At the same time, she reached inwards to the Sufi teaching that was to influence all of her future thinking and writing, ignoring – at least for the present – that the charismatic Shah had some questionable qualities and that his views on Sufism were ignored or rejected by many Sufi scholars.[76]

CHAPTER 12

Victoria
Inner Events, 1970–1979

> I cannot tell much about [outward events], for it would strike
> me as hollow and insubstantial. I can understand myself only
> in the light of inner happenings. It is these that make up the
> singularity of my life.
> C.G. Jung, "Prologue," *Memories, Dreams, Reflections.*[1]

When first reading Jung's autobiography *Memories, Dreams, Reflections*,
Pat Page had written out the above sentences as an epigraph to her copy
of the book, perhaps because they reflected her own sensibility and
situation. In the sixties, she had been frantically busy with external
happenings, but the truly important events for her were internal, and the
same would be true in the seventies.

On 1 January 1970, she learned from Mike Doyle, a young New
Zealander recently hired at the University of Victoria, that the poet and
critic A.J.M. Smith would be lecturing there on 26 March. She was
delighted at the thought of seeing her old friend "jolt UVic into the
realization that there are Canadian poets and that there is Canadian
poetry ... neither of which they seem able to absorb through the thick
filter of English and American Professors."[2] Nonetheless, the seventies
brought about a revolution in schools and universities that was caused
by the recognition that Canada had a culture and a literature of its own.
Students voted with their feet by flocking to "Can Lit" classes to study
Canadian poems and novels in addition to the traditional English or
American offerings, largely because of poems, novels, and short stories
by brilliant younger writers such as Margaret Laurence, Alice Munro,
Margaret Atwood, and Michael Ondaatje. P.K. (as she was now known
in poetry circles) was already acknowledged by established poets such

as A.J.M. Smith and critics such as Northrop Frye. Now, some of the brightest of the younger generation were beating a path to her door.

For P.K., this was the decade in which she spoke publicly of an inner journey that was to last the rest of her life. In her essay in the September 1970 issue of *Canadian Literature*, she announced her search for a new "map": "How to go? Land, sea or air? What techniques to use? What vehicle?"[3] In April 1970 the vehicle for her journey had been poetry, and I happened to be at hand. I had long admired her poems, and having recently been appointed to the English Department at Simon Fraser University, I asked Al Purdy, then a visiting poet, if he would phone P.K. and ask her on my behalf to read to my first-year Canadian poetry class.

She accepted (for many years believing that the invitation had originated with Purdy) but was very, very nervous – this was her first public reading, and she feared she would make a fool of herself.[4] Consequently, she prepared very carefully, timing the poems, practising at home, shopping for the right outfit. She went with Pat Bates to Hudson's Bay in Victoria, finally settling on an English wool skirt and cape in bright purple for her reading.[5] She asked Bates to come along to SFU and record her session so that she could hone her skills. On 2 April, also dressed in an English wool suit, in lavender, I met P.K. at the English Department. As we passed one of the futuristic purple panels in SFU's Academic Quadrangle, she joked that we blended in, disappearing into space.[6]

She read eloquently, old favourites such as "Adolescence" and "The Stenographers," familiar anthologized poems, but also, at the end of her reading, a new poem, "Another Space," based on a dream, which we all found very strange. The poem begins with an "I," implicitly female, who sees a group of people moving in circles on the sand:

> Those people in a circle on the sand
> are dark against its gold
> turn like a wheel
> revolving in a horizontal plane
> ....
> Those people in a circle reel me in.

In the sixth verse, the "headman" takes out what seems to be an arrow and shoots

> to strike the absolute centre of my skull
> *my* absolute centre somehow
> with such skill

such staggering lightness
that the blow is love.

And something in me melts.[7]

It will be recalled that in New York in 1960, P.K. experienced the dream that led to the poem. As retold in "Another Space," the poem becomes a vehicle for psychic integration and higher consciousness: "where now a new / direction opens like an eye." In effect, the action (and writing) of the poem is a kind of spiritual initiation that brings the poet to a consciousness of another dimension. But this was not clear to P.K.'s audience in 1970. When I asked her about the poem, she responded by giving me a draft copied in black ink on yellow paper. I tacked it up on a bulletin board in front of my desk, and there it stayed. For P.K., her first public reading was a revelation. She found that she loved reading her poems and meeting students. She wrote to Smith telling him that "the Simon Fraser event was not too bad … I would certainly accept any reading that came my way on the basis of that experience."[8] As she later explained, "I've got to write some more so I can continue to read!"[9]

This was the decade when Canadian literature suddenly arrived. The first national organizational meeting for the League of Canadian Poets – founded by Frank Scott, Louis Dudek, and Ralph Gustafson – was held in 1968; the first Canadian Poetry Festival was held at Blue Mountain, near Collingwood, in 1972; and the first meeting of the Association for Canadian and Quebec Literatures, co-founded by Robin Matthews, myself, and others, was held in 1974. P.K. was no longer isolated in Victoria, because in 1972 she had joined the League of Canadian Poets, and the league had received a grant to sponsor readings at Canadian universities. Two years later, the Canada Council began its own program of sponsored readings. Both groups invited P.K. to read across the country. She read beautifully. Her voice was clear and resonant, her poems outstanding: each reading was a performance. After one reading, novelist Howard O'Hagan wrote, "It was more than a reading. It was a scene, a ritual, a priestess at the task: the celebration of The Word."[10]

In February 1971 even Robin Skelton invited her to read at the University of Victoria; later in the spring she was reading in Edmonton, and in the fall at Dalhousie University in Halifax. The next year P.K. and Margaret Atwood undertook for the league a joint poetry-reading tour to Lethbridge, Alberta, and Prince George, British Columbia. P.K.

considered Atwood "probably our most talented writer ... only 32 and astonishingly on top of things. Very cool indeed. Very funny. And very generous." She told Florence Bird that although Atwood was the star of the reading circuit, "she began each reading by saying how much she admired my work and how when she first began reading, some of my poems were and still are among her favorite poems. Very sweet of her."[11]

In March 1972 P.K. was invited to read at the University of Calgary. Here her old friend Elizabeth "Fuzz" Carlile, who was now living in England but was visiting Canada, got in touch with her. Also in March she learned from a newspaper that Pocaterra, the former owner of the Buffalo Head Ranch, had just died. This brought back memories of her childhood: "Poky ... lent us horses and joined us in the evenings of camp fires – complete with Indian headdress and tomtom. He was probably the first man who made me realize there was something in the sex thing after all. I sat mute and admiring as he sang and beat his drum."[12]

Through her membership in the League of Canadian Poets, Pat began to meet younger writers, including Michael Ondaatje. In 1972, in Edmonton, they were standing together in line at the cafeteria getting breakfast, at a meeting sponsored by the league: "And he took a cranberry juice, or he took an orange juice, I can't remember, one of us took a cranberry juice, and I said, 'Christ's ichor.' I wasn't at all sure how to pronounce the word, I'd never said it before' ... And Michael said, 'Let's sit together at breakfast.' So we sat together at breakfast, and were sort of tongue tied with each other, and that's when it began, something established itself between us." Ondaatje is an intensely private poet, but this was the beginning of a long and close friendship with Page. He had earlier picked some of her poems for an anthology,[13] and he later stayed with the Irwins in Victoria; and she also wrote letters of reference for him to the Canada Council in support of poetry grants.

P.K. was rapidly becoming a celebrity. Merle Shain wrote an article for *Maclean's* magazine in October 1972 entitled "Some of Our Best Poets Are ... Women" – a novel idea, as the ellipses suggest. The article featured photographs and discussions of Atwood, Page, and Margaret Avison. P.K., echoing her reading in *The Sufis* about mankind being asleep, had quoted Shah: "The important thing is to evolve. To become fully awake is the major task."[14] P.K. was also encountering the new feminism. When writing to Florence Bird about Atwood, considered a feminist, P.K. said that she had been reading a new book on feminism called *The First Sex* (by Elizabeth G. Davis) and had "become much more sympathetic to Women's lib lately. Had a kind of breakthrough in seeing. Graves's *Greek Myths* which I have read ... for years suddenly helped me see the whole thing. God knows I've read his *White Goddess* too. But one goes about blinded by one's conditioning."[15]

Around June 1970, P.K. seems to have encountered Frank Scott at a meeting of the League of Canadian Poets. We know little about this occasion, but the two poets began to write to each other again. At a later meeting of the league, in Edmonton, they were glimpsed sitting on a bench, holding hands. In February 1972 P.K. wrote, "Frank: all coincidences point in one direction. How can I disobey so many signs? Can we try to meet?"[16] They did meet, in February 1973, and P.K. wrote a poem, possibly shortly afterwards, which she later published as "Beside You":

> 1.
> I lay beside you
> soft and white as dough
> put by to rise
>
> I rose and rose and rose ...
> 3.
> My body flowers
> in blossoms
> that will fall
> petal by petal
> all the days of my life[17]

Frank Scott, when receiving the poem, wrote, "Ever lovely" beside it. Later, in 1999, P.K. published a short story in a little magazine about two older lovers meeting after a long and painful separation, who simply lie beside each other on a hotel bed, "subliming," the woman says.[18]

In March 1974 P.K. undertook a tour to the Maritimes and stopped off in Quebec to see Jori Smith in Montreal. On the way back to Victoria, as the plane stopped at Winnipeg, she settled down to write Jori: "The Maritime 'leg' of the trip was a killer – buses, ferries, planes, bad beds, etc. But *very* interesting ... I've seen so many people on this trip it's unbelievable ... friends from the beginning of time."[19] The following month I took a group of graduate students from Simon Fraser University to meet P.K. in Victoria. She was kind to them, made them lunch, and answered their questions about *Preview*. She said she was trying to get a new story on paper, a kind of apocalypse that she had experienced in a dream; this seems to have been the genesis of her allegorical tale "Unless the Eye Catch Fire ..." That afternoon, P.K. took us to visit Alan Crawley, who was living in Sooke in near poverty on the outskirts of Victoria; in profile, he was an emaciated old eagle, hunched over his chair.

Earlier, P.K. had asked librarians in Special Collections at the University of Victoria library to buy Crawley's correspondence with poets such as Jay Macpherson, Margaret Avison, and others whose poetry he had nurtured through *Contemporary Verse*. Her request was turned down. Soon after, at a Victoria reception where she had a few drinks, she bumped into Skelton and learned that he had had some say in the decision. Skelton told her that he considered Crawley's papers "of no historic value at all."[20] P.K., furious, took him to task: "'I said, I don't know what, 'Go and boil your head,' or 'Go back to England ...' The whole party stopped and Skelton and I had a rip-snorting row, publicly."[21]

Skelton's account, which appears in his *Memoirs of a Literary Blockhead*, omits Crawley's papers and says that one day at a reception at the Provincial Museum, "I was attacked by P.K. Page. I had met her previously ... on her first arrival in Victoria and had asked her to do a reading. She told me she no longer was writing poetry, but concentrating on drawing ... Her attack came at me out of the blue. Why was I inviting no Canadian poets to read? It was dreadful. This was Canada, did I realize? And so forth ... I was told later ... that she was aggrieved I had not asked her to read herself, but ... I truly believed that P.K. was no longer interested in poetry."[22] This is disingenuous. P.K. was not writing poetry when she first met Skelton in 1964, but she had published the splendid *Cry Ararat!* by 1967. Despite this, Skelton did not invite her to read at University of Victoria until four years later, after the climate of literary nationalism had accelerated.

Margaret Atwood, in contrast, was a great support.[23] She had earlier sent P.K. a copy of *The Journals of Susanna Moodie*, inscribed "with admiration." In early spring 1973 Atwood wrote to her, "I would adore to work with you on a book; I'd even like to write an introduction. I feel very strongly that you should be widely available in paperback if possible and I agree with you that your stock is high and likely to get higher."[24] Years later, Atwood said that she had first read Page's poems as a student at Victoria College, University of Toronto, in the late 1950s, and found that some of them "blew the top of my head off."[25] In the sixties, when she was facing obstacles to becoming a woman writer in Canada, Atwood was reading P.K. Page, Margaret Avison, and Jay Macpherson: "It was comforting as well as exciting to read these writers

... It was ... like a laying on of hands, a feeling that you could do it because, look, it could be done."[26]

A number of Atwood's early poems show Page's influence.[27] The essence of P.K.'s own early poems "Photograph" and "Landlady" is echoed in Atwood's "This Is a Photograph of Me" (*The Circle Game*, 1966) and "The Landlady" (*The Animals in That Country*, 1968). One of Atwood's most memorable images – the epigraph in *Power Politics*, "you fit into me / like a hook into an eye / a fish hook / an open eye"[28] – may be compared with Page's "Element," which ends with the implied woman speaker as victim, a fish on a line: "silently hurt – its mouth alive with metal."[29]

In 1973 Atwood began editing a paperback collection of P.K.'s prose that included both the early novel *The Sun and the Moon* (1944) – which gave the collection its title – and a group of short stories. Atwood found the novel "one of the weirdest books I've read for some time ... The light it casts on male female roles, among other things, is chilling to say the least ... I think the final section [where the woman protagonist merges with a tree in the northern landscape] really works."[30] Atwood's edition, dated 1973, did not appear until February 1974 with the promised introduction, which notes that the early novella was a "romance" requiring from the reader a suspension of disbelief.[31] Reviews were astute. The *Globe and Mail* identified the title story as a "kind of contemporary tale by Grimm ... But the beautiful heroine is a kind of sorceress who quite unwillingly destroys the soul and the artistic genius of the man she loves."[32] Romany Miller, writing in the *Ottawa Citizen*, suggests a parallel between the young Page and her heroine when the latter is given the perception that "she has either to destroy Karl and obliterate her own identity in the process, or to direct her powers to another dimension."[33]

For *P.K. Page: Poems Selected and New* (1974), Atwood drew upon magazine publications as well as earlier books of poetry, explaining that Page is "a much more socially-oriented, much angrier poet than her previous 'selected' (*Cry Ararat*) [had] revealed." Most of the early popular poems were present, but in Atwood's edition they are given a context. As Atwood pointed out, "The poems on women and love, as well as the ones on social conditions, madness ... are of particular interest now."[34] Atwood speaks of Page as "a supreme artificer, an expert technician ... The danger has been to see her *only* as that, and I believe this collection rescues her from this fate."[35] The collection was dedicated to an enigmatic "S.K." – Stella Kent, who had introduced P.K. to Sufism. P.K.'s letter, thanking Atwood for her work on the book, concludes with a cry

from the heart: "O God. Dreadful poetry. Clumsy. Lazy. Obscure as a result of clumsiness and laziness. But even so I appreciate the work you
have done, the thought you have given."[36] P.K.'s own literary standards
were always stringent.

Poems: Selected and New contained eighty-five poems. As forty-two
had been published in *Cry Ararat!*, approximately half were new and
presented in the last part of the book. They end with "Another Space."
With this book P.K. Page achieved new recognition as a major poet. Her
substantial body of poetry demonstrated integrity, artistic development,
and above all, human relevance. As one reader concluded, "She is a
poet whose work evolves towards a totality of experience."[37] Reviewers were astonished by the scope of her work – lyrical, complex, satiric
– by the depth of her understanding, and by her artistry. Alan Pearson
also recognized the implicit connection between the life and the poetry:
"[H]ers is the world of inner exploration. The poetry rises most naturally out of Miss Page's life. The poems are therefore a subterranean
autobiography."[38]

There was now a new sense of the dimensions of Page's work and of
her achievement. Even Patrick Anderson, her old rival from the *Preview*
days, found that "Another Space" belonged with her "metaphysical
best."[39] Eli Mandel, while affirming Page's status as a major Canadian
poet, said that this new collection provided not only fine poems but the
opportunity to understand "the achievement of a writer who has contributed significantly to what we have come to understand as modernism
in poetry."[40] He had earlier acknowledged Page's influence on his own
work,[41] and his judgment of her status was echoed several months later by
George Woodcock, who called Page "a major modern Canadian poet."[42]

A number of reviewers recognized a mystical side to Page's poetry,
notably Doug Beardsley, who remarked that in "Another Space" and
"Cry Ararat!" she is "a visionary poet ... The dream world of the unconscious is her central theme."[43] George Melnyk was struck by the difference between the early, alienated social poems and the hard-edged
personalism of her later poems, such as "Preparation": "go out of your
mind. / prepare to go mad." He was one of the few readers who wondered whether travel and "the infusion of new cultural mores ... shifted
her poetry away from the social to the deeply personal."[44] The consen-
sus was that Page had become a major poet worthy of international
recognition.

In late February 1974, P.K. undertook an extended reading tour that
began in Detroit (where she spoke of her art and her poetry), then back
to St Lawrence College in Kingston, to Loyola in Montreal, and on to

Charlottetown for a five-day swing of Maritime universities. She reported: "All the readings & talks have gone well so far. Tomorrow I go to London, ONT, & back the same night. Read at noon the following morning at York University."⁴⁵ In May she spoke at the Klein Symposium at the University of Ottawa, reading extracts from A.M. Klein's poem "Portrait of the Poet as Landscape" as well as her own poems. This was an important conference, part of the seventies' reassessment of Canada's modern poets. Irving Layton, Klein's former protégé, attended, as did Leon Edel (the distinguished biographer of Henry James, once the "office boy" of the *McGill Fortnightly Review*, as he liked to describe himself), together with his former office mates F.R. Scott and A.J.M. Smith.

Up to this point P.K. may have felt that her difficulties in getting established in Victoria and elsewhere were personal and related to Skelton, but it is probable that the Blue Mountain Poetry Festival, sponsored by the League of Canadian Poets and others and held at summer's end in Ontario in 1976, led her to see that her problems were shared by others. Over 150 poets and academics came to the festival.⁴⁶ There were three groups of readings, but the focus was on an exchange of ideas about a *Canadian* poetry. Opinions were vigorous, galvanized by a recent article in the *Globe and Mail* by an American reporter, who claimed that Canadians had become increasingly "xenophobic" about "foreign" (meaning American) influences on their culture.⁴⁷

Early in the proceedings, poet and critic Eli Mandel remarked, "There is a poetry explosion in Canada." Tom Wayman agreed, and added, "If you are a poet living in Canada [nationalism] comes up." Poets complained that it was difficult to get their poems published or heard in a market dominated by American presses. Academics complained that it was difficult to find a place for Canadian literature in English Department curriculums where English or American faculty predominated. It was the first wave of a new Canadian literary nationalism. At the end of the festival, participants were asked for their opinions. It is touching to read that P.K. said that for her the Blue Mountain gathering "overcame the loneliness of poets by bringing them together."⁴⁸

If P.K.'s poetry was one vehicle for the psychic journey, her visual art was another. At the start of the decade, and again in November 1971, she was working on a series of black-and-white octagonal drawings based on triangles, or "yantras" as Jung called them.⁴⁹ Made up of straight lines in black ink on white paper, they were difficult to draw.

Any irregularity of line spoiled the symmetry. But the precision of the task may have been soothing, because it distracted P.K. from Arthur's increasing ill health. Throughout their marriage she had supported his career and fitted in her poems and art wherever possible. But in 1970–71 he began to experience severe heart problems, which convinced him to retire from the two Victoria newspapers in June 1971. A year later he had a serious heart attack and, in the next three years, two bladder operations and a prostate operation. P.K. wrote to Florence Bird saying, "What goes on we none of us know. He is alright – but only that."[50]

Now, in fall of 1971, his recovery was slow and P.K. was in turmoil. She needed to keep her mind, and her hands, occupied. She wrote to Florence Bird telling her about her new drawings and included a copy of the autumn 1970 issue of *Canadian Literature*, which contained her essay, a poem, and a pen and ink drawing of "The Dome of Heaven," suggestive of the Persian art that she and Pat Martin Bates had been studying in the late 1960s. The essay, "Traveller, Conjuror, Journeyman," had grown out of George Woodcock's asking her to write about the connections between her poetry and her painting.

As she said, "With a poem I am given a phrase ... And that phrase contains the poem as a seed contains the plant ... Painting or drawing the process is entirely different. I start from no where ... The picture, born at pen-point, grows out of the sensuous pleasure of nib, lead, or brush moving across a surface." But what P.K. emphasized was not artistic process but the beliefs that animated both her poetry and her visual art. The act of creating leads to transportation – the entering of another world. Consequently, the eventual poem or painting are by-products. Writing and painting "are alternate roads to silence."[51]

Bird responded promptly, saying that it wouldn't take a Sherlock Holmes "to detect the Sufi influence" in P.K.'s essay, in which she had remarked, "At times I seem to be attempting to copy exactly something which exists in a dimension where worldly senses are inadequate." Bird asked her, "Did you write 'Traveller, Conjuror, Journeyman' before you were 'given' the octagon?" (It is possible that Idries Shah gave Page permission to copy the Sufi octagon as a figure for contemplation when she visited him in Langton Green in 1969.) P.K. had indeed written the essay before she left for England in 1969. And now a number of her new drawings were of octagons. Bird's letter continues: "I'm sorry 'Variations on a Theme' by Octagon can't yet be seen. Perhaps the time will come"[52] – P.K. had told Bird that she was signing her new artwork "Octagon."

The octagon is by definition an eight-sided geometric figure, but it has larger significance in both Sufi and Jungian thought. In *The Sufis*,

Octagon

Idries Shah says that the number eight is associated with bringing the world into being and that the "eight steps" of Sufi teaching are symbolized by an octagonal diagram.[53] In practice, Sufism offers a discipline for conducting one's life and, like Jungian individuation, for developing one's higher consciousness. I see Page's Sufism as being layered over her earlier readings in Jung. This is suggested in her comment, "A Sufi is an individuated man, to use Jung's terminology."[54] Jung defined "individuation" as the "psychological process that makes of a human being an "individual" – a unique, indivisible unit, or "whole man.""[55] Certainly Idries Shah's Sufism was directed towards individuation.[56] P.K. said repeatedly that she did not claim to be a Sufi. However, from 1965 on she read Sufi books as soon as they were published

Jung's *Psyche and Symbol* includes a discussion of his search for the essential self and its relation to dreams and mandalas – a mandala being a circular image that is drawn, or danced, for the purpose of assisting meditation. Frequently, the inner design of the circle is a "quaternity" (a four-sided figure) in the form of a square, a star, or an octagon.[57] P.K. had been actively seeking individuation for some time. In 1962, when reading Gerhard Adler on Jung in *The Living Symbol: A Case Study on Individuation* (1961), she had written to Jean Fraser: "I'd give an awful

lot to achieve individuation. But apparently one can't do much alone."[58]
Jung's process of individuation – or the achieving of higher consciousness
– is twofold: it is made up of "the spontaneously arising symbol," which
he calls "the *unifying* symbol," followed by an assimilation of its message into consciousness.[59] P.K. had followed this pattern in New York,
when she incorporated her dream of men dancing in a ring in an actual
drawing, and again in Victoria in the poem "Another Space," which depicts
the same symbolic action.

Sufism, "the transcending of ordinary limitations," is also associated
with psychic integration and higher consciousness. Mental activity and
specific exercises, under special conditions, can lead to what is called "a
higher working of the mind, leading to special perceptions whose apparatus is latent in the ordinary man."[60] When, in Mexico, P.K. had read
first drafts of *The Sufis*, she had found helpful, in her words, the "idea
that the meaning of the man is evolutionary and that time place condition and person all have to be right before any work can begin."[61] By
"work," P.K. meant the developing of one's own consciousness, the way
of individuation. She later said, "All my life I had looked for some kind
of spiritual way, and nothing ever pleased me; nothing ever satisfied me
… until I read Shah's teachings, if you call them teachings … nothing
had ever sounded absolutely right."[62]

It seems probable that the thirty-odd octagonal drawings that P.K.
produced in the early 1970s were developed as aids to contemplation, or
mandalas. The black-and-white nature of the drawings also has meaning. Shah explains in *The Sufis*; "Black … is associated with wisdom …
and white, too, stands for understanding."[63] According to a key included
in one of P.K.'s art folders, the first of these drawings was on the theme
of *Target*. In one of the versions of this drawing, the eye is drawn towards the centripetal centre of the drawing, while the title suggests the
homing arrow in "Another Space." One drawing, *The Four-Gated City*,
evokes Lessing's novel. Another grouping is entitled *Square*; like *Target*,
it consists of receding squares that travel by way of an octagon to a circle, again suggesting Jung's "squaring of the circle" – in his view, one of
the most important symbols of the integration of human personality.[64]
Near the end of the series, P.K. drew a new image of the Tree of Life that
unites triangles ("yantras") and squares to a circle by way of an octagon.
The Tree of Life, described by Jung as a transcendent symbol,[65] was important to P.K. In Mexico, she had drawn a plant version of the tree on
the back page of Jung's *Symbols of Transformation*.[66]

In Sufi thought, the octagon[67] is "almost like a circle, but with the
points of one life being part of the circle. Each a centre onto itself."[68] It

P.K. Irwin, black-and-white octagonal series, *Tree of Life.*

is this symbolism that lies behind ancient depictions of the Tree of Life in which a human figure – the primordial Adam – fills the circle. Similarly, the archaic Jungian figures of people dancing "in a circle on the sand" in P.K.'s dream and in the poem "Another Space" are performing a mandala: the observer's consciousness is quickened by the impact of an "arrow" in the poem, and the result is a merging with "another space" in a process quite similar to that described in relation to the Tree of Life, where the crown Kether, the head of man, is touched by the heavens.[69]

P.K.'s poem, and the many black-and-white octagonal drawings from this period indicate her search for a breakthrough in consciousness.[70] This process of deep contemplation – or "entering the mandala," – culminates in finding the Philosopher's Stone, which is the goal of the Sufi quest and signifies the final transformation.[71] In P.K.'s poem "Cullen Revisited," completed by 28 May 1971, Cullen (her old alter ego) finds "a disc, heart-sized and heavy ... / Makeweight, touchstone, lodestar" – the Philosopher's Stone itself.[72] She later titled her octagonal drawings *Pieces of Eight*, giving the individual pieces subtitles pointing towards coins (pirates' currency) and so directing attention away from the octagon as a Sufi or alchemical figure.

In 1973, when writing to George Woodcock, she discussed one of the drawings, *Arcanum*, that she had sent to the Burnaby Art Gallery for a show called "Mystic Circles." She told him, "It is a piece that 'circles the square' by the intervention of the octagon."[73] Here, P.K. is again alluding to Jung. The introduction to this art exhibition, written by artist Jack Wise, also speaks of Jung and mandalas.[74] Babette Gourlay, one of P.K.'s friends attending the show recognized this, telling P.K. that she had been "particularly excited to find your pen and ink drawing *Arcanum*.[75] Your own marvelous and secret mandala?"[76]

This was the first time that P.K. had identified her Sufi art. In May 1972 she had had a good exhibition at the Mido Gallery in Vancouver that included *Bright Fish*, a new painting *Ah, Sunflower* in oil pastel and ink, *Spring Green*, pen and ink and ballpoint, and *That Which Is and That Which Strives to Be*, part of a triptych painted after her return from Mexico. Also included was *Desert Fantasy*, on hand-made paper made from mulberry leaves, in white and black ink, *Ectoplasmic Event* in ink, and *Votive Tablet* in egg tempera and gold leaf. This last painting was divided into four quarters, two of which are Sufi octagons. (A variation of this design was used on the cover of a later book of poetry, *Hologram*.)

In 1976 P.K. and Pat Martin Bates collaborated on a series of miniatures exhibited at the Backroom Gallery in Victoria. Among these were the beautiful *Sun Tree*, a golden heraldic tree on a green background in oil pastel, and *Little One Eye*, oil pastel incised. In April 1978, P.K. again took part in a group exhibition at the Burnaby Art Gallery, entitled "Three Poet Painters: Eldon Grier, P.K. Page and Joe Rosenblatt." Some of her older paintings, including *Night Garden* and *Dark Landscape*, were exhibited together with some new ones, including *Persephone's Flowers* and a number of the *Pieces of Eight* octagons and two versions of the *Four-Gated City*. (She also brought ten copies of *Cry Ararat!* to sell.) A CBC review of the show pointed out that there were similarities between her poetry and drawing, particularly "an iridescent and evanescent quality of metaphor" and suggested that her most recent drawings were "mostly gardens; they have a visual humour, rather like Klee's."[77]

P.K.'s poetry and her visual art were equivalent roads to what she had called "silence" in her essay "Traveller, Conjuror, Journeyman" and what we might call illumination. The question is why? Why draw 64 (8 times 8) octagonal mandalas in the 1970s and 1980s, a process requiring intense concentration, when the first half-dozen might do? When she had first started the octagons she had sent some of her early designs to Ensor Holiday, an Islamicist, whom she had met at Langton Green in 1969. He suggested that she continue to work on her drawings because it would "reveal a principle which at the moment is perhaps not immediately apparent to you."[78]

These precise geometrical drawings demanded an intense focus that took P.K. out of herself. She was now in her fifties, a pivotal point in her life. Two years earlier, at Langton Green, she had exclaimed, "I am oppressed. Help." Reaching out for something more, she again sought the transcendental through contemplation, as she had done in Mexico. Life had not turned out quite the way she had expected. Her husband Arthur was seriously ill and might be dying, and not only was she separated from Frank Scott, but occasional encounters at meetings of the league stirred up old memories. Her life was not complete.

Resolutely, she returned to Sufi symbols and readings for reflection and redirection in her life. This involved coming to terms with a whole new literature on what a human being was. She had begun with Lessing's novels, many of which, as we have seen, draw upon ideas expounded in *The Sufis*. Concurrently, in 1972, P.K. was reading Robert Ornstein's *The Psychology of Consciousness*, which helped provide a physiological basis for what both Gurdjieff and Shah had termed "the Work" on consciousness. Shah had said that to understand Sufism one must "experience," or employ an intuitive intelligence as opposed to a logical intelligence.[79] Ornstein argues that this accords with the structure of the human mind. The brain is divided into two hemispheres; the left hemisphere is directed towards the logical linear thinking associated with Western civilization, and the right hemisphere is directed towards intuitive, artistic, and holistic understanding. Ornstein makes room for transcendental consciousness by showing that normal consciousness has evolved to be drastically limited, shutting out all that is not essential for human survival.

This provides a scientific basis for the Sufi characterization of "ordinary consciousness as a state of 'deep sleep' or 'blindness,'" which can be overcome by the process of meditation that awakens fresh perception.[80] Ornstein offers a drawing of an octagon, which he identifies as a "Sufi contemplation object," to facilitate higher consciousness.[81] This is the octagon that P.K. had encountered in 1969 at Langton Green, and by developing her *Pieces of Eight* series, she was following both Shah's and Ornstein's directives. Throughout *The Psychology of Consciousness*, Ornstein uses Sufi fables to introduce chapters and refers to the "Work of Idries Shah as a new synthesis in process within modern psychology."[82]

P.K. continued to read Ornstein's successive books throughout the seventies, and in the spring of 1974 she attended a seminar on Ornstein's *Psychology of Consciousness* in San Francisco. She went early to help with organizing the seminar, accompanied by some members of a Victoria Sufi-studies group. Idries Shah attended, and P.K. wanted to introduce the group to him. But Shah declined, saying, "I'm just here for the beer and skittles," which P.K. interpreted as a rebuke.[83] In 1975 Ornstein came to Victoria, gave a lecture at the Psychology Department in the University of Victoria, and stayed with the Irwins. P.K. found his teaching fascinating[84] and was especially interested in his Sufi tales, the primary means of conveying Sufi teaching. She sent one of them to Elizabeth Gourlay, who remarked, "It is strange how often my mind has returned to your story of the girl, the boat, the old man, the lovers. I keep changing my mind about the essence of its meaning."[85] This story, as P.K. tells it, is about two lovers who are separated by a wide and threatening river. The young woman submits to an old ferryman's embrace as payment for being taken across the river to see her lover. However, when she explains to the young man that she allowed the ferryman this liberty, he rejects her. Who, then, is the true lover? The girl? The boy? The old ferryman?

In 1976 P.K. read Julian Jaynes's book *The Origin of Consciousness in the Breakdown of the Bicameral Mind* (1976) with enormous excitement. He argues that individual awareness of consciousness did not occur until about three thousand years ago and was associated with the development of language and writing. That same year, P.K. attended two more symposiums organized by Robert Ornstein. The first was held at the University of California, San Francisco, between 8 and 9 May and was entitled "The Psychology of Consciousness." Among the speakers were Dr William Dement, a pioneer in research on sleep, dreams, and sleep disorders, Roger W. Sperry, known for his pioneering research on the split-brain in animals and man, and Idries Shah, described as "the leading contemporary exponent of Sufism." The second, also in San Francisco, was held in November at the Institute for the Study of Human Knowledge and the University of California. It was called "Psychologies East and West." P.K. wrote Jori Smith, "November I go to San Francisco to a symposium where Idries Shah is speaking. The Symposium is organized by Ornstein. Do you remember his *Psychology of Consciousness* that I gave you? It's all very exciting to me – the centre of my universe."[86] Contributors included Charles Tart on "The Assumptions of Western Psychology," who spoke on the relativity of such assumptions as "the nature of man, of the physical world, and man's place in it." Idries Shah stated, "As Western psychologists begin to study the functions of the mind, they may find that many of their problems have been met and answered by those of the East."[87]

Throughout the seventies P.K. continued to read Sufi material and to meet with like-minded friends. Her group, which by the end of the decade seems to have moved to a building on the corner of Cook and Fort Streets,[88] discussed Sufi readings and raised funds for the Institute of Cultural Research. P.K. also continued to absorb Sufi thinking from Doris Lessing. At the heart of the ideal city in *The Four-Gated City* is a square connected to an octagon. In the square, under the library, is a small white octagonal room, where it is believed the governing elite, the saving remnant of the ideal city, resided.[89] (At this point, in her copy of the novel, P.K. had penciled in "Sufis.") In Lessing's *Briefing for a Descent into Hell* (1971), which P.K. was reading in 1970–71, the representative from the gods, entrusted with the task of warning mankind, falls into a sleep when he enters the poisonous atmosphere of Earth and forgets the information that has to be passed on for mankind to survive. Lessing's successive novels in the *Canopus in Argos: Archives*, which P.K. read in the late seventies and throughout the eighties, are very much concerned with the loss of Earth and the attempt to find new worlds in space.

In essence, P.K. was living by and through ideas, but hers was a private quest for illumination. As Jung explains in his autobiography (an explanation carefully copied by P.K.), to follow only "external happenings" is to give no understanding of one's real self.[90] To be sure, some of P.K.'s friends and acquaintances to whom she distributed copies of *The Sufis* (among them Pat Martin Bates, Florence Bird, Elizabeth Brewster, David Jeffrey, Jim Polk, Arlene Lampert, Rosemary Sullivan, and Constance Rooke) glimpsed her deep immersion in the Sufi way.[91] But none of this was apparent to the casual observer. There were few external markings of the ferocious internal journey that she was undertaking.

Throughout the seventies, Pat and Arthur were surrounded by family. Not only were Pat's mother Rose and Aunt Bibbi now relocated in Victoria, but her brother Michael and his wife Sheila followed. In addition, Arthur's daughter Sheila and her husband Edward Irving soon followed when he took a position at the Pacific Geoscience Centre in Victoria and later joined the faculty of the University of Victoria. Pat was now wife, daughter, cook, and housekeeper – as well as poet – continually running from reading to conference to committee and then back home again to Arthur and family. Each day she spent several hours visiting her mother and aunt. Bibbi suffered from dementia (reflected in P.K.'s short story "Victoria" and her poem "Conversation with My Aunt"), and Rose may also have had the beginnings of dementia, developing "a kind of paranoid speech in her as she got older, which was very difficult and so unlike what she was when she was younger." Rose was frequently sharply critical of her daughter, and Pat was hurt and angry: "God! old age."[92] She once expressed her grief to Florence Bird, who responded that she was glad P.K. was facing "disliking"[93] her mother, and advised her to think of Rose the way she used to be: "beautiful, and witty and courageous. And talented I think. Good company until time betrayed her."[94] In 1973 Pat was obliged to move the two sisters to a nursing home, Mount Tolmie Hospital, but she felt unhappy about doing so.

Now, near the end of 1973 – Christmas was always difficult for Pat – her dog Chico died. He had been her faithful companion ever since she had been given him in Mexico. Overtired and emotionally drained, she was plunged into "a black, heavy depression."[95] Having suffered from bouts of depression in the past, she had learned to cope for a few months by retreating, by switching gears from poetry to painting and back again, and then, somewhat rejuvenated, by propelling herself back into a swing of frenetic activity, as indeed she did on her Maritime tour in early 1974, as already described.

Most summers up to 1976, P.K. and Arthur went to the Irwin family cottage at Go Home Lake, Ontario, where they relaxed for several weeks. P.K. and Arthur were fond grandparents, and in August 1974 there were eleven grandchildren at the cottage. She organized activities such as poetry and drawing contests, which generated much excitement, and Arthur distributed Mars bars as prizes. As P.K. explains, "I have offered prizes as in [a] poetry contest & a drawing contest as there is a great deal of work going on with crayons & pencils & much excitement & secrecy." Cottage life was pleasant for P.K. and Arthur. They enjoyed swimming:[96] "first early & nude before anyone was around, later noisily & boisterously with diving splashing grandchildren. Long swims to an island where we climbed up the face of rock like a family of baboons. Gentle paddles in the evening watching the sun sink. It was lovely."⁹⁷ But the couple had no sooner returned to Victoria in September than it was time for P.K. to leave for a reading at Dalhousie University in Nova Scotia.

With the turn of the year, January 1975, P.K. again set out on the circuit, reading to enthusiastic audiences at the University of Toronto, Fanshawe College in London, Ontario, and in Regina and Saskatoon. She spoke at a late afternoon poetry reading series organized by Sam Solecki at St Michael's College. One of her auditors remembered that the good-sized listeners included one of the professors from Victoria, who came in just before the reading began. When P.K. had finished and the audience was beginning to disperse, the professor went up to her and introduced himself: "Hello, I'm Northrop Frye."⁹⁸

By February she was back in Victoria, when Ornstein and his girl-friend came to stay with the Irwins. In June she was again in Saskatoon, where she stayed with Elizabeth Brewster for a week and renewed their old friendship. She also met a promising poet, Anne Szumigalski, gave lectures and readings, and took part in a workshop with Jim Black and Judith Merril. During August 1975, while P.K. was again teaching for the League of Canadian Poets, Arthur began his research in the National Archives for a projected autobiography, "The Making of a Canadian," looking into the Ontario manse of his childhood, his early newspaper days, and his political activism during the Second World War. In October P.K. took part in a group exhibition in the new Student Union Gallery at the University of British Columbia, and in November she read at both Simon Fraser and UBC. At the time, she phoned me to say, "Stop the world, I want to get off!"

By mid-decade P.K. became aware that her mother was slowly dying, and in early 1976 she was reluctant to travel. Rose Page died on 17 April 1976. The night before her funeral, P.K. had been scheduled to give a reading "up-island." She dedicated it to her mother and began with "Arras," Rose's favourite poem. After the reading P.K. nearly fainted (she actually had fainted after her father's death).⁹⁹ A great deal of emotion was bottled up, and it affected her physically. The funeral was held at McCall's Funeral Home, and as P.K. entered the chapel it seemed to glow like gold – she was happy she had not said "No Flowers" – and the navy padre who conducted the service, the Reverend Hugh Mortimer, was the sort of man "mother has known all her life, and the Anglican service is that kind of arm's length service that stops you from getting hysterical."¹⁰⁰ Rose's funeral brought a number of old friends together, including the lieutenant-governor George Pearkes; and Max Bates, whom Rose Page had been so kind to in the Calgary days.[101] Her death brought an outpouring of sympathy as well as a number of anecdotes from the extended Page family.

Aunt Bibbi died a few weeks later, on 2 May 1976. The sisters were buried side by side under a flowering dogwood tree. Beatrice Whitehouse had always said that all she wanted on her gravestone was "M.A. Cantab"[102] – in recognition of the Cambridge degree that she had earned in 1896, studying under Bertrand Russell and Alfred Whitehead, but had not been permitted to receive at that time because she was a woman. P.K. owed a large part of her creative life to this sturdy bluestocking, who had given her a year of intellectual freedom in London and laid the foundations for her understanding of modern art and poetry.

In June 1976 P.K. was on the reading circuit again. She wrote to Shirley Gibson, the executive secretary of the league, describing her visit to Brock University: there was no one to meet her, no posters, and, not surprisingly, no students for the reading. Remarking that it "makes us look like garbage when we allow ourselves to be treated like garbage," P.K. recommended that no future events be scheduled at this university for the season.[103] Also that fall she attended a poetry reading at Blue Mountain. In early October she went on a reading tour to universities around Toronto, and in mid-October was back in Ottawa to join an advisory arts panel for the Canada Council. The high quality of her work was a large factor in her appointment to this panel (on which she served for three years from 1976), which was intended to set the Canada Council's parameters for grants and procedures in relation to creative artists. As Timothy Porteous, then assistant head of the Canada Council recalled, an important part of the council's function was to take advice from practising artists, and it was essential to have on the committee a person like P.K., with her knowledge and skill, to discuss current issues and recommend decisions to the council.[104] Michael Ondaatje was also appointed to this panel, and the two poets, frequently worked together for similar aims.

In the fall of 1977 P.K. again read in Toronto, returned to Victoria, and was back in Ottawa in late October for a Canada Council meeting. She went primed with information from Arlene Lampert, the director of the League of Canadian Poets, about the problems experienced by the league when attempting to place poets for public readings. P.K. had now been elected to the league's advisory council. Later, when the Canada Council tightened up finances, she suggested a program for making poetry tapes, starting with the senior poets. A fine organizer, P.K. chaired the committee, drew up a contract, and had Arthur review it to ensure that it was fair. In 1978 and again in 1979, she was invited by the Canada Council to serve on the writer-in-residence juries and did so again in 1986–87.

⚎

P.K.'s creative life in Victoria had changed for the better. By 1977 there was an active group of younger poets in the city, some former students of Robin Skelton, with whom P.K. stayed in contact. One of these, Marilyn Bowering, wrote to her in February asking if she would like to join a group of poets who were reading at Signal Hill, Victoria. On 27 March 1977 P.K. read there with Doug Beardsley, Bowering, Susan Musgrave, Charles Lillard, and others. This was the beginning of a fruitful relationship with younger poets in Victoria, especially with Bowering, whose poems and interests P.K. recognized were akin to her own. Her relationship with younger poets became closer when novelist David Godfrey, newly appointed head of creative writing at the University of Victoria, asked P.K. in September 1977 if she would teach a course on the subject. Among her students were poets Neile Graham, Gail Harris, Mark Jarman, Harold Rhenisch, and Patricia Young.

Young later spoke of this group and recalled that P.K. introduced the class to poets she loved – Yeats, Stevens, Rilke. She brought copies of their poems to class and read them aloud; she insisted they keep a journal because, she said, it is a well from which they will learn to draw. She gave them weekly assignments, asking them to write poems "using syllable count, half rhyme, hidden rhyme, assonance, dissonance, alliteration." What P.K. was offering, Young recalled, was "the poet's tools."[105] Nonetheless, the young poets balked at P.K.'s suggestion to experiment, to read other poets, to try writing poems that were not "I" centred. Years later, Patricia Young said it had not occurred to her back then that P.K. represented "the possibility of a spiritual or artistic mother."[106] The next year, when the university's Dirk Wynand asked P.K. if she would teach a second class, she refused, disheartened by the closed-mindedness of the students she had recently tried to teach. Teaching a year-long course would have been draining for someone like P.K., unaccustomed as she was to university students, procedures, and paperwork.

P.K.'s poetry readings, her many letters of reference for young poets, her teaching, her participation in workshops, and her appointments to Canada Council committees were all intertwined. Crossing the country on readings, she met younger poets who came to her readings because they loved her poems and wanted to meet her; they included Atwood, Bowering, Eli Mandel, Tom Marshall, Seymour Mayne, Ondaatje, Alan Safarik, Al Valleau – all of whom recognized her distinction as a poet. Many asked her to read their new poems and, inevitably, to write references for them to the Canada Council when they applied for grants. She was already writing references for contemporaries such as George Woodcock and Douglas LePan, but now she began to write for younger writers – Ondaatje, Bowering, Al Purdy, Pat Lane, and Jane Urquhart. P.K. was frantically busy.

The year 1978 began badly for the Irwins. As a result of their decade of living in the tropics, Arthur had a skin ailment that required drastic treatment. P.K. stayed home to look after him and cancelled the first half of a new Maritime tour scheduled for February. In April she put together material for a group exhibition: "Three Poet Artists: Eldon Grier, P.K. Page, Joe Rosenblatt," held at the Burnaby Art Gallery from 5 April to 7 June. When Arthur turned eighty on 27 May, P.K. organized the surprise delivery of a piano, a gift from his son Neal: "such secrecy and excitement as you cannot imagine. It has proved a great success ... and he *adores it.*"[107]

By the late 1970s, P.K. had become one of the best-known and most requested poets on the reading circuit. In the process, she had made two close friends – Gerald and Arlene Lampert. Gerry, a "generous, warm, funny man who had a great love for literature," was the organizer of the League of Canadian Poets' cross-country tours, and his wife Arlene, who became one of P.K.'s closest friends, was secretary and later director of the league. Gerry also organized a series of summer creative-writing workshops for the league, usually held at New College, University of Toronto. In 1973 P.K. had been invited to teach one of the poetry workshops, and she did so for several years. Through these workshops she met younger poets and writers such as Daniel David Moses, Rhea Tregebov, Carolyn Zonailo, and Linda Sandler.[108]

Linda Sandler, who attended the first workshop in poetry from 29 August to 13 September 1974, reported that P.K. taught with reference to the "creative functions of the brain and moved into language games related to the sound qualities of poetry."[109] P.K. had been applying Ornstein's *The Psychology of Consciousness* to help get creative juices flowing. In the midst of one workshop, she wrote to Patrick Anderson: "At the moment I'm at U of T giving a course in creative writing. *Really funny!* Twenty-seven assorted students from (one guesses) hopeless and illiterate to intelligent. When I say really funny – I don't mean the students. I think it's funny that I'm trying to do it after all these years."[110]

Although P.K. enjoyed the poetry workshops – the brief interlude was stimulating rather than draining – the summer of 1978 was frenetic. Gerry Lampert had died suddenly, and Arlene was left not only bereft but with the responsibility of arranging for the poetry workshop. Because funds were scarce, she asked three of the instructors – Page, Elizabeth Salter, an English novelist, and Réshard Gool, a fiction writer from Prince Edward Island – if they would stay in her house to save money. It was a tight squeeze, but a large back garden was available. Lampert recalls P.K. sitting there in the sun reading the students' manuscripts and sometimes reading aloud a few lines from a poem: "Listen to this ..." she would say, "Gorgeous."[111] After the classes were over and the marking done, there was a great deal of joking and laughing.

P.K. was loyal to her friends. After Gerry's death she worked to establish the Gerald Lampert Memorial Fund in his memory by requesting submissions from poets for a book of very short poems called *To Say the Least: Canadian Poets from A to Z* (1979). She persuaded contributors to forgo their normal fee, and the league donated funds, as did the Writers' Union of Canada. In October 1979, she went on an eastern tour to promote the book. The fund started to build and there is now a $5,000 annual prize.

The league had made an arrangement with the secretary of the British league of poets to exchange readers, and this resulted in P.K.'s first international reading tour when she was invited to take part in three weeks of readings in England with Earle Birney and Michael Ondaatje, beginning in early October 1978. At first they had small audiences, as English universities were not yet in session, but there were big audiences at Cheltenham, where they were part of a festival program, and in London where they shared the program with their British counterparts. P.K. thought that the readings in Liverpool, Oxford, and Newcastle also went well.

P.K. summarized the tour's awkward moments for Arlene Lampert. When in Grasmere, Wordsworth's village in the Lake District, she found: "1) kindness overwhelming. 2) politeness likewise. 3) we misbehave." Birney had passed out at Canada House on the first night, and everyone thought he was having a heart attack. In fact, he had not eaten all day because he was too stingy to buy sandwiches, despite a generous per diem allowance. P.K. herself had a miserable cold, "hawking cough, streaming nose, almost useless throat, so I have squeaked and squawcked [sic] through my readings!"[112] The only person doing what he ought to be doing was Ondaatje, who read well and behaved well. P.K. found him very compatible: "Michael and I were good friends on that trip, very good friends ... If you were ready for a walk, he was always ready for a walk, if you wanted to lie down and read, he could lie down and read ... but at the stations, who was first out, and knowing where to find the managers to guide you? ... Where could you find the best bar? He did, he knew, he was alert."[113] After the tour was over, P.K. remained in England for ten days visiting friends. She also went to Kent to stay for a weekend at the Sufi centre and helped in the office and in the garden. In London she once again visited Professor Fry.[114]

By the end of the seventies P.K. had a sustaining philosophy in Sufism and was part of a supportive group of like-minded poets; her poems were widely praised, and her art was finally recognized in Victoria. Indeed, both she and Arthur were known across the country. Arthur's contributions to Canadian culture – as editor of *Maclean's*, as commissioner of the National Film Board, and as a Canadian diplomat abroad – had all been recognized in his appointment to the Order of Canada in 1973. In June 1977 P.K. joined her husband when she too was made an officer of the order. A special coin had been minted to mark the order's tenth anniversary, and it was given to all the new officers and also to Maryon Pearson, widow of Lester Pearson, Norman McKenzie, former president of the University of British Columbia, and Frank Scott, now retired from the McGill law faculty, who was a companion of the order. P.K. found the ceremony very moving – "that extraordinary cross-section of Canadians with their talents & braveries." She spoke with Marian Scott, whom she had not seen for many years: "Thought she had begun to look surprizingly like Frank & also found her very beautiful which I don't remember her as being."[115]

Even the University of Victoria had changed. David Jeffrey, the new head of the English Department, who had been appointed in 1973, spoke up for Canadian academic excellence as represented internationally by such scholars as Northrop Frye and hired Canadians as professors, including Rosemary Sullivan and writer David Godfrey. He was reported in the Victoria *Times Colonist* as criticizing Canadian universities for allowing non-Canadians to control hiring: "What this has meant is that jobs in Canadian universities were regularly filled by people from abroad."[116]

P.K. read the article, phoned Jeffrey, and said in effect, "Good for you! Don't let them bully you." She then invited him to lunch to meet Arthur. He was soon visiting the Irwins regularly, sometimes in company with Walter Young, a professor of political science at UVic who, with his wife Beryl, had become close friends. Occasionally George Pedersen, the new president of UVic, joined the group. All have spoken warmly of the Irwins and the friendship they found in their home, of innumerable good dinners, and of animated evening discussions about things Canadian, especially Arthur's experiences as a gunner in the First World War. All were touched by his observation that although he went to war as a British subject, he came home as a Canadian. During these political discussions Arthur would sit in his chair to the left of the big fireplace while P.K. sat, very quietly, on a far sofa, listening to her husband hold court.

Another UVic friend was Rosemary Sullivan. In 1974, when Sullivan (with her first husband, Doug Beardsley) came to UVic, she as a faculty member and he still a graduate student, she phoned P.K., who received her kindly and invited her to visit. Rosemary became a close and continuing friend. They met regularly, occasionally shopped together, and Rosemary and Doug frequently came to dinner at the Irwins' until Rosemary accepted a position at the University of Toronto in 1977. Knowing that P.K. was very unassuming about her abilities as a poet, Rosemary had told Arthur that P.K. was "really great," meaning world class. Arthur replied, "Do you think so?" Obviously pleased, he nonetheless wanted reasons for this summation.[117] When Rosemary left for the University of Toronto, Constance Rooke (known as Connie), another young professor, became a close friend. Connie valued P.K.'s poetry and enjoyed her high spirits. She found P.K. extraordinarily youthful, full of energy, and gorgeous: "I remember … lots of jewel colours. Her clothing was always dramatic without being excessive." The two women had similar tastes in literature and film, and attended events together. In 1978 P.K. was sixty-two, and on one occasion said, "Connie, don't walk so quickly, you have to remember I'm quite a lot older than you are." For Rooke, it was one of the most important friendships of her life: "The journeys of other people are ways in which we are also moving."[118]

A reassessment of P.K.'s achievement as a poet had already begun. In mid-decade, Joe Rosenblatt had written an article in *Quill and Quire* in which he characterized Page as one of the best and most underrated poets in North America. Then Simon Fraser University's *West Coast Review* published a special issue on P.K. Page. The February 1978 issue included contributions by two of my graduate students, a checklist of P.K.'s poetry by Michele Preston, an MA student, and a critical article by Jean Mallinson, then completing a PH D. Preston's checklist was to lead into

John Orange's later bibliography, *P.K. Page: An Annotated Bibliography* (1985). Also in 1978, Rosemary Sullivan and Connie Rooke wrote pioneering studies of Page's poetry. Sullivan's extensive article, "A Size Larger Than Seeing: The Poetry of P.K. Page,"[119] was submitted before Rooke's, but by the vagaries of publication, Rooke's article, "P.K. Page: The Chameleon and the Center," appeared first. In it she says, "P.K. Page is Canada's finest poet."[120]

Near the end of the seventies P.K. herself took stock of her life, reflecting not on her success but its human costs – her busy and often harried schedule during the decade. She told Jori Smith, "I think I have grown to live in a state of thinking myself in a hurry": "What I am hurrying towards, I don't know ... trying to have meals on time, getting to the stores before they close, not being late for an appointment ... absurd. It began as a child with a military Pappa, was accentuated by all those diplomatic years and now – in my old age for God's sake when there is nothing in the world that really and truly has to be done – except the one important thing which has nothing to do with time – I rush and scramble and struggle to keep on good terms with the clock!"[121] The "one important thing," which is timeless, is perhaps saving one's own soul, an oblique reference to the story of Martha and Mary (Luke 10:42). Like Martha, P.K. was overwhelmed with the requirements of her domestic life but aware that she was neglecting Mary's choice, the one thing needful. P.K. was not happy with the life she was leading, and a year later she refused an invitation by Elizabeth Brewster to read in Saskatoon, explaining that she felt she was running back and forth "like a yo-yo."[122]

CHAPTER 13

Victoria
Transformations, 1980–1989

At the beginning of the decade P.K. was in her mid-sixties but still relatively healthy: "We are not too bad – Arthur less energetic than last year
but still active. My sight is poor. I can no longer drive at night & I'm considering an operation. Also I'm *very* creaky. Quelle vie!"[1] She also felt
that she couldn't write poetry again, "No, never."

All her creative energy was now pouring into her Sufi-studies group.
Working with one's hands was an important part of Sufi group activity,
and P.K. suggested that the group produce a play. In November 1981
she was adapting a Turkish fairy story, retold by Amina Shah (sister to
Idries), as a puppet play for children, which was to be staged the following spring. Called "Prince Attila's Journey to the End of the World,"
it tells of a prince who forgets his divine task but miraculously recovers
his memory to perform it. A member of the group, Grace Williamson,
made the puppets, and P.K. enjoyed helping with the costumes, staging
the play, and projecting the voices of the various characters. "We have
a dragon, if you please, who engages in a fight with our hero. It is a
lovely play and visually very beautiful."[2] The group also produced wall
hangings and puppets to sell as part of its contribution to the Institute
for Cultural Research in London, for which Shah was the director.

She had just finished a major book, *Evening Dance of the Grey Flies*
(1981), published by Oxford. It had its genesis when Rosemary Sullivan
told P.K. that Richard Teleky, then managing editor of Oxford University Press, Toronto, loved her poems and wondered if she had enough
new work for a book. She did – all the poems in *Evening Dance* were
new poems, many of which had immediate appeal. The collection had
five parts. The poems in the first part, set largely in the natural world, include references to individuals (Arthur, Cullen, Mstislav Rostropovich);
those in the second part, inspired by friends (Patrick Anderson, "Ours")
and family who were ill or had died, ends with the title poem; an apoc-

alyptic short story about vision makes up the third part; part four offers introspective poems that include a vibrant response to Pat Lane's "Albino Pheasants," a long poem about P.K.'s childhood called "The First Part," and the semi-autobiographical "Ancestors"; part five, largely metaphysical, alludes to both John Donne and Edith Sitwell.

I reviewed the book for the year's work in poetry for the *University of Toronto Quarterly*: "These are gentle, assured poems of coming to terms with age and death, poems in which the paradigm of rebirth or transfiguration is central ... Hers is an imagination which irradiates matter into metaphor." I found Page's vision a transforming one in which "God is immanent in all creation ... the poems characteristically begin with perception but end in vision ... Page's metaphysic ... is influenced by Sufism."³ Although many of the poems reached for another reality, they were witty and full of wonderful metaphors – some erudite, some homespun, as in "After Reading *Albino Pheasants*":

> And however cool the water my truth won't wash
> without shrinking except in its own world
> which is one part matter, nine parts imagination.
>
> I fear flesh which blocks imagination,
> the light of reason which constricts the world.
> *Pale beak ... pale eye ... pale flesh ...* My sky's awash.⁴

Several of her poems were akin to the seventeenth-century Metaphysicals, but there was a new strain, like the reference to the Sufi saint Rabia El-Adewia in the poem "At Sea." Indeed, all the themes that dominate Page's later writing are contained in *Evening Dance of the Grey Flies*: an insistence on the primacy of the imagination, a preoccupation with Sufi thought as manifested in evolution and transcendence, a new freedom about self and ancestry, and a growing preoccupation with death. Apart from her mother and Aunt Bibbi, she had lost many friends in the past decade: A.M. Klein died in 1972, Stella Kent in 1977, Kit Shaw and Floris McLaren in 1978, Patrick Anderson in 1979, and A.J.M. Smith in 1980.

Some poems refer directly to these deaths and another, "About Death," transforms death into a new birth, suggesting that P.K. had absorbed the Sufi poet Rumi's view of death as a heavenly marriage:⁵

> And at the moment of death
> what is correct procedure?

Cut the umbilical, they said.

And with the umbilical cut
how then prepare the body?

Wash it in sacred water.
Dress it in silk for the wedding.[6]

The grey flies in the title poem are seen on a "sunlit lawn." They gleam, "their cursive flight a gold calligraphy," leading to a moment of sudden illumination when her mother lies dying:

as once your face
grey with illness and with age –
a silverpoint against the pillow's white –

shone suddenly like the sun
before you died.

"Voyager" is a poem about her father. Page tells us that at age fifty-eight, just a few days from 26 August, the anniversary of her father's death in 1944, she was still dreaming about him.[7] He comes back, she tells us, night after night "from some long journey." As in life, he is distant, but on this last occasion she was aware of a change for the better, "he / sought us in other places / studied maps, / set out in search."

It was the closest we have come
to meeting
during thirty years of dreams.[8]

This dream, evoking P.K. as a child learning from her military father how to find her place on a map, now widens into her own life journey, one in which the long-absent father seeks for her.

Now that both parents had died, P.K. had a sense of her own mortality and wanted to write about the past, as she explains in the opening of "The First Part":

Great desire to write it all.
Is it age, death's heavy breath
making absolute autobiography
urgent?[9]

This leads into recollections of childhood: her doll, her mother's ring, the piece of quartz she found, the child's view of a horse and of the story told by P.K. of riding with her father and coming across the terrifying image of the bones of a small Indian child in a grave box,[10] the corpse "picked to the bone." In the poem, the narrating child/older poet cries to the father, asking for love: "Hold me. / Hold me."[11]

"Ancestors," which we have already discussed (chapter 1), invokes powerful figures from the ancestral past. For them, the narrator "had lived in exemplary fashion ... [had] born pain with grace."[12] Her poem to Patrick Anderson, "Ours" – a tribute that moves deftly through gradations of feeling – begins conversationally: "At something over sixty he is dead ... Were we friends?" More like acquaintances who "met each other often, / warmed by the same blaze."

> Sparked by his singular talent
> my small fires
> angered him.

Nonetheless, there were times when their hearts "both leapt / in love with metaphor ... / We were friends." She recognizes that something passed between them, "something memorable and alive – / a kind of walking bird:

> His and mine, that bird. Ours.
> Now
> Unable to fly.[13]

At the heart of *Evening Dance of the Grey Flies* is "Unless the Eye Catch Fire ..." – a tale told in journal entries. Page found her title in lines written by Theodore Roszak in *Where the Wasteland Ends.*[14] The story begins with a woman looking out on her lawn and seeing a flock of quail. Suddenly alarmed, they take flight. Her vision instantly changes – almost as if she were looking through a kaleidoscope and shaking it: instantly all nature shimmers in shining brilliant colours. Another shake intervenes, and the external world is internalized within her. (This "shaking" and "shining" action in conjunction with "colour" has Sufi significance.)[15] For the woman, this vision of beauty is a prelude to a world that is gradually heating up, turning all vegetation – and ultimately all people – into dust. For the narrator, who lives with her dog, the growing heat and world conflagration is of little importance because she has a vision of harmony – "the colours" – and of unity – the "one brain"

that connects all matter, including herself, to some infinite and beneficent source. "We are one with the starry heavens and our bodies are
stars." As she nears death in the fiery conclusion of the story, the narrator of "Unless the Eye Catch Fire ..." experiences a sense of union with
the divine.

As this Sufi "teaching story" indicates (for I read it as such), P.K. continued to follow Shah's books, and a number of poems in this collection
reflect Sufi thought. "Cullen Revisited" itself, an updating of her 1940s
poem about Cullen, incorporates some of P.K.'s new life experiences.
The new poem is "Cullen at Fifty," who finds the kind of "disc" (the
philosopher's stone) that P.K. read about in Jung, Gurdjeiff, and Lessing.
It is "touchstone, lodestar," and when he rubs it, a new world begins
so that he passes from "World One" to "World Two" and glimpses
"World Three."[16]

One of my favourites in the collection is "After Donne," which builds
on John Donne's lament, in a sermon, that his attention even when directed towards "God and his Angels" can be diverted by the buzzing of
a fly or a coach passing.[17] What interests P.K. is the *moment* of transfer
of attention. Her metaphor of a macaw's eye that contracts to become a
vortex – pulling her through to a different reality – is brilliant:

> For the least moving speck
> I neglect God and all his angels,
> yet attention's funnel –
> a macaw's eye – contracts,
> becomes a vortex.
>
> I have been sucked through.[18]

"The Disguises," which begins the last section of the book, was written for Idries Shah, and one of the final poems, "The Trail of Bread,"
can be read as shorthand for the psychic journey. It is a reworking of
Grimm's story of Hansel and Gretel (that P.K. disliked so much as a
child), banished by a cruel stepmother to an "airless wood," who leave
a trail of breadcrumbs behind them, hoping to follow it home. The narrator speaks of finding a few meagre crumbs (many are eaten by birds),
following them until the trail grew clear. Suddenly she was led out of a
"shadowy landscape / into dawn," where she finds not a witch's cottage
but "Rose of the air unfolding ... And sun, up with a rush." The fairy
tale about abandonment is reworked into a journey to paradise: "The
world gold-leafed and burnished."[19]

Evening Dance of the Grey Flies was praised by critics. Bruce Whiteman noted that the book continued the "process of simplification and paring down" noted earlier in Page's poetry; he found her poetry "painterly," but not superficially so, because the sensuousness of the work "arises from a persistent centering on and belief in the senses as the basis for an imaginative apprehension of the world." He identified death as a strong component in the book.[20] A number of reviewers – including Stephen Scobie, Michele Valiquette, and John Bemrose – recognize a supravision in Page's poetry. Scobie also finds that "Unless the Eye Catch Fire ..." is both literally and thematically the centre of the book, praising "the gift of extraordinary perceptions which sets the unknown narrator apart."[21] Similarly, Constance Rooke emphasized perception: "The most persistent, magical turning point of these poems is a kind of metamorphosis or translation from one level of being to another. Yearnings for 'weightlessness,' for the dissolution of boundaries between subject and object ... *lift* the poet into another space."[22]

P.K. was still facing her friends' illness and death. For some years she had been in contact with the novelist Howard O'Hagan, who lived in Victoria and had a crush on her. Every day, at about four in the afternoon – after he had finished his one bottle of Irish whiskey – he would telephone P.K., whom he affectionately called "Piquette," to talk about his day.[23] But now, in 1982, he died. His wife having briefly fled the scene, P.K. was drawn into O'Hagan's death and funeral.[24] Two years later, both Irwins were devastated when Walter Young, a dynamic younger political scientist, died after a brief illness with brain cancer.

Most distressing was Frank Scott's illness. P.K. wrote to Arlene Lampert in 1982 saying; "The situation with Frank doesn't bear thinking about. He's had nurses round the clock since May of this year."[25] In September 1983 several people – including Florence Bird, William Toye, and myself – had alerted her that Scott was dying. When researching Scott's biography earlier that summer I had gone to Clarke Avenue in Montreal to see him, and I wrote P.K.: "His bout with pneumonia, the doctors now think, was followed by a stroke. He certainly recognized me, yet it was as if the filaments in the mind were somehow connected to the wrong terminals ... He looked very frail ... I am afraid that he does not have very much time left."[26] In response, P.K. phoned and asked me to contact Marian Scott: could P.K. come and see Frank when giving a reading in Montreal in mid-October?

Marian agreed. P.K. seems to have visited the Scotts on 20 October 1983, the same day she read at Vanier College. Scott was in an upper bedroom, sitting in his wheelchair in front of the window, his profile silhouetted against the light, looking out at his favourite tree. Marian brought P.K. a drink and tactfully left her alone with Frank to say goodbye. He recognized her but could not speak coherently. She later recalled that he happily took a sip from her drink. A lover of martinis, Scott was reduced in the last few years of his illness to a tomato-juice mixture that he dubbed "a Virgin Mary." A few years later, P.K. published her poem "Goodbye":

We were in a high room
but we were not ourselves ...
At liptip or fingertip
or mindtip where we met
we spoke ourselves a language
as singular as Braille
but wordfull and imagefull ...
We took a little journey ...
and took ourselves beyond.[27]

P.K. broke down and wept as she left the house and made her way down Clarke Avenue to Sherbrooke Street and continued walking to the Ritz-Carlton Hotel. On the plane returning to British Columbia, she wrote to Florence Bird about the poetry tour, adding a brief, poignant sentence with no explanation: "I feel wounded in my very heartbone."[28] Two years later, at the end of January 1985, P.K. received a telegram from Marian Scott: "Frank died peacefully this morning."[29] P.K. found the news literally chilling: "I went so cold – as the heat left his body it left mine. Three days thinking I would never be warm again."[30] With Scott's death a chapter of her life nearly closed, although strong emotions remained: she once said, "I never got over being rejected as I was."[31]

P.K's a group of fellow poets in Victoria, with whom she read, put on performances, and socialized, now included Connie and Leon Rooke, Marilyn Bowering and her husband Michael Elcock, Patricia Young and her husband Terence, Elizabeth Gorrie and her husband Colin (who established and ran Kaleidoscope Theatre in Victoria), Jill Schwartz, and Barry McLean, a filmmaker.

P.K. Page performing "Me Tembro" in Victoria, British Columbia.

On 12 April 1986 P.K. took part in *A Strange Bird, the Angel*, directed by Gorrie for National Book Week. The nature of the production suggests that some of the group understood that P.K. was grieving and were attempting to comfort her. The writers were Marilyn Bowering, Doug Beardsley, Gail Harris, P.K. Page, Derk Wynand, and Patricia Young, who read their own work but also drew upon lines from the poems of Rainer Maria Rilke, William Blake, Wallace Stevens, and Jorge Luis Borges – "Two people who have loved each other on earth become a single Angel."[32] In addition, there were two actors/dancers, a pianist, and a woodwind soloist who improvised.

The performance notes suggest that this was an attempt to answer Rilke's questions about powerful angels, "Who *are* you?," – later reformulated as "Who *are* they?" – in response to Rilke's question: "Who, if I cried out, would hear me among the angelic orders?" This is the first line of J.B. Leishman's translation of Rilke's *Duino Elegies*, a poem that had great resonance for both Page and Scott. The Victoria performance was staged in black and white, with white parachute silk in the background, draped as the gates and throne of heaven. All the readers, were dressed in black, and the actors/dancers wore white body stockings. The first reader was Marilyn Bowering, whose remark recognizes the angel and says, "he can teach us / about parting."[33] Who are angels? There are several poems addressing this question, including the older "Images of Angels" by P.K., who speaks of "a – what of a thing – / primitive as a daisy":

> "Gentlemen, it is thought that they are born
> with harps and haloes
> as the unicorn with its horn.
> Study discloses them white and gold as daisies."[34]

P.K. also read a new poem, "Invisible Presences Fill the Air," with its many references to angels and archangels.[35] It was a moving perform-ance, a first memorial for F.R. Scott.

In the seventies, before "Unless the Eye Catch Fire ..." appeared in book form, Doris Lessing's *Memoirs of a Survivor* (1974) was published. At the time, Page fretted that Lessing might think she had plagiarized the novel, since it describes the last days of a woman who lives with a young girl and her dog. In Lessing's novel, woman, girl, dog, and their closest connections (like Alice in Wonderland) pass through a wall into another world, where they become transcendent beings. After publishing her story again in *Grey Flies* in 1981, Page wrote to Lessing, sending a copy of the book but explaining that her tale had been written earlier. Less-ing responded generously: "I very much like the poems. And I like, too, 'Unless the Eye Catch Fire ...' Perhaps we dreamed the same dream at the same time? It seems to me that ideas and stories go floating around in the air and get 'picked up' by sympathetic minds, like radio re-ceivers."[36] It is unlikely that P.K.'s story was influenced by *Memoirs of a Survivor*,[37] but the fact that she makes this association reminds us of the importance of Lessing in helping P.K. to "set" patterns of thought in her imagination, patterns that both women may have absorbed from the writings of Idries Shah.

Page kept up with her reading of Lessing, including *Shikasta* (1979), which she was "very excited" about in March 1984. Lessing stresses human evolution, especially when she retells the Nativity story. Celes-tial beings from Canopus come from the stars to teach the wretched of Shikasta – a word that in Farsi means "broken" and which Lessing uses for "earth" – that every child has the potential to evolve into the high-est form. (At Christmas for several years, P.K. read this section from

Lessing's book on Peter Gzowski's CBC program *Morningside*.) With *Shikasta*, which Lessing calls "inner space fiction," P.K. felt that the novelist had found a myth to contain all the myths one had been taught (Christianity, Marxism, socialism) and that Lessing saw such myths without distortion. "I felt she was telling me a truth that I'd never really heard before."[38]

In part, what Lessing did for Page was to describe the human journey in its largest sense, as Page herself explained: "I mean there's a personal journey of course, but then there's a racial journey, there's a cultural journey."[39] Furthermore, Lessing's novels "give you a whole cosmos ... She peoples the heavens, the other planets."[40] On these planets are more evolved beings than we are, noted Page. "How did they evolve? ... and is one capable of that evolution?"[41] P.K. especially appreciated Lessing as a novelist of ideas and once remarked, "I am really an ideas person ... I need ideas, and I'm very often reaching for ideas that are quite beyond my intellectual capacities. I haven't had a good education, I don't think I have a very developed left lobe, left hemisphere – a rational, logical [side], which I would be better for having. I don't mean that I value it so highly, but I think we should be in balance ... I think the trouble today with a large number of people is the hypertrophy of the left hemisphere ... the masculine principle."[42]

Longing for a more even distribution of the logical and the intuitive in her own thinking, P.K. objected to the dominance of the male principle – the left lobe – in Western culture. "Women's liberation," as it was called in the seventies and eighties, did not interest her as much as Robert Graves's idea of reinstating the creative principle: "fortifying the feminine principle which seems to me the basis of the whole thing. And the activists [of the seventies and eighties] aren't interested in that, they're busy turning themselves into men."[43] The feminist caucus of the League of Canadian Poets depressed her. To Rosemary Sullivan she wrote, "I am in 2 minds about resigning."[44] She told Arlene Lampert, "The literati shun me. The feminist caucus has created bad feelings here and there, I think. At any rate ... you can't win on the feminist thing. The men don't want any part of me either in case it appears they are supporting an antifeminist."[45] There were various other reasons for moving outside the league, and eventually P.K. joined a new loose association of writers and artists that included Margaret Atwood, Sylvia Fraser, Alice Munro, Michael Ondaatje, and Adele Wisemen (the organizer) and was called "the Loons." It is a pleasant image, the loon being a Canadian water bird with a haunting cry, relatively solitary – not a committee creature. Two groups of these creative artists – poets, visual artists, prose writers

– sprang up in Toronto and Victoria and met regularly, often at lunch, for some years.

In November 1983 P.K. finally underwent much-needed cataract surgery. But she found getting a new lens "unsettling," and she produced "almost nothing" in the first half of the new year. In early March she was invited to visit Australia to speak at Writers' Week in Adelaide with a distinguished group of authors, including Russell Hoban, Angela Carter, Salman Rushdie, and D.M. Thomas. Because it was very hot (over 100° F degrees in the shade), the Australian hosts went to great lengths to provide comfortable surroundings for the writers. They took the group up into the hills and gave them two days to acclimatize. P.K. was bemused at the writers' reactions: Hoban, Rushdie, and Thomas were indignant – they wanted to be in an air-conditioned hotel in Adelaide. But Carter was quite happy because she was there with her husband and child, and the rural surroundings were acceptable. P.K found most of the English "very snooty," but she found common ground with the painter and author Françoise Gilot – Picasso's former mistress and the mother of two of his children – whom she liked despite Gilot's couturier clothing.⁴⁶

On her return to Canada, P.K. stopped off in Toronto. Earlier she had been approached by Martha Butterfield, a young woman who loved her poetry and had become a friend. Martha's husband George was president of the Canadian Club of Toronto and invited Page to introduce Doris Lessing, whom the group had invited to speak at a lunch on 26 March 1984. Page, who very much wanted to meet Lessing, struggled for some time with her preliminary comments, finally managing to put everything she could think of about Lessing in a short, elegant introduction, which concluded, "And she is meat to me."⁴⁷

Lessing spoke from a few brief notes to an audience whom she understood would consist of businessmen. She said she had been talking with a friend and wondered why there had been so few novels about the business world. Perhaps because there were few artists who were business people? Could anyone in the audience suggest why this might be the case? A video of the talk suggests that Lessing was not accustomed to speaking in public and that she was too nervous to appreciate Page's eloquent introduction.

Michael Ondaatje had planned a party for P.K. that night, and Lessing attended with Greg Gatenby, Director of the Harbourfront Reading Series, who had persuaded her to give her first public reading, in Toronto.⁴⁸ The party was attended by a number of P.K.'s friends, including Rosemary Sullivan and Arlene Lampert, as well as Martha

Doris Lessing's address to the Canadian Club. 26 March 1984. Elizabeth Smart,
Doris Lessing, Martha Butterfield, P.K. Page, and Michael Ondaatje.

Butterfield and her husband, Aviva Layton and her husband, the
Rhodesian novelist Leon Whiteside, and Elizabeth Smart. (Years earlier,
in Ottawa, P.K. had met Smart briefly and asked her to autograph a rare
copy of *By Grand Central Station I Sat Down and Wept*, Smart's remarkable novel in the form of a prose-poem, which described her
longtime affair with her married lover, the English poet George Barker.
The book had been kept out of Canada by Smart's influential Ottawa
family, but F.R. Scott had acquired a copy.) As soon as Lessing saw
Whiteside, she went over to talk to him. The men gathered around
Smart, who charmed them with her conversation, her rumpled face, and
attractive hair.[49] Meanwhile, P.K. was in the kitchen telling jokes with
many of the women.[50] Everyone drank rather a lot.

    At one point in the evening Smart followed other guests as they
moved into the kitchen. She approached P.K. in a quarrelsome mood
and declared inexplicably, "I've given you two years of my life, and what
have you done with them?" Later, in Rosemary's car, P.K. was incredu-
lous: "I hardly knew her!"[51] Thinking of Smart years later, P.K. reflected
on their "parallel lives" in the forties – in that both had loved a married

poet. "Although she had lived hers so much more outwardly than I had. Mine had been much more hidden. But I felt that we had great similarities. I certainly struck sparks from her."[52]

Lessing was speaking at Harbourfront, Toronto the following day, and P.K. arranged to have tea with her that afternoon. P.K.'s Oxford editor, Richard Teleky, who also wanted to meet her, drove her to Lessing's hotel, and the three had coffee together. She found Lessing "totally natural, no conceit. Nothing of the celebrity about her."[53] The next day, 28 March, "well nigh dead of all the traveling and carousing," P.K. left Toronto by bus for a quick visit to the United States.[54] David Staines, a young instructor, who later moved to the University of Ottawa, had invited her to speak to his class at Smith College, Northampton, Massachusetts, as had Lee Thompson of the University of Vermont, where she spoke to a Canadian Studies class.

In November 1985, *The Glass Air: Selected Poems* was published by Oxford University Press. As George Woodcock recognized, it was a "selected" that was "clearly moving towards the definitive"[55] and provided readers with a larger sense of Page's complete poetry. For P.K., the "Glass Air" metaphor meant "that moment of heightened vision when it is as if a veil had been peeled away and one sees more vividly – colours more brilliant, forms more sharply defined," bringing to mind the sharp, clear air of her Alberta childhood.[56] She didn't have many new poems to include (only eleven), but Richard Teleky had suggested a more comprehensive book that included her best-known poems, some drawings, and the two essays from *Canadian Literature* discussing her imaginative process. It was an ambitious book and proved to be visually attractive and intellectually challenging. Teleky also encouraged Page to use one of her paintings, *The Glass House*, on the front cover, and nine drawings appeared inside the book. The order is chronological, beginning with a series of poems from 1944–54 and ending with a series dated 1968–85. The book concludes with P.K.'s essays "Traveller, Conjuror, Journeyman" and "Questions and Images."

An excellent introduction to Page, *The Glass Air* contained all her best poems in a paperback format convenient for college and university teaching. One of the new poems – the last one – was "Deaf-Mute in the Pear Tree," a joyous poem about a disabled man up in the branches of a pear tree, clipping, who suddenly sees his wife on the ground below: "then air is kisses, kisses / stone dissolves / his locked throat finds a little door / and through it feathered joy / flies screaming like a jay."[57]

Reviewers concluded that *The Glass Air* was one of the most important books of Canadian poetry published in 1985. One reviewer, Sandra Hutchison, remarked that Page was "an interesting and original artist" and that her constant development and "consistency and complexity of vision" made her not only a poet worthy of serious consideration but "one of our finest and most accomplished poets."[58]

With the publication of *The Glass Air*, P.K. finally felt comfortable in the writing and artistic community not only in Victoria but throughout Canada. She was continuing to exhibit her painting, although she now painted less and wrote more. In October 1983 the Art Gallery of Greater Victoria had put on an exhibition, "Print Making in British Columbia, 1889–1983," which included a version of her earlier Aladdin series but now called "Ship – Nocturnal" (1959). In July 1986 she was again included in an exhibition at the Art Gallery of Greater Victoria and in 1987 at an exhibition at the Maltwood Gallery, University of Victoria.

Skelton had resigned as editor of the *Malahat Review* in 1982, and Connie Rooke, who had taken his place, invited P.K. to join the editorial board in 1985. Lucy Bashford, an editorial assistant, recalls that her future husband, Jay Ruzesky, then a graduate student, was sent by Connie to help P.K. tidy up her basement, which was stuffed with books, magazines, paintings, and manuscripts – a lifetime of work. P.K.'s friendship with Connie had flourished: "She is very bright, a New Yorker married to Leon Rooke, fiction writer – very good friends to us. I guess Connie is the great new friend in this period of my life."[59]

In 1985 P.K.'s old friend Jean Fraser, the widow of Blair Fraser, had died. During the fifties and sixties Jean had become very close to Rose Page and her sister Bibbi Whitehouse, offering the care that P.K. could not provide when she was out of the country. Jean, a follower of G.I. Gurdjieff, had kept P.K. supplied with books when she was in Mexico. The first of Pat's immediate circle to die, she had succumbed to pneumonia in a New York hospital. P.K.'s response was simply, "I miss the thought of her being on this planet."[60] Members of Page's generation were now plagued with health problems. Her own arthritis became progressively worse, but her main concern in the eighties was Arthur. He had experienced a number of unexplained ailments, and by mid-decade they were worried about blocked arteries (he was placed on Digoxin for heart problems). Later in the eighties Arthur had a series of small strokes, but in mid-decade Dr Abram Hoffer, a Victoria doctor with naturopathic interests, placed him on vitamin supplements that helped.

On 23 November 1986 Page celebrated her seventieth birthday. A group of younger poets and friends organized a party at the Rookes'

P.K. Page and Margaret Atwood, University of Victoria, 1980s

home. They put on a spoof of the first meeting of P.K. and Arthur at the National Film Board. Colin Gorrie, who had a British military background, played Arthur. With false nose and glasses, his transformation was startlingly accurate. The other celebrants included Marilyn Bowering and her husband Michael Elcock, the Godfreys, the Purdys, and Carole Sabiston and her husband Jim Munro. Three years later Arthur had his ninetieth birthday, and they had "a great celebration with ninety balloons, a magician and a musical skit on his life. Champagne all the way."[61] To P.K.'s great regret, in 1989 Connie Rooke left UVic to become head of the English Department at Guelph.

When unable to write poetry at the beginning of the eighties, P.K. went back to the journal she had kept in Brazil. She had worked on it sporadically in the sixties and seventies, but the project defeated her. The journal itself was a long manuscript, 238 pages in small single-spaced type, and there were approximately 50 pages of additional travel notes as well as a number of letters sent back to Canada. She requested help from the National Archives, which now housed both her papers and Arthur's. She had earlier sold a portion of her literary papers to the National Archives and from the proceeds had bought a watering system for the garden – Arthur was getting too old to lug hoses – and a new electronic typewriter in order to redraft the journal. She published a long extract from the journal in *Canadian Literature* (Autumn 1981) covering the period from 1 February to 28 August 1960 and giving the flavour of Brazil:"How could I have imagined so surrealist and seductive a world?" It describes the heat, the smells, and the way that life slows down in the tropics. The birds, the flowers, and the people had given her joy and released her creativity.[62]

Shortly after this extract was published, Michael Ondaatje telephoned P.K. with high praise; he had heard a new and different voice in the journals: "Still reeling from your Brazil journal. It was really wonderful and sensual, and even the insects were so well dressed! I haven't enjoyed prose as much for ages and what was interesting was that I didn't hear your voice, it was another voice which I have not heard in the poems. It would be great if you did a book of your journals from all over. Have you thought of that, and if so who will do it? I really think you should. That falling in love with the country happens right in front of our eyes. More! More! Many thanks for that world."[63] Still later, when she published a second excerpt in *Brick*, he again responded enthusiastically. In 1982 Ondaatje published his own autobiographical journal, *Running in the Family.*

Marilyn Bowering was also deeply impressed and asked if she could make a script, "Me Tembro," from the material for performance. This reading was held in Victoria on 12 May 1984 and put on again in 2011. Marilyn had become P.K.'s enduring poet friend. As P.K. had earlier confided to Arlene Lampert, "I'm grateful for Marilyn being here. She is a darling ... I ... feel she has great talent and will probably be one of our best writers before she has finished."[64] P.K. later read one of Marilyn's scripts, "My Grandfather Was a Soldier," written for the BBC, and was very impressed; she wrote to Rosemary Sullivan that Marilyn had done "something so remarkable with time. And images linger on in my head – the white chests of young men, the white petals of apple blossom – animal and vegetable intermingling, fragile, underlining the brutality ... and presenting it as if through a series of scrims. Impossible to describe. Very understated. No sob stuff but heart-rending none the less. Marvelous girl."[65]

P.K. had told Ondaatje that she was having great difficulty with the journal and he offered to help her edit it and find a publisher. He worked with P.K. in Victoria in mid-September 1982, staying with her and Arthur. During the visit, he may have heard Arthur holding forth on his experiences in France as a gunner during the First World War and on his later joy in viewing Michelangelo's glorious paintings on the ceiling of the Sistine Chapel. If so, some of Arthur's memories may have funnelled into Ondaatje's later novel, *The English Patient*, together with his other literary sources. The year Ondaatje visited the Irwins, his *Running in the Family* appeared and was read by Page. She loved it. It did not occur to her that the distinctively personal style and voice of her Brazilian journal may have influenced Ondaatje's own travel writing.

On Ondaatje's recommendation, by late June 1985 Page was working with the publisher Lester & Orpen Dennys, who assigned Gena Kay Gorrell, a careful copy editor, to work on P.K.'s manuscript. Editing is always tricky, and P.K. balked at some of her suggestions, becoming uncomfortable and unwilling to work. Arthur stepped in: "Look, why don't we do it together. I'll pace you so we maintain a speed on this ... Don't take on any other appointments until we've got it done. We're just going to do this."[66] Arthur set up a routine by which they initially worked separately. He would go to his study in the basement and work through twenty pages at a time. When he had finished, he would bring them up to P.K., sitting at the kitchen table. She would then decide whether or not she wanted to accept his editorial changes. Arthur was an accomplished editor, and for P.K. working with her husband was a joy. "It was Arthur who did the real editing on that book ... A speed, and a rhythm, and [we] just got through it. It was wonderful. It was one of the happiest times of my life in a way, working in that kind of harmony with Arthur."[67] Ultimately, he made it possible for her to finish the book. Arthur always expressed his affection by doing rather than saying, though, on their anniversary a few years later, he wrote laconically: "Dear Pat: It's been a good thirty-eight years & Thanks for everything X I love you X Arthur."[68]

Brazilian Journal was well received by readers and critics alike. William French, writing in the *Globe and Mail*, praised it as "a love story, but not the usual kind." He suggested that the book showed Page to be "a woman of wit, perception and sensibility ... with a mind and heart open to new experience." He responded to her vivid metaphors, the books she was reading, and her reflections on what it was like to be an ambassador's wife.[69] George Galt, writing in *Saturday Night*, spoke of the book as "an intricate triptych of her Brazil: on one panel the rich narrative of everyday life, on another the inner world of metaphor and memory, and on the third her sketches and paintings." He suggested that Page's metaphors, together with her intense perceptions, appeared "about to break into the magic-realist prose of South America," a product of her deep immersion in Brazilian culture.[70]

Brazilian Journal was shortlisted for the British Columbia Hubert Evans Non-Fiction prize in 1988 and for the Governor General's Award. The citation for the BC prize read: "Page fell in love with Brazil and this is her vivid, sympathetic and intensely personal diary recounting her time there. Fascinating, funny, beautifully written – this is a window into a special place." As it happened, my book, *The Politics of the Imagination: A Life of F.R. Scott*, was shortlisted for the same prize, and P.K. sent me a postcard saying, "I want us *both* to win!"[71] Of course, *Brazilian Journal* received the prize. Nonetheless, this coincidence may have encouraged P.K. to think of me as a possible biographer. A year later in Vancouver, when I was driving her to the bus for the Victoria ferry, she began to speak of a dream about her military father as a tall upright figure on a horse. The image stayed with me – perhaps because I remember my father, a captain in the Canadian Merchant Marine during the Second World War, as a similar figure on the bridge of his ship. Later, in the early nineties, after again hearing P.K. speak of her father affectionately but sadly, at a writers' festival on Granville Island, I began to wonder about P.K.'s life story. Would she have a biography?

The process of preparing *Brazilian Journal* led P.K. down to the basement on Exeter Road where her early Brazilian sketches were stored. She showed them to Shushan Egoyan, who suggested cheerfully that the best way to clean out one's basement was to have an exhibition. In November 1987 P.K. showed her work at UVic's Maltwood Gallery. It was a splendid retrospective because it contained much of her early work and demonstrates how she emerged as an artist up to the end of her time in Brazilian. There are early felt pen sketches of the embassy grounds and gardens, of the mountains dominating Rio and the many native plants. As she began to experiment with colour, the black and white felt pen drawings were tempered by watercolour or, most often, gouache, as in *Sala Grande* and *Pink Embassy* (the cover of the published *Brazilian Journal*) and the wonderful umbers and yellows of the embassy "Stairwell." Her strengths are architectural rather than figurative, and the renderings of nature and place are increasingly assured; but the occasional human figures, as in bathers at the beach in *Striped Umbrellas*, are less accomplished. Curiously, she does not appear to have shown any of her later Brazilian oil paintings in this exhibition.

⸎

During the last half of the decade, P.K. was increasingly reflecting upon the larger questions of man's relation to nature. In early January 1985 she had begun to watch a TV series featuring David Suzuki, entitled *A Planet for the Taking*. The first episode questioned man's colonizing attitude to nature and discussed Darwinism with the paleoanthropologist Richard Leakey. In response to Suzuki's question about when man separated from the apes, Leakey responded, "In my view, it hasn't happened. We are apes. The similarities are so great." When describing the program to Florence Bird, P.K. repeated Leakey's comment: "We are still apes." It interested her very much in relation to Shah's saying: "The first thing is to become human." P.K. had thought that Shah was referring to individuals, meaning that they should rise above their petty selves. But after hearing Leakey, she wondered if Shah's remark carried a double meaning, that "he may have meant individually but he perhaps means *in evolutionary terms* too."[72] Earlier, she had read a prose piece by Shah entitled "Report on the Planet Earth," which is included in his *Reflections*, a small book of Sufi readings.[73] P.K. had always responded to nature, but now Suzuki's *A Planet for the Taking* focused her interest on Planet Earth in a new way.

Shah's fable of "The Islanders," which opens *The Sufis*, is one of apocalyptic loss of home and memory, and includes the possibility of escape. Lessing invokes both aspects of this theme in *The Four-Gated City* and *Briefing for a Descent into Hell*. However, in her successive *Canopus* novels she widens the possibilities for escape from the island.[74] For various reasons, which Lessing attributes to racial pride, war, pestilence, and other intergalactic catastrophes, Earth is moving towards its own destruction, despite the valiant efforts of a progressive chosen few. These superior individuals from a higher plane (from "the Stars," as Lessing says in *Shikasta*) attempt to influence the inhabitants of Planet Earth for the better.[75]

Sufi writings, whether by Shah or Lessing, had brought Page to think more deeply about human evolution. She thought, "[I]f I could get a fix on my genetic background, that might be a clue to finding out who I was and to coming to terms with myself, not necessarily psychological terms but something bigger ... both the evolution of the species and the evolution of the individual."[76] She undertook genealogical research, attempting to find out more about her ancestors, the Pages and the Whitehouses, but this was time-consuming and expensive.

She also continued to be interested in the evolution of the modern individual. Martha Quest and Lynda Coldridge in Lessing's *The Four-Gated City*, and Johor in *The Sirian Experiments*, were examples of individuals who had developed new capacities in response to cosmic upheaval. Lessing frequently wrote of a small group of progressive left-wingers, newspaper commentators, artists, and political figures – both male and female – attempting to ameliorate the problems of an overindustrialized and degenerating planet. Similarly, P.K. and Arthur Irwin found their deepest friendships in a group of politically oriented Canadian nationalists – though saving the planet was less an issue than saving Canada, especially after the 1984 election of Prime Minister Brian Mulroney, when the proposed free trade agreement with the United States threatened the integrity of Canadian sovereignty. Young poets and intellectuals of the period, particularly Margaret Atwood and Dennis Lee, were also greatly troubled by these changes in the national scene.

In 1989 P.K. published with Oxford University Press her first children's book, *A Flask of Sea Water*. A traditional fairy tale with Sufi overtones, it was handsomely produced with beautiful illustrations by Laszlo Gal. A goatherd glimpses a beautiful princess and they fall in love. Her fairy godmother proposes a contest to the king, her father, in which the princess's hand will be given to the candidate who brings back to this land-locked kingdom "a flask of sea water." The suitors are the usual trio of fairy tale, and predictably two fall by the way because of their unkindness to supernatural helpers. The third is the goatherd, who is generous to everyone he meets and therefore is helped. Despite this, the goatherd (like Prince Attilla) is enslaved by a wizard, who takes away the memory of his quest. His memory is providentially restored when the fairy godmother reappears. He reaches the sea, finds the sea water, and wins the princess's hand.[77] Although the book sold reasonably well, P.K. was a little miffed about its reception. "The few reviews of 'Flask ...' are short but sweet but my literary friends are inclined to behave as if I've made a bad smell. Children's literature is not literature clearly."[78] Four years later she published a sequel, *The Goat That Flew* (1993), illustrated by Marika Gal. The goat, the wizard, and the flask of sea water continue from the first story, and again the quest is to reach the sea – but in this case so that the goat, put under a spell by the wizard, can again become a young man and marry the girl he loves.

☰

P.K.'s day-to-day activities had changed. She now rarely went to meetings of the League of Canadian Poets and told Elizabeth Brewster in 1989, "I've never been a joiner and even to join the League when it was small took some effort. I was just about to de-join when they made me a life member!"[79] A larger milestone occurred in the same year with a breakdown in communications from Idries Shah. The newsletters and cassettes regularly sent from the Sufi centre in England to small groups in North America abruptly stopped. P.K. wrote to Florence saying that "Langton is sold and Shah has moved to Burgundy. He is not well ... We have given up our room and await (hopefully) new instructions. My personal contacts are now one – a friend in England ... And perhaps I could count Lessing with whom I have a tenuous connection. I always feel she is a developed Sufi, but how can one tell?"[80]

CHAPTER 14

Victoria
Acclaim, 1990–1999

P.K.'s creativity exploded in all directions in the nineties – poetry, fiction, plays, children's stories – and was promptly acknowledged. She published three fine books of poetry: *The Glass Air: Poems Selected and New* (1991; a new edition of the 1985 collection), *Hologram: A Book of Glosas* (1994); and the two volumes of *The Hidden Room: Collected Poems* (1997). She also undertook three poetry tours. She was the subject of a film, *Still Waters*, by Donald Winkler of the National Film Board, and her poetry was featured in several musical programs in Toronto, Montreal, and San Francisco. In 1996 the *The Malahat Review* devoted a special issue to her work in celebration of her eightieth birthday. She was also honoured by her peers. Her work was featured at the Sunshine Coast Festival of the Written Arts in Sechelt, British Columbia in 1998 and the Vancouver International Writers Festival in 2000; in 1999 she was also invited to read her poetry at the prestigious International Festival of Authors at Harbourfront, Toronto.

Recognition had also come from the academic world. In May 1985 she had been awarded an Honorary DLITT. from the University of Victoria. Four years later, in 1989, she received another honorary doctorate, from the University of Calgary, and a third came from Simon Fraser University in 1991. Degrees are granted at SFU in an outdoor mall partially covered by a glass roof, and because concrete resounds, there is always a hum of conversation, a shuffling of feet, and a shifting of seats. Robed in burgundy and royal blue, P.K. Page was a regal figure as she stood on the platform and began to speak, enunciating each word. The hum died away as the audience strained to listen. They had suddenly realized – despite the colloquial swing of her diction – that she was not speaking in prose:

What do I have to tell you? I could wish
today was fifty years ago for then,
chock-full of schooling and high spirits, I
knew what was what. And where. And even when.

Instead of the usual convocation speech to the graduates, P.K. had written a poem, "Address at Simon Fraser." She spoke of the clear-cutting
of forests and of extremes in weather; of global warming and its opposite, the bitterly cold BC winter in 1989. She had never before felt that
the writer had a role "beyond the role / of writing what he/she *must*
write." But now the future of our planet – "the whole great beautiful
caboodle" – hangs in doubt. Eloquently she spoke of the stars and
warned her audience that "our break with nature is the source / of all
that's out of kilter." Furthermore, "This turning world / we call our
home … could / become inimical to humankind." Her concluding message was simply this:

"Imagination is the star in man."
Read *woman*, if you wish. And though we are
trapped in the body of an animal,
we're half angelic, and our angel ear,
which hears the music of the spheres, can hear
the planet's message, dark, admonishing,
as the archaic torso of Apollo
admonished Rilke, "You must change your life."

Art and the planet tell us. Change your life.[1]

The poem was all the more effective because P.K. rarely wrote of public
issues. It was also a farsighted speech for 1991, and the concepts informing this poem – human evolution, Planet Earth, and ecology – provided themes for P.K.'s next two decades of writing.

To some degree her sense of Suzuki's presentation in *A Planet for the
Taking* had fused with a new book by Robert Ornstein and Paul Ehrlich
entitled *New World, New Mind*. Ornstein argues that humans are still
evolving, but they must make great changes to incorporate a larger understanding of the world, especially the tradition represented by Sufism.
In the last chapter, "Changing the World Around Us," he argues for "a
new kind of synthesis between the modern scientific understanding …

and the essence of religious or esoteric traditions." What Ornstein was advocating is now known as a "sustainable future." Can we win through to a better world? Yes, he argues, "With luck, we will have started to change your mind."[2]

P.K.'s Simon Fraser poem, dedicated to Arlene Lampert, was included as the last poem in *The Glass Air: Poems Selected and New*. This edition included a number of new poems: "Kaleidoscope," "The Hidden Components," "Lily on the Patio" (for Connie Rooke), "Conversation," "I – Sphinx" (P.K.'s dramatization of the aging Sibelius for a CBC radio program), "Winter Morning," "The Gift," "The World," "Eden," "Chinook," and "The Sky" as well as "Address at Simon Fraser." Of these, the Simon Fraser poem is the most important as a statement of PK.'s developing ecological views. The poems are arranged in three groups, headed roughly by the dates of the period when they were first published. The book contains the same nine drawings and two concluding essays that were in the first *Glass Air*.

This new edition of *The Glass Air* generated a flurry of critical attention. Douglas Barbour called Page "a visionary poet" and referred to the collection as containing "some of our finest poetry," but he considered "Address at Simon Fraser" too polemical.[3] George Johnston was disappointed that readers had been presented with a selected book instead of a collected works; but he praised "Address at Simon Fraser" as a "confirmation of all we had admired and loved in this poetry."[4] Cynthia Messenger regretted the lack of an introduction and the somewhat inconsistent chronology – some poems are in the wrong group (as they were in the first edition).[5]

The launching of this edition of *The Glass Air* sent P.K. on tour in eastern Canada. In mid-October 1991 she undertook a reading at the University of Toronto and a number of surrounding venues. In November she was interviewed by the *Toronto Star* and in December by the *Globe and Mail*, where Val Ross described P.K. Page's poems as "sensitive, fine-lined, nervy, elusive." The article included a tribute from Michael Ondaatje: "She's a very important touchstone for writers. She's raucous and funny in person but her head is another reality. She has a very odd-angled vision of the world, tragic and comic, the imagined world lying side by side with the real."[6]

In early August 1993 the English poet Ted Hughes came to Victoria to speak to the Steelhead Society of British Columbia. He also gave a public poetry reading. Susan Musgrave, then living in Victoria, had come to know Hughes in England, and Clive and Christine Tanner, the owners of Tanner's Books in Victoria, gave a lunch on 12 August for the Victoria poets and their spouses to meet Hughes. Invited were P.K., Patrick Lane and Lorna Crozier, Marilyn Bowering and Michael Elcock, and Musgrave and Stephen Reid. P.K. had a wonderful time because the group treated her as the senior poet and seated her beside Hughes, whose poems she had long admired. She felt that Hughes was "on the Sufi beam" because she recalled he had once said that the Sufis must be the greatest body of intelligent men the world had ever produced. Also, he had chosen one of P.K.'s poems, "Portrait of a Salt Mine," for an anthology, *School Bag*, which he had edited with Seamus Heaney. P.K. found Hughes himself "wonderful, immediate, I knew that we could have been friends given any chance."[7] That night, at his public reading, Hughes read a number of poems without explanation, including a number about his first wife, Sylvia Plath.[8] They were later published in *Birthday Letters* (1998), which P.K. read and to some degree emulated in her later *Hand Luggage*.

Unless the Eye Catch Fire performance at the Belfry Theatre, Victoria, British Columbia. Joy Coghill, P.K. Page, and Robert Cram.

In May 1994, Joy Coghill produced and acted in a special production of "Unless the Eye Catch Fire ..." at Victoria's Belfry Theatre in honour of the Commonwealth Games. Coghill, a veteran actor and former director of the Vancouver Playhouse, had wanted to set some of P.K.'s poems to music. She contacted Robert Cram, a flutist and a founding member of the National Arts Centre, and invited him to accompany her while she read from the text. Page suggested they try "Unless the Eye Catch Fire ..." Reworking this fable in a different medium was a tightrope experience for Cram. Although he had often improvised, this time, as he said, "I was trying to carry a line in a story, not getting in the way of it – that's a hard one – of finding sounds that worked in a narrative context without taking away from the narration." He recognized that his flute music at times had to rise up and take over the narrative, but then disappear again. "It was a wonderful challenge. And working on it with Joy was one of the most intense experiences I've ever had."[9]

They spent some time at the Banff School of Fine Arts working on the performance: Cram attempting to develop improvisations that were original and would complement Coghill's spoken voice. Coghill was determined to keep her narrative true to Page's text, whittling down the story by two-thirds and then checking the result with Page. The performance was given at the Belfry Theatre on a bare stage on which the props consisted of a chair and table with a telephone. But Coghill was a consummate performer and carried the story to its transcendent conclusion. It was a highly successful production, running three nights. On the last night, a voice from the balcony called out, "Author, Author," and P.K. stood up. Later, as the Page and Irwin families were discussing this, someone joked, "That was Théa" (presumably because Théa Gray always insisted that P.K. receive due credit for her poems and had once protested indignantly during a musical performance when this had not happened). "No," said P.K., "It wasn't. Théa was sitting beside me and for one of the few times in our friendship, she was firmly under my thumb."[10]

P.K. and Théa Gray had been close friends ever since Théa had urged her sister Dagmar, who lived in Victoria, to introduce them in early 1992. The sisters were daughters of Brigadier H.F.H. Hertzberg, a professional soldier in the Canadian army who had been the district officer in command in Halifax, 1934–37. Lionel Page had worked under him in the mid-1930s. Théa met P.K. for lunch in March when she and her husband Duggan were visiting in Victoria. The two women talked non-stop about poetry all afternoon. Théa had a list to cover: she wanted P.K. to define technique ("It's knowing just exactly what word to put beside another word, and exactly what rhythm is the one to use in this particular situation. It's know-how.") and to speak of her favourite poets (Wallace Stevens, Rilke, Rumi, T.S. Eliot). She asked P.K. if she knew W.S. Merwin's "Elegy."[11] No, said P.K. Théa picked up a scrap of paper and wrote out the whole poem. It was just one line: "Who would I show it to?" At that instant they forged a bond.

Théa loved music and knew a great deal about literature, especially the classics, including Homer and Dante. A graduate of McGill University, she had begun reading poetry in the 1960s. Starting with Chaucer, she had worked her way up to the Romantics, finally encountering the moderns and Canadian poetry. When she discovered P.K.'s poems, she determined to meet her. Théa shared with P.K. many of the disciplined values generated by an army childhood: she believed in doing one's duty and getting things done without complaint. She was also intelligent, empathetic, and down-to-earth. She filled the great void in P.K.'s life left by the departures of Rosemary Sullivan and Connie Rooke.

In the spring of 1992 when they first met, Théa and P.K. went to Point-No-Point at Sooke for a week of respite while Arthur's daughters looked after him. They read books to each other and talked about poetry in a cottage by the sea. It rained all the time, but that didn't seem to matter: Théa recalls that she was "dazzled" to have access to P.K.'s mind,[12] and P.K. was delighted to have found a travelling companion. Their next jaunt was to Seattle to see the Debussy opera *Pelléas et Mélisande*. Thereafter, Théa accompanied P.K. on all her trips east and facilitated her attendance at poetry festivals. Although she would disagree with this statement, she also entered into the creative process, at first as an empathetic reader but increasingly as a critical third eye.[13]

Ironically, it was Robin Skelton who provided P.K. with the poetic form, the glosa, for which she became known in the nineties through her collection *Hologram: A Book of Glosas*. On 9 January 1992, Skelton urged Marilyn Bowering to write what he called a "Glose," a complicated poetic form because it consists of an opening four lines from another poet's work, followed by four ten-line stanzas, their concluding lines taken consecutively from the initial quatrain, their sixth and ninth lines rhyming with the borrowed tenth. Marilyn read her glosa, "Letter from Portugal," derived from the Egyptian poet Cavafy, at a June reading in the Malahat Reading Series in Victoria's Market Square.[14] P.K. and a number of other poets, including Patricia Young, were present. As Marilyn

was reading, Patricia recognized that it was a really good poem, and she
saw "P.K. almost visibly gasping. As though she couldn't get home fast
enough to write a glosa."[15]

P.K. found the form challenging.[16] After Marilyn had explained the
glosa rules, P.K. told her that she "had been seized by the glose form and
was writing madly – as she hadn't for years."[17] Within a month she had
written her first glosa, "Hologram." It was comparatively easy to write,
and she published it promptly in the *Malahat Review* (September 1992).
For the next two years she and Théa had fun looking for poems that
could be used in glosas. Théa helped find Sappho's "Alone" and suggested changes in some of the glosa titles. For example, P.K. had written
a glosa that began with W.H. Auden's "Elegy for W.B. Yeats." P.K. had
originally intended to call the glosa "R.I.P." – possibly because F.R. Scott
(its subject) had written a poem with this title.[18] But Théa suggested that
"In Memoriam" would be a better title for the glosa, and it was.[19]

By November 1993, P.K. had found a publisher, Brick Books, and
was in the process of preparing *Hologram* for publication. Her editor, the
poet Jan Zwicky, saw at once that this would be a wonderful book: "The
final stanzas almost without exception move with a cumulative sureness
that takes my breath away." Zwicky recognized the increasingly powerful cadences of P.K.'s voice and her mastery of the glosa form: "These
poems are so generous, so visionary in their conception, and so exacting
in their execution ... They're true." She found the order convincing, with
"lovely echoes and throws, poem to poem, and threadings through the
whole manuscript. The intertwining of themes – love, the planet, loss – is
so completely achieved."[20] By Christmas Day 1993, P.K. was able to write
Rosemary Sullivan that *Arthur Irwin: A Biography* by David MacKenzie[21] was out and that she was now putting her glosas together with Jan
Zwicky – "what a great girl she is."[22] In January 1994 P.K. went to visit
Théa in the Okanagan, where they jointly read proofs of the new book.

P.K.'s personal experience of the hologram (a three-dimensional image
that has depth, produced by light and radiation) anticipates her Seferis
poem, called "Hologram," and seems to have come by chance. She
dreamed of, or was actually visiting, the old National Gallery in Ottawa,
on Elgin Street: "A gallery-length away I either dreamed or saw a miniature gothic building, flying buttresses and all, floating in the air. I was
drawn to it as if pulled. I had no idea what I was seeing. It might have
been a hallucination. I walked round its three-dimensional presence –
perfect, made as it were from densities of air." It was one of the most
amazing visual experiences in her life.[23]

The book *Hologram* is a collection of fourteen glosa, and each poem is followed by one of P.K.'s black-and-white octagonal drawings. These are mandalas with Sufi undertones and augment P.K.'s vision of love in its largest sense. The glosa was a particularly appropriate form for P.K. to use to honour the poets she admired because it allowed her to borrow their lines. And she found the exercise of writing these poems demanding, a good thing for an older poet whose life experiences were now diminishing and less vivid. Astonishingly, the form itself unearthed deep personal emotion and brought to light – like a hologram – a new intertwined sense of the universe. Writing in response to another poet's poem allowed P.K. to express her own emotions more freely.[24]

The title poem, "Hologram," borrowed lines from George Seferis's poem "The King of Asine," which begins: "*All that morning we looked at the citadel from every angle.*" It came easily, taking the form of a hologram of the citadel/castle.

It was astonishing, larger by far than we could imagine,
larger than sight itself but still we strained to see it.
It was Kafka's castle in a dream of wonder,
nightmare transmuted, black become golden,
buttresses disappearing in the cloud and azure:
a new geometry of interlocking octangles
and we, watching it, interlocked in a strange dimension –
that neither your heart nor mine could have invented –
of multiple images, complex as angels.
All that morning we looked at the citadel from every angle.[25]

To the watchers, over time, as explained in this and succeeding stanzas, the landscape moves from darkness to light, from morning to noon, and suddenly – in a flash, from infrared to ultraviolet – the one-dimensional citadel is "rainbowed" and immediate. It is a hologram that "*received us like time that has no break in it.*" The references to octangles (octagons), angels, love, a strange dimension, and time without break – all evoke Sufi thought, as indeed do many poems in this book.

P.K. liked the idea of constructing a poem backwards, as allowed by the glosa form, the final line of each stanza being in effect "the starting line." She discovered a second example in "Credences of Summer" by Wallace Stevens, but it was extremely difficult to find a third example until she came across Rilke's "Autumn Day" in a contemporary translation: curiously, she did not remember that as an eighteen-year-old she had published her first poem, "The Moth," next to this poem by Rilke in the London *Observer*. Her glosa on Elizabeth Bishop's "Sandpiper," which she calls "Poor Bird," speaks of the poor bird (herself? all of us? – certainly the bird of *And You, What Do You Seek?* that had served as the cover painting of *Cry Ararat!*) who is "*looking for something, something, something.*"

> But occasionally, when he least expects it,
> in the glass of a wave a painted fish
> like a work of art across his sight
> reminds him of something he doesn't know
> that he has been seeking his whole long life –
> something that may not even exist![26]

Some poems in *Hologram*, specifically "Planet Earth" and "The End," will be discussed later in the book. "In Memoriam," "Alone" and "Exile" were written for Frank Scott. Another poem, "The Answer," which begins with a quatrain from "The Vow" by Robert Graves, raises the discussion of love to a wider, more encompassing Sufi plane.

> *For whom do you live? Can it be yourself?*
> *For whom then? Not for this unlovely world ...*
>
> 'but love, only for love, the love that is
> so focused on its object that I die ...'[27]

This poem again alludes to "that beam of love which clothes us in." In 1968 P.K. and Arthur had been travelling in the BC interior, in the mountains. She told Marilyn Bowering that she suddenly felt "an all-encompassing beam of love," an experience that stayed with her for several weeks.[28] It was this experience that P.K. craved and found in Sufi thinking, especially the chapters on "Fariduddin Attar" and "Omar Khayyam" in *The Sufis*, which emphasize the importance of Love.

A number of the poems in *Hologram*, especially "The End," emphasize this larger Sufi concept of Love as the final stage of a journey, or quest. Shah, when quoting Attar, alludes to the "Traveler," or "Seeker," and the relation of Love to the seven stages of Sufi development as portrayed in the latter's Sufi poem the "Parliament of Birds." The first stage is the Valley of the Quest, where the Traveler must face peril and renounce personal desires. Although the Valley of Love follows, the Traveler cannot rest in mere ecstasy but must continue on to the Valley of

Intuitive Knowledge (where the heart directly receives the illumination of Truth) until he finally reaches the Valley of Detachment and is liberated from desire. The fifth valley is the Valley of Unification, where the Seeker understands that what he had understood to be different ideas and things are actually one. This is followed by the Valley of Astonishment, where the Seeker finds both "bewilderment" and "Love": he no longer understands knowledge in the old way, "something which is called Love replaces it." The last valley is that of Death, where the Seeker understands the mystery of how an individual "drop can be merged with an ocean, and still remain meaningful."[29]

Hologram was published in the spring of 1994. A year later, P.K. sent a copy of the book, along with several of her children's books, to Idries Shah. From her perspective, she was sending her work to her spiritual guide. His response was devastating. Shah appears to have rebuked her sharply, possibly for using a variant of the octagon (associated with his Sufi publications) on the cover of *Hologram*, and she replied contritely, regretting her "heedlessness."[30] It is probable that Shah was ill at this point – he died the following year – but it is also apparent that he did not respond positively to the fine poetry of *Hologram*, nor does he seem to have acknowledged what a large part his writings, especially *The Sufis*, had played in her perception of infinite Love.

P.K.'s *Hologram* poetry tour was postponed until the fall of 1994 because of a scheduled hip operation. Her hip had been very painful for some years and she now suffered from osteoporosis. She had an operation in August 1994, but it was only partially successful; she still had difficulty walking. She continued to suffer from chronic pain that persisted to the end of her life. In July she cancelled an Ontario reading tour and in August withdrew from the North American Literary Arts Festival.

⊟

In September, P.K. and Théa journeyed east to launch *Hologram* at the Eden Mills Writers' Festival, organized by Connie and Leon Rooke. The reading took place at the home in Eden Mills, Ontario, of writer Janice Kulyk Keefer and her husband Michael. It provided a natural amphitheatre, with a lawn at the back of the house and a big hill with rocks and grass. P.K. stood on the verandah, propped by her cane, facing a packed audience. Approximately a hundred people reclined on the lawn, and others found space up the back. Esta Spalding, stepdaughter of Michael Ondaatje, preceded P.K. and said what an honour it was to be on the same stage as P.K. and Thomas King. P.K. read "Hologram," "The Gold Sun," and "Autumn" from *Hologram*, as well as "Intraocular Lens," "A

Little Reality," and "Spring Tree." Théa recalls that at the end, all the people leapt to their feet: "It was one of those real standing ovations ... everybody rose as one ... I can see her standing ... the sun was dappled on her face."[31] P.K. just stood there, not knowing how to respond; finally, she put her cane up in the air and waved back at the audience. On 5 November, back in Victoria, a launch for *Hologram* was held at the Majestic Café, where P.K. read four poems, including "Autumn."

Hologram is a powerful book. Bruce Whitman, again reviewing Page, remarked that the language and metre of each poem mirrors its source, but in the best poems "Page is so engaged in her own poetic urgencies that ... she ... feels [the glosa form] as the nearest gossamer enclosure to her flight."[32] Kevin McNeilly pointed out that Page was not just imitating the poets she chose to write on but was taking part in "a music's recreation to her own ear." In so doing, she was participating in "the process of response."[33] The book started a trend in Canadian writing, a "glosa revolution," as Patricia Young later commented: "I mean back East they're all writing them. Everywhere you go, every magazine you pick up ... She's the queen of glosas. Nobody can touch her!"[34]

P.K. made friends with the Canadian-born American poet Mark Strand through *Hologram*. When reading at McMaster, she met Jeffrey Donaldson, a faculty member whom she recalled as writing: "I've given Mark Strand your *Hologram*, he is delighted with it, and says he's so pleased to be in it, and he would very much like to exchange books with you, if you would like to do that."[35] P.K. sent Strand *The Glass Air*, and he responded with a new book of his called *Dark Harbour*.[36] Strand later wrote P.K. saying, "I love *Hologram*."[37]

Ever since her new edition of *The Glass Air*, P.K. had been thinking that the time had come to gather her work together. She briefly considered publishing a journal that she had kept intermittently when travelling in Australia. This had been suggested by Ronald Hatch – a professor in the English Department at UBC and the publisher of Ronsdale Press – when she read at UBC in the early nineties. After Hatch had read parts of the journal, he suggested that she might consider changing some of the language used in Australia in the fifties – "Abo" for Aborigine, for example. But as P.K. later reflected, rewriting history is always a mistake. She attempted to deal with the problem by constructing a "Then and Now" alternation in journal entries, incorporating her visit to Australia in 1984. But this didn't work either, and eventually the project lapsed. Nonethe-

less, sections from the journal were published in *Brick* and in Keath
Fraser's *Bad Trips* (1991).[38]

Collecting her poems was a more pressing issue, in view of her advanced age. She approached both Oxford University Press and McClelland and Stewart, but neither publisher was interested. Indeed, Oxford
had ceased publishing collections of poetry. At McClelland and Stewart
the proposal had gone to poetry editor Stan Dragland, who deeply
regretted the press's decision. He admired P.K.'s poetry, had attended the
"amazing open-air reading" by P.K. at Eden Mills, and took it upon
himself to contact John Metcalf, the senior editor for the Porcupine's
Quill; he asked Metcalf if publishers Tim and Elke Inkster would be
interested in publishing P.K.'s collected poems.[39] They were.

Dragland made preliminary arrangements and recounted all this to
P.K. in a letter of December 1995. She was delighted: "What a wonderful Christmas present – your letter with the enclosure from John Metcalf.
You persuade me! Objections overruled."[40] Early in the New Year P.K.
again wrote to Dragland: "It sounds as if we're in it for real and it gives
me quite a turn! But how wonderful to have you in it with me." P.K. had
taken a shine to Dragland, who had introduced her at a poetry reading
at the University of Western Ontario when she was on a tour for *Hologram*. In his letter of reply in mid-January 1996, Dragland spelled out
his vision of the book: a comprehensive edition but not every poem: "I
think we should be looking at everything we think is good. Allowing for
development, of course. We should display P.K. at all, or at least all significant, stages."[41] P.K. sent copies of her published books to Dragland
and raised the issue of including unpublished early verse and magazine
publication. The process of deciding which poems to include became a
joint process shared by Dragland, P.K., and Théa Gray.[42] Théa chose
several poems from the unpublished early verse.

The first "assemblage" was a collation of poems from the unpublished, published, and magazine work. Stan made a list of everything,
allowing for a checkmark as a positive response. When all three of them
checked a poem, it was in. Then there was the question of arrangement:
In what order should they be presented? Dragland suggested that there
be section titles, and P.K. thought this a good idea. She proposed: "'To
Begin Before I was Born' would be good, I think, if there is such a section ... [as] I was not really born prior to *As Ten as Twenty*, in the forties. If you think *Evening Dance* and *Hologram* stand alone, there is no
reason that I can see against letting them do so." She also agreed to add
some additional poems to the roughly chronological sections.

Dragland chose the thematic units and their titles by fanning out the
poems on the living-room floor – like playing cards – where he could see
them. There was a great deal of shifting, with sections emerging in the
process. Once all the poems had been assembled, it became clear that the
first and last sections, "To Begin Before I Was Born and "Now That I Am
Dead," were, as he later pointed out, "temporal book ends, being selec-
tions of early and late poems, respectively." He asked P.K. for a chronological listing of the uncollected and unpublished poems. Dragland soon
found, however, that it was "impossible to make chronologically based
units without muddling the thematic families into which the poems fell."[43]

P.K. fully approved of the format. As she said in the acknowledgments, Dragland "tackled material spanning sixty years and threaded it
together in a manner uniquely his own." He faxed P.K. the table of contents, and when she had considered it she responded, "You are brilliant,"
saying that both of his "hemispheres were flashing" as he made the
arrangement.[44] These sections trace significant themes in P.K.'s poetry
and constitute, by their arrangement, a critical commentary. "Generation"
(1), for example, is a personal view of the war years and slightly beyond.
The title poem – a new poem – acts as a prologue to the collection. Théa
Gray suggested that the first poem in volume one (after "The Hidden
Room") should be "Grand Manan," retitled "Emergence," and that the
last poem be "This Heavy Craft." P.K.'s dedication, "To All My Family
/ and Beyond," suggests not only that her "family" has a larger than
usual context but also that some are "beyond" in a metaphysical sense.

This process of compiling the book continued from January 1996 to
May 1997, when Tim and Elke Inkster received the completed manuscript. Elke wrote P.K.: "We are all rather intimidated – it's gigantic, but
it does indeed *look* like a life-time's worth of marvelous work."[45] Shortly
afterwards, "Tim the printer" added what amounted to a P.S.: "*The Hidden Room* is quite a bit bigger than Stan had thought. Could we publish
this as a matching two-volume set? Such a plot would double the public funding, make it easier to bind, increase the retail price!"[46] Tim was
also concerned about reproductions of P.K.'s art: "Are there any origi-
nals still around?" He did not think that reproductions in her past books
of poetry were as good as they could be.[47]

P.K. had still not signed a publishing contract with the Porcupine's
Quill. In the past, she had always been scrupulous about retaining her
full copyright wherever possible. But she was very grateful to Tim and
the Porcupine's Quill for publishing this final collection when other publishers would not. Over the years the Porcupine's Quill had regularly
published good poetry at a loss. On 2 May 1997 she reached an agree-

ment with Inkster in which the press retained 20 per cent on present and future royalties on the publication of P.K.'s poems. With this agreement, the book could now go to press.

Four months later, in early September, the two volumes of *The Hidden Room: Collected Poems* arrived in Victoria. P.K.'s letter to Tim was brief and heartfelt: "The book has just arrived and it is BEAUTIFUL! Thanks for your art and skill and care."[48] Shortly afterwards, on 4 September, she and Théa left Victoria for Ontario. They arrived at Eden Mills, near Guelph, on the fifth, and P.K. stayed with Connie and Leon Rooke. The highlight of the tour was P.K.'s reading at Eden Mills on Sunday afternoon, 7 September. The festival began with the popular Peter Gzowski, former host of the CBC morning show, who told the audience that they were lucky – P.K. Page would be reading that afternoon. Her reading of old poems and new was a triumph. Théa recalls that as P.K.'s reading came to an end, the whole audience rose to shout and cheer their approval – just as they had done here three years earlier. Photographs show a triumphant P.K., wearing white pants and top, again waving her cane. As before, she had packed a field full of poetry enthusiasts. She was the first – and only – person in the history of the festival to receive a standing ovation from the huge crowd attending. Tim Inkster, as publisher, was astonished and delighted to (almost) sell out the first printing of the book so soon after publication. He had set out an ambitious schedule for launching *The Hidden Room* that included a number of readings in Toronto, Ottawa, and Montreal, as well as a recording by the CBC and several interviews.

On the ninth P.K. and Théa travelled by car to Toronto, where they stayed until the tenth. There she read at the Rivoli restaurant on Queen Street West. Just before the reading began, Margaret Atwood came down the aisle with an armful of flowers, which she placed on the platform as a tribute. Their next stop was Ottawa, from 12 to 14 September, where P.K. read at the old Fire Station in a series organized by John Metcalf. Somehow she fitted in visits with Florence Bird, Jori Smith, and Anne Goddard of the National Archives and had lunch with David Staines of the University of Ottawa. At a dinner in P.K.'s honour given by the Porcupine's Quill, P.K.'s conversation with fellow poet John Newlove was recorded for the *Ottawa Citizen*'s weekly books column.

Page and Newlove had recounted their youthful enthusiasm for the written word and the creative process. Their discussion turned to old poet friends such as Scott, Anderson, and Klein, and then to science fiction. Page said, "I adore science fiction. It stretches my awareness of possibilities." Newlove was dismissive, but Page countered by describing a conference organized by science-fiction writer Arthur C. Clarke in which the mathematician Benoît Mandlebrot had demonstrated multiplying fractals (a figure that contains a smaller version of itself, with a smaller version within that, ad infinitum). Page said that when Benoît Mandlebrot attempted to explain fractals, "I honestly thought I'd seen the fingerprint of God."[49] Fractals had become a new fascination.

P.K. and Théa spent the nights of the 15 and 16 September in Montreal. On the second day, Page again met with Jori Smith and at noon appeared at the Simone de Beauvoir Institute, Concordia University. At 7:30, at the Double Hook bookstore, she gave a reading that was taped by CBC Radio for *Art Talks*. She was introduced by an enthusiastic Brian Trehearne, a Canadianist from McGill University who subsequently published a book on the Montreal poets of the forties, with a chapter on Page.[50] He urged P.K. to consider a scholarly edition of her poems.

Early the next morning, P.K. and Théa left for Victoria. P.K. was worried about Arthur. He had been ill; he needed her at home. And she herself was very tired. Throughout her triumphant tour, she had been in great pain from the earlier hip operation, bone grating against bone. She wrote of this, satirically, in "Pain to His Helper":

Just one more turn, said Pain.
Hand me the tool –
screwdriver, silly! –
no, the heavy one.
I want to screw it tight.[51]

Back home in Victoria, *The Hidden Room* was given a launch at Hawthorne Books. It was a pleasant occasion, attended by a large number of Victoria poets. Marilyn Bowering and Patricia Young, among others, spoke. Arthur, who now rarely went anywhere, came to hear P.K. read for the last time, escorted by his daughter Sheila Irving.

The Hidden Room was an enormous achievement. Some of the section headings reflect Page's quirky sensibility, as does the first of several drawings, including "To Begin Before I Was Born," which implies the infinite. The "room" in the title poem is located, like Virginia Woolf's space for creation, in "a house / deeply hidden in my head." It is not only Woolf's "room of one's own" but a secret place for alchemical transformation, "a magic square / the number nine" (in Sufi thinking the number eight, or the octagon, leads to nine, or occult knowledge). Many of the poems in the first section are familiar – early poems that had already been published, such as "The Crow," "Ecco Homo," "Desiring

Only," and "As on a Dark Charger."Others, such as "The Clock of Your Pulse" (May 1942), "The Understatement" (1939), and "Death" (c.1937–38), are new to the reader, having been culled from little magazine publications.

P.K. had kept all her unpublished poetry manuscripts. To her astonishment, Stan Dragland had chosen a large number of them for publication. Volume one consists of the very best poems, including all those in *Evening Dance of the Grey Flies,* and volume two contains a number of fine earlier poems, all of the splendid *Hologram,* and a section entitled "Now That I Am Dead," which includes the generous "But We Rhyme in Heaven" for Dorothy Livesay (who was known to be quarrelsome):

But her anguished, defiant phrase –
"we rhyme in heaven!"
is like a balloon
that carries our anger up
to a rarefied air
where rancour is blown away ...[52]

The critical response to this extensive collection stretched over two years. The rationale of the collection was deftly explained by W.J. Keith when he said, "These two volumes of P.K. Page's collected poems are designed for poetry lovers rather than for academic scholars."[53] Dragland's editing was praised for its creative order in which each poem was linked to its immediate neighbours. Esta Spalding wrote: "They show us how ideas and images resonate within her whole *oeuvre.* Like tuning forks struck together, the poems sound a new music."[54] Sue McCluskey remarked: "The arrangement of the collection is structured like a poem. As [Page] says, the [sections] 'begin me and end me outside time.'"[55]

For some readers, the lack of temporal clarity was a problem. As Libby Scheier wondered, "One does not know if the book is chronological, or if the section headings are subject groupings or titles from Page's books. It's rather disorienting."[56] Kenneth Sherman, who recognizes Page as an alchemist of "marvelous complexity," stated flatly, "The only proper way to organize a poet's collected work is chronologically."[57] But poet-critic Richard Outram distinguished an inherent unity: "While the overall drift is chronological, the poems have been so intelligently interwoven that each of the volumes is a realized entity, as each is a reflection of the whole."[58] This issue is addressed by Dragland in an essay on the making of *The Hidden Room,* in which he suggested that it might

284   VICTORIA

have been a mistake to call the volume a "collected" as it raised in some
readers "expectations of a completeness and a linearity that the book wasn't
trying for," whereas in fact he was editing a book for and with Page.[59]

All critics agreed on the excellence of the poetry. Carmine Starnino,
reporting on Page's poetry tour to Montreal, observed that "there is
something terrifying about this book, the judgment it casts on our feck-
less literary age: both in how it recuperates the technical artistry that has
been abandoned in this country and in how it refurbishes poetry's bygone
ambition of fitting together, as palpably and as precisely as possible,
experience and language." He also accepted A.J.M. Smith's designation
of P.K. Page as "among the fine poets of this century."[60] W.J. Keith
concluded: "Constance Rooke once called P.K. Page 'Canada's finest poet.'
After a reading of *The Hidden Room*, I know she is right."[61] Marnie
Parsons, writing the year's review of poetry for the *University of Toronto
Quarterly*, characterized the book as "the essential collection of one of
the country's finest poets." She noted that three other poets publishing
books in 1997 – Pat Lane, Sandy Shreve, and Patricia Young – all acknowledged a connection with Page.[62]

For over a decade the idea of a biography had been percolating in P.K.'s
mind. While reading Isak Dinesen's biography in the early eighties, she
had written to George Johnston about point-of-view in biography. In response, Johnston had remarked that *he* did not expect a biography, but
"I might be willing to wonder about your biography, I am sure there will
be one. Very exotic."[63] Although P.K. frequently declared that she did not
want one, she was interested in the progress of the F.R. Scott biography,
which I was completing in the eighties. I sometimes visited the Irwins in
Victoria to ask about events that had occurred in the forties in Montreal
and Ottawa. While taping P.K. on Canadian poetry, I also taped Arthur
about the Canadianizing of *Maclean's* and his role as an investigative
journalist in bringing to light the Bren Gun scandal when Canadian
troops of the Second World War had been issued faulty guns.

During this period, P.K. became increasingly interested in autobiography and her own genealogical history. This had been reflected in her
past writings, especially the longer poetic sequence "Melanie's Nite-
book," which first appeared in the *Canadian Forum* in 1976 and included "Ancestors." There, she describes quasi-autobiographical figures,
somewhat distorted, of father, mother, brother – but all containing some
psychological truth. The mother, for example, is described as giving her
daughter "a diamond heart, / a splinter of ice for either eye." "Totally

untrue," P.K. said later.[64] Yet there was a sense in which Rose Page, in her last years, had been cruel (like the icy snow queen of Hans Christian Andersen); her "paranoid speech," as P.K. described it, made her daughter weep. And there are several poignant lines in one of the "Father" poems. P.K. believed that her strict father, devoted to her beautiful mother, had to some degree rejected *her*.[65] The awkwardness of her poetic line (so unusual for P.K.) expresses some of her pain: "I still crave thy praise / striving for thy approval / to appear / beautiful in thine eyes / or talented?" The language is formal and liturgical, and P.K.'s pronouns evoke the power of the patriarchy – "thy praise," "thy approval" – and concludes: "Father, Father / can we call a truce?"

P.K.'s resolution with her father may be related to her growing interest in human and social evolution in the mid-1980s. On 12 March 1985 P.K. had phoned me and mentioned in passing that she had been at a teacher's meeting earlier in the month listening to a paper on "brutal fathers and dominated daughters." She thought that perhaps this concept was an evolutionary spiral, of which she and her father were a part. Twenty years later, P.K. recalled her father as "a small, crumpled figure" on his deathbed in her essay in Sandra Martin's *The First Man in My Life: Daughters Write about Their Fathers*. "It was hard to believe it was my larger-than-life father. For the first time, I saw him as a human being. Mortal ... He was not superman; he was life-sized, an amateur, like me."[66]

Although P.K. had spoken to me of her father as a tall figure on a high horse in the late eighties, I did not become a candidate to write her biography until early 1996, when she asked me to contribute to a special issue of the *Malahat Review* in honour of her eightieth birthday: "You might like to do something for it and it might get us both used to the idea of further work." As she said earlier in the same letter, a biography would be "better now [rather] than after I've lost my marbles or am dead. Also *now* there are people alive who knew me when I was young." But she emphasized that this was "in no way a commitment."[67] In the fall of the same year, John Orange, professor of English at the University of Western Ontario – who had published the first Page bibliography, *P.K. Page and Her Works* (1989) – contemplated a critical book for ECW Press. P.K. phoned me to ask if I would mind, suggesting that it would be a work preliminary to an eventual biography.

After we hung up, the penny dropped. P.K. had now decided to have a biography, and she was implying that I would write it. But if so, the work must start right away, while her memory was good and support might be available from the Social Sciences and Humanities Research Council of Canada. I wrote back, explaining this, and on 21 December

1996, just before Christmas, P.K. phoned and formally asked me if I would write her biography. We agreed that I would come to Victoria at the beginning of the New Year and we would discuss arrangements regarding interviews, access to files, and permission to quote from her poetry and prose. On 27 February she drafted a summary contract and on 14 October 1997 wrote a formal agreement saying that her biography would be "one in which you would be free to interpret as you see fit ... You also know a great deal about the age in which I have lived ... I have total confidence in your painstaking research and ability to get on top of a body of material."

⚏

In the late 1990s, P.K.'s reputation as a poet was increasingly acknowledged in the media and elsewhere. On May 14 and 15 1996, the CBC *Ideas* series aired two programs on P.K.'s poetry. Entitled "The White Glass: Conversations with P.K. Page," they were produced by Ann Pollock, a freelance Vancouver writer and broadcaster. As mentioned at the beginning of this chapter, in late November 1996 a special "P.K. Page" issue of the *Malahat Review* appeared in celebration of her eightieth birthday. Edited by Jay Ruzesky, it contained excerpts from P.K.'s "Australian Journal," a fantasia by Leon Rooke on P.K.'s childhood, my biographical interview with Page, and tributes from a number of poets and writers – all interspersed with photographs and drawings. P.K.'s granddaughter Christine Irwin spoke affectionately in "My Grandmother's Luggage" of her earliest memories of her grandmother, in which "she is always a traveller ... Her greatest gift to me has been this closeness which we share, something thicker than blood, thicker than thieves."[68] Jay Macpherson recalled P.K. in Ottawa in the forties, Rosemary Sullivan wrote on *Hologram* and Constance Rooke on female friendship. Anne McDougall wrote "P.K. Irwin, the Painter," and Don Fisher explored "Eastern Perspectives in the Work of P.K. Page." There were also excerpts from Ann Pollock's CBC Radio program. And old friends such as Elizabeth Brewster, George Johnston, Margaret Atwood, Al Purdy, and Michael Ondaatje wrote poems in tribute. Atwood's poem spoke of "Mystical, practical P.K. ... Not 80! No, / impossible! Say, rather, ageless."[69] At a launch of the *Malahat Review* special issue at the University of Victoria, a number of close friends, including Arlene Lampert and Rosemary Sullivan, spoke to the large audience assembled there.

In early December 1996 P.K. travelled to Mexico with a group of Canadians, including Rosemary Sullivan and Linda Spalding, Michael Ondaatje's wife. Rosemary had arranged for P.K. to attend the Mexican

Canadian Studies conference in Mexico City, prior to the Guadalajara Book Fair. Page had been invited to read some of her poems at this gathering but was interrupted in the middle of her reading when the Canadian ambassador appeared to give a closing address. After he had finished, Rosemary informed the ambassador that he had interrupted the guest of honour. When he apologized, saying he had not realized what was going on, Page responded tartly, "When my husband was ambassador here forty years ago, if his staff had made such a mistake he would have changed his staff."[70] She then remounted the stage to thunderous applause. At the Guadalajara Book Fair, both P.K. and Rosemary read Canadian poems. Rosemary and Lesley Krueger, a Canadian writer who was with the group, were both struck by how much fun P.K. was having during this visit to Mexico. She was exuberant, opening up, making witty jokes, and reminiscing about old friends.[71]

In Mexico City, P.K. attended the opening of a large and important show of paintings by Leonora Carrington. She found her paintings as exquisite as ever – and astronomical in price. Leonora was now much more relaxed, enjoying her success. The next day, P.K. went to see Leonora in the old apartment that she remembered. There had been an earthquake, and although the house containing the apartment was still standing, none of the buildings around it had been rebuilt; they were just rubble. P.K. also found Leonora greatly changed and thought she looked evil: "All those demons she had been living with: her face very white, her eyes dark – awful, all in grey."[72] She also realized, meeting after so many years, that she and Carrington were estranged and could not seem to reconnect.[73]

In June 1998 P.K. was nominated for an honorary LLD at the University of Toronto, where Rosemary Sullivan was now teaching. It was a wonderful occasion, and many of P.K.'s friends gathered at a luncheon before the ceremony to speak exuberantly about her life and work. Her address to the students was radical in a university context – she told them not to listen to authority.[74] On 30 June and 1 July there was a gala opening of Festival Canada at the National Arts Centre in Ottawa in which P.K.'s lyrics for "A Children's Hymn" (in commemoration of the fiftieth anniversary of the United Nations) were sung in a composition by Harry Somers.

In October 1998 P.K. was invited to read her poems at the International Festival of Authors in Toronto. She read them on 29 October at the large dance theatre at Harbourfront. The auditorium was packed with friends and supporters – all poetry lovers – and the warmth of the audience's response was apparent. On the thirtieth Rosemary interviewed her on stage, and P.K. spoke eloquently of the early days in Montreal. The following night, 31 October, P.K. and Théa donned full Hallowe'en costume to visit P.K.'s stepson Neal Irwin and the grandchildren. P.K. "just happened to have" Hallowe'en masks in her luggage.

In February of the next year, P.K. and Théa travelled to Ottawa. P.K. was to be made a Companion of the Order of Canada, the highest civilian honour, and had invited her nephew Tim Page to attend. The ceremony began at 4.30 PM, with citations and the presentations of the medal of the Order of Canada, followed by a dinner. P.K. was seated in the front row with Peter Gzowski, who also was being made a companion.[75] Governor General Roméo LeBlanc said during the presentations, "It is an honour for us, for me, to be able to give you these awards. You are the makers of this country."[76] When the bus was about the leave for the Château Laurier, P.K. was delayed, talking with the governor general, and as they went out the door, LeBlanc called out to P.K., "Now you go on writing those poems; it's very important." When they reached the hotel, P.K. and Théa threw off their formal clothes, fell on their respective beds, and burst out laughing. They stayed awake until about 3 AM, reliving every minute of the occasion.[77]

For over a year P.K. had been involved in a new dramatization of "Unless the Eye Catch Fire …" A young Victoria filmmaker, Anna Tchernakova, had approached her in 1998, asking for permission to film the story and inviting P.K. to take part in the production. The distinguished English composer Gavin Bryars had agreed to write music for it. P.K. enjoyed the filmmaking process. The video begins with a highly flattering image of her as the older narrator in the garden – her large grey eyes luminous under a floppy hat. She was, however, woefully disappointed with the film, shown on 19 June 1999 at Alix Gooden Hall in Victoria. She felt that Tchernakova had not followed the action of the story and had made meaningless changes; more important, she had not respected the transcendental conclusion. P.K. therefore withdrew her permission to publish, and for some time the distressed Tchernakova doubted if she could show the completed film at all. Eventually, however, agreement was reached, and the film was distributed with a new title, *Last Summer*. The real difficulty may have been that for P.K. the tale was implicitly a Sufi teaching story, but she had not managed to convey this – or what it would mean in terms of filmmaking – to Anna Tchernakova.

Companion of the Order of Canada. Théa Gray, Roméo LeBlanc,
Mrs LeBlanc, P.K. Page, and Tim Page.

Throughout the nineties Arthur's health had been slowly failing. Throughout the decade there had been a number of special features on Arthur's life and work in *Maclean's*, *Saturday Night*, and the *Globe and Mail*. In 1996 he was frail and his memory very thin. On 27 May 1998 the family celebrated Arthur's hundreth birthday with a song (sung to the tune of Gilbert and Sullivan's "For He Is an Englishman")

For in spite of all temptations
To belong to other nations
He remains Canadian
For he might have been a Russian
An Englishman, or Prussian ...

Or perhaps American!
But in spite of all temptations
To belong to other nations
He remains Canadian
He remains Cana-a-a-a-a-a-a-a-dian.

Hooray!

Arthur Irwin, as his son Neal remarked, had "survived two world wars, a Great Depression, a red scare, the coming of the automobile, freeways and smog, radio, movies, television, commercials, and talking heads, but also rampant commercialism, the 'me' generation and global warming." More importantly, he had been a staunch Canadian who had brought a sense of duty to the common good from the nineteenth-century into the twentieth.[78]

He had now been diagnosed with Alzheimer's, but P.K. firmly believed that "Arthur must be able to do what he wants to do," and by and large he did. Each morning he rose, dressed himself in a vest and dark business suit, and prepared for the day. His invariable greeting to visitors was succinct: "What do you think about the state of Canada?" – a question sufficiently broad for all social occasions. One morning in the late nineties, I arrived in Victoria for an interview and found P.K. exhausted and Arthur not yet dressed – he had fallen during the night and she could not lift him off the floor.

During the third week of July 1999, Arthur fell again, and this time P.K. wondered if he had had a slight stroke. In early August, for the first time Arthur said he did not want to get out of bed. And he did not want to eat. He became worse later in the week, and on Thursday, 5 August, P.K. telephoned Neal, who left Toronto for Victoria on the following Saturday with his daughter Chris, a nurse. On Sunday, Arthur's mind was clear, but by the following Monday he was feeling very sleepy. He died on 9 August at 101 years of age, surrounded by his family. When he suddenly stopped breathing, P.K. burst into tears: "He turned to white marble in front of our eyes," she told me. Still at his bedside, the family began talking about Arthur, reminiscing and telling stories, laughing and crying. The next afternoon, P.K. explained, they had a wake at the funeral parlour and "there was something holy in the room."[79] The following day the family gathered in an anteroom at Royal Oak Funeral Chapel.

On 12 August P.K. held a small reception at home for friends, a casual gathering with drinks. She was obviously exhausted but made a brave attempt to be cheerful, wearing a bright top and white pants. It was raining dismally and she was sad and tired. The Page and Irwin families were there: her brother Michael and his wife Sheila; Neal and his wife Carol and their children; Sheila, Arthur's daughter, and her husband. Also a number of P.K.'s poet friends, including Marilyn Bowering and Patricia Young, and old friends from Victoria: Shushan Egoyan, her daughter Eve and husband David, and others, including Erika and Burton Kurth, and Mavor Moore and his wife Alexandra Browning,

Carol Matthews from Malaspina, Beryl Young, myself, and my husband Lalit Srivastava from Vancouver.

Théa was present and agreed to stay with P.K. When the funeral was over and the family had left, she proposed that they get away from the empty house by going up-island for ten days to a bed and breakfast called Whistle Stop. Afterwards, Arlene Lampert volunteered to come from Toronto to help P.K. respond to the letters of condolence; and Connie Rooke, who had just become president of the University of Winnipeg, flew in for several days.

As most of Arthur's family connections were in Ontario, P.K felt there should be a gathering in Toronto in the fall when family and friends could meet. She left Victoria on 10 October for Toronto where, two days later, old friends John Fraser and Ann Saddlemyer (master and former master of Massey College, respectively) had arranged a memorial service and reception at Massey College, University of Toronto. Many of Arthur's and P.K.'s old friends attended, but afterwards P.K. felt sick and went back to her hotel and to bed. The following day a service took place at Mount Pleasant Cemetery, where Arthur's ashes were interred. He had chosen a grave plot in a little copse of trees, such a pleasant place that P.K. felt a little less sad about leaving him there.[80] She returned to Victoria feeling utterly bereft – she and Arthur had been married for forty-nine years. She also felt ill – her bones ached constantly. Worse, she was now facing the last stretch of her journey alone.

CHAPTER 15

Victoria
Endings, 2000–2010

> It is not only that she is lonely … Lonely for Heaven, she thinks …
> But what is the story she wants to tell? And to whom? She wants
> to tell the one in which she is an onlooker, behind some veil. She
> wants to tell the story of her life alone – invisible in a glass house
> on the sands of an endless ocean, washed in light. But is it true?
> Does a story demand truth?
> P.K. Page, "Shipwreck," 2002

A sense of apocalypse hung over P.K. during her last decade. It was partly her age – she was now eighty-three – and for the first time in nearly fifty years Arthur was no longer by her side, a buffer against the world. Just after his death, having gone away with Théa Gray for a brief respite, she returned to an empty house, later writing "Empty House Blues":

> My house is empty but I don' want no one here
> My house is empty but I don' want no one here
> My bed is empty and the friggin' fridge is bare
> there ain't no scrap fer a starvin' cat in there
> no scrap for this cat neither
> no scrap for this ol' cat
> this ol' grey rundown cat

The house cries out at night: "Ain't no one to hold me tight / No other cat in sight / To fight me, hold me tight."[1]

To be sure, she had some family still at hand. Her brother Michael and Arthur's daughter Shelia and their families had moved to Victoria. P.K. was very fond of her nieces and nephews and of Arthur's son Neal, who lived in Toronto but visited her as often as he could. She also had a wide circle of good friends and soon acquired a live-in housekeeper. Théa phoned every day, as did Rachel Wyatt, a Toronto writer and a former director of the writing program at Banff, now living in Victoria. P.K. still saw her oldest friends Pat Martin Bates and Shushan Egoyan, but now less frequently. There was also Mavor Moore and his wife, the opera singer Alexandra Browning Moore. She also reconnected with old friends, the Irish literature scholar Ann Saddlemyer and her partner Joan Coldwell, formerly of McMaster University who had retired to Victoria. She continued to delight in the company of younger poets such as Marilyn Bowering, Jay Ruzesky, and Patricia Young, and Lucy Bashford helped P.K. with her papers. Carol Matthews, dean of instruction at Malaspina College (and a former student of Connie Rooke) had been asked to keep an eye on P.K. – and she did. Beryl Young of Vancouver regularly telephoned and visited.

All of P.K.'s longtime friends, including Rosemary Sullivan, Connie, and Arlene Lampert in Toronto were keeping in touch by phone and by electronic mail. Early in 1999 I had persuaded P.K. to go online for the purpose of her biography. She agreed reluctantly, protesting all the way: "I am connected, ha ha! But don't send me joyful notes. Only real communications. Got it? As you know I am against the whole thing."[2] But P.K. discovered a new universe in the World Wide Web. In her last decade, she spent much of the day at her computer, composing, checking facts, playing solitaire, and replying to an astonishing number of e-mails from younger writers, translators, puppeteers, and filmmakers – Margaret Atwood, Dionne Brand, Atom Egoyan, Patrick Friesen, Timothy Gosley, Steven Heighton, Lesley Kreuger, and Jaspreet Singh, Jane Urquhart, and others. Instantly, the computer itself had become a friend that made it easier for her to stay in touch.

P.K. the writer was flourishing, but P.K. the person was becoming a little more difficult to get along with. She had never suffered fools gladly and was sometimes sharp even with her oldest and closest friends. She became irritated with me when I checked information from our interviews against letters from the period, as biographers must. Why? It was partly that she wanted to tell her own story but also that she developed a transcendental view of her own life – and a pressing desire to have her story told in this form. More importantly, a tendency towards irritability was intensified in her last years by the fact that she was so often in great pain. Early in the decade it was thought that she had fibromyalgia; but she was later diagnosed with polymyalgia, a lesser but still painful disease. Her hip operation had gone awry, and she now suffered continual pain in all her joints, which impeded walking. In March 2000 she fell and broke her wrist; in November she fell again, further injuring her hip. Pat Martin Bates tried to cheer her up by e-mail, saying rumour had it that P.K. had fallen and that this was "not cool, indeed it is very, very uncool. Desist."[3]

Worst of all was an ailment that her doctors were unable to identify. It began with a high fever and chills that sent her to bed and knocked her out for several days. Tests seemed to rule out tropical diseases, or *Cryptococcus gatti*, a fungus-like infection that had recently been discovered on Vancouver Island, though some of her symptoms were similar. As she remarked, "Odd, isn't it? The vaguely tropical qualities and the distribution fits, also the night sweats and the fact that it can be carried by dogs and cats."[4] (Two of her housekeepers had pets, and P.K. later acquired two graceful but shy white Siamese kittens.)

Finally, she felt increasingly uneasy about the state of the world, especially world politics, and this sense of dis-ease was heightened after 9/11. It was partly the loss of human life – the grotesque images of television reinforcing the horror of bodies hurtling down from the towers to destruction – but, more importantly, for P.K. the tragedy seemed to signal a breakdown in world order. Many of the recurring themes in P.K.'s post-2000 writing are apocalyptic.

Unfortunately, she was away from home at the time of 9/11, which added to her sense of vulnerability. P.K. and Théa Gray had left Victoria on 3 September for a third reading at Eden Mills, Ontario. They were staying at the Elora, a pleasant old stone inn on the edge of a peaceful river. P.K. read excerpts from *Alphabetical/Cosmologies* (2000). *Alphabetical* has fun, treating words (and related ideas) that begin in turn with each letter of the alphabet. The volume begins with A:

A curious concept – *afterwards*
bearing the phantom of *before* within it.
Old-fashioned novelists fell back
on *afterwards*
to conjure up the sexual act
or when referring to religious conversion:
"afterwards her life was entirely changed."[5]

She also read from *And Once More Saw the Stars* (2001) a book that had begun in the late nineties, when she learned that Philip Stratford, a poet and academic, was convalescing after a bout with cancer. She proposed that they write a *renga* together, each writing alternate stanzas, which became their joint book.[6] P.K.'s stanza began: "Open your door and step outside – the garden / becomes a Persian miniature ... / So far, no sign of canker in the rose."[7] Stratford riposted: "Yet what were Paradise, I'd like to know, / without the gate, the sword, the snake ..."[8] The crowd at Eden Mills, as always, was highly enthusiastic.

Théa and P.K. had planned to return to Victoria on 12 September, but the terrorist attack occurred the day before their departure. Flights were cancelled, the Toronto airport was a madhouse, and P.K. could not have endured the crowds or the line-ups. She was now travelling by wheelchair, and the two women had to contend with luggage. They were stranded for more than a week until a new flight was booked. P.K. was greatly worried about Arthur's grandson Alex Irwin, who lived and worked close to the World Trade Center.

Several days after 9/11, Alex sent the whole Irwin family, including "GramPat," a first-hand account of the tragedy. When he got up on the morning of 11 September, he looked out his window and thought a bomb had exploded. He set out for work, but Canal Street, just outside his apartment, was filled with running people. He walked south towards the towers until he was about ten blocks away and stared up at the flames: "I could see into the burning holes – see the floors exposed and raw." One of the towers fell before his eyes, and in the streets people were screaming and "falling to their knees, covering their faces. Great clouds of debris and dust came down on the streets, and dense clouds began to rush up at terrifying speed towards us – shooting up the street at a heart-stopping pace." It felt as if the towers and the sky were falling down upon him. "Terrified and in disbelief ... I ran to my apartment and barely looked back." He felt so totally disconnected – it just couldn't be real.[9]

Shortly after returning to Victoria, P.K. e-mailed Carol Matthews: "On this bleak day. What a time! I feel wordless."[10] Carol responded, "Everyone seems to be operating under a shadow. We ARE operating under a shadow. What Martin Amis called 'species shame.'"[11] P.K. also sent an e-mail to a new young friend in New York, Susan MacRae, asking how she was. Susan replied, "It is the most horrific scene I have ever seen in my life. I am reading 'Love's Pavilion' from your book *Hologram* and I have to let you know that I find a lot of solace in that poem right now."[12]

When I went to see P.K. shortly after 9/11, she said the previous night she had nightmares about the world on the brink of disaster and had woken up frightened: "It makes me sick what goes on in the world." She held that the American invasion of Afghanistan was predicated on nineteenth-century thinking – that force and rhetoric could conquer. But other forces were working: "The Sufis say there's a hidden directorate, and it is not concerned with the world particularly, except inasmuch as the world is part of the whole. And it is very concerned with the whole. And if the world is out of line, the hidden directorate will step in ... Is this to wake us up, smarten us up and save us? Or is it to destroy us because we're not performing as we should? But I woke up scared this morning."[13]

In December 2001 she e-mailed me, agreeing to a visit the following month, adding: "I've been intermittently sick for about a month – high fevers and chills ... But by then I should be OK. Or dead! ... I think we are seeing the end of a civilization ... Bush's refusal to sign any of the agreements – Kyoto, land mines, etcetcetc. Lunacy."[14] The war in Afghanistan (the home of Sufism) begun on 7 October, weighed heavily on P.K.'s consciousness. Her sense of international political collapse accelerated in early spring 2003 with the invasion of Iraq on 20 March.

A number of Canadian writers had signed a petition against this invasion, and P.K. had e-mailed Margaret Atwood expressing her concern. Atwood responded that she didn't think that writers' petitions whizzing about the Internet would make any difference to American intervention: "The folks won't win and they're so far down the road they can't see the way back. They'll have to spill some blood, if only to justify the expense." She added, "Don't get too discouraged. This too will pass."[15] But P.K. *was* discouraged. Commiserating with Patrick Lane, she wrote, "I am depressed too. And I've had one more war than you have – parents and brothers and boyfriends all involved. And now we're deep in it again. And this war may never [end]. The last crusade."[16] To P.K., these events represented a confirmation of Doris Lessing's prophecies in the *Canopus in Argos* series of novels – the end of planet Earth as we know it. Nonetheless, P.K. and a Victoria storytelling group, some of whom were members of the Victoria Sufi-studies group, organized a benefit for Afghan relief and raised $7,300 for Oxfam, an organization for channelling aid to developing countries.

Despite fears and continuing illness, P.K. created and published a remarkable body of work in her last decade – nineteen books in all: nine books of poems, three books of fiction, six children's books, and one book of non-fiction. She recognized that the time had come to consolidate her literary and artistic reputation. In the early nineties, she had initiated the collecting of her poems; in the mid-nineties she had appointed a biographer; and in the late nineties, she began to assemble all her prose. Always receptive to younger writers and scholars, she became friends with Farouk Mitha, a graduate student then taking a PH D in education at the University of Victoria. He was "surprised and honoured" when she asked him if he would search out her uncollected prose, both fiction and non-fiction.[17] From 1999 to 2000, Farouk scanned hard copies of stories and articles in her possession and tracked down references for others. In the process, he assembled a large draft manuscript for possible publication.

Now came thoughts of a scholarly edition of her poems, as suggested by Brian Trehearne of McGill University. In 2000, when P.K. began to ask friends about scholarly editors, I suggested Zailig Pollock, who had edited the *Complete Poems: A.M. Klein*, and wrote to him on Page's behalf.[18] Pollock and Page began to correspond, and P.K. set out her parameters: "I don't want this project ... to take up all my time. I am still alive and working after a fashion and that is where my priorities lie."[19] In mid-July, Pollock and I met at P.K.'s house in Victoria, where the discussion broadened to include her unpublished journals and art. Pollock and I agreed to undertake a scholarly edition of her work,[20] and Page agreed to provide access to published and unpublished work. Several years later we were joined by a third general editor, Dean Irvine of Dalhousie University.

Work on P.K.'s biography, initiated in the late nineties, continued throughout the decade. In late March 2000, we had exchanged a series of e-mails about the differences between her perspective on her life (non-linear and symbolic) and her biographer's, which she saw as linear and literal. To P.K., a chronological, date and place emphasis indicated that we lived in different universes. Her Boswell wanted to know *when* she did *what*. But from the Sufi perspective, all time and events are simultaneous. As she would sometimes remind me, speaking of the creative process and its reflection, "The process is not linear. And I can't but feel you think it is. Everything we read and experience is, of course, part of the compost heap that produces the flowers, the weeds. But there is another – and much larger – source, the collective unconscious to use Jung's term; or to quote myself, that there are other dimensions to the mind beyond those we already recognize."[21]

To be sure, the artist experiences "other dimensions"– and expresses them in her work – but the biographer's task frequently begins on a more mundane level with the attempt to establish the main events of a life. P.K. eschewed dates in many of her early letters, and in interviews she would cheerfully say, "That's your job!" As many of the Page family papers were lost in storage during the Second World War, the first hurdle in writing her biography was to construct a timeline by consulting a number of archives, military records, and census reports – both here and in Great Britain – to fix dates. Only when the main events had been charted was it possible to speculate on the curve of the artist's creative life. Although a chronological approach is helpful to readers of biography, in this last chapter I am approaching P.K.'s final years first through the various genres of her own creative work and the timeless vision they express – her poems, non-fiction, short fiction, children's writing and art – and only then suggesting how they might mesh with the events of her life.

⚏

P.K. was still writing fine poetry. In the late nineties she had written two long poems, *Alphabetical* and *Cosmologies* that were published as paperback chapbooks in 1998; then, in 2000, in a beautiful special edition by Rhonda Batchelor and Alexander Ladovsky[22] through Poppy Press.[23] In 2002 a selection of P.K.'s poems was published – *Planet Earth: Poems Selected and New*, selected and edited with a fine introduction by Eric Ormsby, a poet and a professor of Islamic studies at McGill.[24] The title poem, "Planet Earth," is a glosa that develops from a poem by Pablo Neruda; it expresses, in warmly domestic terms, that we must learn to love and cherish the earth,

> It has to be loved the way a laundress loves her linens,
> the way she moves her hands caressing the fine muslins
> knowing their warp and woof,
> like a lover coaxing, or a mother praising[25]

This poem had earlier received a flurry of international attention when, in March 2001, Susan MacRae, a young writer who was taking an MA at the City College of New York, submitted the poem to her professor, Marilyn Hackett, for consideration for the United Nations Dialogue among Civilizations through Poetry. The poem was chosen to be the centrepiece of the United Nations program and was read aloud from 25 to 29 March 2001 at several international sites. These included the United Nations, the summit of Mount Everest, the Antarctic, the West Philippine Sea, and the International Space Station.[26] The poem was also sent whizzing around the earth in a space shuttle. In Victoria, Jay Ruzesky read "Planet Earth" at a special celebration of poetry.

In early 2003 the book *Planet Earth* was shortlisted for the Griffin Poetry Prize, along with books by Margaret Avison and Dionne Brand. This was a prestigious prize of forty thousand dollars for the Canadian winner. The judges included Michael Longley, an Irish poet; Sharon Olds, an American poet; and Sharon Thesen, a Canadian poet. P.K.'s hopes were high when the finalists read their poems on 11 June at Harbourfront. But the prize went to Avison for *Concrete and Wild Carrot*. P.K. sensed this immediately when she entered the Griffin banquet room and was led to her table – not the one where Governor General Adrienne Clarkson and Avison were sitting. P.K. was devastated. She had been identified as Canada's "National Treasure" in the *Ottawa Citizen* after the publication of *The Hidden Room* in 1997,[27] but this epithet was now applied to Avison in a brief summary of the poet's work. In the forties there had been some rivalry between the two poets, and P.K. had not forgotten. On the day and night of the Griffin presentation, she was suffering from a new attack of chills and fevers. She went home early from the dinner, depressed. To P.K., the Griffin prize represented a long-hoped-for recognition of her outstanding poetic career.

I wrote to her saying that the prize, awarded for one book, was not a judgment on her reputation. She was not comforted: "If your analysis is right, then it is a judgment ... for my book is a distillation of a life's work and Avison's is a collection of poems written in her recent old age."[28] Yet the formal elegance of some of P.K.'s poems may have been a disadvantage in a competition where judges might "trace their descent from a simpler, more immediate sprig of wild carrot ... and the immediate process of making the poem ... or, so I think. Plus a high degree of sympathy for Avison's present position."[29] Avison had been ill; she was thought to be older than Page (actually, she was younger), and she had not been adequately recognized. Of greater importance, the prize was for a specific book and *Planet Earth* contained a number of P.K.'s older poems, thus slighting her newer post-nineties poems. Unfortunately, the award carried overtones of poetic reputation. Page felt this keenly, for it seemed to suggest that Avison was the better poet. Nonetheless, as Arthur had so often admonished her to do during his lifetime, P.K. put aside her disappointment and kept on working. She was greatly encouraged a year later by a glowing reference to her work by American critic Joseph Hirsch.[30]

In the fall of 2004, P.K. was invited by David McKnight, curator of the McGill University library, to read at McGill. She and Théa left Victoria for Montreal on 11 October, and a week later, on the nineteenth, she read from the Montreal section of what she was then calling "the

Long Bad Poem" – the developing *Hand Luggage* – to an enthusiastic crowd of one hundred McGill students and faculty.[31] The excerpts referred to A.M. Klein, A.J.M. Smith, and F.R. Scott, and she also spoke of Leonard Cohen and Philip Stratford. That night, McKnight and Brian Trehearne took the two women for supper at the Faculty Club. As McKnight recalls, "She seemed bright, and after whisky seemed relaxed, especially that the reading was over." On the way out, P.K. fell on the tricky, winding Faculty Club stairs (it had once been a private residence) but fortunately didn't injure herself. Two days later, she and Théa took a journey north, into the Laurentians, towards Saint-Sauveur-des-Monts, where Montrealers had regularly skied in the 1940s. For P.K. as for Théa, the past was still in the air in the Laurentians: both women knew they were saying goodbye to Quebec.[32]

From 2002 to 2006 P.K. continued to draft *Hand Luggage: A Memoir in Verse*, which suggests a selection, the highlights of a life (poignantly, hand luggage was now all that she could carry). The title is highly suggestive, echoing three forms of hand luggage: "My Grandmother's Luggage" (the title of Christine Irwin's talk at the *Malahat* celebration of P.K.'s eightieth birthday); "Black Luggage," in a poem on Arthur's death;[33] and the "baggage" of F.R. Scott's "On Saying Goodbye to My Room in Chancellor Day Hall." (Scott, facing retirement, had catalogued his life from the "Old baggage" in his office – an Oxford oar, a picture of J.S. Woodsworth, a cardboard padlock: "Old baggage, I wish you goodbye and good housing. / I strip for more climbing.")[34] *Hand Luggage* is in the same genre, a retrospective poem, a selection of primary events from "a full and passionate life" written to emphasize climactic moments.[35] The poem, a rollicking tetrameter, is divided into twelve sections identified by the places where P.K. had lived. The last section allows us to see into the poet's mind circa 1 August 2004.

P.K. is now writing her own story, and the ongoing narrative is the making of a transcendental artist, one intrigued by the metaphysics of other worlds. Her relationship with Scott is included – but de-centred from the central story of her life by typography – the three verse paragraphs alluding to him are moved to the right-hand side of the page. The long-legged Scott, to whom P.K. looked up to as a poet (she admired his poems in *New Provinces* long before they met) is introduced as "one on stilts":[36]

> Then like a mirage one on stilts appeared
> who spoke my tongue with no interpreter

and when I came to walk at such a height
and match his stride and travel at his side
someone in me was born and someone died.[37]

Scott is the primary figure of her time in Montreal, and their love affair
leads to both a birth and a death (in an undated poem written in 1950
after their break-up, Scott wrote, "We gave birth to selves, not to sons").[38]
P.K. tells us obliquely that the lesson painfully learned during the Montreal period is one of loss, by alluding briefly to Elizabeth Bishop's poem
"One Art," a poem that she knew by heart:

(Re-reading "One Art," I realize loss
is the ultimate art. And you learn it by heart.)[39]

But as she affirms, in Montreal she became "a real writer."[40] Now, reflecting on her past, she finds that "chronology's merely a temporal
squint" – everything coexists simultaneously.[41]

By the 1950s she was "thirtyish" and married to Arthur Irwin, whom
she describes as reticent, truthful, and accomplished. Would he have preferred a less outspoken wife? She records his gallant response – that "a
wife less outspoken would not have been me."[42] In Brazil she was one of
the last of a generation of wives that accepted their husbands' careers as
their own. She wonders now "if 'Brazil' / was destined to happen wherever I'd been":

(... I suspect there's a sphere where all possible things
co-exist – like the Noosphere [Chardin]. Or perhaps
a hologram's nearer the concept I seek.
Or do I mean Borges' "The Aleph"? Alas,
I clearly don't know how to formulate this!)

Again, she emphasizes the existence of a larger dimension where all
ideas, all shapes, indeed all creation, co-exist. When Arthur's diplomatic
posting to Brazil is over, she recognizes herself as translated into another
medium: "living there, I was italicized."[43] In Mexico she was introduced
to surrealist painting and alchemy by "Leonora-incredible-Carrington
... both angel and devil," and to Idries Shah by Leonora's circle: "Something in me was stilled. Some thirst was assuaged."[44]

Back home in Canada, P.K. alludes to the "Eden" that Arthur constructed in their Victoria garden and to her poetry readings: but the

sections on the eighties and nineties are brief. The conclusion of the book, which covers much of her last decade in Victoria, begins on 1 August (Scott's birthday) 2004:

> I write this today as the world falls apart –
> two thousand and four, August first. It is hot,
> not unseasonable – it is summer – but hot
> for this northerly hemisphere; full of freak storms
> and assorted disasters – floods, wildfires, and drought.[45]

She wonders whether it is "age or a sharpened perception that sees / world's end?" To her, "Rice. Cheney. And Rumsfeld … And Bush" infect the body politic. She had hoped "that a critical mass would up-tilt the whole mess, / … Alas! I can see no such thing. / 'Things' only get worse – or such my dark view."[46] P.K. no longer seems to think that a critical mass, or elite, can change the world for the better. What most interests her now is beyond her: "the hologram, fractals, and 'god'" – further defined as the space "where discreteness dissolves and the many are one." The end of the poem brings us back to the poet and those closest to her, when she records that sickness and death "take their terrible toll."[47] When publishing this poem, P.K. was saddened by the illness of Jori Smith, who died in 2004, and that of of Mavor Moore, who died in December 2006 (P.K. spoke at his funeral).

In 2008 Arlene Lampert and Théa Gray edited *The Essential P.K. Page*, a selection of Page's representative poems, which they described as "a sort of pocket P.K. Page," a sampling of the poet's best poems which the editors hoped would make its way into backpacks and carry-on luggage.[48] Two years later, Zailig Pollock edited the first scholarly edition, *Kaleidoscope: Selected Poems of P.K. Page*,[49] as a part of the larger P.K. Page collected works. The book includes a fine introduction to the poet and the context of the poetry. (P.K.'s one suggestion was that Pollock add to the collection "Your Slightest Look," a poem for F.R. Scott.)

There were three new books of poetry by the end of the decade. Two were launched at the opening of the Page Irwin Colloquium Room at Trent University on 2 May 2009. Alan Stein had prepared a special hand-printed copy of Page's *The Golden Lilies*, a selection of eight glosas with ten wood engravings, including a hand-coloured frontispiece. And Tim and Elke Inkster, her publishers, had worked frantically to bring to publication *Coal and Roses: Twenty-One Glosas* (2009), Page's last collection of new poetry. This book has a surprising variety of tone, from the philosophical poem "Each Mortal Thing" (which asks, "Essence, inner being, soul, heart's core, / quiddity ... are they one?")[50] to the flippant "Paradise," where heaven is compared to the British class system: "For God cannot hobnob / with any old Tom, Dick or Harry."[51] "Domain of the Snow Queen" is a return to the terrifying Hans Christian Andersen tale of P.K.'s childhood: "Imagine then her heart, a block of ice / unmelting, permafrost."[52] Most affective is "The Last Time": "Everything slips away. The street I lived on / ... And all those years in barracks, teenage travels. / ... And there are mirrors in which I am forgotten ... / ... I am grey, without lustre. / I refuse to look at myself in any glass."[53] The narrator conjures the end of the world, when the holy are taken to heaven and the wicked, "us" are left behind: "Shall I lie with my nails painted, my hair curled / awaiting my beloved, as of old? / Will darkness snuff me out in the blink of an eye?"[54]

In early November 2009 Jay Ruzesky brought P.K. the proofs of a new chapbook, *Cullen: Poems*. Over the years, P.K. had developed two Cullen poems with a male narrator whose generation and experience largely reflected her own. A third was added to this group when Zailig Pollock found an unfinished Cullen poem from the Australian period in her papers at Library and Archives Canada. P.K., who had forgotten this poem, decided to finish it and titled it "Cullen Revisited" (the previous poem with this title became "Cullen at Fifty"). To this sequence she added "Cullen in the Afterlife," a new poem that she had written in 2008–09 and published in *Poetry* in June 2009, and "Cullen in Old Age," which seems to have been written about June of the same year and appeared in the summer edition of the *Malahat Review*.[55]

The five poems were prepared for publication in the fall of 2009 by Ruzesky's press, Outlaw Editions, with an afterword by Pollock. This chapbook is dedicated to F.R.S., a Leo. Several phrases in one of the new poems, the new "Cullen Revisited," allude to Cullen's encounter with the lion: "... the claw marks that the lion / left near his heart ... / he calls his birth marks."[56] In "Cullen in Old Age," the fourth poem of the sequence, Cullen dies, "... his life was spent / like a silver coin that slipped from a hole in a pocket." Finally, in "Cullen in the Afterlife," he finds himself in new dimensions – the fourth? the fifth? – "bathed in some unearthly light":

> Engulfed by love. Held in a healing beam
> of love-light. Had he earned such love?
> And how partake of such a gift when he
> was handicapped by earthshine – wore the stars,
> badges and medals of privilege and success?[57]

"Earthshine" is negative, suggesting earthly success and "sleep." But a "beam / of love-light" forces Cullen to recognize that he must start his mortal journey again (the Sufi poet Rumi's evolution from "mineral, to vegetable, to animal, to man" – and from there to "angels and beyond"). For now, other worlds beckon: "What a rush of wings / above him ... / angels were overhead, and over them / a million suns and moons."[58] Pollock's "Afterword," which cautions against a one-to-one equation of Cullen with Page, suggests that he represents a "fictional, and not uncritical, portrait of a fellow pilgrim through the journey of life."[59]

Increasingly P.K.'s poems inspired new musical compositions. On 30 May 2000, Derek Holman's oratorio *The Invisible Reality*, which drew on P.K.'s poetry, was performed at Roy Thomson Hall in Toronto by tenor Ben Heppner, the Toronto Symphony Orchestra, the Toronto Children's Chorus, and the Toronto Mendelssohn Choir. The oratorio had been commissioned in celebration of Canada's centenary by impresario Nicholas Goldschmidt as part of music Canada 2000. Holman's title *The Invisible Reality* refers, as he says in the program notes, to Plato's metaphor of the cave where man sees only the shadow of reality. "Planet Earth" became the second movement of the oratorio, and Holman drew on seven other Page poems, including "Single Traveller" and "Love's Pavilion." It was a stunning performance and in response to the audience's cry of "Author! Author!," P.K. – enormously pleased – took her bow on the stage, regal in a white caftan that shimmered gold under the lights. Goldschmidt had requested P.K. also to write "A Millennium Children's Song" for the opening of the Trans-Canada Trail, with music by Oscar Peterson. On 9 September 2000 this song was performed by the Central Children's Choir of Ottawa. But P.K. could rarely write poetry to order, and her trail verse was halting.[60] Furthermore, she found the Ottawa opening ceremony embarrassing: "Political speeches, commercials from sponsors, amateur acts in dance and song ... Interminable."[61]

P.K. ventured into opera when she was approached by Anna Höstman, a young musician associated with UVic and the Victoria Symphony Orchestra, who asked her if she would be interested in writing a libretto for an opera on dementia, for which Höstman would compose the music. The result was the chamber opera *What Time Is It Now?*, performed on 24 October 2004 at the University of Victoria. P.K.'s libretto is a dialogue between an old lady and her twenty-year-old self, who are joined on stage by a male caregiver. The old woman, who suffers from Alzheimer's, continually asks, "What time is it now?" As she tells and retells her life story, she is echoed by her younger self. Both speak of a lover who was killed at war, an abortion, and the lover's watch that was sent to them after his death. Their shared experiences culminate in an "aha" moment when their two voices chime on "liquefaction" in the first stanza of Robert Herrick's poem "Upon Julia's Clothes": "Whenas in silks my Julia goes, / Then, then, methinks, how sweetly flows / That liquefaction of her clothes."[62] As their characters overlap in harmonious pitch, their unity is revealed. The story has pathos but also humour: the old woman, acknowledging her state, says, "I've grown old, a hard-boiled, cracked, old-addled egg. An old, old lady."[63]

While completing *Hand Luggage*, P.K. turned once again to the manuscript compiled by Farouk Mitha to cull the fiction and non-fiction. The occasional non-fiction essays she sent to a number of people, including Zailig Pollock, who agreed to edit it for publication. It became *The Filled Pen: Selected Non-Fiction* (2007) and was dedicated to Connie Rooke, now gravely ill with cancer. It is an impressive collection, largely because of P.K.'s comments on poetry, poets, and artists, on both her own work and that of others. The major essay, "A Writer's Life," given as the Margaret Laurence Lecture to the Writers' Union of Canada, in Halifax in 1999, reflects her sixty-five years as a writer. Other essays speak of her memories of poet A.M. Klein and isolate the skaldic qualities of George Johnston's poems, which she greatly admired. Her comments on the art of Pat Martin Bates are highly suggestive, because P.K.'s essay "Darkinbad the Brightdayler," originally written for *Canadian Art*, links Bates's colours and geometrical figures with their informing Sufi content.

Farouk Mitha's compilation provided the basis for two books of fiction. The first, entitled *A Kind of Fiction* (2001),[64] was dedicated to the memory of *Preview*. Its eighteen stories comprise a "kind" of fiction, in that many of the stories have autobiographical or Sufi relevance. The architecture of the book, especially the framing first and last stories, offers shifting perspectives on reality. The title story is a powerful depiction of old age and the transcending of limitations: Veronika, an old woman, witnesses a fall by another frail old lady and feels her pain as if it were her own; indeed, as she discovers, it was she herself who fell. P.K. is now utilizing in her fiction a technique for developing consciousness advocated by Gurdjieff and Shah – that of standing back from the self and observing the self perform. For P.K.'s alter ego narrators, "imagination" is all-important. This is signalled by the last paragraph of "Victoria," where "the cosmos" enters an aunt's sickroom and "angels" surround her.[65] Similarly, the final story in *A Kind of Fiction* is the transcendental "Unless the Eye Catch Fire ..." (1979), a story that asserts the primacy of a vision that perceives, holds, and is part of all creation: "We are one with the starry heavens."[66] Here, as in much of her later work, P.K. is affirming versions of her own story as an artist.

During the decade, P.K. had written the occasional short story, and she now she put several of them together with some of the stories from Mitha's collection for a second book of prose, *Up on the Roof* (2007), a collection of eleven old and new stories, which she had dedicated to Rosemary Sullivan. P.K. sent a copy of the book to Margaret Atwood, who responded: "You are quite simply amazing and a model to us all."[67] "Crayons" and "Up on the Roof" represent earlier writing, while the new stories are "Ex Libris," "True Story," "Shipwreck," "Eatings," "A Biography of You," and "Stone." Also included is the one-act opera *What Time Is It Now?* It was broadcast by the CBC as part of a birthday celebration for P.K.'s ninetieth birthday in 2006. In "Birthday," an old woman's dream of birth (not dissimilar from P.K.'s birthing dream in New York) transforms the moment of her own death into life: she a "rush of air" and feels "the exquisite movement of its currents stirring the small down on her incredible wings."[68]

"Ex Libris" is developed from a metaphor expressed by the Persian Hakam Sanai: "[T]he human's progress is that of one who has been given a sealed book written before he was born."[69] In this story Ivor, born into a family of avid readers, has nightmares when growing up in a house so crammed with books that they block out the light. But he learns that he has a capacity for out-of-body experiences. Tall and lanky, he becomes a basketball star, the only white on a black team. Inevitably, he falls in love with a "black orchid," Esmeralda: "To love her was my career."[70] Just as inevitably, she leaves him. After his parents die, Ivor works through his losses by gathering their books to form a magnificent library, a vast glass-ceilinged atrium. Just before the startling conclusion of the story, he remembers the book of his life that his mother had read to him as a baby – and how it ends – with his death. (P.K. herself had a recurring dream of a book-lined corridor, a kind of hidden room, where she felt complete bliss. It ultimately turned into a light-filled atrium that she liked less because it was more exposed, but the feeling of bliss remained the same.)[71]

"Stone" tells the story of a woman artist, C.D. Stone, better known as "Cass" (Cassandra?), who submits a large marble sculpture to a gallery in Los Angeles and then discovers that there is no such gallery. The loss of the sculpture becomes another of the great losses in her life.

As she tells her new boyfriend, Joe: "I had an abortion ... I couldn't bring a child – especially a fatherless child – into this world ... Now, that loss has become part of a pattern of losses: the baby, the head, the marble. I feel I must fill those great holes in my life by making things. At the same time, another part feels the world itself is a loss – this beautiful, dying world. What greater loss could there be than the loss of the world?"[72]

Cass believes that for women, in the past, having and raising a baby was "an enormously creative act"– in effect, a substitute for art – but "Somewhere between then and now, we've been given permission," meaning that women can now be artists as well as mothers.[73] She parallels art and childbirth: "[T]he original idea ... provides the energy and the growth of a piece. For it does grow, very often unexpectedly, rather like a child."[74] After the loss of her sculpture, Cass sinks into a deep depression, accentuated by her alienation from her mother. A letter offers the possibility of their reconciliation, but Joe has just given Cass a new block of white marble. In this marble she sees great possibilities: "An enormous egg floated before her. Egg of the World."[75] (This suggests P.K.'s 1960 painting of a huge glowing egg, titled *A Kind of Osmosis*.) Although Cass wants to read her mother's letter, "the urge to work was even stronger. The letters could wait. The egg couldn't."[76]

"Shipwreck," first published in 2002, is an evocative new story. The female narrator acknowledges her increasing age and her longing for transcendence. But what is the story that she wants to tell? It is the story of her life "alone – invisible in a glass house on the sands of an endless ocean." If we read these last sentences as we might read a line of poetry, we recognize that not only is the narrator alone but she feels that she alone can tell her story, perhaps because onlookers (friends, family, biographers) cannot really see her. Even if she sits in a glass house, they cannot see through the façade to the real person – shall we say P.K.? She is "invisible" because we lack the intuition and deeper insight, perhaps to be found in Sufi study, to comprehend her. She invokes the "endless ocean" because she views the sea as both all-creating and infinite – both are part of P.K.'s personal myth, her sense of her own position in relation to her past life. The narrator's asks, "Does a story demand truth?"[77] This is an important question. A short story is fiction, yet what we think of as good fiction is often "good" because it expresses human truth. Several autobiographical themes recur in these stories of the artist – difficulties with the mother, depression, the equation of art and a child, a perception of "this beautiful, dying world." Primarily, however, the stories affirm the healing role of art in relation to the many losses that life brings.[78]

You Are Here, her last book of fiction, dated 2008, was actually published in 2009. An older narrator, in many aspects a frailer P.K. in her
nineties, meditates on life, death, and identity. The book was launched
at the Winchester Galleries. Despite a new injury and her great fragility
(she now had to allow for hours of rest after each visit or activity), P.K.
was gracious and smiling in a navy jacket and a white blouse with a bright
scarf. She read sections from the book, including "Name," "Horo-
scope," "The Third Eye," "Coincidence," and "Second Identity Joke."

It is a remarkable book for the casual way in which P.K. introduces
very large concepts – concepts that she herself was now exploring. The
story begins with "Mimi" at a shopping mall looking at the dot on the
directory that says "YOU ARE HERE," which she reads metaphysically:
"How does she move away from the dot that holds her? It is as if she is
in a board game and until released by some other player she has to stay
in place."[79] Mimi asks the large questions that all humans face: Where
did I come from? Who am I? – Margaret, Maggie, Marg, Meg, even?
[Patricia, Patty, Patsy, Pat, P.K., even?] She insists this questioning "is
about identity, and identity is close to consciousness ... And consciousness is what? A matter of the soul?" What entity formed the embryo that
became her? Although she has been daughter, sister, writer, wife, aunt,
housekeeper, cook, and gardener, she questions "writer" (a title P.K. had
always resisted) and "wife." Mimi has never felt married: "This is not a
subject she could bring up with her husband ... Is she his mistress? His
housekeeper? His cook? *His* ... marriage has not changed her identity."[80]

You are Here offers familiar topics: childhood memories, a sense of
immortality induced by a revenant, the "beam of love" that P.K. experienced when travelling with Arthur in 1968, her work on Philip Glass,
the difference between right-brainers and left-brainers. There are glimpses
of new interests (crop circles, fractals, an experiment with marijuana) and
reminders of continuing interests (Flatland, dreams, and synchronicity).
But P.K. knew this would be her last book and her last public reading.
She e-mailed me saying, "This will probably be the last ever."[81] She later
e-mailed her publisher, Joan Coldwell: "I think you've attended my last
reading. It nearly killed me ... the stress of getting there and coping is absurd at 92."[82] She had broken three ribs in January 2008 and now in,
April 2009 at the reading, was recovering from a cracked tailbone. Nonetheless, her final book was an affirmation – reflected in virtually the entire paper cover of *You Are Here*, which reproduces P.K.'s beautiful
painting *Star Burst*, a study from the early nineties, created with gel pens.

P.K. Page's last public reading from *You Are Here*.

P.K. had continued to publish plays and picture-story books for children throughout the decade: in 2003 *A Grain of Sand,* a gloss on William Blake's lines "To see a World in a Grain of Sand," and in 2005 *A Brazilian Alphabet for the Younger Reader* (2005), illustrated with old engravings. In mid-decade, she became increasingly active in endorsing the Sufi teaching story. Although such stories may appear to be simple fairy tales, they are designed, as Robert Ornstein writes, "to embody – in their characters, plot and imagery – patterns and relationships that nurture a part of the mind that is unreachable in more direct ways."[83] In 2004 the Institute for Cross-Cultural Exchange (ICE) had been founded in Canada to distribute books for children in support of literacy. Titles that promoted cross-cultural understanding were to be distributed to school libraries. P.K. agreed to become honorary chairperson of the association, and letters went out under her name in 2005 and 2006 urging members of the League of Canadian Poets, among others, to support this project.

She also wrote a series of fables for younger readers. *Jake the Baker* (2008) is a tale of a young baker who sells his smile and his laugh but recants when he finds that money doesn't make him happy. In 2008 she published both *The Old Woman and the Hen* and *There Was Once a Camel*. More thematically ambitious was a trilogy, *The Sky Tree*, illustrated by Kristi Bridgeman (2009), bringing together the story of that name and two earlier stories: *A Flask of Sea Water* and *The Goat That Flew*. It tells us of the continuing quest of the goatherd Galaad, who had defeated a wizard to marry Princess Meera. This final story describes the elderly Galaad and Meera, nearing the end of their human journey, anxious to meet again with the transformed wizard, visualized as a figure clothed in light – an "astonishing golden being."[84]

Shortly afterwards, P.K. completed *Uirapurú* (2009). It was published as a children's book but can be read as a fable for adults that unites several versions of a Brazilian folk tale. In P.K.'s story a group of boys enter the Brazilian rainforest wanting to catch the fabulous Uirapurú bird, renowned for its wonderful song: "Oor a poor oo." One night the boys hear such a sweet sound that they believe it must be the bird but find instead an old man, sitting at the foot of a tree and playing a flute. He tells them that he cannot play the Uirapurú's song perfectly and that the bird will only respond to another of its own species. He adds there is only one Uirapurú left in the world, and if his song dies the world will end. This story angers the boys, and they drive the old man away.

After some time in the rainforest the boys are awakened one night by astonishing sounds. They see a young woman, "as shining and white as the moon itself," and flapping around her the creatures of the night. They hear overhead the fabulous song of the Uirapurú. Suddenly the young woman shoots an arrow up into the darkness, hitting the bird. In a flash the bird turns into a tall handsome young man, who takes her hand. The boys become fearful and run away. Just as the young man and woman are about to walk out of the rainforest, they hear the notes of the old man's flute, which calls "oorapurooo," each note now rounded and perfect. The young man, in a rage, turns on the old man, who responds by shooting him through the heart. Instantly, the young man disappears and a small bird flies up into the branches and again sings its beautiful song.

We understand the young man's anger – the old man has stolen his song – yet why do the young woman and the old man so ruthlessly shoot the bird? All the characters seem to act rashly. I wrote to P.K. saying that it felt like a Sufi story.[85] She responded, "It is probably my last song. I guess I see it as the necessity for art."[86] She meant, perhaps, that it is an old man (and indeed an old woman) who seeks to keep art alive.[87] The story also suggests that the artifact – the art object itself – supersedes life, thus validating the role of the artist who conserves art and by so doing makes society possible.

≡

P.K. was becoming increasingly aware that her time was running out. She began by sorting the remaining paintings and books stored in her basement on Exeter Road. Some art work had been sold at the Maltwood Gallery exhibition at the University of Victoria, but there was still a large number of paintings remaining. In October 2000, at the BC International Writers' Festival honouring P.K. Page, there was an accompanying exhibition of her work. A wide variety of paintings and genres were represented, including familiar titles: *The Dance, Stairwell, Dark Kingdom, How Is the Gold Become So Dim*, and *And You, What Do You Seek?* There were versions of her earlier etchings *Ghost Ship*, "Heart," a miniature in pen and ink, and *The Golden Bough* in oil pastel.

An exhibition put on a year later, on 26 October 2001 at the Windsor Art Gallery, had wider dimensions. Curated by Barbara Godard of York University, it included important paintings such as *Who in This Bowling Alley Bowl'd the Sun?, World Within World*, and *Party at Intamarity*, a gouache with vivid red touches of a Brazilian diplomatic party mentioned in *Brazilian Journal*.

Shushan Egoyan had put P.K. in contact with the Winchester Galleries, and plans for a large retrospective of Page's art were put in motion. With the help of her niece, artist Wendy Page, many of P.K.'s remaining paintings were framed for exhibition. These included gouaches, watercolours, oils, pen-and-ink drawings, and sketches of various kinds. There was a gala opening for "A Retrospective: P.K. (Page) Irwin" at the Winchester on 10 March 2002. Included from the Brazilian period were *Brazilian Dolls*, oil on board; *Fiesta*, a cheerful carnival in oil on canvas; and *Woman's Room*, an impressive early painting in oil. The show remained open for several weeks and was reviewed enthusiastically by art critic Robert Amos. For the opening, P.K. posted an artist's statement that emphasized the process of painting: "the tooth [rough surface] of the paper I worked on, the colour of the ink, the thickness of the nib, the sound of the nib on the paper … and then the different ways of applying colour pastel." On the first day she sold one drawing, and a first refusal was put on a second, a record that P.K. considered "not displeasing."[88] Peter Redpath of the gallery characterized sales as quite good.[89]

In October 2002 at "Extraordinary Presence," a symposium held in Page's honour, Barbara Godard curated a still larger retrospective at the Art Gallery of Peterborough, which ran from 25 October to 8 December.

This was the first exhibition to bring together Page's works from across the country, spanning the whole of her career and documenting them in a catalogue. The exhibition included approximately fifty works (etchings, egg tempera, oil pastel, pen and ink, punch, gouache, and mixed media, representing all aspects of her visual art since the 1950s. It displayed early examples of her Brazilian work from the fifties – *Stairwell*, in felt pen and gouache, and the vivid *Party at Itamarity* in gouache. There were two samples from the *Aladdin's Ship* etching series in New York at the end of the decade, and a number of brilliant paintings from Mexico, notably *Cosmos* and *Who in This Bowling Alley Bowl'd the Sun?* as well as *And You, What Do You Seek?* in egg tempera with scratchboard. There were examples from some of her Victoria work, *Shape of the Flower Is Yellow* in egg tempera; and the seventies' *Dome of Heaven* in pen and ink. Included also was a late *Doodle* in pen and ink.

The overall impression is of vivid colour and enormous energy. In her introduction to the exhibition catalogue, Godard compares Patricia Page/Irwin's work to that of Chagall, in that it is situated "between the concrete and the abstract, the physical and the metaphysical." Godard sees in the artist's later work a "dynamic cosmology, one in which a change of lenses, a kaleidoscopic swirl of colours, a momentary flash of an alternate vision, induces boundary play. One thing becomes another; something shifts or merges in metamorphosis or osmosis. A change in thickness of line or tone of colours alters space, bringing new worlds to light."[90]

There was a second Winchester showing at the opening of an Oak Bay gallery on 28 September 2003 and a third exhibition, "The Three Pages," held in April 2006 in which P.K. exhibited jointly with Wendy and Mike Page, her niece and nephew. She held another solo exhibition, "P.K. (Page) Irwin *Selected Works*" from 3 to 24 May 2008. One of the more interesting paintings exhibited on this occasion was a self-portrait in gouache, painted while she was still in Brazil.

Honors and distinctions piled up in P.K.'s last decade. Her importance as a BC poet was acknowledged in October 2000 when the thirteenth annual Vancouver International Writers (& Readers) Festival sponsored a special tribute to Page that included an exhibition of her visual art. All of the tributes were wholehearted, and many poets acknowledged P.K.'s enormous influence on their work. Dennis Lee and Esta Spalding both spoke of P.K.'s importance on the national scene, (Spalding recalling

Michael Ondaatje, her stepfather, referring to P.K. as one of Canada's great poets). In the early fall of 2001 the University of Windsor had sponsored a conference on women and Canadian modernism entitled "Wider Boundaries of Daring," where more papers were presented on P.K. Page than on any other writer.

The following year, at Trent University in October 2002, a fuller assessment began in "Extraordinary Presence: The Worlds of P.K. Page," a symposium on Page's work, organized by Zailig Pollock and others to celebrate Page's lifelong achievement and to initiate a new critical edition of her collected works.[91] Papers on her life, poetry, and art were given by a dozen critics, including Stan Dragland, Dean Irvine, Cynthia Messenger, and Brian Trehearne, and conference papers were later collected in a special issue of *Canadian Studies* (38, no. 1). As previously mentioned, Barbara Godard assembled an exhibition and produced a catalogue, for which she wrote an introduction linking P.K.'s poems and paintings. A musical evening featured Eve Egoyan, whom P.K. had encouraged as a child. Excerpts from *Unless the Eye Catch Fire* ... were again performed by Joy Coghill and Robert Cram, and several poems by Page were set to music by various composers.

P.K. was inducted as a member of the Order of British Columbia on 25 June 2003. It was an impressive ceremony followed by a dinner given by the premier of the province, Gordon Campbell, and the lieutenant governor, Iona V. Campagnolo. The following year, on 1 May, Campagnolo instituted BC's Lieutenant Governor's Award for Literary Excellence, and P.K. Page was the first recipient. In the following month she was also awarded the Terasen Lifetime Achievement Award at the Vancouver Public Library in recognition of her many contributions to Canadian letters. A tile with her name engraved on it was added to the sidewalk of fame near the library. The presentation and award took place in 2004, and P.K. gave a talk at the library to a large crowd. But in 2005, after one division of Terasen Gas (formerly BC Hydro and Gas) was sold to a Texas group, Kinder Morgan, she renounced the award on principle, donated the $5000 prize to charity, and asked that her name be taken off the award plaque outside the library. (It was not.) The Council of Canadians issued a special brochure praising her courage in objecting to the sale of parts of Canadian utilities to foreign nationals.

This string of honours culminated in May 2005 when P.K. was awarded an honorary degree, Doctor of Letters, by the University of British Columbia, which was conferred by the chancellor, Allan McEachern. The convocation was held on a bright, sunny afternoon, and as P.K.

later recalled, "I got up to speak and burst into tears – a great involuntary sob that came from nowhere I was. Still don't understand it. And so forgot to address chancellor, president et al. But the poems went well I think."[92] Academic recognition had come in the last two decades of her life, and P.K. was overcome by that joy that sometimes masquerades as sorrow. There was a similar moment in February 2007 when she was inducted into the Royal Society of Canada at the University of Victoria.

⚏

If P.K. looked back at her literary career – and surely she did – she had much to be proud of. As early as 1946 the influential *Poetry* (Chicago) had reviewed her first book, *As Ten, As Twenty*, acknowledging that she had made the modern idiom her own.[93] In 1952 Cid Corman, the respected American poet and editor, who greatly admired her work, had wanted to feature her poems in his avant-garde journal *Origin*. As he said, he would take ten, twenty, forty ... as many of her poems she could give him.[94] In response to her second book, *The Metal and the Flower* (1954), Northrop Frye wrote, "If there is any such thing as 'pure poetry,' this must be it: a lively mind seizing on almost any experience and turning it into witty verse."[95] Shortly afterwards, the *Times Literary Supplement* pronounced: "Miss P.K. Page is the most original Canadian poet writing today."[96] A.J.M Smith and other poets concurred, including Stephen Spender, when visiting Canada in the late fifties.

Of her third book of poetry, *Cry Ararat!* (1967), Eli Mandel observed that not only did it contain excellent poems but it provided readers the opportunity to understand "the achievement of a writer who has contributed significantly to what we have come to understand as modernism in poetry."[97] He might have specified "modernism in Canada," because so many major younger poets in the seventies and eighties – including Margaret Atwood, Michael Ondaatje, and Mandel himself – looked to Page's work. *The Glass Air* (1985) consolidated her national reputation: "Page is clearly one of our finest and most accomplished poets, as well as an interesting and original artist."[98] A newspaper tribute by Ondaatje confirmed her continuing influence on the younger generation: "She's a very important touchstone for writers."[99] *Hologram* (1994) is not only an example of a poet sensitively and wittily responding to the international poets who had shaped her own early poetic but is a remarkably fine poetry in its own right.

Her collected poems, *The Hidden Room* (1997), prompted Richard Outram to describe Page as "a *force majeure* in Canadian life, a National Treasure,"[100] and Carmine Starnino to reiterate A.J.M. Smith's recognition that Page was not merely a splendid Canadian poet but was internationally recognized and "among the fine poets of this century."[101] In 2009, in the *Cambridge Companion to Canadian Literature,* Kevin McNeilly remarked that P.K. Page was "probably English Canada's most important poet of the last fifty years."[102] He concluded, "Preeminent among Canadian poets, P.K. Page produces work that is nonetheless *sui generis.*"[103]

These distinctions came as P.K.'s life was slowing down. She had come to realize that she would never see the Alhambra in Grenada, with its Moorish lattices and reflecting pools. In the summer of 2008, just after an operation for breast cancer, she catalogued her activities sardonically: "I really don't have a life now. I write when I can. I read. I see the occasional person for a drink or lunch. There are no love affairs or involvements in public events. Art Makosinski who was doing a little film on me has coverage of readings, etc. My engagements ... are a weekly session with an acupuncturist."[104] Arthur Makosinski, who worked at UVic, was preparing a video on Ravi Shankar's daughter, and another on Shankar himself. He greatly admired Page's poems "Poor Bird" and "Planet Earth" and began to film her readings after October 2005 in a video entitled *Looking for Something.* Khosrow Fasihi, a respected Victoria acupressurist, was the only person able to bring relief to P.K.'s continual pain in the last years of her life. "Koz" was Iranian, knowledgeable about Sufism, and the grandson of a poet laureate of Iran. P.K. was very fond of him.

P.K.'s friends in eastern Canada all worried about her health. In the spring of 2005 Rosemary Sullivan and Connie Rooke had come out for a joint visit. A year later, in October, Arlene Lampert sent a heartfelt e-mail: "I'm getting the miserable feeling that we're all lining up to say goodbye to you and I'm so not there yet."[105] In 2007 Rosemary and Connie again planned to come to Victoria for P.K.'s birthday. P.K. hoped that she wouldn't "celebrate with an attack! It is tiresome."[106] It was the younger Connie, however, whose ovarian cancer metastasized and became fatal: "But she is valiant. No wailing. No self-pity. Extraordinary."[107] And she did manage to visit Victoria for P.K.'s birthday that fall. Alexandra Browning Moore, who shared P.K.'s birthday, decorated a cake, Carol Matthews composed a birthday song, and everyone – Victoria friends Lucy Bashford, Marilyn Bowering, Camilla Turner, and Rachel Wyatt – sang. This was the last time that Connie met with P.K., the "dearest woman of my heart," as Connie called her.[108]

Connie Rooke died the following year, on 5 October 2008. Her death was devastating for P.K.: "I've slept almost solidly since I've learned of Connie's death and behaved in a very strange manner."[109] P.K. spoke of Connie as a "seeing glass" and e-mailed columnist Sandra Martin and Carol Matthews referring to her as a "comet" who flashed through her life.[110] P.K.'s Victoria friends Jay Ruzesky and Lucy Bashford noticed a great difference in her attitude after Connie's death: she grieved and took less interest in things. Connie, like Rosemary Sullivan, Eve Egoyan, and Marilyn Bowering, had become a daughter figure to P.K.

P.K.'s correspondence throughout 2008–09 reflects an increasing loss of control and a growing certainty that she must wind up her affairs. In spring 2008 she had had a request from Sandra Martin of the Toronto *Globe and Mail* for an obituary interview and she subsequently spoke to Sandra forthrightly about Frank Scott and their love affair, knowing that this information would be published after her death. For over a decade she had been slowly dismantling the house on Exeter Road, dispersing her artworks, selling many of her books, and indicating to several friends and relatives that she wanted them to have cherished objects. In the spring of 2009 she accelerated arrangements to send relevant books and paintings to Trent for the opening of the Page Irwin Colloquium Room at Trent University, arranged by Zailig Pollock. Peter Redpath of the Winchester Galleries in Victoria helped by boxing the paintings for shipping. As P.K. had felt too ill to attend in person, she pre-recorded a video explaining Arthur's role at *Maclean's* magazine in developing closer relations between all parts of Canada. Neal Irwin spoke biographically, provoking affectionate chuckles as he recollected the joint life of the couple.

P.K.'s "attacks" were now happening more frequently. She had a fall one night in late May, followed by an attack and had to take to her bed for several days. Then, in the summer of 2009 there were more alarming symptoms. She began to experience periods when whole afternoons, and indeed days, would disappear from her memory. On 11 July she attended the wedding of her nephew Tim Page, but the next day she had no memory of the event. As she later explained to her editor for *The Sky Tree*, "I am told I behave normally during the events, but afterwards have no memory of anything. It's as if I've forgotten to hit the 'record' button, so the event is not on tape ... These memory blanks are sometimes associated with unnatural sleeping – excessive sleeping – 36 hours for instance ... I could cope with it more easily if I had more energy and was working at something in my normal periods."[111]

During this last summer of 2009 Théa Gray spent a fair amount of time with P.K. – all of July and the first week of August. During the hot days they packed a picnic lunch and drove down to the little park at Willows Beach, just below Exeter Road and Beach Drive. The two women would sit in the car and eat their lunch – P.K. could no longer walk to the shore – and look out to the deep sea.

In the fall, P.K.'s bouts of forgetfulness became more frequent, and she redoubled her efforts to find out what was the matter, writing to a number of doctors and contacting a specialist she had heard on the CBC. In late September, Eve Joseph, a poet and later the wife of Patrick Friesen, suggested that she might have transient global amnesia.[112] P.K. was happy with this suggestion, in part because the name of the disease suggested it might go away of its own accord. But there were good days and bad days – intervals when her chills and fevers sent her to bed, others when she wrote to neurologists asking for further information on her problems. She tried vigorously to understand what was happening to her on an intellectual level. But there were still other days when the content of her e-mails indicate she could no longer handle the computer keyboard. On 1 October 2009 she wrote to me as follows: "I have a atrage memoryloss – very rare so it' had to tree; I've no much energy so if you want to know anything, ask it mow."

In October 2009 P.K. told Jay Ruzesky about her "memory blackouts," saying that she seemed to be lucid in the moment but later could not remember what had happened – which, as he observed, was very distressing for someone with such a fine mind. But as she told Jay, what concerned her most was not so much her memory loss as her possible alteration in consciousness: "I've always wanted to be fully conscious at the moment of death, and now I'm not certain that I will be." This troubled her. She wasn't afraid of death, indeed she was ready for it. "But she wanted to go into it with her eyes open. She wanted to *know* death and to experience it."[113]

Théa visited P.K. again at the beginning of November. They talked, read, and enjoyed each other's company. In the past they had always read aloud to each other from Virginia Woolf, E.M. Forster, and others – José Saramago's *The Cave* was their favourite book. But P.K. could no longer do this. Now Théa read to her from a light novel, *The Anthologist* by Nicholson Baker, about a man writing an introduction to a poetry anthology. Théa was in Victoria for the celebration of P.K.'s ninety-third birthday. On 22 November Carol and Mike Matthews and Patricia and Terence Young came in the afternoon with champagne and presents: "A happy time for this old crone."[114] And as the twenty-second was Alexandra Browning Moore's birthday, P.K. and Théa were invited to a birthday dinner at Moore's house. One of the other guests was a former Canadian ambassador, and P.K. was her old self – laughing and joking and telling stories about army and diplomatic life. Her actual birthday, on 23 November, was a quiet celebration with her brother Michael, his wife Sheila, and their son Michael Peter. It was a disappointment when P.K.'s good friend Rachel Wyatt, also invited, did not attend, having become lost in the maze of winding streets surrounding Exeter Road.

Cullen was launched in Victoria in December, but P.K. was not well enough to attend. Later, Jay Ruzesky came to the house to celebrate, but P.K. was sound asleep: "I think I must be a bear as it's very hard to stay awake."[115] A new problem with copyright now blew up. An interior decorator had copied one of Page's poems – "Your Slightest Look" (a glosa based on a poem of the same name by e.e. cummings)[116] – on wallpaper for a prize home in Kitsilano, to be awarded in a lottery for the Vancouver Children's Hospital. One of P.K.'s friends, Beryl Young, visited the house, recognized the poem, and notified her.[117] P.K. couldn't deal with it herself, didn't want to get a lawyer, and finally contacted Tim Inkster at the Porcupine's Quill. The issue dragged on, with e-mails flying back and forth.

P.K. found Christmas worse than usual in 2009 because in mid-December she had an injection for the HINI virus that made her extremely sick, and she was unable to move for five days. Consequently, she did "NOTHING" in preparation for Christmas. Writing to Rachel Wyatt, she said, "I miss seeing you. A big gap in my life but I find I get slower and slower and slower. 93 is ten years older than 92."[118] Worst of all, she had discovered that transient global amnesia is often a prelude to Alzheimer's, and when she consulted a Victoria neurologist she was diagnosed as having Alzheimer's – a revelation that gave her great distress. She spoke of this on the telephone to Elizabeth Brewster, one of her oldest poet friends from early days in New Brunswick, saying that if she could no longer write she did not want to go on living.[119]

On Christmas Day a formal Christmas dinner was scheduled at the home of her brother Michael Page and his wife Sheila, with their extended family and Alexandra Browning Moore. Carol Matthews had given P.K. a strange mask with a labyrinth upon it for her birthday and, feeling a little antic, P.K. brought it to the Christmas dinner. It was a pleasant

occasion, but to everyone's astonishment P.K. began to speak in salty language. The next day on the telephone Michael told P.K. this was the kind
of language he had last heard as a young sailor, below decks.[120] P.K. was
horrified. She had no memory of this. It didn't matter if she spoke this
way at her brother's house, but what if it were a public occasion?

As the new year of 2010 began, P.K. was facing the fact that her mind
was failing. For her, mind and consciousness were primary – essential
qualities for life. A decade earlier, in *Alphabetical*, she had considered the
nature of consciousness, whether it could exist without understanding:

> Or does the brain
> Deliberate as a hand
> Turning a tap,
> Turn consciousness off …
>
> The very me of me gone?
>
> Who then?
> Then what?

For P.K. her periods of amnesia were a time when "The very me of me"
was absent. Her later intellectual life had been centred on developing
mindfulness, on the understanding of right-brain, left-brain knowledge,
on the search for a higher reality. Much of her late poetry and fiction
explores the question of what happens at the moment of death, and as
she had told Jay Ruzesky, she very much wanted to be conscious when
death came. Aside from her Sufi interests, this desire also reflects a conviction from the early sixties. At that time she had been reading an interview with the English writer Cyril Connolly and had copied his words
into her diary: "I regard it as my duty to cling to consciousness until the
last possible moment" – this Connolly defined as his duty to his consciousness "as an artist."[121]

At intervals during her last month there were days when P.K.'s mind
was clear, when she talked with visitors, spoke to friends on the telephone, and send out e-mails. She had a quiet pleasant New Year's Eve
dinner at home with Farouk Mitha and his wife Mehmoona. On 7 January 2010, Eve Egoyan and her five-year-old daughter Viva came to visit.
In the past, P.K. would sit with Viva on her knee, reading from her books
for children. But now she entertained from her bed, explaining to Eve
that she was taking a chance in seeing her, and spoke of brain seizures
and her language at Christmas. But they had a lovely afternoon: P.K.

was "absolutely present, chatting normally and popping back cookies" in competition with Viva. Eve and her small daughter left happily, but afterwards P.K. could not remember their visit.[122]

Her mind was quite clear on the last day of her life, 13 January, when she contacted both Arlene Lampert and Rosemary Sullivan in Toronto. For Rosemary, she agreed to write a description of her illness to be sent to Oliver Sacks, the neurologist who wrote *The Man Who Mistook His Wife for a Hat*. As Rosemary recalls, "I'd seen Louise Dennys before Christmas and she'd asked about PK and I told her about PK's bouts of amnesia. She said Oliver Sacks was interested in writers and amnesia etc, and she wrote him about PK. PK was keen to talk with him. Ours was such an immediate, warm conversation ... She had, as always, things she planned to do."[123] To Arlene, P.K. sent an e-mail to make sure that Tim Inkster got his case of beer in grateful payment for handling the breach of copyright issue with the Vancouver interior decorator. It was agreed that the decorator would contribute $800 to the Vancouver Children's Hospital lottery on P.K.'s behalf.

On the last night of her life P.K. went to bed before nine as usual. What was unusual was that one of her white Siamese cats, Prince Henry, climbed up onto the bed to keep her company. She was delighted. For the last two years, both cats had seemed to avoid her, but it is thought that some pets sense death. P.K. seemed to sleep relatively comfortably until about 1:30, when she woke briefly, called for her housekeeper Luisa, and then went back to sleep. But the next morning, when Luisa came in to wake her, she found that P.K., having risen from her bed, had died during the night. It is possible that she did meet death in full consciousness.

P.K. had specified that she was to be cremated and her ashes to be divided – half to go to the Irwin family plot in Mount Pleasant, Toronto, that green space amid a copse of trees where Arthur was interred, and half to be scattered on the sea at Cattle Point in Victoria. This was a rocky outcrop near Willows Beach, not far from the house on Exeter Road, where P.K. had sometimes walked down to the water, looking out to the deep sea on the Strait of Georgia. With this division, P.K. seems to be acknowledging the two great loves of her life: Arthur Irwin and Frank Scott. In spring 1944, when P.K. had first left Scott for Halifax, he had jotted the first lines of the poem "Departure," assuring her that each would find "the deep sea, in the end."[124] In the nineties, P.K. had herself written a poem called "The End" that echoes both Scott's words and the title of another poem with the same name by Mark Strand.

P.K.'s "The End" begins by alluding to a story that she first came across in the seventies, possibly in Jung's writings:

> In the story, you come at last to a high wall.
> Some who have scaled it say they were stricken blind ...
> One girl I know clambered up and gazing over
> saw the familiar universe reversed ...[125]

This story, which she sometimes called "the Jung game," describes a series of questions asked by an interlocutor to a listener about a number of things, including a house, a tree, a path, a key, a cup, a body of water and, at the end, a very high wall. The listener is asked how he/she sees each object and what he/she would do with it. Most people have no difficulty with the first objects, but when they get to the end they pause, recognizing instinctively that the high wall is death. Echoing Strand, P.K. writes in her poem, "*Not every man knows what he shall sing at the end.*"

In the second stanza P.K. alludes to "one, composed of light, came back, he said / to tell me it was *not* everlasting there / as once he had assumed, that I was right / Was he not proof?" This is the second time that P.K. recounted a vision of a loved one returning after death. The first occurred after the death of her friend Tommy Ross,[126] but here it is a male figure[127] and seems to refer to Scott, in the first instance, and to that larger Sufic concept of Love that he had come to embody to her.[128] A radiant and lifelike presence kisses her and puts her mind at ease: "there was nothing to fear / ... *when he's held by the sea's roar, motionless, there at the end.*"

> For he belongs to the sea – we all do. We are part of its swell.
> And only the shoreline grounds us. Yet we stand
> hands tied, deluded, seemingly earthbound
> imagining we belong to the land
> which is only a way-station, after all.
> We are the sea's, and as such we are at its beck.
> We are the water within the wave and the wave's form.[129]

Life on the land, she reminds us, is merely a "way-station" but the sea endures as promised in Scott's "Departure."

> We shall find, each, the deep sea in the end
> A stillness, and a movement only of tides
> That wash a world, whole continents between,

Flooding the estuaries of alien lands.
And we shall know, after the flow and ebb,
Things central, absolute and whole.
Brought clear of silt, into the open roads,
Events shall pass like waves, and we shall stay.[130]

Acknowledgments

My greatest debt is to P.K. Page, who put aside time for interviews for over a decade and provided access to her personal books and papers. Arthur Irwin, a committed Canadian, generously shared his knowledge of the literary and political climate of the twenties and forties. I am also grateful to the Page, Irwin, and Scott families for their continuing help and cooperation. Neal Irwin, Lorraine Larkin, and Michael Page, trustees for the P.K. Page estate, granted permission to quote from P.K. Page's published work, her archival papers, and from those of Lionel Page, W.A. Irwin, and Florence Bird (Bird's letters are contained within Page's collection) at Library and Archives Canada (LAC). Zailig Pollock, literary executor for P.K. Page, has been unfailingly helpful.

I would like to thank Tim and Elke Inkster, publishers of the Porcupine's Quill, for permission to quote from *The Hidden Room: Collected Poems* and from P.K. Page's poetry and prose included in post-1997 publications by the Porcupine's Quill. Extracts from F.R. Scott's poems, diaries, and letters are reprinted with the permission of William Toye, literary executor for the estate of F.R. Scott. Quotations from the diaries of Marian Scott, also at LAC, are reprinted through the kindness of Peter Dale Scott. Many thanks to Graham Fraser for permission to quote from the P.K. Page/Jean Fraser correspondence. Margaret Atwood generously shared her personal and archival Page correspondence and gave permission to publish sections of her poems. Mavis Gallant shared her memories of Page in the forties in Montreal, and Alice Munro her meetings with Page in Victoria in the sixties.

William Toye read successive versions of this manuscript with un-flagging energy and a keen editorial eye; he helped shepherd this book to the press and I am profoundly grateful to him. My deepest thanks also to W.J. Keith, who read the final version of the manuscript; his suggestions were invaluable. For help of various kinds when writing this biography I would especially like to thank Marilyn Bowering, Joan Givner, Théa Gray, Arlene Lampert, John Orange, Peter Redpath, Rosemary Sullivan, Brian Trehearne and Rachel Wyatt. This book would have been far more difficult to write without Zailig's Pollock's careful scholarship. His editorial dating of successive versions of Page's poems and his listings of Page's visual art are reflected in this manuscript. He also read a final version of the manuscript and offered new insights. Dean Irvine generously provided textual information and advice with the dating of a number of F.R. Scott's poems, as did Robert G. May. In addition to Pollock and Irvine, other members of the editorial team for the "Collected Works of P.K. Page," especially Suzanne Bailey and Margaret Steffler, have been of great help in confirming journal dates and archival numbers for newly deposited Brazilian and Mexican journals.

Throughout the years I was assisted by many friends, colleagues, and students, including Mike Doyle, G.D. Fulton, Joan Givner, Sherrill Grace, Janice Helland, Marlene Kadar, James King, Kitty Lewis, Sandra Martin, Fred Moseley, Kirk Niergarth, Colin Partridge, Michael Peterman, Harley and Nancy Schwartz, Robert Scott, Tom Smart, Sam Solecki, David Staines, Richard Teleky, Christopher Varley, Tracy Ware, Alan Wilkinson, and Stephen Wright. Researcher and editor Perry Miller helped me to begin and conclude this biography. Simon Fraser University students Rachel Friederich, Jason Le Heup, Rhiannon Jones, Tillie King, Bronwyn Scott, Sarah Spear, and Chris Turnbull helped with research questions, the dating of letters, and the transcription of tapes. Michelle Valiquette (later Preston) then an SFU graduate student, in an early MA checklist of P.K. Page's poetry, commented on the importance of the journey motif. Dorothy Chala, Barbara Marshall, Bronwyn Scott, and Natasha Stegemann typed the manuscript.

Above all, I want to thank Jean Wilson and Linda McKnight, committed editors, who helped guide this manuscript to the right publisher. It has been a pleasure to work with all the editors at McGill-Queen's University Press who brought their knowledge, experience, and dedication to the various aspects of scholarly book production. I am especially grateful to Philip Cercone, Ryan Van Huijstee, Jessica Howarth, and the exceptional Carlotta Lemieux, my manuscript editor. Jane Cowan helped compile the bibliography, and Mary Newberry prepared the index.

This book has been enriched by the patience and good advice of a number of librarians and archivists at Library and Archives Canada, especially Archivist Catherine Hobbs, but also Archivists Anne Goddard,

Maureen Hoogen, and Michael MacDonald; University Archivist Paul
Banfield, Heather Home, and Susan Office at Queen's University
Archives; Richard Virr of McGill Libraries, Rare Books and Special
Collections division; Head Librarian Bruce Whiteman, Clark Library,
University of California at Los Angeles; Manuscripts Librarian, Jennifer
Toews, Albert Masters, and John Shoesmith of the Thomas Fisher
Rare Book Library, University of Toronto; Michael Dawe, Garth
Clarke, and Jillian Staniec, Red Deer Archives; Shelley Sweeney, Head
of Archives and Special Collections, and Archivist Brian Huber,
University of Manitoba Special Collections; Jodi Aoki, Archivist and
Art Collection Coordinator, and Christine Walsh of Trent University
Archives; University Archivist Lara G. Wilson, Christopher G. Petter,
Nadica Lora, and John Frederick of the University of Victoria Archives;
Lisa Sherlock, head of Reader Services, Victoria University Library;
Emma McDonald, Museum of the Regiments, Calgary; Corporal Lee
J. Ramsden, Archivist, LDSH(RC) Museum Lord Strathcona Archives;
Shelley Sweeney, University of Manitoba Archives; Jack Corse, Sylvia
Roberts, Liaison Librarian (English and History) Rebecca Dowson,
and Reference Librarian Andre Iwanchuk, all of the Simon Fraser
University Library; and Amanda Faehnel of Special Collections and
Archives, the Kent State University Libraries.

The research for this biography was supported by grants from the
Social Science and Research Council of Canada for research, research
travel, and student support, by several SSHRC Small Grants from Simon
Fraser University, and by a grant from the Victoria Arts Council.

The following persons or their executors have given permission
to quote from letters and interviews: Margaret Atwood, Pat Martin
Bates, Florence Bird, Earle Birney, David Blackwood, Hiro Boga,
Marilyn Bowering, Elizabeth Brewster, Elizabeth Carlile, Joan Cold-
well, Cid Corman (Kent State University Libraries Special Collections
and Archives), Robert Cram, Alan Crawley (courtesy of Queen's
University Archives), Erica Deichmann (Provincial Archives of New
Brunswick), Jeffrey Donaldson, Stan Dragland, Atom Egoyan, Eve
Egoyan, Shushan Egoyan, Jean Fraser (Graham Fraser), Mavis Gal-
lant, Elizabeth Gourlay, Théa Gray, Forbes Helem, Norah Helliwell,
Tim and Elke Inkster, Alex Irwin, Neal Irwin, George Johnston, Arlene
Lampert, Patrick Lane, Doris Lessing (by permission of Jonathan
Clowes, Ltd.), Lois Lord, Jay Macpherson, Susan MacRae, Eli Mandel
(University of Manitoba Archives), Carol Matthews, Floris McLaren
(from Diane McLaren), Farouk Mitha, Alice Munro, Grant Munro,
Michael Ondaatje, Michael Page, Myfanwy Pavelic, Landon Pearson,

Zailig Pollock, Arlene Perly Rae, Constance Rooke (Leon Rooke),
Jay Ruzesky, Juliana Saxton, Harley and Nancy Schwartz, F.R. Scott
(William Toye, literary executor), Marian Scott (Peter Dale Scott),
Kushwant Singh, A.J.M. Smith (Michael Peterman and Trent University
Archives for post-fifties letters; Fisher Library, University of Toronto
for earlier letters), Jori Smith (Dr Heather Hume Cameron, executor),
Rosemary Sullivan, Rachel Wyatt, and Jan Zwicky.

I am grateful to the following people who contributed to interviews
and discussions for the purposes of this biography: Margaret Atwood,
Toronto; Rhonda Batchelor, Victoria; Pat Martin Bates, Victoria; Lucy
Bashford, Victoria; Douglas Beardsley, Victoria; Anjali Bhelandi, Van-
couver; Florence Bird, Ottawa; Marilyn Bowering, Victoria; Elizabeth
Brewster, Victoria; Martha Butterfield, Toronto; Evelyn Calow, Al-
berta; Elizabeth Carlile, London, UK; Joy Coghill, Vancouver; Joan
Coldwell, Vancouver Island; Elaine Corbet, West Vancouver; Robert
Cram, Ottawa; Noni Crawley, Victoria; Annecke Deichmann, Rothe-
say; Erica Deichman, Rothesay; Louis Dudek, Montreal; Atom Egoyan,
Toronto; Eve Egoyan, Toronto; Shushan Egoyan, Victoria; Michael
Elcock, Victoria; Mimi Fogt, Spain; Graham Fraser, Vancouver; Mavis
Gallant, Vancouver; Myron Galloway, Montreal; Barbara Godard,
Toronto ; Ellen Godfrey, Victoria; Elizabeth Gourlay, Vancouver;
Théa Gray, Okanagan; Christian and Henriette Hardy, Ottawa; Forbes
Helem, Vancouver; Norah Helliwell, North Vancouver; Sheila Irving,
Victoria; Neal and Carol Irwin, Toronto; David Jeffrey, Texas; Judith
Koltai, Victoria; Khosrow Fasihi, Victoria; Lesley Kreuger, Toronto;
Arlene Lampert, Toronto; Jay Macpherson, Toronto; Mary Mawer,
Calgary; Judith McCoombs, Maryland, US; Floris McLaren, Victoria;
Alexandra Browning Moore; Alice Munro, Clinton, ON; Grant
Munro, Montreal; Diana Neil, Fife, Scotland; Michael Page, Victoria;
Myfanwy Spencer Pavelic, Victoria; Geoffrey and Landon Pearson,
Ottawa; Constance Rooke, Toronto; Bruce Ruddick, New York; Jay
Ruzesky, Victoria; Ann Saddlemyer, Vancouver Island; Frank Schaeffer,
Rio de Janeiro; Khushwant Singh, New Delhi; Juliana Saxton, Victoria;
Jori Smith, Montreal; Rosemary Sullivan, Toronto; William Toye,
Toronto; Jane Urquhart, Stratford, Ont.; Joyce Williams, Calgary;
Beryl Young, Vancouver; Patricia Young, Victoria.

Notes

LAC   Library and Archives Canada
PANB   Provincial Archives of New Brunswick
QUA   Queen's University Library
TFRBL   Thomas Fisher Rare Book Library
TUA   Trent University Archives

All interviews are with the biographer unless otherwise indicated.

CHAPTER ONE

1 P.K. Page to Tom Marshall, letter, n.d. [c. early 1976], LAC R11777-0-3-E (cataloguing in process).

2 P.K. Page, "Ancestors," in *Hidden Room*, 1:150-1. Wherever possible P.K.'s poetry citations are to P.K. Page, *The Hidden Room: Collected Poems*, vols. 1 and 2.

3 P.K. Page, interview, 3 November 1997.

4 In 1879 Lizzie (Elizabeth Jones) had married a Major Edward Girdlestone Graham, with whom she had a daughter, Violet. But in 1886, the same year as Henry's death, Lizzie had divorced her husband, and in 1891 the two sisters, their two children, and their mother Emily were living together in Hollington, Sussex. By the 1901 census most of the extended Jones family had moved to London.

5 Margot Peters, when writing *Mrs. Pat: The Life of Mrs. Patrick Campbell*, did not find any connection between the two families (Margot Peters to Sandra Djwa, e-mail, 12 January 2002). However, as Michael Holroyd, Bernard Shaw's biographer, had earlier observed to me in conversation during the 1999 Harbourfront International Festival of Authors, in Toronto, he had found "Mrs. Pat elusive about her living arrangements during this period."

6 Subsequently I found death and census confirmations of connections between the two families. In 1897 Emily Augusta Jones, Lionel's grandmother, died at 2 Glebe Place with her daughter Augusta Page present. Four years later, Augusta's unmarried sister, Charlotte Jones, was living with Mrs Pat's mother and sister nearby at 22 Glebe Place in the same London square.

7 On the flyleaf of a Bible that Lionel Page kept as a child is written "Fairseat, Wrotham, Kent"

8 Williams. *A History of Berkhamsted School: 1541–1971*, 225.

9 Gaetz, *The Park Country: A History of Red Deer and District*, 92–3.

10 P.K. Page, interview, 10 September 1998.

11 P.K. Page, interview, 14 February 2002.

12 "Major-General Lionel F. Page," unidentified newspaper clipping, "Red Deer Pioneers," Red Deer Archives.

13 Lionel Page to Patricia Kathleen Page, letter, 18 November 1917, LAC, MG30 D311, vol. 20, f. 13.

14 R[ose] & L[ionel] Page, *Wisdom from Nonsense Land*, facsimile of original (1918).

15 There may have been some connection between the Whitehouses and the Tenniels through the first wife, name unknown, of P.K. Page's great-grandfather, Robert Whitehouse. Both the Whitehouses and the Tenniels were members of St Marylebone Church in London and appear to have belonged to the same social set. Tenniel painted several members of the Whitehouse family.

16 R. & L. Page, *Wisdom*.

17 P.K. Page, interview, 14 February 2002.

18 P.K. Page, interview, 10 September 1998.

19 Esme James, "Col. L.F. Page's Welcome Home," *Red Deer News*, 18 June 1919.

20 P.K. Page, interview, 3 November 1997.

21 Ibid.

22 P.K. Page, "Canada's Poetry," Melbourne, Australia, 15 June 1954, LAC, MG30 D311, vol. 17, f. 7.

23 In 1922 Sylvestre Clark Long assumed the name Chief Buffalo Child Long Lance and in 1928 published *Long Lance: Autobiography of a Blackfoot* (London: Faber & Gwyer), a fictional work that was widely read.

24 P.K. Page, interview, 10 September 1998.

25 P.K. Page, interview, 27 June 2001.

26 P.K. Page, "The First Part," in *Hidden Room*, 1:218.

27 This drawing is located in the Page Irwin Colloquium Room at Trent University.

28 This drawing is also located in the Page Irwin Colloquium Room at Trent University.

29 P.K. Page, interview, 8 January 1999.

30 P.K. Page, "Safe at Home," in *Filled Pen*, 24.

31 P.K. Page, "Max and My Mother," in *Filled Pen*, 104.

32 Snow, *Maxwell Bates*, 1.

33 P.K. Page, "Max and My Mother," 103.

34 P.K. Page, interview, 9 November 1998.

35 P.K. Page, interview, 10 September 1998.

36 P.K. Page, interview, 10 November 1998.

37 Elizabeth Wordsworth, "Good and Clever," in Larkin, ed., *The Oxford Book of Twentieth-Century English Verse*, 26.

38 P.K. Page, interview, 21 May 1996.

39 P.K. Page, "Crayons," in *Up on the Roof*, 43.

40 Ibid., 43–4.

41 P.K. Page, "Safe at Home," 24.

42 P.K. Page, "The Neighbour," in *The Sun and the Moon and Other Fictions*, 138.

43 P.K. Page, interview, 3 November 1997.

44 P.K. Page, "Safe at Home," 25.

45 P.K. Page, interview, 18 February 1999. See "Birthday," in Page, *A Kind of Fiction*.

46 P.K. Page, interview, 9-10 September 1998.

47 Ibid.

48 Ibid.

49 P.K. Page, interview, 9 November 1998.

50 P.K. Page, interview, 9–10 September 1998.

51 Michael Page and P.K. Page, discussion, 4 October 2001.

52 P.K. Page, interview, 9–10 September 1998.

53 P.K. Page, interview, 4 October 2001.

54 Ibid.

55 P.K. Page, interview, 19 February 1998.

56 Ibid.

57 P.K. Page, interview, 9–10 September 1998.

58 "P.K. Page," in Rae, *Everybody's Favourites*, 54.

59 P.K. Page, interview, 19 February 1998.

60 Ibid.

61 P.K. Page, interview, 21 May 1996.

62 P.K. Page, interview, 22 February 2001.

63 P.K. Page, interview, 21 May 1996.

64 Lively, *Oleander, Jacaranda*, 95.

CHAPTER TWO

1 P.K. Page, "The First Part," in *Hidden Room*, 1:218.
2 P.K. Page, "Max and My Mother," in *Filled Pen*, 102.
3 Ibid., 101.
4 P.K. Page, "Canada's Poetry," LAC, MG30 D311, vol. 17, f. 7.
5 P.K. Page, "Max and My Mother," 106.
6 Snow, *Maxwell Bates*, 5.
7 P.K. Page, "Canada's Poetry," LAC, MG30 D311, vol. 17, f. 7.
8 P.K. Page, "The First Part," in *Hidden Room*, 1:219.
9 P.K. Page, interview, 21 May 1996.
10 P.K. Page (Patsy), "A Day's Fishing," *The Ammonite*, LAC, MG30 D311, vol. 2, f. 34
11 P.K. Page (Patsy), "The Autobiography of an Alarm Clock," *The Ammonite*, LAC, MG30 D311, vol. 4, f. 32
12 Mary Mawer, interview, 28 January 1999.
13 Stratton-Porter, 1909, *A Girl of the Limberlost*.
14 P.K. Page, interview, 7 July 2000.
15 P.K. Page, interview, 8 January 1999.
16 P.K. Page, interview, 26 April 1997.
17 Ibid.
18 P.K. Page, interview, 9–10 September 1998.
19 Ibid.
20 Ibid.
21 Mary Mawer, interview, 28 January 1999.
22 P.K. Page (Pat), "On Being Ill," *The Ammonite*, LAC, MG30 D311, vol. 6, f. 16.
23 Pat Page, "My First Ministry," *The Ammonite*, LAC, MG30 D311, vol. 12, f. 16.
24 Juliana Saxton to Sandra Djwa, interview, 11 November 2011.
25 Cost, *A Man Called Luke*.
26 Morgan, *The Fountain*, 117.
27 P.K. Page, interview, 3 December 1998.
28 O'Connor, *Alec Guinness: The Unknown*, 67.
29 Elizabeth Carlile to Sandra Djwa, letter, 8 March 1999.
30 P.K. Page, interview, 22 February 2001.
31 Elizabeth Carlile and Pearl King to Sandra Djwa, e-mail, 13 October 2001.
32 P.K. Page, "Chinook," in *Hidden Room*, 2:128.
33 Elizabeth Carlile to Sandra Djwa, letter, 8 March 1999.
34 Finch, *R.M. Patterson*, 171.
35 Elizabeth Carlile to Sandra Djwa, letter, 8 March 1999.

36 P.K. Page, interview, 8 January 1999.

37 P.K. Page, "Max and My Mother," 104.

38 P.K. Page, "Written during Exams," Poetry Notebook, LAC, MG30
D311, vol. 1, f. 1, 24.

39 P.K. Page, "The Hidden Room," in *Hidden Room*, 1:11. This poem
evokes a letter written by Elizabeth Carlile to P.K. Page, 25
December 1995: "I wonder if you remember the little cubby-hole we
constructed for ourselves in our basement which was our studio – a
sort of bolt-hole in which our creativity was to have a little womb in
which it could grow."

40 P.K. Page, "Beauty," Poetry Notebook, LAC, MG30 D311, vol. 1, f. 1,
45–6.

41 P.K. Page, "The Effects of Life," Poetry Notebook, LAC, MG30
D311, vol. 1, f. 1, 10-11.

42 P.K. Page, "Individuality," Poetry Notebook, LAC, MG30 D311, vol.
1, f. 1, 26.

43 P.K. Page, *Hand Luggage*, 10.

44 P.K. Page, "The Woods Are Full of Them," Poetry Notebook, LAC,
MG30 D311, 1-1: 34-35.

45 St. Vincent Millay, "First Fig" in *Selected Poems*, 19.

46 P.K. Page, interview, 21 February 2001.

47 Class prediction, *The Ammonite* (1934), LAC, MG30 D311, vol. 7, f.
11.

48 P.K. Page, "Ambition," Poetry Notebook, LAC, MG30 D311, vol. 1,
f. 1, 36.

49 Lionel Page to P.K. Page (Pat), letter, July 1934, LAC, MG30 D311,
vol. 20, f. 13.

CHAPTER THREE

1 Henry James, preface to *The Portrait of a Lady*, 8.

2 P.K. Page, interview, 3 October 2001.

3 P.K. Page, "The Moth," *Observer* (London), 2 December 1934.

4 P.K. Page, interview, 3 October 2001.

5 Ibid.

6 Ibid.

7 P.K. Page, interview, 4 December 1998.

8 Djwa, "P.K. Page: A Biographical Interview," 33–54.

9 Rossetti, "Sudden Light," in *Dante Gabriel Rossetti*, 174.

10 P.K. Page, interview, 3 October 2001.

11 Anthony Blunt in the *Spectator*, 15 March 1935, as quoted in
Gardiner, *Epstein*, 340–1.

12 P.K. Page, "Ecce Homo," in *Hidden Room*, 1:17.

13 P.K. Page said "James Agee" in our interviews, but given the fact that James Agate was the primary drama critic during the early thirties it is probable that she confused the two.

14 P.K. Page, interview, 30 September 1997.

15 Ibid.

16 Myra Jehlen, quoted in Carolyn Heilbrun's, *Writing a Woman's Life*, 16–17.

17 Woolf, *A Room of One's Own*, 78.

18 Field (Marion Milner), *A Life of One's Own*, 64.

19 Woolf, *A Room of One's Own*, 112.

20 Field, *A Life of One's Own*, 67–8.

21 P.K. Page, interview, 3 October 2001.

22 Monro, ed., *Twentieth Century Poetry*, 11.

23 Wollman, ed., *Modern Poetry*, viii.

24 Edith Sitwell, "Aubade," in ibid., 37.

25 P.K. Page, "On Discussing Canada with the English," Poetry Notebook "Nineteen & Twenty," LAC, MG30 D311, vol. 1, f. 1, 65–6.

26 P.K. Page, "Spring," Poetry Notebook "Nineteen & Twenty," MG30 D311, vol. 1, f. 1, 92–3.

27 I have not been able to find an occasion when Mackenzie King took part in a public parade in England while Page was there. However, she may have seen King in a film in 1935 in London. Alternatively, she may be recalling a similar incident when Bruce Hutchison described King at the coronation of King George VI in *The Incredible Canadian* – a book that she read closely: "Stuffed into gold braid and a double-ended hat, King was a Tenniel drawing out of *Alice in Wonderland*, a very caricature of the Frog Footman. As the round and gleaming face was thrust out of the coach window, as the preposterous hat was waved at the crowds of Canada House, they replied … with a hoarse cheer. He might not look it but he was for the moment the incarnate spirit of Canada," 221. Page may have absorbed Hutchison's description by reading it aloud. In a letter from Ottawa in early 1953, she told Alan Crawley: "Arthur and I are reading aloud to each other Bruce Hutchison's book on King which I am finding a fascinating tale. What an incredible little guy King was. I certainly don't like him but there is a kind of open minded amazement for me in almost every page. And in view of the fact I know little or nothing of recent Canadian political history – it's got all of the suspense of a mystery for me" (P.K. Page to Alan Crawley, letter, n.d. [c. early spring 1953], QUA, 2010, box. 1, f. 20. In either case, this recollection affirms how strongly Page had begun

to feel her Canadian roots in London. Her memory of seeing King in London is again cited in P.K. Page, "Safe at Home," in *Filled Pen*, 26.

28 P.K. Page, "To Violet [The Change]" Poetry Notebook, LAC, MG30 D311, vol. 1, f. 1, 67–8.

29 Raymond Patterson was an intrepid Englishman who had explored western Canada and the Nahanni River and he bought Pocaterra's Buffalo Head Ranch in 1933–4.

30 Mark Shepherd, "Perseverance" by Turbot and Vulligan, a Cochran Review, 2001, 12 December 2005, http://www.cris.com/~oakapple/gasdisc/mdpersev.htm

31 P.K. Page, unpublished short story, "The Middleman," LAC, MG30 D311, vol. 44, f. 6.

32 Ibid.

33 P.K. Page, interview, 3 October 2001.

CHAPTER FOUR

1 P.K. Page, interview, 4 December 1998.

2 P.K. Page, interview, 22 February 2001.

3 P.K. Page, interview, 10 October 2002.

4 P.K. Page, "Depression," Poetry Notebook "Nineteen & Twenty," LAC, MG30 D311, vol. 1, f. 1, 8–9.

5 P.K. Page "A Writer's Life," in *Filled Pen*, 10.

6 P.K. Page, interview, 16–17 November 2000.

7 Ben Brantley, *New York Times*, quoted in *Globe and Mail*, 25 September 1999.

8 Lionel Page to P.K. Page, letter, [c. June 1941], LAC, MG30 D311, vol. 20, f. 13.

9 Pat Page kept a scrapbook in which she pasted a clipping from an unidentified English newspaper dated London, 11 December 1936, a day after Edward VIII's abdication. Edward is quoted as saying, "I have found it impossible to carry the heavy duty of responsibility and to discharge my duties as King as I would wish to do without the help and support of the woman I love," LAC, MG30 D311/R2411.

10 P.K. Page, interview, 22 February 2001.

11 Ibid.

12 Herbert, *Holy Deadlock*.

13 P.K. Page, interview, 22 February 2001.

14 Lionel Page to P.K. Page, letter, [c. 23 November 1937], LAC, MG30 D311, vol. 20, f. 13.

15 P.K. Page to Erica Deichmann, letter, 23 June 1963, PANB, MC497 MS1-521.

16 P.K. Page, "This Happiness," LAC, MG30 D311, vol. 4, f. 50.

17 Erica Deichmann later expressed this view to her daughter, Anneke Gichuru, who recorded the statement in her own diary, 17 May 1955. Diary in the possession of Anneke Gichuru.

18 Mansfield, "To J.M. Murry" (May 1921), *Letters of Katherine Mansfield*, 2:112.

19 P.K. Page, interview, 26 June 2001.

20 P. K. Page, "A Letter to K.S.," Poetry Notebook "Twenty," LAC, MG30 D311, vol. 1, f. 3, 32–3.

21 P.K. Page, interview, 22 February 2001.

22 P.K. Page, interview, 3 October 2001.

23 Ibid.

24 Mansfield, "To Richard Murry" (3 February 1921), *Letters of Katherine Mansfield*, 2:91.

25 P.K. Page "To Katherine Mansfield," Poetry Notebook "Twenty-Two," LAC, MG30 D311, vol. 1, f. 2, 86.

26 Mansfield, "To S.S. Koteliansky" (17 May 1915), *Letters of Katherine Mansfield*, 1:27.

27 Mansfield, "At the Bay," in *The Garden Party and Other Stories*, 35.

28 P.K. Page, "Untitled," story about New River Beach, LAC, MG30 D311, vol. 4, f. 23.

29 P.K. Page, interview, 26 June 2001.

30 P.K. Page, interview, 19 February 1998.

31 Blagrave, "Community Theatre in Saint John between the Wars," 109–10. Rittenhouse was later superintendent of the Protestant School Board of Greater Montreal.

32 P.K. Page, interview, 9 September 1998.

33 P.K. Page, interview, 22 February 2001.

34 P.K. Page to Erica Deichmann, letter, 1 December 1939, PANB, MC497 MS1-521.

35 P.K. Page, interview, 8 July 1999.

36 Ibid.

37 P.K. Page, "Sonnet," Poetry Notebook, LAC, MG30 D311, vol. 1, f. 4, 65.

38 P.K. Page to Erica Deichmann, 12 March 1940, PANB, MC497 MS1-521.

39 Lionel Page to P.K. Page, 6 June 1940, LAC, MG30 D311, vol. 20, f. 13.

40 P.K. Page, interview, 9 November 1998.

41 P.K. Page, "For V.W.," Poetry Notebook, LAC, MG30 D311, vol. 1, f. 4, 136–7.

42 P.K. Page, interview, 26 June 2001.

43 P.K. Page to Erica Deichmann, letter, 10 February 1940, PANB, MC497 MS1-521.

44 P.K. Page (Mrs. W.A. Irwin) to Murray Barnard, letter, 20 March 1972, LAC, MG30 D311.

45 P.K. Page to Erica Deichmann, letter, 10 February 1940, PANB, MC497 MS1-521.

46 P.K. Page to Erica Deichmann, letter, 4 March 1940, PANB, MC497 MS1-521.

47 P.K. Page, interview, 30 September 1997.

48 P.K. Page, interview, 3 November 1997.

49 David Blackwood expressed his opinion to Peter Redpath of the Winchester Galleries, Victoria, BC (Peter Redpath to Sandra Djwa, e-mail, 13 June 2011).

50 P.K. Page. "Victoria." *Tamarack Review* 69 (Summer 1976): 50–3.

51 Brewster, "Essence of Marigold," in her *The Invention of Truth*, 93–4.

52 P.K. Page to Elizabeth Brewster, letter, c. 1 April [1941], LAC, MG30 D370, vol. 19A.

53 P.K. Page to Elizabeth Brewster, letter, 7 June [1941], LAC, MG30 D370, vol. 19A.

54 P.K. Page, interview, 3–4 December 1998.

55 P.K. Page to Elizabeth Brewster, letter, c. 1 May 1941, LAC, MG30 D370, vol. 19A.

56 Powys, *Wolf Solent*, 407–8.

57 P.K. Page, interview, 3 October 2001. Page describes herself as experiencing the atomic structure of a chair. This is a parallel to an experience described by Joanna Field [Marion Milner] in *A Life of One's Own*. Field describes "putting herself out" into a chair in the room: "at once the chair seemed to take on a new reality I 'felt' its proportions and could say at once whether I liked its shape," 64.

58 Ezra Pound, "A Girl," in Monro, ed., *Twentieth Century Poetry*, 230.

59 See Relke, "Tracing a Terrestrial Vision in the Early Work of P.K. Page," 21. Relke notes the connection between "Reflection" and Page's novella *The Sun and the Moon*, but does not link it with the Ezra Pound poem.

60 P.K. Page, "Reflection," *Canadian Poetry Magazine* 4 (July 1939): 23.

61 Kay Smith to Sandra Djwa, letter, c. May 1997.

62 Margaret Atwood, introduction in *The Sun and the Moon and Other Fictions*, i.

63 P.K. Page, *The Sun and the Moon,* 82.

64 Ibid., 120–1.

65 P.K. Page, "Ecce Homo," in *Hidden Room*, 1:17–18.

CHAPTER FIVE

1 P.K. Page, "Alphabetical," in *Planet Earth*, 128.

2 Jori Smith, interview, 14 March 1997.

3 P.K. Page, interview, 10 November 1998.

4 P.K. Page to Jori Smith, letter, 7 January [ca. 1947], LAC, MG30 D249, vol. 4, f. 5.

5 P.K. Page, "Looking for Lodgings," LAC, MG30 D311, vol. 4, f. 44.

6 Priscilla (Hazen) Pritchard, interview, 12 June 2003.

7 P.K. Page to Alan Crawley, letter, 1 December [1941], QUA, Crawley fonds 2010 1-20.

8 P.K. Page, "The Crow," in *Hidden Room*, 1:16.

9 John Sutherland to P.K. Page, letter n.d., [c. September–October 1941] LAC, MG30 D311, vol. 8, f. 71.

10 P.K. Page, interview, 3 October 2001.

11 P.K. Page, "Desiring Only," in *Hidden Room*, 1:20. First published in *Preview*, April 1942.

12 P.K. Page, interview, 9 November 1998.

13 Ibid.

14 P.K. Page, interview, 20 July 1975.

15 P.K. Page and Théa Gray, discussion, 23 March 2000.

16 P.K. Page, "F.R. Scott," *Brick* 29 (Summer 1987): 36.

17 P.K. Page, "The Bones' Voice," Poetry Notebook, March 1942, LAC, MG30 D311, vol. 1, f. 5.

18 P.K. Page, "Desiring Only," in *Hidden Room*, 1:20.

19 P.K. Page, interview, April 1974.

20 Ibid.

21 Irvine, "Gendered Modernisms," 127–80.

22 [Patrick Anderson], "Statement," *Preview*, March 1942, 3.

23 P.K. Page, untitled, Poetry Notebook, 1940–44, LAC, MG30 D311, vol. 1, f. 15.

24 P.K. Page and Arthur Irwin, interview, 20 July 1975.

25 John Sutherland [as Jack Hakaar], "Why George Left College," *First Statement*, April 1944, 14–18.

26 Frank Scott, Leon Edel, Neufville Shaw, and A.J.M. Smith discussing *Preview* on 19 February 1966. Later published as "Four of the Former *Preview* Editors: A Discussion" as part of "Three Documents from F.R. Scott's Personal Papers," *Canadian Poetry: Studies, Documents, Reviews* no. 4 (Spring-Summer 1979): 73–119.

27 P.K. Page, "Canadian Poetry 1942," *Preview*, October 1942, 8–9.

28 John Sutherland, "P.K. Page and *Preview*." *First Statement* 6 (October 1942), 6.

29 F.R. Scott, 13 March 1944, Notes on *Preview* meeting, LAC, MG30 D211, vol. 21, f. 84.

30 Klein, "Montreal," in *Complete Poems: A.M. Klein*, 2:621–3.

31 P.K. Page, "The Sense of Angels: Reflections on A.M. Klein," in *Filled Pen*, 64.

32 Ibid., 68.

33 P.K. Page, interview, 9 November 1998.

34 P.K. Page, "A Writer's Life," Margaret Laurence Memorial Lecture, Halifax, 1999, in *Filled Pen*, 11.

35 P.K. Page, interview, 1 April 1974.

36 Patrick Anderson to P.K. Page, letter, [c. July–August 1942], LAC, MG30 D311, vol. 6, f. 7.

37 Laura Killian has discussed Page's general use of impersonality, in "Poetry and the Modern Woman," 105. For a sensitive updating of this topic, see also Irvine, "The Two Giovannis: P.K. Page's Two Modernisms," 23–45.

38 T.S. Eliot, "Hamlet and His Problems," 100.

39 P.K. Page, interview, 10 October 2002.

40 P.K. Page, "The Stenographers," in *Hidden Room*, 1:102–3.

41 P.K. Page, interview, 9 November 1998.

42 P.K. Page to A.J.M. Smith, letter, n.d. [ca. early spring 1943], TFRBL, 00015, vol. 2, f. 38.

43 Ibid.

44 P.K. Page, interview, 9 November 1998.

45 P.K. Page, "The Bands and the Beautiful Children," in *Hidden Room*, 2:14.

46 Gagnon, *Paul-Émile Borduas*, 114–15.

47 P.K. Page, interview, 10 November 1998.

48 Jori Smith to P.K. Page, letter, [c. July 1995], LAC, MG30 D311.

49 Jori Smith to P.K. Page, letter, n.d. [ca. summer 1943], LAC, MG30 D311, vol. 11-3

50 Jori Smith, interview, 14 March 1997.

51 Ibid.

52 P.K. Page, "Photograph," in *Hidden Room*, 2:40.

53 Margaret Atwood chose "Photograph" for *P.K. Page: Poems Selected and New* (1971).

54 "The Stenographers" appeared in *Preview*, July 1942, and *Canadian Forum*, September 1942, 177.

55 P.K. Page, interview, 10 November 1998.

56 P.K. Page's poem "Landscape of Love" was later known as "Personal Landscape." It first appeared in *First Statement*, August 1942. I suspect that the phrase "the landscape of love" is derived from the

poem "Time and Again" by Rainer Maria Rilke in the following
translation by J.B. Leishman (Rainer Maria Rilke: *Poems,
1875–1926*):

> Time and again, however well we know the landscape of love,
> and the little church-yard with lamenting names,
> and the frightfully silent ravine wherein all the others
> end: time and again we go out two together,
> under the old trees, lie down again and again
> between the flowers, face to face with the sky.

57 P.K. Page, "Personal Landscape," in *Hidden Room*, 1:38.
58 P.K. Page, interview, 10 November 1998.
59 In 1942 F.R. Scott published "What Did No Mean?" (*Canadian
Forum*, June 1942), an article in response to the national plebiscite
on conscription in which the majority of the English provinces voted
in favour of conscription whereas in Quebec 73 percent voted "no."
He explained to English Canadians that a large factor in the "no"
vote was against "the continuing colonialism of Canada's relation to
Great Britain." With this article, Scott stirred up a hornet's nest. See
Djwa, *The Politics of the Imagination*, 200–1.
60 F.R. Scott, "Metamorphosis," in "The Auto-Anthology of F.R. Scott"
(Montreal 1939). Copy in the possession of the author. The
manuscript was not published and "Metamorphosis" was not
selected for Scott's subsequent books. It reads:

> I married a woman.
> She could do the things I did
> And go with me.
>
> We climbed high rocks together
> And in dark pools
> Bathed
> Swimming out into strong currents.
>
> But suddenly she turned into a mother.
> Life used our love as a tool
> For its own selfish ends.
> Life overreached us.
>
> Now I have to take care of her.

She is not the woman I married.

I do not like this thing.

61 F.R. Scott, diary, 13 November 1950, LAC, MG30 D211, vol. 92, f. 3.

62 Russell, *The Right to Be Happy*. Russell's chapter on "The Rights of Human Beings" separates sex and parenthood, pointing out that "the impulse to sexual pleasure has never yet had its rightful place in shaping our society, because it has not been allowed recognition" (131). "What hinders us from establishing a social system in which young men and women who are out in the world earning may enter into open temporary sex partnerships without harm" (154). "The idea of sin must be banished ... There would be passionate grieves, disappointments and broken ideals, but none of this is so damaging to a human personality as atrophy. We must have freedom and courage to learn if we are to be worth anything as human beings" (155).

63 Scott spoke of his marital life to Leon Edel, the biographer of Henry James and a close friend since the late 1920s. Edel mentioned this conversation to me on 25 October 1982 when I was preparing Scott's biography, remarking that wives sometimes become mother figures after the birth of a child.

64 Trépanier, *Marian Dale Scott*: "The intellectual and literary circles the Scotts frequented might be compared to the Bloomsbury group in England, in their commitment to modernity and their acceptance of sexual freedom. As Marian Scott so often said in her dry way, 'Creative minds need a variety of experiences ... especially men!' Frank Scott was certainly a case in point. Although Marian, no less creative than her husband, had some close friendships with men, including those in the thirties with King Gordon and Norman Bethune, she was nonetheless hurt by Frank's numerous affairs," 94.

65 Marian Scott, diary, LAC, MG30 D399, vol. 2.

66 Rilke, *Duino Elegies*, trans. with an introduction by J.B. Leishman and Stephen Spender, 21.

67 Strachey, "Digging for Mrs. Miller," *New Statesman and Nation*, 9 November 1940, 466.

68 Scott, "Recovery," *Preview*, Spring 1942, 6. See also *The Collected Poems of F.R. Scott*, 105.

69 F.R. Scott, in *Collected Poems of F.R. Scott*, 141.

70 Dean Irvine, Scott's editor, dates the writing of "Departure" as beginning c. 1945 and completed in 1950.

71 Mavis Gallant to Sandra Djwa in conversation, Simon Fraser University, Burnaby, BC, 28 October 1997.
72 Herbert, *Holy Deadlock.*
73 P.K. Page, interview, 25 January 2006.
74 P.K. Page to F.R. Scott, letter, 1 July 1944, LAC, MG30 D211, vol. 115, f. 7.
75 P.K. Page, interview, 11 January 2000.
76 Ibid.
77 P.K. Page, interview, 10 November 1998.
78 F.R. Scott, "Departure," in *Collected Poems of F.R. Scott,* 142.

CHAPTER SIX

 1 P.K. Page to F.R. Scott, letter, [c. 10 June 1944], LAC, MG30 D211, vol. 115, f. 7.
 2 P.K. Page to F.R. Scott, letter, [c. 19 June 1944], LAC, MG30 D211, vol. 115, f. 7.
 3 P.K. Page to F.R. Scott, letter, [c. 28 June 1944], LAC, MG30 D211, vol. 115, f. 7.
 4 F.R. Scott, "Windfall," in *Collected Poems of F.R. Scott,* 144.
 5 P.K. Page to Jori Smith, letter, n.d. [c. July 1944], LAC, MG30 D249, vol. 4, f. 5.
 6 P.K. Page to F.R. Scott, letter, n.d. [c. 17 July 1944], LAC, MG30 D211, vol. 115, f. 7.
 7 P.K. Page, "The Lion's Shadow," unpublished manuscript, [c. 1943], LAC, MG30 D311, vol. 4, f. 38.
 8 P.K. Page, interview, 9 September 1998.
 9 Michael Page, interview, 6 May 2006.
10 P.K. Page, "For My Father," unpublished manuscript, [c. 1944], LAC, MG30 D311, vol. 3, f. 33.
11 P.K. Page, interview, 10 November 1998.
12 P.K. Page, interview, 11 January 2000.
13 P.K. Page, interview, 10 October 2002.
14 When the Page family prepared to move to Victoria they discovered that some of their more important belongings, including vital family papers and photographs, had gone missing while in storage.
15 Graham, *Earth and High Heaven.*
16 P.K. Page to Jori Smith, letter, 22 October [1944], LAC, MG30 D249, vol. 4, f. 5.
17 P.K. Page, interview, 10 November 1998.
18 Ibid.

19 F.R. Scott to P.K. Page, drafted letter, 12 October 1944, LAC, MG30 D211, vol. 115, f. 16.
20 P.K. Page, "Element," in *Hidden Room,* 1:90.
21 Djwa, "P.K. Page and Margaret Atwood," 81–93.
22 Leila Sejur, "Addressing a Presence: An Interview with Phyllis Webb," *Prairie Fire* 9, no. 1 (1988), 31.
23 W.S. Milne, "Two First Novels," *Saturday Review,* 2 December 1944, LAC, MG30 D311, vol. 15, f. 3.
24 P.K. Page, *The Sun and the Moon,* 63.
25 Ibid., 76.
26 P.K. Page, in Hambleton, ed., *Unit of Five,* 37.
27 P.K. Page, "Summer Resort," in *Hidden Room,* 1:108–9.
28 P.K. Page, "Snap Shot," in *Hidden Room,* 1:77.
29 P.K. Page, "Cullen," in *Hidden Room,* 1:127–9.
30 B.K. Sandwell, "Four Very Angry Poets in a *Unit of Five,*" *Saturday Night,* 10 February 1945, 21–2.
31 P.K. Page, "No Flowers," in *Hidden Room,* 1:119.
32 P.K. Page, interview, 10 November 1998.
33 Ibid.
34 P.K. Page, "Stories of Snow," in *Hidden Room,* 1:53–4.
35 F.R. Scott, "Advice," in *Collected Poems of F.R. Scott,* 153.
36 F.R. Scott, "Villanelle for Our Time," ibid., 106.
37 P.K. Page to Jori Smith, letter, 2 May [1945], LAC, MG30 D249, vol. 4, f. 5.
38 P.K. Page to Jori Smith, letter, nd. [ca. May 1945]. LAC, MG30 D249, vol. 4, f. 5.
39 Mwfanwy Pavelic-Spencer, interview, 20 February 2001.
40 P.K. Page, interview, 10 November 1998.
41 PK Page to Jori Smith, letter, 8 November [ca. 1945], LAC, MG30 D249, vol. 4, f. 5.
42 PK Page, "Election Day," in *Hidden Room,* 1:116–17
43 P.K. Page, interview, 10 November 1998.
44 P.K. Page, "The Glass Box," in *A Kind of Fiction,* 114.
45 Ibid., 116

CHAPTER SEVEN

1 P.K. Page, interview, 3 December 1998.
2 Evans, *John Grierson: Trailblazer of Documentary Film,* 50–1.
3 Arthur Irwin "A View from the Top," 37–41. Irwin, government film commissioner, recalls Film Board employees: "They tend to be

radical, they tend to be unconventional in their behaviour, even their clothes – plump women came to work in purple slacks – for God's sake, purple slacks in a government office in 1950" (40).

4 P.K. Page, interview, 19 February 1998.

5 Jay Macpherson, interview, 28 October 1998.

6 Grant Munro, interview, 4 March 1999.

7 P.K. Page, interview, 10 November 1998.

8 Norah Helliwell, interview, 23 January 1998.

9 P.K. Page, "Introducing Filmstrips," a talk given at the National Film Board, n.d. [c. 1947], LAC, MG30 D311, vol. 15, f. 11.

10 P.K. Page, interview, 21 May 1996.

11 Forbes Helem, interview, 29 August 1997.

12 John McKay, "Cannes honours animator, NFB," *Vancouver Sun*, 12 May 2006.

13 Grant Munro, interview, 4 March 1999.

14 Ibid.

15 Ibid.

16 Crawley, "P.K. 1946," in Rogers and Peace, eds., *P.K. Page*, 129–30.

17 P.K. Page, interview, 10 November 1998.

18 Djwa, *The Politics of the Imagination*, 259.

19 P.K. Page, interview, 9 November 1998.

20 Mavis Gallant, in conversation, 28 October 1997.

21 Meredith, "A Good Modern Poet and a Modern Tradition," 208–11.

22 P.K. Page, "Generation," in *Hidden Room*, 1:125–6.

23 Auden, "September 1, 1939," in Mendelson, ed., 245–6.

> There is no such thing as the State
> And no one exists alone;
> Hunger allows no choice
> To the citizen or the police;
> We must love one another or die.

24 P.K. Page, "As Ten, As Twenty," in *Hidden Room*, 2:23. The poem was called "Love Poem" in the book *As Ten, As Twenty* (Toronto: Ryerson, 1946) but when it was reprinted in *Cry Ararat!* (Toronto: McClelland & Stewart, 1967), the title was changed to "As Ten, As Twenty."

25 P.K. Page, "If it Were You," in *Hidden Room*, 1:65-7

26 P.K. Page, "Personal Landscape," ibid., 38. Page's line seems to precede "The optic heart must venture" of Margaret Avison's "Snow," in *Winter Sun* (1982), 27.

27 P.K. Page, "Waking," in *Hidden Room*, 1:134.

28 A.J.M. Smith, "New Canadian Poetry," *Canadian Forum*, February 1947, 250–2.
29 Ibid., 250.
30 P.K. Page, "Round Trip," in *Hidden Room*, 1:30–5.
31 P.K. Page to Alan and Jean Crawley, letter, 4 November [1946], QUA, 2010, box 1, f. 20.
32 A.J.M. Smith to P.K. Page, letter, c. November-early December 1946, LAC, MG30 D311, vol. 17, f. 8.
33 P.K. Page to Alan and Jean Crawley, letter, 3 December [1946], QUA, 2010, box 1, f. 20.
34 Earle Birney to P.K. Page, letter, 17 August 1946, LAC, MG30 D311, vol. 6, f.
35 Earle Birney to Alfred Purdy and Curt Lang, letter, 15 March 1955, in Purdy, *Yours, Al: The Collected Letters of Al Purdy*, 29–31.
36 P.K. Page to Alan Crawley, letter, "Thursday," [c. October 1946], QUA, 2010, box 1, f. 20.
37 Alan Crawley to Earle Birney, in McCullagh, *Alan Crawley and Contemporary Verse*, 27–8.
38 Sutherland, "The Poetry of P.K. Page," in *John Sutherland*, 101–12.
39 Ibid., 103. Sutherland refers specifically to a "leprechaun" in this article. When both Sutherland and Page were still in New Brunswick, Sutherland had placed second in a competition sponsored by the Canadian Authors Association in which Page's poem "The Moon-Child" (with it's leprechaun), had received honourable mention.
40 P.K. Page to Jori Smith, letter, 17 January [ca. 1947], LAC, MG30 D249, vol. 4, f. 5.
41 Sutherland, "Robert Finch and the Governor-General's Award," in *John Sutherland*, 144–7.
42 P.K. Page to Jean Crawley, letter, n.d. [c. 1948], QUA, 2010, box 1, f. 20.
43 P.K. Page to Elizabeth Brewster, letter, 13 December 1947, LAC, MG30 D370, 19A.
44 P.K. Page to Jori Smith, letter, 7 January 1948, LAC, MG30 D249, vol. 4, f. 5.
45 Singh, *Truth, Love & a Little Malice*, 128.
46 Khushwant Singh to Jagpal Tiwana, e-mail, "Canada is the Most Beautiful Country," 18 February 2005. LAC, MG30 D311/R4211/R4211, 2006-0941, 3. (Khushwant Singh e-mailed T. Sheer Singh who e-mailed the message to Jagpal Tiwana.) See also Khushwant Singh, interview, New Dehli, India, 13 February 2005.
47 P.K. Page, interview, 10 November 1998.
48 Ibid.

49 Ibid.

50 P.K. Page, "Portrait of Marina," in *Hidden Room*, 1:72–3.

51 P.K. Page, interview, 7 January 1999.

52 P.K. Page, interview, 26 February 2004.

53 Northrop Frye speaks of "Portrait of a Marina" as a little novelette in itself: "a spinster bullied by a sailor-father and 'antlered with migraines' in consequence" ("Letters in Canada: 1954," 40).

54 P.K. Page interview, 10 November 1998: "Anyhow we drove down, Florence and I to Rhode Island, and it was an interesting drive because Florence was a very masterful woman. I think I've attracted a lot of very bossy women in my life."

55 P.K. Page to Eve Friesen, e-mail, 27 September 2009.

56 P.K. Page to Alan Crawley, letter, 11 November 1948, QUA, 2010, box 1, f. 20.

57 P.K. Page, interview, 11 January 2000.

58 P.K. Page to Jean Crawley, letter, n.d. [c. 1947], QUA, 2010, box 1, f. 20.

59 Abelard, *The Letters of Abelard and Heloise*, 13.

60 Ibid., 149

61 Money et al., *The Art of Margot Fonteyn*, n.p.

62 P.K. Page, interview, 16 February 1999.

63 P.K. Page, interview, 11 January 2000.

64 Ibid.

65 Scott, "Return," in *Collected Poems of F.R. Scott*, 145.

66 Alan Crawley to Anne Wilkinson, letter, 10 August 1949, TFRBL, 0029, box 4, f. 9.

67 "Noted Young Canadian Poet Finds Inspiration in Province," unidentified Vancouver newspaper clipping, [c. August 1949].

68 P.K. Page, interview, 3 December 1998.

69 Wilkinson, "Journals," 31.

70 P.K. Page to Anne Wilkinson, letter, 11 August [c. 1949], TFRBL, 29, box 4, f. 54.

71 The Scotts had spoken of their marital situation to a number of their friends. Frank Scott spoke to Leon Edel (Leon Edel to Sandra Djwa, discussion, 25 October 1982); Marian Scott told Florence Bird and Lois Lord, a New York photographer and friend of the family (Florence Bird, interview, 20 March 1997). Lois Lord to Sandra Djwa, discussion, 28 December 1999, Vancouver.

72 Conversation with Frank and Marian Scott, Montreal, after a recording session, c. June 1976. The date when Norman Bethune and F.R. Scott travelled back to Canada from England on the same ship

is cited in Stewart and Stewart, *Phoenix: The Life of Norman Bethune*, 116.

73 Marian Scott, diary, 11 February 1944. LAC, MG30 D399, vol. 1, f. 30.

74 Myron Galloway, interview, 16 March 1997.

75 Marian Scott, diary, 3 March 1950. LAC, MG30 D3992, vol. 2, f. 4.

76 Evans, *John Grierson*, 99.

77 Ibid., 103.

78 P.K. Page, interview, 8 January 1999.

79 P.K. Page, interview, 19 February 1998.

80 Jori Smith, interview, 7 January 1999.

81 Mary Ferguson to P.K. Page, letter, 14 December 1975, LAC, MG30 D311.

82 P.K. Page, interview, 10 November 1998.

83 Scott, "Message," in *Collected Poems of F.R. Scott*, 141.

84 F.R. Scott, diary, 16 July 1950, LAC, MG30 D11, vol. 92, f. 3.

85 P.K. Page, interview, 11 January 2000.

86 Marian Scott, diary, 13 August 1950, LAC, MG30 D399, vol. 2, f. 7.

87 Jori Smith, interview, 14 March 1997.

88 Arthur Irwin, interview, 10 November 1998.

89 P.K. Page, interview, 10 November 1998.

90 P.K. Page, interview, 11 January 2000.

91 Arthur Irwin, in conversation, 28 December 1983.

92 Neal Irwin, interview, 3 March 1998.

93 Norah Helliwell, interview, 23 January 1998.

94 F.R. Scott, diary, 31 October 1950, LAC, MG30 D11, vol. 92, f. 3.

95 F.R. Scott, diary, 13 November 1950, LAC, MG30 D11 vol. 92, f. 3.

96 Ibid.

97 F.R. Scott, diary, 20 November 1950, LAC, MG30 D11 vol. 92, f. 3.

98 Ibid.

99 P.K. Page to F.R. Scott, letter, 10 June 1944, LAC, MG30 D211, vol. 115, f. 7.

100 F. R. Scott, "Departure," in *Collected Poems of F.R. Scott*, 142.

101 P.K. Page, interview, 11 January 2000.

102 P.K. Page, interview, February 1998.

103 Arthur Irwin, "A View from the Top," 41.

104 McKay, "Cannes honours animator, NFB." According to McKay, George Lucas, the director of *Star Wars*, was later to acknowledge his indebtedness to National Film Board shorts like *Neighbours*. McKay also says that when François Truffaut viewed some of McLaren's pioneer animations, he wrote to him, "I was amazed and also very moved. I had tears in my eyes watching your films."

105 P.K. Page, interview, 19 February 1998.

106 P.K. Page to Jori Smith, letter, n.d. [ca. 1952], LAC, MG30 D249, vol. 4, f. 5.

107 Lester B. Pearson "Memorandum for the Acting Secretary of State for External Affairs," 7 November 1951, LAC, RG25 86–9/160 38 4533–40.

108 P.K. Page, interview, 8 January 1999.

109 P.K. Page to Alan Crawley, letter, n.d. [c. February 1953], QUA, 2010, box 1, f. 20.

110 P.K. Page, "Australian journal," 29 November 1953, LAC, MG30 D311, vol. 113, f. 4.

CHAPTER EIGHT

1 P.K. Page, "Australian journal" (1952–53), 20 June [1953], LAC, MG30 D311, vol. 113, f. 4.

2 P.K. Page to Jean Fraser, letter, 8 August [1953], LAC, MG31 D184, vol 2, f. 16.

3 Ibid.

4 Ibid.

5 P.K. Page to Jean Fraser, letter, n.d. [August 1953], LAC, MG31 D184, vol 2, f. 16.

6 P.K. Page, "Then," revisions to "Australian journal," August 1953, LAC, MG30 D311/R2411, vol 96, f. 8–9.

7 P.K. Page, interview, 19 February 1998.

8 P.K. Page to Jean Fraser, letter, n.d. [1955], LAC, MG31 D184, vol 2, f. 16.

9 P.K. Page revisions to "Australian Journals," August 1953, LAC, MG30 D311/R2411, vol 96, f. 8–9.

10 Ibid.

11 P.K. Page to Jean Fraser, letter, 3 October [c. 1954], LAC, MG31 D184, vol 2, f. 16.

12 P.K. Page to Jack McClelland, letter, 5 December 1953, LAC, MG30 D311, vol. 15, f. 9.

13 P.K. Page, interview, 17 February 1999.

14 P.K. Page to Jean Fraser, letter, 3 October [c. 1954], LAC, MG31 D184, vol 2, f. 16.

15 P.K. Page, interview, 7 January 1999.

16 P.K. Page, interview, 19 February 1998.

17 Ibid.

18 Shute, *In the Wet*.

19 P.K. Page to Jean Fraser, letter, 15 March [1954], LAC, MG31 D184, vol 2, f. 16.

20 P.K. Page, interview, 8 January 1999.

21 P.K. Page to Jean Fraser, letter, 15 March [1954], LAC, MG31 D184, vol 2, f. 16.

22 P.K. Page to Jean Fraser, letter, 3 October [c. 1954], LAC, MG31 D184, vol 2, f. 16.

23 P.K. Page to Jean Fraser, letter, 15 March [1954], LAC, MG31 D184, vol 2, f. 16.

24 Frye, *The Bush Garden*, 40.

25 Young, *P.K. Page: Essays on Her Works*, 30.

26 P.K. Page, "Arras," in *Hidden Room*, 1:46–7.

27 P.K. Page, "I think of it as the life force. The creative force" (Djwa, "P.K. Page: A Biographical Interview," 47).

28 P.K. Page, "F.R. Scott," 36: "Great brilliance is not something universally loved, is it? There's a kind of icy quality to it. And you know, he looked like the King of Diamonds – that look, sharp. His profile could have cut." Continuing Page's metaphor of the royal cards we might consider that Leo, Scott's astrological sign, is the King of Beasts and the heraldic sign of English royalty.

29 In Australian Aboriginal lore, which Page was now learning, to "point a bone" is to threaten with death. A secondary reading of "to point a bone" is sexual in nature, as in the seventeenth-century phrase "little death."

30 A.J.M. Smith to P.K. Page, letter, 24 April 1956, LAC, MG30 D311, vol 8, f. 65.

31 P.K. Page, "Arras," in *Hidden Room*, 1:46–7.

32 A number of references in "Arras" suggest Lewis Carroll's *Alice in Wonderland*: Alice sees a vista through an aperture and puts her eye to the keyhole where she sees a garden beyond; she enters into it as does the female narrator in "Arras"; at the conclusion of the Alice story, Alice dismisses the Red Queen ("Sentence first, verdict afterwards") saying, "Who cares for *you*? ... You're nothing but a pack of cards" (78). The concept of the aperture, the reference to playing cards, and the question about caring all seem to be part of the structure of "Arras."

33 P.K. Page to Jori Smith, letter, 31 May [c. 1955], LAC, MG30 D249, vol 4, f. 5.

34 P.K. Page to Jean Fraser, letter, 3 October [c. 1954], LAC, MG30 D184, vol 2, f. 16.

35 Cid Corman to P.K. Page, letter, 3 December 1952.

36 Cid Corman to P.K. Page, letter, 21 January 1953, LAC, MG30 D311 vol 6, f. 40.

37 P.K. Page to Alan Crawley, letter, n.d. [c. 1953], QUA, 2010 box 1, f. 20.

38 Cid Corman to P.K. Page, letter, 27 February 1953, LAC, MG30 D311, vol 6, f. 40.

39 P.K. Page to Jori Smith, letter, 27 January 1955, LAC, MG30 D249 vol 4, f. 5.

40 P.K. Page to Anne Wilkinson, letter, n.d., TFRBL, 29, vol 4, f. 54.

41 P.K. Page to Jack McClelland, letter, 7 July 1954, LAC, MG30 D311, vol 15, f. 9.

42 P.K Page, "The Metal and the Flower," in *Hidden Room*, 2:39.

43 P.K. Page, "Australian journal" 1952–53, 2 August 1954, LAC, MG30 D311/R2411, vol 113, f. 4.

44 P.K Page, "Photos of a Salt Mine," in *Hidden Room*, 1:48–9.

45 Anne Wilkinson to P.K. Page, letter, 14 November 1954, LAC, MG30 D311, vol 9, f. 6.

46 P.K. Page to Anne Wilkinson, letter, nd. [c. 1955], TFRBL, 29, vol. 4, f. 54.

47 Floris McLaren to P.K. Page, letter, [c. 1955], LAC, MG30 D311, vol. 8, f. 16.

48 Frye, *The Bush Garden*, 39–40.

49 P.K. Page, interview, 1 April 1974.

50 P.K. Page to Jean Fraser, letter, n.d. [c. 1955], LAC, MG31 D184, vol. 2, f. 16.

51 Rose Page to P.K. Page, letter, 23 March 1954.

52 Alan Crawley to P.K. Page, letter, 13 April 1955, LAC, MG30 D311, vol. 13, f. 5.

53 David Thomson to P.K. Page, letter, c. November 1954, LAC, MG30 D311, vol. 13, f. 5. The judges were Roy Daniells of UBC, Ira Dilworth of the CBC, and W.J. Alexander from Queen's University.

54 P.K. Page, "The Map," in *Hidden Room*, 2:49–50.

55 Floris McLaren to P.K. Page, letter, 4 January 1955. LAC, MG30 D311, vol. 8, f. 16.

56 P.K. Page prefers "cayouse."

57 P.K. Page, address at the Australian-American Association, Melbourne, Victoria, Australia, 15 June 1954, LAC, MG30 D311, vol. 17, f. 17.

58 P.K. Page, "Canada's Poetry," LAC, MG30 D311, vol. 17, f. 17.

59 Ibid.

60 P.K. Page, Address at the Australian-American Association.

61 Hope, "Soledades of the Sun and the Moon: For P.K. Page," in his *Collected Poems*, 109–10.

62 Marilyn Bowering to Sandra Djwa, e-mail, 11 October 2010. Bowering had been visiting Australia and met Hope on 8 March 1985. She recorded his remarks in her journal.

63 P.K. Page to Anne Wilkinson, letter, n.d. [c. 1955], TFRBL, 29, vol 4, f. 54.

64 P.K. Page to Jean Fraser, letter, n.d. [c. 1955], LAC, MG31 D184, vol. 2, f. 16.

65 P.K. Page, interview, 10 November 1998.

66 P.K. Page, address at the Australian-American Association. Another Australia poem, "Frieze of Birds" is interesting both for the catalogue of Australian birds that caught Page's eye, but also because it makes an explicit connection between birds, tapestry, and Dom Robert, indicating that Page was indeed thinking of the monk's tapestry designs while in Australia. An early version begins "This frieze of birds encloses / Dom. Robert and his explicit tapestry." In this poem, she contrasts the freedom of the birds in flight with the rigidity of those contained within one of Dom Robert's designs (P.K. Page to Floris McLaren, letter, [c. 1956]).

67 P.K. Page, interview, 8 January 1999.

68 P.K. Page, "After Rain," in *Hidden Room*, 2:109–10.

69 Floris McLaren to P.K. Page, letter, 20 May [c. 1956], LAC, MG30 D311, vol. 8, f. 16.

70 Alan Crawley to P.K. Page, letter, 13 April 1955, LAC, MG30 D311, vol. 13, f. 5.

71 P.K. Page to Jean Fraser, letter, 29 May [1954], LAC, MG31 D184, vol. 2, f. 16.

72 P.K. Page, "Riel," unpublished manuscript, LAC, MG30 D311, vol. 3, f. 72.

73 Ibid.

74 P.K. Page, "The First Part," in *Hidden Room*, 1:216–19.

75 Trehearne, *The Montreal Forties*, 95.

76 P.K. Page, "Australian journal," 1956, 27 March. LAC, MG30 D311/R2411, vol. 113, f. 7.

77 P.K. Page, "Cullen Revisited," in *Cullen: Poems*. (This title was formerly applied to an earlier poem when it was first published in 2010.)

78 Rooke, "P.K. Page: The Chameleon and the Centre," 165–95.

79 This began in April 1954 when Vladimir Petrov, third Secretary in the Soviet Embassy in Canberra but also a colonel in the Soviet Secret Police, the MVD, defected to Australia, offering to provide evidence of Soviet espionage in exchange for political asylum.

80 P.K. Page to Jean Fraser, letter, 5 July 1955, LAC, MG31 D184, vol. 2, f. 16.

81 P.K. Page, interview, 17 February 1999.
82 P.K. Page to Jean Fraser, letter, 31 December 1955, LAC, MG31 D184, vol. 2, f. 16.
83 P.K. Page, interview, 7 January 1999.
84 P.K. Page, June 1956, "On the Road, North Coast," LAC, MG30 D311/R2411, vol. 96, f. 1–6.
85 Ibid.
86 P.K. Page, "On the Road Again," n.d., LAC, MG30 D311/R2411, vol. 96, f. 1–6.
87 Ibid.
88 P.K. Page, "Australian journal," 1956, 10 August, LAC, MG30 D311/R2411, vol. 113, f. 9.
89 P.K. Page to Jean Fraser, letter, 31 December [1955], LAC, MG31 D184, vol. 2, f. 16.
90 P.K. Page, interview, 19 February 1998.

CHAPTER NINE

1 P.K. Page, *Brazilian Journal*, 3 February 1957, 9.
2 P.K. Page, *Hand Luggage*, 48.
3 P.K. Page, *Brazilian Journal*, 21 January 1957, 5.
4 Bishop, "On the Railroad Named Delight," 30.
5 P.K. Page, "Questions and Images," in *Filled Pen*, 36.
6 P.K. Page, *Brazilian Journal*, 18 February 1957, 15.
7 Ibid., 8 April 1957, 34.
8 P.K. Page, "Questions and Images," 36.
9 P.K. Page, *Brazilian Journal*, 15 June 1957, 59. This account does not occur in the Brazilian journals but is added, as "insert B" part way through the revision process.
10 P.K. Page, "Questions and Images," in *Filled Pen*, 36.
11 P.K. Page, *Brazilian Journal*, 3 February 1957, 10.
12 Ibid., 30 May 1957, 56.
13 Ibid., 18 February 1957, 15.
14 Ibid., 15 June 1957, 59.
15 Ibid., 12 October 1958, 177.
16 Ibid., 31 March 1957, 29.
17 P.K. Page, interview, 16 February 1999.
18 P.K. Page, *Brazilian Journal*, 14 April 1957, 35.
19 Ibid., 6 July 1957, 62.
20 P.K. Page, "Brazilian Fazenda," in *Hidden Room,* 2:123
21 P.K. Page, *Brazilian Journal*, 6 June 1957, 57.
22 Ibid., 58.

23 Ibid., 14 April 1957, 34.

24 P.K. Page, interview, 16 February 1999.

25 Ibid.

26 P.K. Page, "Brazilian journal," 4 August, 57, LAC, MG30
    D311/R2411, vol. 113, f. 14.

27 P.K. Page, *Brazilian Journal*, 12 May 1957, 46.

28 Ibid., 14 July 1957, 64.

29 Ibid., 17 August 1957, 72.

30 Ibid., 15 August 1957, 70.

31 Heaps, "P.K. Page's Brazilian Journal: Language Shock": "By
    drawing and painting everything she saw, Page constructed a bridge
    over the [space] of the culturally and linguistically unfamiliar … In
    so doing she makes Brazil culturally intelligible to herself, and her
    own autobiography captures this process of making the culturally
    unintelligible intelligible" (355).

32 P.K. Page, *Brazilian Journal*, 10 July 1959, 238. *"Divino Espírito
    Santo, Alma da minha alma, eu Vos adoro …"*

33 P.K. Page, interview, 30 September 1997.

34 P.K. Page, *Brazilian Journal*, 21 August 1957, 74.

35 Ibid., 12 May 1958, 151.

36 P.K. Page to Jean Fraser, letter, n.d. [c. June 1958], LAC, MG31 D184,
    vol. 2, f. 18.

37 P.K. Page, "Brazilian journal," 25 February 1958, LAC, MG30
    D311/R2411, vol. 113, f. 14.

38 P.K. Page to Jean Fraser, letter, 10 March [c. 1958], LAC, MG31
    D184, vol. 2, f. 17.

39 P.K. Page, *Brazilian Journal*, 1 June 1958, 158.

40 Ibid.

41 P.K. Page exhibited *Woman's Room* at the Winchester Galleries in
    2003.

42 P.K. Page, "Could I write a poem now?" LAC, MG30 D311, vol. 3, f.
    17.

43 See also Messenger, "But How Do You Write A Chagall?" 102–17.

44 A.M. Klein's growing knowledge of the Holocaust, developed while
    he was working on *The Second Scroll*, did contribute to his
    breakdown, but undoubtedly there were other causes.

45 P.K. Page, *Brazilian Journal*, 2 January 1959, 195.

46 Trehearne, *The Montreal Forties*, 95–105. Trehearne sensitively
    explores a number of reasons for P.K. Page's poetic silence in
    Australia, Brazil, and Mexico.

47 In her "Brazilian journal" P.K. Page writes simply that "M" probed
    about why she no longer wrote poems. It is likely that this "M" was

Molly McKay, with whom she had lunch a few weeks later, on 10 March, and "talked almost non-stop of God." But it could also have been Molly Hendrickson, a Brazilian of Germanic extraction, whom Page described in an interview as keenly interested in her art and who bought Pat's painting, *Holy Ghost*. In her diaries Page refers on several occasions to Molly McKay but later speaks of "both Mollies," meaning Hendrickson and McKay.

48 P.K. Page, "Brazilian journal," 17 February 1959, LAC, MG30 D311/R2411, vol. 113, f. 17.

49 P.K. Page, *Brazilian Journal,* 23 February 1959, 209–10.

50 Ibid., 29 March 1959, 217.

51 Ibid., 16 November 1958,181–7.

52 Ibid., 23 May 1959, 231.

53 Ibid., 14 April 1959, 218.

54 Ibid., 16 April 1959, 221.

55 Ibid., 23 May 1959, 228.

56 Ibid., 2 January 1959, 194.

57 P.K. Page, "Brazilian journal," 27 December 1957, LAC, MG30 D311/R2411, vol. 113, f. 14.

58 P.K. Page, *Brazilian Journal,* 14 July 1957, 64.

59 Ibid., 17 August 1957, 72.

60 Ibid.: "I lay naked on the bed" (1956, 1). "A.[rthur] and I, stark naked on single beds" (4 December 1957, 100); "Am sitting stark naked in the heat" (10 March 1959, 213).

61 P.K. Page, ibid.: "Bought a *figa* as a present for one of the girls at the office. The literature that accompanied it cannot be paraphrased: *Figa* is one of the oldest charms against evil eyes and spirits: the human hand with the thumb between the indicator and the middle-finger, it's the symbol of reproduction which annuls the negative influences of sterility and adversity in life" (*Brazilian Journal,* 20 May 1957, 54).

62 P.K. Page, ibid.: "the red banana-flower, heavy as male genitals" (17 August 1957, 71); "He asked me to touch a particular spot and I was promptly attacked by a small yellow object ... 'The penis of the plant,' they explained to A." (23 May 1959, 231).

63 Ibid. In April, Page visited the Israeli ambassador's wife, who explained that "she found Rio difficult at first, but now, after nine months, she finds it easier. (Like a pregnancy?)" (8 April 1957, 34).

64 Ibid. P.K. describes the convalescence from her uterine operation in relation to children: "The child of one of the servants is staying here for the Christmas holidays and she is a perfect convalescent present

for me. We sit together on the patio and draw, or take slow walks in the garden – two children, really … Very beautiful, very static – a painting, perhaps" (27 December 1957, 108).

65 Ibid., 2 January 1959, 192–3.

66 Ibid., 29 July 1959, 239.

67 Ibid., 10 July 1959, 238.

68 P.K. Page, "Brazilian journal," 30 January 1959, LAC, MG30 D311/R2411, vol. 113, f. 16.

69 Ibid., 21 August 1959, LAC, MG30 D311/R2411, vol. 113, f. 18.

CHAPTER TEN

1 P.K. Page to Alan and Jean Crawley, letter, August 1963, QUA, 2010, box 1, f. 20.

2 P.K. Page, "Traveller, Conjuror, Journeyman," in *Filled Pen*, 44.

3 P.K. Page, "Mexican journal," 10 March 1960, LAC, MG30 D311/R2411, vol. 113, f. 26.

4 P.K. Page, interview, 7 July 1999.

5 Ibid., 24 February 2003.

6 Ibid., 7 July 1999.

7 P.K. Page to Jori Smith, letter, 28 March [1960], LAC, MG30 D249, vol. 4, f. 5.

8 P.K. Page, "Mexican journal," 26 April 1960, LAC, MG30 D311/R2411, vol. 113, f. 26.

9 Ibid.

10 Ibid.

11 P.K. Page, interview, 12 January 2000.

12 P.K. Page, revisions to her Mexican journal, 20 March 1960, LAC, MG30 D311/R2411, vol. 113, f. 26.

13 Geoffrey and Landon Pearson, interview, 11 November 1999.

14 P.K. Page, interview, 3 October 2001.

15 P.K. Page, "Mexican journal," 20 November 1960, LAC, MG30 D311/R2411, vol. 113, f. 26.

16 Jung, *Modern Man in Search of a Soul*, 71.

17 P.K. Page, "Mexican journal," 7 April 1961, LAC, MG30 D311/R2411, vol. 113, f. 26.

18 P.K. Page, interview, 24 February 2003.

19 P.K. Page, "Mexican journal," 23 July 1960, LAC, MG30 D311/R2411, vol. 113, f. 26.

20 Orenstein, *The Theater of the Marvelous*, 124.

21 Orenstein, ("Leonora Carrington: Another Reality," 30) notes:

"André Breton, in the second of his *Manifestoes of Surrealism*, observed that Surrealism and alchemy really had analogous goals – the transformation of man in his quest for spiritual enlightenment."

22 P.K. Page, interview, 24–25 February 2003.

23 P.K. Page, interview, 7 July 1999.

24 P.K. Page, "Mexican journal," 31 July 1960, LAC, MG30 D311/R2411, vol. 113, f. 26.

25 Ibid., 11 October 1961, LAC, MG30 D311/R2411, vol. 113, f. 26.

26 Ibid., 31 July 1960, LAC, MG30 D311/R2411, vol. 113, f. 26, (Page's spelling: "schitzophrenia" and "exctasy").

27 Jung, *Symbols of Transformation*.

28 P.K. Page, "Phone Call from Mexico," in *Hidden Room*, 1:173–4.

29 P.K. Page's Mexican art exhibition was reported by Carlos Valdés as "Dreams and Superstitions at the Juan Martin Gallery," in *Novedades*, 18 June 1961: "It could be said that certain designs which appear in her work have been inspired by Klee, but it is not an imitation, rather it is the artist who has the same plastic concept as Klee; the creation of poetic and mysterious symbols which represent the world of concrete reality."

30 P.K. Page, "Mexican journal," 9 June 1961, LAC, MG30 D311/R2411, vol. 113, f. 26.

31 Anne Francis [Florence Bird], "P.K." *Canadian Art* 20 (January–February 1963), 42–5.

32 P.K. Page, "Mexican journal," 9 June 1961, LAC, MG30 D311/R2411, vol. 113, f. 26.

33 P.K. Page to Jori Smith, letter, 3 November 1961, LAC, MG30 D249, vol. 4, f. 5.

34 P.K. Page to Jori Smith, letter, n.d., c. 1960–62, LAC, MG30 D249, vol. 4, f. 5.

35 P.K. Page, interview, 22 February 2001.

36 P.K. Page, interview, 7 January 1999.

37 P.K. Page to Jean Fraser, letter, c. 12 May 1958, LAC, MG31 D184, 2-18.

38 P.K. Page, interview, 7 January 1999.

39 P.K. Page, interview, 17 November 2000.

40 P.K. Page, "Mexican journal," 14 November 1960, LAC, MG30 D311/R2411, vol. 113, f. 26.

41 Ibid., 18 October 1960, LAC, MG30 D311/R2411, vol. 113, f. 26.

42 P.K. Page, interview, 7 July 1999.

43 Khushwant Singh, interview, New Delhi, 13 February 2005.

44 P.K. Page, "Mexican journal," 8 July 1962, LAC, MG30 D311/R2411, vol. 113, f. 26.

NOTES TO PAGES 189–93

45 P.K. Page, interview, 7 July 1999.

46 Kennedy placed a naval "quarantine" on Cuba on 24 October to prevent further Soviet shipments of military weapons.

47 P.K. Page, "Mexican journal," 25 October 1962, LAC, MG30 D311/R2411, vol. 114, f. 3.

48 Ibid., 9 December 1963, LAC, MG30 D311/R2411, vol. 114, f. 3.

49 Ibid., 5 May 1961, LAC, MG30 D311/R2411, vol. 114, f. 3.

50 Ibid., 3 April 1961, LAC, MG30 D311/R2411, vol. 114, f. 3.

51 Orenstein (*Theater of the Marvelous*, 136) gives the first date of production as 1957.

52 P.K. Page, "Mexican journal," 9 July 1961, LAC, MG30 D311/R2411, vol. 113, f. 26.

53 Ibid., 11 September 1961, LAC, MG30 D311/R2411, vol. 113, f. 26. Like D.H. Lawrence's story *The Rocking Horse Winner*, *Pénélope* is a tale about a nursery and a rocking horse. Carrington's bizarre fantasy tells of an eighteen-year-old girl confined to the nursery. She loves her rocking horse but hates her father, an exaggerated symbol of masculine authority. The girl receives advice from a celestial being (a cow representing the Moon Goddess) and rebels. In the transcendental conclusion, both girl and rocking horse turn into white colts – forms of the White Goddess – and fly out through the nursery window.

54 P.K. Page, interview, 27 February 2004.

55 P.K. Page to Jori Smith, letter, n.d. [c. mid-June 1962], LAC, MG30 D249, vol. 4, f. 5.

56 Jung, *Memories, Dreams, Reflections*, 158–9.

57 Smith, *The Classic Shade*, 96

58 "The Sephiroth ... are a medium between the divine, the absolute (Ain-Soph) and the physical world as we know it ... Ain-Soph is the infinite." Below it is the Ain Soph Aur, which retracts itself to a light point and brings "substantiality out of nothing." The first Sephiroth to be created is the Kether, or "crown," "the first Sephira at the top of the Tree of Life." It is the "primal vibration of the universe" which will follow," http://www.soul-guidance.com/houseofthesun/treeoflifetraditional.htm

59 P.K. Page, "Mexican journal," 18 November 1960, LAC, MG30 D311/R2411, vol. 113, f. 26.

60 P.K. Page, "Another Space," in *Hidden Room*, 2:170–1.

61 Ouspensky, *In Search of the Miraculous*, 202.

62 P.K. Page, "Mexican journal," 7 April 1961, LAC, MG30 D311/R2411, vol. 113, f. 26.

63 Suzuki, *An Introduction to Zen Buddhism*.

64 P.K. Page to Jean Fraser, letter, 4 November [1962], LAC, MG31 D184, vol. 2, f. 17.

65 P.K. Page, "Mexican journal," 18 November 1962, LAC, MG30 D311/R2411, vol. 114, f. 3.

66 Ibid., 20 November 1962.

67 Ibid., 3 January 1963.

68 Ibid., 17 April 1963.

69 Ibid., 27 October 1963.

70 Roger Shattuck, Introduction to René Daumal's *Mount Analogue,* 106.

71 Ibid.,11.

72 P.K. Page, interview, 8 July 1999.

73 P.K. Page, "Traveller, Conjuror, Journeyman," in *Filled Pen,* 43.

74 P.K. Page, "Mexican journal," 13 January 1963, LAC, MG30 D311/R2411, vol. 114, f. 3.

75 Ibid.

76 Ouspensky, *In Search of the Miraculous,* 116–40.

77 P.K. Page, interview, 3 December 1998.

CHAPTER ELEVEN

1 P.K. Page, "Canadian journal: Ottawa 1964, Victoria [1964–65]," 18 October 1964, LAC, MG30 D311/R2411, vol. 113, f. 23.

2 Ibid., September 1964, LAC, MG30 D311/R2411, vol. 113, f. 23.

3 Arthur Irwin, interview, 17 February 1999.

4 P.K. Page, "Election Day," in *Hidden Room,* 1:116–17

5 P.K. Page to Jori Smith, letter, 13 November 1964, LAC, MG30 D249, vol. 4, f. 5.

6 P.K. Page, conversation, 14 February 2002.

7 Ann Saddlemyer, for example, later master of Massey College, was hired in the sixties at Victoria College with an MA but was encouraged by Roger Bishop to undertake a PHD.

8 Roger Bishop, interview, 9 January 1996.

9 Alice Munro, interview, 18 June 2008.

10 Alice Munro to Sandra Djwa, letter, 15 September 1997.

11 P.K. Page to Jack McClelland, letter, 28 June 1965, LAC, MG30 D311, vol. 15, f. 4.

12 P.K. Page recalled that Skelton once asked her if she had some poetry for the *Malahat Review,* a journal that then stressed "international" rather than Canadian poets. Pat responded truthfully that she did not, that she was now painting most of the time. Skelton, who

seemed to admire her poetry, took offence (P.K. Page, interview, 16–17 November 2000).

13 P.K. Page to Jori Smith, letter, 16 March [c. 1965], LAC, MG30 D249, 4-5.
14 P.K. Page to Jean Fraser, letter, 19 October [c. 1965], LAC, MG31 D184, vol. 2, f. 17.
15 P.K. Page to William Toye, letter, 24 August 1965, in the possession of the recipients.
16 Pat Martin Bates, interview, Victoria, 20 February 2001.
17 Francis, "P.K.," 42–5.
18 Pat Martin Bates, interview, Victoria, 20 February 2001.
19 Ibid.
20 Jung, et al., *Man and his Symbols*; P.K. Page, "Canadian journal: Victoria 1964–65," 24 August 1965, LAC, MG30 D311/R2411, vol., 113, f. 22-5.
21 Shushan Egoyan, interview, 29 July 2008.
22 P.K. Page, interview, 22 February 2001.
23 Alice Munro, interview, 18 June 2008.
24 Atwood, "If You Can't Say Something Nice, Don't Say Anything at All," 17.
25 P.K. Page, "Canadian journal: Victoria 1964–65," 12 December 1965, LAC, MG30 D311/R2411, vol., 113, f. 23.
26 One of the descriptions of this painting says "oil gesso," but Page at one point says "tempera."
27 P.K. Page, "Canadian journal: Victoria 1964–65," 18 December 1965, LAC, MG30 D311/R2411, vol., 113, f. 23.
28 Myfanwy Spencer-Pavelic, interview, 20 February 2001.
29 Robin Skelton, "Emily Carr Book an Insult – Don't Buy It," *Daily Times* (Victoria) 22 October 1966.
30 Skelton later told Pat Martin Bates that the title had been invented by a copyeditor (Pat Martin Bates, interview, 28 July 2001).
31 Pat Martin Bates, interview. 28 July 2008.
32 At this time George Woodcock's literary interests were divided between British and Canadian literature. Yet as late as 1974, when I was organizing the inaugural meeting of the Association for Canadian and Quebec Literatures at the University of Toronto, he refused to advertise the event in *Canadian Literature* because, as he said, the association represented "narrow nationalism"; his objective in editing *Canadian Literature* was to emulate the English journal *Encounter*, which that was directed towards the "general reader."
33 P.K. Page, interview, 26 February 2004.

34 Page sent Smith "Element," "Images of Angels," "Man with One Small Hand," and "Arras" [Smith published 6 of his own poems, Scott was given 6, Anne Wilkinson was given 7, Margaret Avison was given 6].

35 A.J.M. Smith to P.K. Page, letter, 7 February 1965, LAC, MG30 D311, vol. 8, f. 65.

36 F.R. Scott's "Lakeshore" in turn was a response to P.K. Page's "Divers," which begins: "Remet, the pair, double in water, / wet and dyed with leaves under the sun. / Sailed on themselves, silken and twice one, / four with love – nailed to the shot self."

37 F.R. Scott, diary, 1 December 1956, LAC, MG30 D11, vol. 91, f 6.

38 Scott, "Lakeshore," in *Collected Poems of F.R. Scott*, 50–1.

39 Anon. "Oh Western Wind."

40 F.R. Scott, diary, 20 April 1968, LAC, MG30 D211, vol. 91, f. 11. A year later, in February of 1969, Scott added: "Notice how the "Love Poem" in P.K. Page's *As Ten, As Twenty*, written to me has been replaced in *Cry Ararat* by a memory of "love poem," which speaks, and must have been meant to speak, directly to me. And thus I muse, alone, on Ararat on this St. Valentine's Day" (F.R. Scott, diary, 14 February 1969, LAC, MG30 D211, vol. 114, f. 2).

41 P.K. Page, "Cry Ararat!" in *Hidden Room*, 2:183–6.

42 P.K. Page to A.J.M. Smith, letter, 8 February 1967, TUA, 78-007, box 2, f. 6.

43 P.K. Page to Jori Smith, card, "Christmas 1967," LAC, MG30 D249, vol. 4, f. 5.

44 A.J.M. Smith to P.K. Page, letter, 17 December [1967], LAC, MG30 D311, vol. 8, f. 65.

45 Floris McLaren to P.K. Page, letter, 8 November 1967, LAC, MG30 D311, vol. 8, f. 16: "Mac, who never [takes] friendship or any relationship, for granted waited until I passed the book to him, then read the inscription and could not help showing that he was touched and pleased – 'to me, too??'"

46 Atom Egoyan, interview, 10 May 2010. P.K. thought the film *Calendar* the best of all his work, perhaps because it was a poetically structured piece. Egoyan wondered if Page's geometric shapes and drawings might not have influenced *Calendar*, which is "very severely divided ... almost geometric in its construction ... and prismatic." Page's and Egoyan's sensibilities were different: nonetheless, each recognized in the other "that sense of yearning, that sense of trying to strive for something beyond ourselves and using our art forms to do that, even if we didn't have the same sensibility much of the time." One of Page's last gifts to Egoyan

acknowledged the nature of his creative urge when she gave him *Mexican Poetry: An Anthology*, translated by Samuel Beckett, with "Love P.K." What P.K. and Arthur may have contributed to Egoyan was a sense of the transforming power of art and the fact that it can be politically directed.

47 Skelton, "A Poet of The Middle Slopes," 40–4.

48 P.K. Page to A.J.M. Smith, letter, 13 March [c. 1967], TUA, 78-007, vol 2, f. 6.

49 Joan Finnigan, "Poetry at the Convention," *Ottawa Journal,* 9 April 1969.

50 P.K. Page to A.J.M. Smith, letter, 8 February 1967, TUA, 78-007, box 2, f. 6.

51 Margaret Atwood to P.K. Page, letter, 2 April 1969, LAC, MG30 D311, vol. 14, f. 4. In this letter Atwood distinguishes between the use of metaphor by P.K. Page and Jay Macpherson. I interpret her comment to mean that "Macpherson, in a poem like 'Mary in Egypt,' begins by identifying the myth in her title but transforms the story to contemporary images. Page, in poems like 'Photos of a Salt Mine,' usually does the reverse, working from an image, or a series of images, to imply a larger structure" (Djwa, "P.K. Page and Margaret Atwood, 81–93).

52 Margaret Atwood to Sandra Djwa, letter, 7 August 1997.

53 P.K. Page to George Woodcock, letter, 12 November n.d. [probably 1968], thanking him for the invitation, QUA 2095 box 2, f. 75.

54 P.K. Page, "Questions and Images," in *Filled Pen,* 35–42. Page tells us that her search had led her through a myriad of esoteric books: *The Collected Works of Jung*, *The Perennial Philosophy*, *The Doors of Perception*, Zen, C.S. Lewis, and St John of the Cross, 39. In retrospect, we can see that Page's reading shares the quest of Aldous Huxley when he explains: "The Perennial Philosophy … is expressed most succinctly in the Sanskrit formula, *tat tvam asi* ('That art thou'); the Atman, or immanent eternal Self, is one with Brahman, the Absolute Principle of all existence; and the last end of every human being, is to discover the fact for himself, to find out Who he really is" (Huxley, *The Perennial Philosophy*, 1–2).

55 P.K. Page, "Questions and Images," in *Filled Pen,* 40.

56 P.K. Page, interview, 12 January 2000.

57 P.K. Page, "Questions and Images," in *Filled Pen,* 40.

58 Robert Graves, Introduction to *The Sufis,* vii–viii.

59 Shah, *The Sufis,* 32–3.

60 P.K. Page, interview, 21 May 1996.

61 Ibid.

62 Marilyn Bowering notes in her diary of 15 June 2000 (in the possession of the owner) that P.K. had spoken to her of Idries Shah and that he had told Stella Kent that "if P.K. wanted to continue her studies she had to form a group and lead it" (Marilyn Bowering to Sandra Djwa, e-mail, 13 October 2011).

63 Pat Martin Bates, interview, 28 July 2008.

64 Hilmi, "The Sufi Quest," 196.

65 P.K. Page, "Canadian journal: Victoria, England, Victoria" 1969–72, 14 April – 1 May 1969, LAC, MG30 D311/R2411, vol., 113, f. 25.

66 Ibid.

67 Ibid.

68 Lessing, "An Elephant in the Dark," 373–5.

69 Robert Graves wrote an enthusiastic introduction to *The Sufis*, Doris Lessing pledged to Shah royalties from books she had yet to write, and Geoffery Grigson and Ted Hughes wrote favourably about Sufism.

70 P.K. Page to Jori Smith, Christmas card, 1965, LAC, MG30 D249, vol. 4, f. 5.

71 Lessing, *The Four-Gated City*, 111.

72 Ibid., 640.

73 Ibid., 461.

74 P.K. Page, interview, 26 February 2004.

75 P.K. Page to Jori Smith, card, n.d. Christmas [c. 1969], LAC, MG30 D249, vol. 4, f. 5.

76 Idries Shah, Doris Lessing, and Robert Graves have stated in various venues that the Sufism that Shah advocated is not Islamic and not a sect. Yet Shah's organization fulfilled much of the criteria for a sect in that it was led by a charismatic individual who received funds from followers pledged to a degree of secrecy. His teachings, however, do narrow traditional Sufism by divorcing it from Islam and placing it firmly in the context of psychic development as advocated by Carl Jung and G.I. Gurdjieff. Shah may have initially shaped his message in this fashion to appeal to Gurdjieff's substantial European following. There is evidence of this intention in *The Teachers of Gurdjieff*, written by Shah (under the pseudonym of Rafael Lefort), which is structured in imitation of Gurdjieff's *Meetings with Remarkable Men*. In it Shah suggests that the great Sufis of the East who had authenticated Gurdjieff now regarded him as superseded by a new European teacher – presumably Shah himself. P.K. Page bought *The Teachers of Gurdjieff* in 1966 and read it carefully, underlining key passages.

CHAPTER TWELVE

1 Jung, *Memories, Dreams, Reflections*, 5.
2 P.K. Page to A.J.M. Smith, letter, n.d. [c. 1970], TUA, 78-007, vol. 2, f. 6.
3 P.K. Page, "Traveller, Conjuror, Journeyman," 44.
4 Al Purdy greatly admired Page. Pat Martin Bates recollected that he had led both women to believe that the invitation to speak at my poetry class at SFU was at his instigation (Pat Martin Bates to Sandra Djwa, e-mail, 5 April 2000).
5 P.K. Page, interview, 22 February 2001.
6 Ibid.
7 P.K. Page, "Another Space," in *Hidden Room*, 2:170–71.
8 P.K. Page to A.J.M. Smith, letter, April 1970, TUA, 78-007, vol. 2, f. 6.
9 P.K. Page to A.J.M. Smith, letter, 5 March 1971. TUA, 78-007, vol. 2, f. 6.
10 Howard O'Hagan to P.K. Page, letter, 22 December 1974, LAC, MG30 D311, vol. 8, f. 35.
11 P.K. Page to Florence Bird, letter, 7 November [1972], LAC, M31 D63, vol. 13, f. 20.
12 P.K. Page, "Canadian journal: Victoria, England, Victoria," 31 March 1972, LAC, MG30 D311, vol. 113, f. 25. The newspaper clipping of Pocaterra's death is dated 13 March 1972.
13 Ondaatje, ed., *The Broken Ark: A Book of Beasts*, with drawings by Tony Urquhart.
14 Shain, "Some of Our Best Poets Are … Women," 48–50, 103–7.
15 P.K. Page to Florence Bird, letter, 7 November [c. 1972], LAC, MG31 D63, vol. 13, f. 20.
16 P.K. Page to F.R. Scott, letter, 2 February 1972, LAC, MG30 D211, vol. 116, f. 9.
17 P.K. Page, "Beside You," in *Hidden Room*, 2:56.
18 P.K. Page, "Even the Sun, Even the Rain," *Malahat Review* 127 (Summer 1999), 103–5. Reprinted in *A Kind of Fiction*, 73.
19 P.K. Page to Jori Smith, letter, "En route, Saturday" [ca. 16 March 1974], LAC, MG30 D249, vol. 4, f. 5.
20 P.K. Page, interview, 26 April 1997.
21 Ibid.
22 Skelton, *The Memoirs of a Literary Blockhead*, 11–13.
23 Djwa, "P.K. Page and Margaret Atwood," 81–93.
24 Margaret Atwood to P.K. Page, letter, 2 March 1973, LAC, MG30 D311, vol. 6, f. 6.

25 Atwood, "Address in Honour of Mimmo Paladino / P.K. Page."

26 Atwood, "If You Can't Say Something Nice." Atwood called this
    "the Canadian complication," that is, "Could you be a female, a
    writer, be good at it, get published, not commit suicide, and be a
    Canadian too?" (17).

27 A.J.M. Smith, when he chose a selection of Page's poetry for *Modern
    Canadian Verse in English and French*, 1967), placed "Element"
    first. In 1982, when Atwood edited *The New Oxford Book of
    Canadian Verse*, she omitted "Element" but included "Stories of
    Snow," "Photos of a Salt Mine," and "The Snowman," and added
    new poems (Atwood, *The New Oxford Book of Canadian Verse in
    English*, 179–88).

28 Atwood, "you fit into me," in *Power Politics*, 1.

29 P.K. Page, "Element," in *Hidden Room*, 1:90.

30 Margaret Atwood to P.K. Page, letter, 20 April 1973, LAC, MG30
    D311, vol. 12, f. 3.

31 Atwood, "Introduction," in Page, *The Sun and the Moon and Other
    Fictions*, i.

32 Review of *The Sun and the Moon* (1973), *Globe and Mail*, 9 March
    1974.

33 Romany Miller, review, *Ottawa Citizen*, 9 February 1974.

34 Margaret Atwood to Shirley Gibson, letter, Saturday [c. December
    1973], LAC, MG30 D311, vol. 12, f. 31.

35 Ibid.

36 P.K. Page to Margaret Atwood, letter, 2 January [1974], LAC, MG30
    D311, vol. 12, f. 3.

37 Arthur Adamson, review of *Poems: Selected and New*, by P.K. Page,
    Contemporary Verse, Spring, 1975, 9.

38 Alan Pearson, review of *Poems: Selected and New*, by P.K. Page,
    Canadian Forum, May–June 1974, 17–18.

39 Patrick Anderson, "Poet's Progress," review in unidentified source.

40 Eli Mandel, "Tactility Page. Nervous and Fluid as Ever," *Globe and
    Mail*, 27 April 1974.

41 Eli Mandel to P.K. Page, letter, 17 July 1973, LAC, MG30 D311, vol.
    33, f. 22: "Please accept this belated letter of gratitude for comment
    on *Crusoe* [*Selected Poems 1973*]. You will understand how very
    much I appreciate and value those comments when I say that it was
    your own work – the poems I read in *The Metal and the Flower* and
    earlier – that sustained and encouraged me. One day maybe I'll be
    able to show you some of my inept imitations of your style."

42 George Woodcock, "P.K. Page – Collected but Incomplete," Victoria
    Times, 7 September 1974.

43 Douglas Beardsley, review of *Cry Ararat!* by P.K. Page, *Northern Journal*, 6 June 1976.

44 George Melnyk, "The Social and Personal Views of Poetry," *Edmonton Journal*, 22 July 1974.

45 P.K. Page to Rose Page and Aunt Bibbi, letter, 1 August 1974, LAC, MG30 D311, vol. 20, f. 15.

46 Besides Page, the poet group included Milton Acorn, Elizabeth Brewster, Fred Cogswell, Garry Geddes, George Johnston, George Jonas, D.G. Jones, Douglas LePan, Eli Mandel, Steve McCaffery, Susan Musgrave, Michael Ondaatje, Al Purdy, Joe Rosenblatt, and Tom Wayman.

47 Stephen Overbury, "Explosion of Poetry in Canada," *Leader-Post* (Regina), 13 August 1976.

48 Ibid.

49 Yantra is a Sanskrit term for an instrument, often used to refer to geometric figures and symbols. In Jungian thought the yantra is discussed in relation to psychological symbolism and "the union of opposites," that is, the union of the ego with the "non-personal, timeless world" or "the union of the soul with God," and as such is representative of the wholeness of the psyche or self. Aniela Jaffé also discusses yantras in reference to a form of mandala composed of nine linked triangles (Aniela Jaffé, "Symbolism in the Visual Arts," in Jung's *Man and his Symbols*, 267–68).

50 P.K. Page to Florence Bird, letter, 7 November 1972, LAC, MG31 D63, vol. 13, f. 20.

51 P.K. Page, "Traveller, Conjuror, Journeyman," in *Filled Pen*, 46–7.

52 Florence Bird to P.K. Page, letter, 4 March 1971, LAC, MG30 D311, vol. 10, f. 6.

53 Shah, *The Sufis*, 222: "The world was created through a word from Thoth [Hermes] – eight characteristics ... The eightfold character of Sufi teaching is symbolized by the octagonal diagram for the word *hoo*, the Sufi sound."

54 P.K. Page, interview, 21 May 1996.

55 Jung, *Psyche and Symbol*, xxvii.

56 See note 71, below.

57 Carl Jung believed that a "rearranging of the personality is involved, a new kind of centering over time as the mandala-making process continues." He also affirmed that meditation on the mandala helped to bring psychic order out of chaos and states that "the goal of psychic development is the self. There is no linear evolution; there is only a circumambulation of the self" (*Memories, Dreams, Reflections*, 196).

58 P.K. Page to Jean Fraser, letter, 4 November 1962, LAC, MG31 D184, vol. 2, f. 17.

59 Jung defines the term individuation as the psychological process that makes of a human being an "individual" – a unique, indivisible unit, or "whole man" (John Freeman, introduction to Jung, *Psyche and Symbol*, xxvii).

60 Shah, *Way of the Sufi*, 14–15

61 P.K. Page, "Mexican journal," LAC, MG30 D311/R2411, vol. 114, f. 3.

62 P.K. Page, interview, 21 March 1996.

63 Shah, *The Sufis*, 212.

64 Jung discusses the squaring of the circle in *The Collected Works of C.G. Jung*, 404.

65 P.K. Page, interview, 6 December 2007. Jung also speaks of the tree as a symbol of psychic life (*Psyche and Symbols*, 151–2).

66 In 1962 Page was reading Jung's *Symbols of Transformation* in Mexico, and it seems likely that the version of the Tree of Life that she drew on the back page was done at this time. Her Tree of Life incorporates "Solomon's Seal" as two interlocking triangles, further subdivided into eight by the plant (Solomon's Seal is a form of lily), making an octagon. To this plant, also a symbol of man, Pat has appended notes showing that it spans the distance from "Earth" and a "Lower Level" to "Heaven" and a "Higher Level."

67 Shah, *The Sufis*. Shah states that the number eight symbolizes the number of perfect expression, the octagon, and quotes a saying that "the eight (balance) is the way to the nine." Nine in Arabic stands "for the letter *Ta*, whose hidden meaning is 'secret knowledge,'" 214.

68 Pat Martin Bates, interview, 28 July 2008.

69 "Tree of Life," http://en.wikipedia.org/wiki/Tree_of_life.

70 The interlocking triangles and octagonal domes of this drawing function as Jungian "yantras," joining earth to heaven (Jung, *Psyche and Symbol*, xxvii).

71 "According to Sufi teaching the search for the 'Philosopher's Stone' is an encoding for the Sufi quest for integration of inner and outer levels of perception expressed in chemical terms" (Fahim, *Doris Lessing: Sufi Equilibrium*, 108).

72 P.K. Page, "Cullen Revisited," This poem (together with the essay "Traveller, Journeyman, Conjuror") was first published in *Canadian Literature* 50 (Fall 1971): 33–4. "Cullen Revisited" was reprinted in *The Hidden Room*, 1:165–6.

73 P.K. alludes to the squaring of the circle in her letter to George

Woodcock and continues by saying that her octagon drawings are "hard-edge and I think a lot of people – not Jack [Wise], surely – confuse 'mystic' with 'soft or hazy'" (P.K. Page to George Woodcock, letter, 11 September 1973, QUA 2095, box 2, f. 75).

74 J.W. [Jack Wise], "Foreward to Exhibition."

75 This drawing, *Arcanum*, now unavailable, was completed by 11 July 1970. A pen and ink drawing, it appears to have been part of the octagonal group. "Arcanum," is defined as "a secret known only to the members of a small select group," or "a secret of nature, of the kind that was sought by alchemists," which ties in with Shah's remark on secret knowledge in *The Sufis* and that contemplation of the octagon, or figure eight, "leads to the nine," or secret knowledge (*The Sufis*, 214).

76 Elizabeth Gourlay to P.K. Page, letter, 6 January 1974, LAC, MG30 D311, vol. 10, f. 15.

77 Russell Cazeire, "P.K. Page, a well-known Canadian poetess," CBC review, Burnaby Art Gallery, 5–7 April 1978.

78 P.K. Page to Lois Crawley, letter, 14 August [1970], in the possession of the recipient.

79 Shah, *The Sufis*, xxiii–xxvii.

80 Ornstein, *Psychology of Consciousness*, 132–3.

81 Ibid., 164.

82 Ibid., 224.

83 P.K. Page later told this anecdote to Marilyn Bowering (Marilyn Bowering to Sandra Djwa, e-mail, 5 February 2010).

84 P.K. Page to Jori Smith, letter, 3 March 1975, LAC, MG30 D249, vol. 4, f. 5.

85 Elizabeth Gourlay to P.K. Page, letter, 13 March 1974, LAC, MG30 D311, vol. 10, f. 15.

86 P.K. Page to Jori Smith, letter, n.d. [ca. 1976], LAC, MG30 D249, vol. 4, f. 5.

87 Information from conference posters in the possession of the writer.

88 Harley and Nancy Schwartz, interview, 6 February 2010.

89 Lessing, *The Four-Gated City*, 152.

90 Jung, *Memories, Dreams, Reflections*, 5.

91 Florence Bird, interview, 20 March 1997: "[Page's] Sufism, she passed it on to me and I found it very useful."

92 P.K. Page to Florence Bird, letter, 7 November [1972], LAC MG31 D63, vol. 13, f. 20: "Mother furious because she isn't 90 – insists she *is* and when I tell her her birth certificate says when she was born and that is pretty well conclusive she slyly, next day, asks me to bring her birth certificate so she can destroy it – nobody needs to clutter

their lives up with useless, bits of paper and if I won't get rid of it, she will!"

93 Florence Bird to P.K. Page, letter, 20 March 1974, LAC, MG30 D311, vol. 10, f. 6.

94 Florence Bird to P.K. Page, letter, 24 April 1976, LAC, MG30 D311, vol. 10, f. 7.

95 Florence Bird to P.K. Page, letter, 2 December 1973. Bird is referring to P.K.'s remark in an earlier letter (LAC, MG30 D311, vol. 10, f. 6).

96 P.K. Page to Rose Page and Beatrice Whitehouse, letter, n.d. [c. August 1974] LAC, MG30 D311, vol. 20, f. 16.

97 P.K. Page to Jori Smith, letter, 14 September [1974], LAC, MG30 D249, vol. 4, f. 5.

98 G.D. Fulton to Sandra Djwa, conversation, 17 November 2011.

99 P.K. Page to Jean Fraser, letter, "Sunday" [c. April 1976], LAC, MG31 D184, vol. 2.

100 Ibid.

101 Ibid.

102 P.K. Page to Dolly Holt, letter, 5 May 1976, LAC, MG30 D311, vol. 20, f. 16.

103 P.K. Page to Shirley Gibson, letter, 12 October 1976. LAC, MG30 D311, vol. 14, f. 9.

104 Timothy Porteous, former head of the Canada Council, interview, 2 December 2009.

105 Patricia Young, "P.K. In the Classroom" in *P.K. Page: Essays on Her Works*, 33.

106 Ibid., 34.

107 P.K. Page to Jori Smith, letter, 29 June 1978, LAC, MG30 D249, vol. 2, f. 4.

108 The creative writing courses would have approximately ten instructors: four people for poetry, four for prose, and two for plays. The instructors and students stayed in dormitories and the students paid $140 for two weeks' instruction.

109 Sandler, "A Report on the Handicraft School of Writing," 40–1.

110 P.K. Page to Patrick Anderson, letter, 13 August 1974, LAC, MG30 D177, vol. 18.

111 Arlene Lampert, interview, 7–8 February 2000.

112 P.K. Page to Arlene Lampert, letter, 1 October 1978, in the possession of the recipient.

113 P.K. Page, interview, January 1999.

114 P.K. Page to Arlene Lampert, letter, 31 October 1978, in the possession of the recipient.

115 P.K. Page to Florence Bird, letter, 1 July 1977, LAC, MG31 D63, vol. 13, f. 20.

116 David Jeffrey, "The Issue is Cultural Integrity," Victoria *Times*, 18 March 1976.

117 Rosemary Sullivan, interview, 15 November 2008.

118 Constance Rooke, interview, 27 April 2004.

119 Sullivan, "A Size Larger than Seeing: The Poetry of P.K. Page," 32–42.

120 Rooke, "P.K. Page: The Chameleon and the Centre," 169–95.

121 P.K. Page to Jori Smith, letter, 29 June 1978, LAC, MG30 D249, vol. 2, f. 4

122 P.K. Page to Elizabeth Brewster, letter, 29 November 1979, LAC, MG30 D370, 13-0406, vol. 19.

CHAPTER THIRTEEN

1 P.K. Page to Florence Bird, letter, 27 November [1980], LAC, MG 31 D63, vol. 13, f. 21.

2 P.K. Page to Florence Bird, letter, 23 March [1982], LAC, MG 31 D63, vol. 13, f. 20.

3 Djwa "Poetry," *University of Toronto Quarterly*, Summer 1982, 347–8.

4 P.K. Page, "After Reading *Albino Pheasants*," in *Hidden Room*, 1:213–14.

5 Rumi, "105," *Mystical Poems of Rumi*: "Our death is an eternal wedding-feast; what is the secret of this? *He is God, One.*"

6 P.K. Page, "About Death," in *Hidden Room*, 1:179.

7 Lionel Page was born on 17 December 1886 and died on 26 August 1944. As P.K. was born in 1916, presumably she began the poem in late August or early September 1974.

8 P.K. Page, "Voyager," in *Hidden Room*, 1:183–4.

9 P.K. Page, "The First Part," in *Hidden Room*, 216–19.

10 P.K. Page, interview, 21 May 1996.

11 "The First Part," in *Hidden Room*, 1:216–19.

12 P.K. Page, "Ancestors," in *Hidden Room*, 1:150–1.

13 P.K. Page, "Ours," in *Hidden Room*, 181–2

14 Roszak, *Where the Wasteland Ends*, 296.

15 P.K. Page, "Unless the Eye Catch Fire … ," in *Hidden Room*, 1:187–207. The "shaking" metaphors in this story seem to me to be derived from *The Sufis*. There, Shah refers to the celebrated Sufi poem *The Parliament of Birds*, by twelfth-century Persian poet Farid ud-Din

Attar, in which birds in the thousands congregate and decide they need a king. The hoopoe agrees to guide them to the Simurgh, a mystical bird who will be their king. After a long and dangerous journey, only thirty survive. When the birds ask to see the Simurgh, they see an image of themselves, since "si murgh" in Persian means thirty birds. The poem is an allegory of the Sufi journey to a realization of the nature of God.

Page draws upon Shah's translation into English of various words and phrases in the poem: "to flash (light); to twinkle; shining (color); to be shaken by the wind," to describe the roots of one of the descriptive words used. "The flash refers to intuition, the shining to the projection of teaching and the use of colors by the Sufis. The shaking, used in this root as of a plant in the wind, means the movement of the exercises of the dervish ... The wind which is taken as shaking the plant is the divine wind" (*The Sufis*, 199).

16 Gurdjieff, *Beelzebub's Tales to His Grandson*. In this allegorical work, Beelzebub explains Planet Earth to his grandson and refers to passing from worlds one, two, and three.

17 John Donne, "Preached at the funerals of Sir William Cokayne Knight, Alderman of London, December 12. 1626," in Simpson and Potter, *The Sermons of John Donne*, 264: "I throw my selfe downe in my Chamber, and I call in, and invite God, and his Angels thither, and when they are there, I neglect God and his Angels, for the noise of a Flie, for the ratling of a Coach, for the whining of a doore."

18 P.K. Page, "After Donne," in *Hidden Room*, 1:225.

19 P.K. Page, "The Trail of Bread," in "Melanie's Nite-Book," *Hidden Room*, 1:153–4.

20 Bruce Whiteman, review in *Queen's Quarterly*, Spring 1982, 223–5.

21 Stephen Scobie, "More Than Meets the Eye," *Books in Canada*, March 1982.

22 Constance Rooke, "A Unique Voice," undated review.

23 P.K. Page to Sandra Djwa, interview, August 1997.

24 P.K. Page, "Hospital/Howard O'Hagan journal 1982," LAC, MG30 D311/R2411, vol. 114, f. 13.

25 P.K. Page to Arlene Lampert, letter, 21 December 1982, in the possession of the recipient.

26 Sandra Djwa to P.K. Page, letter, 2 September 1983.

27 P.K. Page, "Goodbye," *West Coast Review* 2 (Fall 1987): 41.

28 P.K. Page to Florence Bird, letter, nd. [c. 25 October 1983], LAC, MG31 D63, vol. 13, f. 20.

29 The telegram was dated the thirty-first but F.R. Scott died on the thirtieth. (LAC, MG30 D311, vol. 33, f. 29).

30 P.K. Page, telephone conversation, 12 March 1985.

31 P.K. Page to Sandra Djwa, interview, 10 November 1998.

32 Borges, "Swedenborg's Angels," 215–16.

33 Marilyn Bowering, reading from typescript, "A Strange Bird, the Angel," in the possession of the owner.

34 P.K. Page, "Images of Angels," in *Hidden Room*, 1:41–3.

35 P.K. Page, "Invisible Presences Fill the Air," in *Hidden Room*, 2:169.

36 Doris Lessing to P.K. Page, letter, 10 December 1982, LAC, MG30 D311, vol. 30, f. 99.

37 Lessing's *The Memoirs of a Survivor* was published early in 1974. Page subscribed to Octagon Press, but many of the the similarities between Lessing's novel and Page's story can be accounted for by the fact that her woman protagonist, like P.K. herself, kept journals and had a dog.

38 P.K. Page, interview, 26 February 2004.

39 Ibid.

40 Ibid.

41 Ibid.

42 P.K. Page, interview, 22 February 2001.

43 Ibid.

44 P.K. Page to Rosemary Sullivan, letter, 7 March [c. 1981], Thomas Fisher Rare Book Library, 325.

45 P.K. Page to Arlene Lampert, letter, 27 October [c. 1982], letter in the possession of the recipient.

46 P.K. Page, interview, 24 February 2003.

47 P.K. Page, introduction at Doris Lessing's talk to the Canadian Club, LAC, MG30 D311/R2411, vol. 115, f. 2.

48 P.K. Page, interview, 30 September 1997.

49 Rosemary Sullivan, interview, 14 October 2000.

50 Ibid.

51 Rosemary Sullivan to William Toye, conversation, c. December 2010.

52 P.K. Page, interview, September 1997

53 P.K. Page to Arlene Lampert, letter, 20 June [c. 1984], letter in the possession of the recipient.

54 Ibid.

55 George Woodcock, *Poetry Canada Review* 7 (Summer 1986), 51–2.

56 P.K. Page to Richard Teleky, letter, 3 December 1990, LAC, MG30 D311, vol. 37, f. 62.

57 P.K. Page, "Deaf-Mute in the Pear Tree," in *Hidden Room*, 2:107–8

58 Hutchison, "Diamond Panes," *Canadian Literature* 113–14 (Summer/Autumn 1987): 247–9.

59 P.K. Page to Florence Bird, letter, 30 July 1985, LAC MG31 D63, vol. 13, f. 20.

60 Ibid.

61 P.K. Page to Elizabeth Brewster, letter, 12 June 1989, LAC, MG30 D370, 13-0406, vol. 19.

62 P.K. Page, "Extracts from a Brazilian Journal," *Canadian Literature* 90 (Autumn 1981): 40–59.

63 Michael Ondaatje to P.K. Page, letter, 6 July 1982, LAC, MG30 D311, vol. 8, f. 36.

64 P.K. Page to Arlene Lampert, letter, 21 December 1982.

65 P.K. Page to Rosemary Sullivan, 19 February 1987, TFRBL, 00366, vol. 42, f. 2.

66 P.K. Page, interview, 16 February 1999.

67 Ibid.

68 Arthur Irwin to P.K. Page, personal note, 16 December 1988, LAC, MG30 D311, vol. 49, f. 30.

69 William French, "Tropical Dreaming," review of *Brazilian Journal*, by P.K. Page. *Globe and Mail,* 27 June 1987.

70 George Galt, "The Poet in the Pink Palace," review of *Brazilian Journal*, by P.K. Page, *Saturday Night*, September 1987, 61–3.

71 P.K. Page to Sandra Djwa, postcard, 27 April 1988, in the possession of the recipient.

72 P.K. Page to Florence Bird, letter, n.d. [c. February 1985], LAC, MG31 D63, vol. 13, f. 20.

73 Shah, "Report on the Planet Earth," 26. Shah, tongue-in-cheek, speaks of a group of celestial beings that wanted to develop their influence upon the people of earth. They hired an investigator, who recommended that they simply lie and manipulate. "But this is terrible," said the celestials, such treatment would turn humans into automata. "Now listen," said the expert, "do you, or do you not want to extend your territory?"

74 Lessing, *Canopus in Argos*, (1980), *The Marriages between Zones Three, Four and Five* (1980), and *The Sirian Experiments* (1980) all refer to Planet Earth, known as Rohanda in its Edenic state and Shikasta in its degeneration.

75 Lessing, *Shikasta*, 211–12.

76 P.K. Page, interview, 10 September 1998.

77 Page explains that the story came into being when the phrase "blue blood" triggered in her mind "sea-blue blood." Being "a blue blood," she concluded, had little to do with lineage but everything to do with wisdom; thus the goatherd's ascendency signified natural aristocracy.

78 P.K. Page to Florence Bird, letter, 26 October 1989, LAC, MG31 D63, vol. 13, f. 21.

79 P.K. Page to Elizabeth Brewster, letter, 12 June 1989, LAC, MG30 D370, 13-0406, vol. 19.

80 P.K. Page to Florence Bird, letter, 26 October 1989, LAC, MG31 D63, vol. 13, f. 21.

CHAPTER FOURTEEN

1 P.K. Page, "Address at Simon Fraser," in *Hidden Room*, 2:99–104.

2 Ornstein and Ehrlich, *New World New Mind*, 264–5.

3 Douglas Barbour, "Three Poets Make Complex Music," review of *The Glass Air*, by P.K. Page, *Toronto Star*, 27 July 1991.

4 George Johnston, review of *The Glass Air*, by P.K. Page, *Antigonish Review* 89 (1992): 53–6.

5 Cynthia Messenger, "Selecting P.K. Page," review of *The Glass Air*, by P.K. Page, *Canadian Poetry* 35 (Fall/Winter 1994): 115–21.

6 Val Ross, "Rifling through the Pages," *Globe and Mail*, 23 December 1991.

7 P.K. Page, interview, 7 January 1999.

8 Marilyn Bowering to Sandra Djwa, e-mail, 25 March 2010.

9 Robert Cram, interview, 11 June 2004.

10 Théa Gray, interview, 18 September 2000.

11 Merwin, "Elegy," 137.

12 Théa Gray, interview, 17 September 2000.

13 Théa Gray, interview, 18 September 2000.

14 Marilyn Bowering to Sandra Djwa, e-mail, 28 May 2010.

15 Patricia Young, interview, 29 July 2008.

16 P.K. Page, "Foreword," in *Hologram*, 9.

17 Marilyn Bowering to Sandra Djwa, e-mail, 28 May 2010.

18 The poem speaks of "his radically altered syntax / the total absence of verbs," which Page had experienced on her last visit to Montreal before F.R. Scott's death.

19 Théa Gray, interview, 20 May 2010.

20 Jan Zwicky to P.K. Page, letter, 28 November 1993. LAC, MG30 D311, vol. 37, f. 62.

21 MacKenzie, *Arthur Irwin*.

22 P.K. Page to Rosemary Sullivan, letter, 25 December 1993, TFRBL, 00366, vol. 42, f. 2.

23 P.K. to Rosemary Sullivan, letter, 12 April 1996, TFRBL, 00366, vol. 42, f. 2.

24 Kevin McNeilly, "Graceful Clarities," review of *Hologram*, by P.K. Page, *Canadian Literature* 157 (Summer 1998): 160–3.
25 P.K. Page, "Hologram," in *Hidden Room*, 2:189–90.
26 P.K. Page, "Poor Bird," in *Hidden Room*, 2:195–6.
27 P.K. Page, "The Answer," in *Hidden Room*, 2:213–14.
28 P.K. Page told Marilyn Bowering about this journey to the British Columbia interior and her sense of a beneficent "beam of love" (Marilyn Bowering, interview, 5–6 February 2010). Page alludes to this experience again in *You Are Here* and also in a late glosa, "The Answer."
29 Shah, *The Sufis*, 123.
30 P.K. Page to Idries Shah, letter, 31 July 1995. LAC, MG30 D311 /R2411/R2411, 2010-0191, 5. The quality of "heedlessness" used by Page in her letter of apology to Shah may carry a double meaning. In the introduction to his parable of "The Islanders," Idries Shah quoted a couplet from Dhu'l-Nun Misri: "The ordinary man repents his sins: / the elect repent of their heedlessness" (*The Sufis*, 1).
31 Théa Gray, interview, 18 September 2000.
32 Bruce Whiteman, "Extraordinary Presences," review of *Hologram* by P.K. Page, *Canadian Forum*, November 1994, 57–8.
33 McNeilly, "Graceful Clarities," 160–3.
34 Patricia Young, interview, 29 July 2008.
35 P.K. Page, interview, 21 May 1996.
36 Ibid.
37 Ibid.
38 P.K. Page, "The Australian Outback," *Brick* 42 (Winter–Spring 1992): 61–4. See also P.K. Page, "On the Road Again, in Fraser, ed., *Bad Trips*, 82–91.
39 Dragland, "Hidden Out in the Open," 167.
40 P.K. Page to Stan Dragland, letter, 31 December 1995.
41 Dragland, "Hidden Out in the Open," 172.
42 Théa Gray, interview, 18 September 2000.
43 Dragland, "Hidden Out in the Open," 172.
44 Stan Dragland to Sandra Djwa, e-mail, 26 May 2010.
45 Elke Inkster to P.K. Page, letter, 9 May 1997.
46 Tim Inkster to P.K. Page, letter, 11 May 1997.
47 Ibid.
48 P.K. Page to Elke and Tim Inkster, letter, 3 September 1997.
49 Jenny Jackson. "Verbatim," *Ottawa Citizen*, 21 September 1997.
50 Trehearne, "Imagist Twilight: Page's Early Poetry," in his *Montreal Forties*, 41–105.
51 P.K. Page, "Pain to His Helper," in *Hidden Room*, 2:230.

52 P.K. Page, "But We Rhyme in Heaven," in *Hidden Room*, 2:231.

53 Keith, *Canadian Book Review Annual, 1997*, 237.

54 Spalding, "Through the Looking Glass," 70.

55 McCluskey, "Forging Her Own Vision," 23.

56 Libby Scheier, "Showcasing a Most Talented Pair," *Toronto Star*: 22 November 1997.

57 Kenneth Sherman, "Alchemist with Dutch Cleanser," *Books in Canada* 27 (February 1998): 34.

58 Richard Outram, "A Life's Work: P.K. Page's Collected Work," *Ottawa Citizen*, 21 September 1997.

59 Dragland, "Hidden Out in the Open," 174.

60 Carmine Starnino, "Sentimentality Is a Horror," *Gazette* (Montreal), 27 September 1997.

61 Keith, *Canadian Book Review Annual 1997*, 237.

62 Parsons, "Poetry," 275–306.

63 George Johnston to P.K. Page, letter, 28 April 1983. LAC, MG30 D311, vol. 11, f. 11.

64 P.K. Page, interview, 11 May 1996

65 P.K. Page to Sandra Djwa, conversation, 12 March 1985.

66 P.K. Page, "The Change," in *The First Man in My Life*, 175.

67 P.K. Page to Sandra Djwa, letter, c. early January 1996, in the possession of the recipient.

68 Christine Irwin, "My Grandmother's Luggage," 55–7.

69 Atwood, "P.K. Page as a Non-Snow Angel," 100–1.

70 Lesley Kreuger to Sandra Djwa, interview, 18 October 2000.

71 Arlene Lampert and Rosemary Sullivan, interview, 14 October 2000.

72 P.K. Page, interview, 24–25 February 2003.

73 P.K. Page, interview, 16–17 November 2000

74 P.K. Page, interview, 19 February 1998.

75 Théa Gray, interview, 18 September 2000

76 Théa Gray, interview, 25 May 2010.

77 Ibid.

78 Neal Irwin to Sandra Djwa, e-mail, 5 December 2011.

79 P.K. Page, interview, 26 October 1999.

80 Ibid.

CHAPTER FIFTEEN

1 P.K. Page, "Empty House Blues," LAC, MG30 D311/R2411 2010-0191.

2 P.K. Page to Sandra Djwa, e-mail, 28 February 1999.

3 Pat Martin Bates to P.K. Page, e-mail, 3 November 2000, LAC, MG30 D311/R2411, vol. 88, 3–5.

4 P.K. Page, e-mail to Sandra Djwa, 30 November 2004.

5 P.K. Page, "Alphabetical," in *Planet Earth*, 125–35.

6 A renga is a Japanese form usually written by several poets sitting together and composing successive stanzas. Page proposed that she and Philip Stratford compose by mail.

7 Ibid., 79

8 Ibid. Subsequent titles were "Wilderness," "Sea," and "Stars," in the first stanza of which Stratford writes: "I take a sip / and swallow galaxies, gamma rays, tons / of cosmic dust, fires leaping into space." He died in 1999. After consultation with his widow, P.K. wrote a final stanza and published their poems and correspondence as *And Once More Saw the Stars: Four Poems for Two Voices* (2001). Her final stanza ends: "Oh Philip, do you rage in space? Do you?" Anne Simpson, reviewing the book, remarked that the reader becomes "a fly on the wall of poetic process," (Simpson, "Poetry as Ping Pong," 23–5).

9 Alex Irwin, e-mail to P.K. Page, 14 September 2001. Copy provided by the sender.

10 P.K. Page to Carol Matthews, e-mail, 21 September 2001, LAC, MG30 D311/R2411, vol. 71, 22–4.

11 Carol Matthews to P.K. Page, e-mail, 21 September 2001, LAC, MG30 D311/R2411, vol. 71, 22–4.

12 Molly Starlight and Susan MacRae to P.K. Page, e-mail, 26 September 2001, LAC, MG30 D311/R2411, vol. 71, 20–21.

13 P.K. Page, interview, 3 October 2001.

14 P.K. Page to Sandra Djwa, e-mail, 17 December 2001.

15 Margaret Atwood to P.K. Page, e-mail, 21 February 2003, LAC, MG30 D311/R2411, vol. 88, 1.

16 P.K. Page to Patrick Lane, e-mail, [c. March 2003], LAC, MG30 D311/R2411, vol. 80, 4–8.

17 Farouk Mitha to Sandra Djwa, e-mail, 26 May 2011.

18 Sandra Djwa to Zailig Pollock, e-mail, 23 March 2000.

19 P.K. Page to Zailig Pollock, e-mail copied to Sandra Djwa, 28 March 2000.

20 Sandra Djwa to Zailig Pollock, e-mail, 23 March 2000: "My belief is that [Page] is the person next to Pratt & Klein deserving of this."

21 P.K. Page to Sandra Djwa, e-mail, 26 March 2000.

22 P.K. Page, *Alphabetical/Cosmologies*.

23 Rhonda Batchelor, interview, 28 July 2008.

24 An American edition of the *Planet Earth* was also published: *Cosmologies: Poems Selected and New* (Boston: David R. Godine, 2002).

25 P.K. Page, "Planet Earth," in *Planet Earth*, 14–15.

26 "Arts Notebook," *Globe and Mail*, 8 March 2001.

27 Richard Outram, "A Life's Work," *Ottawa Citizen*, 21 September 1997.

28 P.K. Page to Sandra Djwa, e-mail, 19 June 2003.

29 Sandra Djwa to P.K. Page, e-mail, 19 June 2003.

30 Edward Hirsch, "Poet's Choice," *Washington Post*, 8 August 2004.

31 P.K. Page to Sandra Djwa, e-mail, 1 October 2003. She described the developing work as a "Long, Bad Poem."

32 Théa Gray, telephone discussion, 31 May 2011.

33 P.K. Page, "Black Luggage," LAC, MG30 D311/R2411, 2010-0191, 8: "Even Lucifer wears mourning today / Black Luggage / Black Luggage / For a good man gone in a puff of smoke."

34 Scott, "On Saying Goodbye to My Room in Chancellor Day Hall," in *Collected Poems of F.R. Scott*, 218–19.

35 P.K. Page, *Hand Luggage*, 22.

36 "One on stilts" implies that the figure is not as tall or as great as one thinks at first view. Elsewhere P.K. Page speaks of Scott as a "conjuror," a term that also has circus overlays ("F.R. Scott," 36).

37 *Hand Luggage*, 19.

38 F.R. Scott, untitled poem in six parts, beginning "Come, fill the glass cage of my hollow heart," QUA, 5021.7, box 3, f. 11.

39 *Hand Luggage*, 22.

40 Ibid., 17

41 Ibid., 19

42 Ibid., 25

43 Ibid., 70

44 Ibid., 82

45 Ibid., 91

46 Ibid., 91–2

47 Ibid., 93

48 Lampert and Gray, eds., *The Essential P.K. Page*, 7.

49 Pollock's *Kaleidoscope: Selected Poems of P.K. Page* was published by Porcupine's Quill in 2010.

50 P.K. Page, "Each Mortal Thing," in *Coal and Roses*, 20.

51 "Paradise," in *Coal and Roses*, 52.

52 "Domain of the Snow Queen," in *Coal and Roses*, 56.

53 "The Last Time," in *Coal and Roses*, 64–5.

54 Ibid., 65.

55 P.K. Page, "Cullen in the Afterlife," *Poetry* 194 (June 2009): 212–13.

56 P.K. Page, *Cullen: Poems*, 10.

57 Ibid., 23

58 Ibid., 23–4

59 Pollock, "Afterword," *Cullen Poems*, 25–6. He adds, however, "If there is a retrospective narrative to these poems, perhaps it is the story of 'scars' and 'claw marks' becoming 'birth marks' through a process of struggle, renunciation and transcendence – a story that echoes Page's own 'upward anguish.'"

60 "All across our country the trail of dreams is winding. / It winds across the mountains and the prairies to the sea," LAC, MG30 D311/R2411, vol. 67, f. 12–13.

61 P.K. Page to Sandra Djwa, e-mail, 15 September 2000.

62 Herrick, "Upon Julia's Clothes," in *Seventeenth Century Prose and Poetry*, 822.

63 P.K. Page, "What Time Is It Now?" in *Up on the Roof*, 140. In its first version, the lines occur as quoted in the text. In its abbreviated version for publication, the line reads "Who am I? ... a cracked old egg?"

64 *A Kind of Fiction* was published by Porcupine's Quill in 2001.

65 P.K. Page, "Victoria," in *A Kind of Fiction*, 85.

66 P.K. Page, "Unless the Eye Catch Fire ..." in *A Kind of Fiction*, 184.

67 Margaret Atwood to P.K. Page, letter, 7 January 2008, LAC, MG30 D311/R2411, vol. 2008-1147, 1 4a.

68 P.K. Page, "Birthday," in *Up On the Roof*, 94.

69 P.K. Page, "Ex Libris," in *Up On the Roof*, 23.

70 Ibid., 13.

71 Marilyn Bowering, interview, 6 February 2010.

72 P.K. Page, "Stone," in *Upon on the Roof*, 116.

73 Ibid., 116

74 Ibid., 107

75 Ibid., 127

76 Ibid., 131

77 P.K. Page, "Shipwreck," in *Up on the Roof*, 57–8.

78 These stories shed light on P.K.'s own aesthetic. In 1973 P.K. interviewed the artist Maxwell Bates in Victoria. She asked, "Do you get panicky when you're not painting?" Bates replied, "Not at all." P.K. then asked "How do you fill the time? ... Isn't there a large gap?" She wonders whether Bates can write when he can't paint. This discussion – together with the short story "Stone" – suggests that for P.K. the creating of art helped to fill an emotional void. ("A Conversation with Maxwell Bates," 1973. LAC, MG30 D311/R2411/R2411 2010-1054, 60 1B, 2A and B).

79 P.K. Page, *You Are Here*, 1.

80 Ibid., 11.

81 P.K. Page to Sandra Djwa, e-mail, 21 April 2009.

82 P.K. Page to Joan Coldwell, e-mail, 24 April 2009, LAC, MG30 D311/R2411/R2411 2010-0191, 60 1B 4–5.

83 "Robert Ornstein to Speak at Library of Congress, 16 October 2002, LAC, MG30 D311/R2411 2006-0941 2A 11.

84 P.K. Page, *The Sky Tree: A Trilogy of Fables*, 83.

85 Sandra Djwa to P.K. Page, e-mail, 11 November 2009.

86 P.K. Page to Sandra Djwa, e-mail, 11 November 2009.

87 Yet paradoxically she sees the bird itself as art. P.K. Page wrote to Kristi Bridgman, the illustrator of *The Sky Tree*: "I see the bird as art – those who want to kill it, those who want to save it, etc. As it is a Brazilian fable, I would set it there. P.K." (P.K. Page to Kristi Bridgman, 21 December 2009. LAC, MG30 D311/R2411/R2411 2010-0191, 60 1A 16).

88 P.K. Page to Sandra Djwa, e-mail, 3 October 2003.

89 Peter Redpath to Sandra Djwa, e-mail, 7 June 2011.

90 Godard, "Kinds of Osmosis," 66.

91 "*The Complete Poems of P.K. Page*, as a critical edition, will include all of P.K. Page's poems, including her juvenilia, arranged chronologically. It will contain one version of each poem – the latest published version – except in cases where poems exist in such radically different versions that there is justification for printing more than one. There will be a critical introduction to Page's work and the work's relation to its milieu, and a textual introduction laying out editorial principles and procedures" (Sandra Djwa to Kathryn Mulders, e-mail, 18 February 2002).

92 P.K. Page to Constance Rooke, e-mail, 30 May 2005, LAC, MG30 D311/R2411 60, 2A 15.

93 Meredith, "A Good Modern Poet and a Modern Tradition," 208–11.

94 Cid Corman to P.K. Page, letter, 3 December 1952.

95 Frye, "Letters in Canada: 1954," in *The Bush Garden*, 40.

96 *Times Literary Supplement*, August 1955.

97 Eli Mandel. "Tactility Page. Nervous and Fluid as Ever," *Globe and Mail*, 27 April 1974.

98 Hutchison, "Diamond Panes," 247–9.

99 Val Ross, "Rifling through the Pages," *Globe and Mail*, 23 December 1991.

100 Richard Outram, "A Life's Work," *Ottawa Citizen*, 21 September 1997.

101 Carmine Starnino, "Sentimentality Is A Horror," *Gazette* (Montreal), 27 September, 1997.

102 McNeilly, "Poetry," 423.

103 Ibid., 437.

104 P.K. Page to Sandra Djwa, e-mail, 7 August 2008.

105 Arlene Lampert to P.K. Page, e-mail, 31 October 2006, LAC, MG30 D311/R2411/R2411, 2008-1147, 1 6-L.

106 P.K. Page to Patrick Friesen, e-mail, 21 November 2006, LAC, MG30 D311/R2411/R2411, 60, 2B 15.

107 P.K. Page to Marilyn Bowering, e-mail, 31 March 2008. LAC, MG30 D311/R2411 2010-0191, 3.

108 Constance Rooke to P.K. Page, e-mail, 24 December 2006, LAC, MG30 D311/R2411/R2411, 60, 1B 3.

109 P.K. to Carol Matthews, e-mail, 9 October 2008, LAC, MG30 D311/R2411/R2411 2008 1147, 2B.

110 P.K. to Carol Matthews, e-mail, 8 October 2008, LAC, MG30 D311/R2411 2008-1147, 2B.

111 P.K. Page to Hiro Boga, e-mail, 23 July 2009, LAC, MG30 D311/R2411/R2411, 2010-0191 60, 2A 4.

112 Eve Joseph to P.K. Page, e-mail, 27 September 2009, LAC, MG30 D311/R2411/R2411, 2010-0191 60, 1B 3.

113 Jay Ruzesky, interview, 5 February 2010.

114 P.K. Page to Patricia Young, e-mail, 22 November 2009, LAC, MG30 D311/R2411/R2411, 2010-0191 60, 1A 11.

115 P.K. Page to Jay Ruzesky, e-mail, 8 December 2009, LAC, MG30 D311/R2411/R2411, 2010-0191 60, 1A 11.

116 P.K. Page, "Your Slightest Look," in *Coal and Roses*, 32.

117 Beryl Young to P.K. Page, e-mail, 8 December 2009, LAC, MG30 D311/R2411/R2411, 2010-0191 60, 1B 5.

118 P.K. Page to Rachel Wyatt, e-mail, 10 December 2009, LAC, MG30 D311/R2411/R2411, 2010-0191 60, 1B 5.

119 Elizabeth Brewster to Sandra Djwa (by way of Nancy Senior), e-mail, 24 December 2011.

120 Michael Page, interview, February 2011.

121 P.K. Page, "Mexican journal," 11 September 1961, LAC, MG30 D311/R2411, 113–26.

122 Eve Egoyan, interview, April 2010.

123 Rosemary Sullivan to Sandra Djwa, e-mail, 19 January 2010.

124 Dean Irvine dates the writing of the poem between 1944 and 1950; it was collected in Scott's *Events and Signals* (1954).

125 P.K. Page, "The End," in *Hidden Room*, 2:215–16. See also P.K.'s jotted notes on "The Test," LAC, MG30 D311/R2411/R2411, 2010-0191 60, 8.

126 As a young woman in Saint John, P.K. had a vision of her dear friend "Tommy" Ross. P.K. believed there was life after death, but Tommy

did not. "So when I saw her alive in the room, I said, 'So I was right after all.' And she said, 'Yes, that's what I came back to tell you,'" (P.K. Page to Sandra Djwa, interviews, 8 July 1999 and 26 June 2001).

127 The message is also slightly different in that place is connected to duration. The Tommy Ross story suggests only that there is life after death, whereas the second story in "The End" invokes a male figure and the statement that it is not "everlasting there."

128 See Rumi, Book 1, "Prologue," 3: The Beloved is all in all, the lover only veils Him; / The Beloved is all that lives, the lover a dead thing." These lines are echoed by Idries Shah when he explicates the Parliment of the Birds, showing that human love is one of the first steps in the quest for transcendent Love (*The Sufis* 120–3).

129 P.K. Page, "The End," in *Hidden Room*, 2:215–6. The last line, "We are the water within the wave and the wave's form" is suggestive of Shah's depiction of the Sufi as a drop in the ocean of truth (see *The Sufis*, 123).

130 Scott, "Departure" in *The Collected Poems of F.R. Scott*, 142.

Bibliography

ARCHIVAL SOURCES

Kent State University, Kent, Ohio
  Cid Corman papers
Library and Archives Canada, Ottawa
  Florence Bird fonds
  Jean Fraser fonds
  Arthur Irwin fonds
  George Johnston fonds
  Tom Marshall fonds
  P.K. Page fonds
  F.R. Scott fonds
  Marian Scott fonds
  Jori Smith fonds
  Rachel Wyatt fonds
Provincial Archives of New Brunswick, Fredericton, New Brunswick
  Keld and Erica Deichmann fonds
Queen's University Archives, Kingston, Ontario
  Alan Crawley fonds
  Tom Marshall fonds
  F.R. Scott fonds
  George Woodcock fonds
Red Deer Archives, Red Deer, Alberta
  Page family papers and pioneer life
Thomas Fisher Rare Book Room, University of Toronto, Toronto, Ontario
  Margaret Atwood fonds
  Earle Birney fonds
  A.J.M. Smith fonds
  Rosemary Sullivan fonds
  Anne Wilkinson fonds

Trent University, Trent, Ontario
   Page and Irwin papers, Page Irwin Colloquium Room
   A.J.M. Smith fonds

                              P.K. PAGE

Alphabetical. Victoria, BC: Published for the Hawthorne Society by Refer-
   ence West, 1998
Alphabetical/Cosmologies. Victoria: Poppy Press, 2000
And Once More Saw the Stars: Four Poems for Two Voices. With Philip
   Stratford. Ottawa: Buschek Books, 2001
As Ten, As Twenty. Toronto: Ryerson, 1946
"The Australian Outback." *Brick: A Journal of Reviews* 42–3
   (Winter/Spring 1992): 61–4
A Brazilian Alphabet for the Younger Reader. Erin, ON: Porcupine's Quill,
   2005
Brazilian Journal. Toronto: Lester & Orpen Dennys, 1987
"Canadian Poetry 1942." *Preview*, October 1942, 8–9
"The Change." In *The First Man in My Life: Daughters Write about Their
   Fathers*, edited by Sandra Martin with a foreword by Margaret Atwood,
   171–5. Toronto, Penguin, 2007
Coal and Roses: Twenty-One Glosas. Erin, ON: Porcupine's Quill, 2009
Cosmologies: Poems Selected & New by P.K. Page. Edited and introduced
   by Eric Ormsby. Boston: David R. Godine, 2003
Cry Ararat! Poems New and Selected. Toronto: McClelland & Stewart,
   1967
"Cullen in the Afterlife." *Poetry* (Chicago), 194 (June 2009): 212–13
Cullen: Poems. Afterword by Zailig Pollock. Victoria: Outlaw Editions,
   2010
"Desiring Only." *Preview*, April 1942
"Ecce Homo." *Contemporary Verse* 1 (September 1941): 5–6
The Essential P.K. Page. Edited by Arlene Lampert and Théa Gray. Erin,
   ON: Porcupine's Quill, 2008
Evening Dance of the Grey Flies. Toronto: Oxford University Press, 1981
"Even the Sun, Even the Rain." *Malahat Review* 127 (Summer 1999):
   103–5
"The First Part." *West Coast Review* 13 (February 1979): 5–6
A Flask of Sea Water. Illustrated by Laszlo Gal. Toronto: Oxford Univer-
   sity Press, 1989
"F.R. Scott." *Brick: A Journal of Reviews* 29 (Summer 1987): 36
The Filled Pen: Selected Non-fiction. Edited by Zailig Pollock. Toronto:
   University of Toronto Press, 2007

The Glass Air: Selected Poems. Toronto: Oxford, 1985

The Glass Air: Poems Selected and New. Toronto: Oxford University Press, 1991

The Goat That Flew. Illustrated by Marika Gal. Toronto: Oxford University Press, 1993

The Golden Lilies: Poems by P.K. Page. Illustrated by Alan Stein. Parry Sound, ON: Church Street Press, 2009

"Goodbye." *West Coast Review* 2 (Fall 1987): 41

A Grain of Sand. Illustrated by Vladyana Krykorka. Markham, ON: Fitzhenry & Whiteside, 2003

Hand Luggage. Erin, ON: Porcupine's Quill, 2006

The Hidden Room. 2 vols. Erin, ON: Porcupine's Quill, 1997

Hologram: A Book of Glosas. London, ON: Brick Books, 1995

"Invisible Presences Fill the Air." *Malahat Review* 67 (February 1984): 5

Jake the Baker Makes a Cake. Illustrated by Ruth Campbell. Lantzville, BC: Oolichan Books, 2008

Kaleidoscope: Selected Poems of P.K. Page. Edited with an introduction by Zailig Pollock. Erin, ON: Porcupine's Quill, 2010

A Kind of Fiction. Erin, ON: Porcupine's Quill, 2001

"Landscape of Love." *First Statement,* August 1942, 7

"Max and My Mother." In Page, *The Filled Pen,* 101–8

The Metal and the Flower. Toronto: McClelland & Stewart, 1954

Mimmo Paladino/P.K. Page: Works on Paper Inspired by the Poetry of P.K. Page. Exhibition catalogue. Toronto & Vancouver: Istituto Italiano di Cultura, 1998

"The Moth." *Observer* (London), 2 December 1934

The Old Woman and the Hen. Woodcuts by Jim Westergard. Erin, ON: Porcupine's Quill, 2009

"On the Road Again: The Australian Outback, June 1956." In *Bad Trips,* edited by Keath Fraser, 82–91. New York: Vintage, 1991

Planet Earth: Poems Selected and New. Edited with an introduction by Eric Ormsby. Erin, ON: Porcupine's Quill, 2002

Poems: Selected and New. Edited by Margaret Atwood. Toronto: Anansi, 1974

"Questions and Images." In Page, *The Filled Pen,* 35–2

"Reflection." *Canadian Poetry Magazine* 4 (July 1939): 23

Rosa dei venti: Compass Rose. Poems by P.K. Page. Edited by Branko Gorjup, illus. Mimmo Paladino., trans. Francesca Valente. Ravenna, Italy: A. Longo Editore snc, 1998

"Safe at Home." In Page, *The Filled Pen,* 23–8

"The Sense of Angels: Reflections on A.M. Klein." In Page, *The Filled Pen,* 62–88

The Sky Tree: A Trilogy of Fables. Lantzville, BC: Oolichan Books, 2009
"The Stenographers." *Canadian Forum*, September 1942, 177. First pub-
    lished in *Preview*, July 1942, 5–6
"Summer Resort." In Page, *The Hidden Room*, 1:119
[Judith Cape, pseud.]. *The Sun and the Moon.* Toronto: Macmillan, 1944
The Sun and the Moon and Other Fictions. Toronto: Anansi, 1973
There Once Was a Camel. Illustrated by Kristi Bridgeman. Victoria, BC:
    Ekstasis Editions, 2008
To Say the Least: Canadian Poets from A to Z. Edited with an introduc-
    tion by P.K. Page. Toronto, ON: Press Porcépic, 1979
"Traveller, Conjuror, Journeyman." *Canadian Literature* 46 (Autumn
    1970): 35–40. Reprinted in Page, *The Filled Pen*
The Travelling Musicians. Retold by P.K. Page. Illustrated by Kady Mac-
    Donald Denton. Toronto: Kids Can Press, 1991
Uirapurú. Illustrated by Kristi Bridgeman. Fernie, BC: Oolichan Books,
    2010
*Unit of Five: Louis Dudek, Ronald Hambleton, P.K. Page, Raymond
    Souster, James Wreford.* Edited with a foreword by Ronald Hambleton.
    Toronto: Ryerson, 1944
Up on the Roof. Erin, ON: Porcupine's Quill, 2007
"Victoria." *Tamarack Review* 69 (Summer 1976): 50–3
"What Time Is It, Now?" In Page, *Up on the Roof*, 133–40
"A Writer's Life." Margaret Laurence Memorial Lecture. Halifax, 1999.
    In Page, *The Filled Pen*, 3–22
You Are Here. Sidney, BC: Hedgerow Press, 2008

                         SECONDARY SOURCES

Abelard, Peter. *The Letters of Abelard and Heloise.* Translated by C.K.
    Scott-Moncrieff. New York: Knopf, 1933
Adamson, Arthur. Review of *Cry Ararat!* by P.K. Page. *Contemporary
    Verse* 11 (Spring 1975): 9
[Anderson, Patrick]. "Statement." *Preview*, March 1942
Atwood, Margaret. "Address in Honour of Mimmo Paladino/P.K. Page."
    Toronto: Italian Cultural Institute, 1998
– "Death by Landscape." In *Wilderness Tips.* Toronto: McClelland &
    Stewart, 1998
– "If You Can't Say Something Nice, Don't Say Anything at All." In *Lan-
    guage in Her Eye: Views on Writing and Gender by Canadian Women
    Writing in English*, edited by Sarah Sheard, Libby Scheier, and Eleanor
    Wachtel, 15–25. Toronto: Coach House Press, 1990

– Introduction to *The Sun and the Moon and Other Fictions*, by P.K. Page.
    Toronto: Anansi, 1973
– "P.K. Page as a Non-Snow Angel." *Malahat Review* 117 (December
    1996): 100–1
– *Power Politics*. Toronto: Anansi, 1971
– ed. *The New Oxford Book of Canadian Verse in English*. Toronto:
    Oxford University Press, 1982
Auden, W.H. *The English Auden: Poems, Essays, and Dramtic Writings
    1927–1939*. Edited by Edward Mendelson. New York and Toronto:
    Random House, 1977
Avison, Margaret. *Winter Sun/The Dumbfounding: Poems 1940–66*.
    Toronto: McClelland & Stewart, 1982
Barbour, Douglas. "Three Poets Make Complex Music." Review of *The
    Glass Air: Poems Selected and New* (1991), by P.K. Page. *Toronto Star*,
    27 July 1991
Beardsley, Douglas. "A Trial Immortality: Recent Canadian Poetry,"
    Northern Journey, 6 June 1976, 124–5
Bishop, Elizabeth. "On the Railroad Named Delight." *New York Times
    Magazine*, 7 March 1965, 30
Blagrave, Mark. "Community Theatre in Saint John between the Wars."
    In *Theatre in Atlantic Canada*, edited by Richard Paul Knowles,
    109–10. Sackville, NB: Centre for Canadian Studies, Mount Allison
    University, 1988
Borges, Jorge Luis. "Swedenborg's Angels." In *The Book of Imaginary
    Beings*, edited by Norman Thomas di Giovanni in collaboration with
    the author. New York: Dutton, 1970
Brewster, Elizabeth. *The Invention of Truth*. Toronto: Oberon, 1991
Carroll, Lewis. *Alice in Wonderland*. London: Macmillan, 1865
Cost, March. *A Man Named Luke*. London: Collins, 1932
Crawley, Lois. "P.K. 1946." In *P.K. Page: Essays on Her Works*, edited by
    Linda Rogers and Barbara Colebrook Peace, 129–30. Toronto: Guer-
    nica, 2001
Djwa, Sandra. "P.K. Page: A Biographical Interview." *Malahat Review*
    117 (December 1996): 33–54
– "P.K. Page and Margaret Atwood: Continuity in Canadian Writing."
    In *Margaret Atwood: The Open Eye*, edited by John Moss and Tobi
    Kozakewich, 81–93. Ottawa: University of Ottawa Press, 2006
– "Poetry" for "Letters in Canada," *University of Toronto Quarterly* 51
    (Summer 1982): 343–58
– *The Politics of the Imagination: A Life of F.R. Scott*. Toronto: McClel-
    land & Stewart, 1987

Dragland, Stan. "Hidden Out in the Open: Editing and Reading P.K. Page's *The Hidden Room.*" *Journal of Canadian Studies* 38, no. 1 (2004): 166–88

Eliot, T.S. "Hamlet and His Problems." In *The Sacred Wood: Essays on Poetry & Criticism.* London: Methuen, 1960

Evans, Gary. *John Grierson: Trailblazer of Documentary Film.* Montreal: XYZ Publishing, 2005

Fahim, Shadia S. *Doris Lessing: Sufi Equilibrium, and the Form of the Novel.* London: Macmillan, 1994

Field, Joanna. *A Life of One's Own.* London: Chatto & Windus, 1935

Finch, David. *R.M. Patterson: A Life of Great Adventure.* Calgary: Rocky Mountain Books, 2000

Finnigan, Joan. "Poetry at the Convention." *Ottawa Journal,* 9 April 1969

Francis, Anne [Florence Bird]. "P.K." *Canadian Art* 20 (January–February, 1963): 42–5

Fraser, Keath, ed. *Bad Trips,* New York: Vintage, 1991

French, William. "Tropical Dreaming." Review of *Brazilian Journal,* by P.K. Page. *Globe and Mail,* 27 June 1987

Frye, Northrop. "From 'Letters in Canada,' *University of Toronto Quarterly.*" In *The Bush Garden: Essays on the Canadian Imagination,* 33–44. Toronto: Anansi, 1971

Gaetz, Annie L. *The Park Country: A History of Red Deer and District.* Vancouver: Wrigley Printing, 1948

Gagnon, François-Marc. *Paul-Émile Borduas.* Montreal: Montreal Museum of Fine Arts, 1988

Galt, George. "The Poet in the Pink Palace." Review of *Brazilian Journal,* by P.K. Page. *Saturday Night,* September 1987, 61–3

Gardiner, Stephen. *Epstein: Artist against the Establishment.* London: Michael Joseph, 1992

Globe and Mail. Review of *The Sun and the Moon,* by P.K. Page, 9 March 1974

Godard, Barbara. "Kinds of Osmosis," *Journal of Canadian Studies* 38, no. 1, (2004): 65–75

Graham, Gwethalyn. *Earth and High Heaven.* New York: Lippencott, 1944

Gurdjieff, G.I. *Beelzebub's Tales to His Grandson: An Objectively Impartial Criticism of the Life of Man.* New York: Dutton, 1973

– *Meetings with Remarkable Men* [1963]. Reprint, New York: Dutton, 1969

Hambleton, Ronald, ed. *Unit of Five: Louis Dudek, Ronald Hambleton, P.K. Page, Raymond Souster, James Wreford.* Toronto: Ryerson, 1944

Heaps, Denise Adele. "P.K. Page's *Brazilian Journal*: Language Shock." *Biography: An Interdisciplinary Quarterly* 19, no. 4 (1996): 355–70

Heilbrun, Carolyn G. *Writing a Woman's Life*. New York: Ballantine Books, 1988

Herbert, A.P. *Holy Deadlock*. London: Methuen, 1934

Herrick, Robert. "Upon Julia's Clothes." In *Seventeenth Century Prose and Poetry,* 2nd edn. Edited by Alexander M. Witherspoon and Frank J. Warkne, 822. New York: Harcourt Brace and World, 1963

Hilmi, Ustad. "The Sufi Quest." In *Thinkers of the East: Studies in Experimentalism*, edited and arranged by Idries Shah. London: Jonathan Cape, 1971

Hirsch, Edward. "Poet's Choice." *Washington Post*, 8 August 2004

Hope, A.D. *Collected Poems 1930–1965*. New York: Viking, 1966

Hutchison, Bruce. *The Incredible Canadian: A Candid Portrait of Mackenzie King: His Works, His Times, and His Nation*. Toronto: Longmans Green, 1953

Hutchison, Sandra. "Diamond Panes." *Canadian Literature* 113–14 (Summer-Autumn, 1987): 247–9

Huxley, Aldous. *The Perennial Philosophy*. New York: Harper & Row, [1944], 1970

Irvine, Dean. "Gendered Modernisms: Montreal Toronto Vancouver, 1941–1956." In *Editing Modernity: Women and Little-Magazine Cultures in Canada, 1916–1956,*" 127–80. Toronto: University of Toronto Press, 2008

– "The Two Giovannis: P.K. Page's Two Modernisms." *Journal of Canadian Studies* 38 (Winter 2004): 23–45

Irwin, Arthur. "A View from the Top." *Cinema Canada* 56 (June–July 1979): 37–41

Irwin, Christine. "My Grandmother's Luggage." *Malahat Review*. Winter 1996, 55–7

James, Esme. "Col. L.F. Page's Welcome Home." *Red Deer News*, 18 June 1919

James, Henry. *The Portrait of a Lady*. Edited by Leon Edel with an introduction. Cambridge, MA: Riverside Press, 1956

Johnston, George. Review of *The Glass Air: Poems Selected and New* (1991), by P.K. Page. *Antigonish Review* 89 (1992): 53–6

Jung, C.G. *The Collected Works of C.G. Jung*. Vol. 7, 2nd edn. Translated by R.F.C. Hull. Princeton: Princeton University Press, 1966

– *Memories, Dreams, Reflections*. Recorded and edited by Aniela Jaffe and translated from the German by Richard and Clara Winston. New York: Vintage, 1963

– *Modern Man in Search of a Soul*. London: Routledge & Kegan Paul, 1961
– *Psyche and Symbol: A Selection from the Writings of C.G. Jung*. Edited by Violet S. de Laszlo. Garden City, NY: Doubleday Anchor Books, 1958
– *Symbols of Transformation: An Analysis of the Prelude to a Case of Schizophrenia*. Translated by R.F.C. Hull. New York: Harper 1956
– Jung, C.J., M.L. von Franz, Joseph L. Henderson, Jolande Jacobi, and Aniela Jaffe. *Man and His Symbols*. New York: Dell, 1964
Keith, W.J. *Canadian Book Review Annual 1997*. Edited by Joyce M. Wilson, 237. Toronto: CBRA, 1998
Killian, Laura. "Poetry and the Modern Woman: P.K. Page and the Gender of Impersonality." *Canadian Literature* 150 (Autumn 1996): 86–105
Klein, A.M. *Complete Poems: A.M. Klein*. Edited by Zailig Pollock. Toronto: University of Toronto Press, 1990
Lampert, Arlene, and Théa Gray, eds. *The Essential P.K. Page*. Erin, ON: Porcupine's Quill, 2008
Larkin, Philip, ed. *The Oxford Book of Twentieth-Century English Verse*. Oxford: Clarendon Press, 1973
Lessing, Doris. *Canopus in Argos: Archives. Re: Colonised Planet 5 Shikasta*. Toronto: Granada, 1980
– "An Elephant in the Dark." *Spectator*, 18 September 1964, 73–5
– *The Four-Gated City*, St Albans: Granada, 1972
– *The Memoirs of a Survivor*. London: Octagon, 1974
– *The Sirian Experiments*. St Albans: Granada, 1982
Lively, Penelope. *Oleander, Jacaranda: A Childhood Perceived*. London & New York: Viking, 1994
McCluskey, Sue. "Forging Her Own Vision." *Saint John Telegraph Journal*, February 1998
McCullagh, Joan. *Alan Crawley and Contemporary Verse*. Vancouver: University of British Columbia Press, 1976
McKay, John. "Cannes Honours Animator, NFB: Norman McLaren Subject of Festival Retrospective." *Vancouver Sun*, 12 May 2006
MacKenzie, David. *Arthur Irwin: A Biography*. Toronto: University of Toronto Press, 1993
McNeilly, Kevin. "Graceful Clarities." Review of *Hologram*, by P.K. Page. *Canadian Literature* 157 (Summer 1998): 160–3
– "Poetry." In *The Cambridge History of Canadian Literature*, edited by Coral Ann Howells and Eva-Marie Kröller, 422–40. New York: Cambridge University Press, 2009
Mandel, Eli. "Tactility Page. Nervous and Fluid as Ever." *Globe and Mail*, 27 April 1974

Mansfield, Katherine. *The Garden Party and Other Stories* [1922].
    Reprint, Harmondsworth, UK: Penguin, 1997
– *The Letters of Katherine Mansfield*. Edited by J. Middleton Murry. 2
    vols. London: Constable, 1928
Melnyk, George. "The Social and Personal Views of Poetry." *Edmonton
    Journal*, 22 July 1974
Meredith, William. "A Good Modern Poet and a Modern Tradition."
    Poetry 70 (July 1947): 208–11
Merwin, W.S. "Elegy." *The Carrier of Ladders*. New York: Atheneum,
    1970
Messenger, Cynthia. "'But How Do You Write a Chagall?': Ekphrasis and
    the Brazilian Poetry of P.K. Page and Elizabeth Bishop." *Canadian Liter-
    ature* 142–3 (Fall–Winter 1994): 102–17
– "Selecting P.K. Page." Review of *The Glass Air: Poems Selected and New*
    (1991), by P.K. Page. *Canadian Poetry* 35 (Fall–Winter 1994): 115–21
Millay, Edna St. Vincent. *Selected Poems*. Edited by Colin Falck. New
    York: HarperCollins, 1991
Miller, Romany. Review of *The Sun and the Moon and Other Fictions*, ed.
    Margaret Atwood. *Ottawa Citizen*, 9 February 1974
Milne, W.S. "Two First Novels." *Saturday Review*, 2 December 1944
Money, Keith, et al. *The Art of Margot Fonteyn*. New York: Reynal, 1966
Monro, Harold. *Twentieth Century Poetry: An Anthology*. London:
    Chatto & Windus, 1929
Morgan, Charles. *The Fountain*. New York: Knopf, 1932
O'Connor, Garry. *Alec Guinness: The Unknown: A Life*. London: Pan
    Macmillan, 2002
Ondaatje, Michael. *Running In the Family*. Toronto: McClelland &
    Stewart, 1982
– ed. *The Broken Ark: A Book of Beasts*. Drawings by Tony Urquhart.
    Ottawa: Oberon Press, 1971
Orenstein, Gloria. "Leonora Carrington: Another Reality." *Ms. Magazine*,
    August 1974, 27–31
– *The Theater of the Marvelous: Surrealism and the Contemporary Stage*.
    New York: New York University Press, 1975
Ornstein, Robert. *Psychology of Consciousness*. San Francisco: W.H.
    Freeman, 1972
Ornstein, Robert, and Paul Ehrlich. *New World New Mind: Moving
    towards Conscious Evolution*. New York: Doubleday, 1989
Ouspensky, P.D. *In Search of the Miraculous*. New York: Harcourt, Brace,
    1949
Outram, Richard. "A Life's Work: P.K. Page's Collected Work." *Ottawa
    Citizen*, 21 September 1997

Overbury, Stephen. "Explosion of Poetry in Canada." *Leader-Post*
    (Regina), 13 August 1976
Page, R., and L. Page. *Wisdom from Nonsense Land*. Facsimile of 1918
    original. Victoria, BC. Porcepic Books 1991
Parsons, Marnie. "Poetry," from "Letters in Canada." *University of
    Toronto Quarterly* 69 (Winter 1999/2000): 275–306
Peters, Margot. *Mrs. Pat: The Life of Mrs. Patrick Campbell*. New York:
    Knopf, 1984
Powys, John Cowper. *Wolf Solent*. London: Jonathan Cape, 1929
Purdy, Al. *Yours, Al: The Collected Letters of Al Purdy*. Edited by Sam
    Solecki. Madeira Park, BC: Harbour Publishing, 2004
Rae, Arlene Perly. *Everybody's Favourites: Canadians Talk about Books
    That Changed Their Lives*. Toronto: Penguin, 1997
Relke, Diana. "Tracing a Terrestrial Vision in the Early Work of P.K.
    Page." *Canadian Poetry* 35 (Winter 1994): 11–30
Rilke, Rainer Maria. *Duino Elegies*. Translated with an introduction by
    J.B. Leishman and Stephen Spender. New York: Norton, 1939
Rogers, Linda, and Barbara Colebrook Peace, eds. *P.K. Page: Essays on
    Her Works*. Toronto: Guernica, 2001
Rooke, Constance. "P.K. Page: The Chameleon and the Centre." *Malahat
    Review* 45 (January 1978): 169–95
Ross, Val. "Rifling through the Pages." *Globe and Mail*, 23 December
    1991
Rossetti, Dante Gabriel. *Dante Gabriel Rossetti: Collected Poetry and
    Prose*. Edited by Jerome McGann. New Haven: Yale University Press,
    2003
Roszak, Theodore. *Where the Wasteland Ends*. Garden City, NY: Double-
    day, 1972
Rumi. Jalal-al-Din. *Mystical Poems of Rumi, First Selection Poems, 1–200*.
    Translated from the Persian by A.J. Aberry. Persian Heritage Series no.
    3. Chicago: University of Chicago Press, 1968
– "Prologue." *The Masnavi: The Spiritual Couplets of Maulana Jalaulu'd-
    din Muhammad Rumi*. Translated by E.H. Whinfield [1898]. Reprint,
    New York: Cosimo Classics 2010
Russell, Dora. *The Right to Be Happy*. Garden City, NY: Harper, 1927
St. Vincent Millay, Edna. "First Fig." In *Selected Poems*, ed. Colin Falck.
    New York: HarperCollins, 1991
Sandler, Linda. "A Report on the Handicraft School of Writing." *Books
    in Canada*, November 1974
Sandwell, B.K. "Four Very Angry Poets in a *Unit of Five*." *Saturday
    Night*, 10 February 1945, 21–2

Scheier, Libby. "Showcasing a Most Talented Pair." *Toronto Star*, 22 November 1997

Scobie, Stephen. "More Than Meets the Eye." *Books In Canada*, March 1982

Scott, F.R. *The Collected Poems of F.R. Scott*. Toronto: McClelland & Stewart, 1981

– *Events and Signals*. Toronto: Ryerson, 1954

– "What Did 'No' Mean?" *Canadian Forum* 22 (1942): 71–3

Sejur, Leila. "Addressing a Presence: An Interview with Phyllis Webb." *Prairie Fire* 9, no. 1 (1988): 30–43

Shah, Idries. "Report on the Planet Earth." In *Reflections*. London: Octagon, 1968

– *The Sufis*, with an introduction by Robert Graves [1964]. Reprint, New York: Random House, Anchor Books, 1971

– [Rafael Lefort]. *The Teachers of Gurdjieff*. London: Gollancz, 1966

– *The Way of the Sufi*. Harmondsworth, UK: Penguin, 1979

Shain, Merle. "Some of Our Best Poets Are ... Women." *Chatelaine*, October 1972, 48–50, 103–7

Shattuck, Roger. Introduction to René Daumal's *Mount Analogue*. San Francisco: City Lights Books, 1952

Shepherd, Mark. *"Perseverance"* by Turbot and Vulligan, a Cochran Review. 2001. http://www.cris.com/-oakapple/gasdisc/mdpersev.htm (accessed 12 December 2005)

Sherman, Kenneth. "Alchemist with Dutch Cleanser." Review of *The Hidden Room: Collected Poems* by P.K. Page. *Books in Canada*, February 1998, 34–6

Shute, Nevil. *In the Wet*. London: Heinemann, 1953

Simpson, Anne. "Poetry as Ping Pong." Review of *And Once More Saw the Stars*, by P.K. Page. *Antigonish Review* 12 (Winter 2002): 23–5

Singh, Khushwant. *Truth, Love and a Little Malice*. New Dehli: Penguin, 2002

Skelton, Robin. "Emily Carr Book an Insult." *Daily Times* (Victoria), 22 October 1966

– *The Memoirs of a Literary Blockhead*. Toronto: Macmillan, 1988

– "A Poet of the Middle Slopes." *Canadian Literature* 31 (Winter 1967): 40–4

Smith, A.J.M. *The Classic Shade: Selected Poems*. With an introduction by M.L. Rosenthal. Toronto: McClelland & Stewart, 1978

– "New Canadian Poetry." *Canadian Forum*, February 1947, 250–2

– ed. *Modern Canadian Verse in English and French*. Toronto: Oxford University Press, 1967

Snow, Kathleen M. *Maxwell Bates: Biography of an Artist*. Calgary: University of Calgary Press, 1993

Spalding, Esta. "Through the Looking Glass." *Border Crossings* 17 (February 1998): 70

Starnino, Carmine. "Sentimentality Is a Horror." *Gazette* (Montreal), 27 September 1997

Stewart, Roderick, and Sharon Stewart. *Phoenix: The Life of Norman Bethune*. Montreal & Kingston: McGill-Queen's University Press, 2011

Strachey, John. "Digging for Mrs. Miller." *New Statesman and Nation*, 9 November 1940

Stratton-Porter, Gene. *A Girl of the Limberlost* [1909]. Reprint, Bloomington: Indiana University Press, 1984

Sullivan, Rosemary. "A Size Larger than Seeing: The Poetry of P.K. Page." *Canadian Literature* 79 (Winter 1978): 32–42

Sutherland, John. "P.K Page and *Preview*." *First Statement*, (October 1942), 6

– "The Poetry of P.K. Page." In *John Sutherland: Essays, Controversies and Poems*, ed. Miriam Waddington, 101–12. Toronto: New Canadian Library, McClelland & Stewart, 1972

– "Robert Finch and the Governor-General's Award." In *John Sutherland*, 144–7

– [as Jack Hakaar]. "Why George Left College." *First Statement*, April 1944, 14–18

Suzuki, Daisetz Teitaro. *An Introduction to Zen Buddhism*. London: Rider, 1949

Trehearne, Brian. *The Montreal Forties: Modernist Poetry in Transition*. Toronto: University of Toronto Press, 1999

Trépanier, Esther. *Marian Dale Scott: Pioneer of Modern Art*. Quebec: Musée du Québec, 2000

Valdés, Carlos. "Dreams and Superstitions at the Juan Martin Gallery." *Novedades*, 18 June 1961

Whiteman, Bruce. "Extraordinary Presences." Review of *Hologram* by P.K. Page. *Canadian Forum*, November 1994, 57–8

– Review of *Evening Dance of the Grey Flies*, by P.K. Page. *Queen's Quarterly* 89 (Spring 1982): 223–5

Wilkinson, Anne. "Journals." In *The Tightrope Walker: Autobiographical Writings of Anne Wilkinson*. Edited by Joan Coldwell, Toronto: University of Toronto Press, 1992

Williams, B.H. Garnons. *A History of Berkhamsted School, 1541–1972*. Aylesbury, UK: Hazell Watson & Viney, 1980

[Wise, Jack]. Foreword to exhibition. *Mystic Circle*. Vancouver: Burnaby Art Gallery with Talonbooks, 1973

Wollman, Maurice, ed. *Modern Poetry 1922–1934* [1934]. Reprint, London: Macmillan, 1937

Woodcock, George. "Introduction to Canadian Poetry." *Poetry Canada Review* 7 (Summer 1986): 51–2

– Review of *Cry Ararat!* by P.K. Page. *Times* (Victoria), 7 September 1974

Woolf, Virginia. *A Room of One's Own* [1929]. Reprint, Harmondsworth, UK: Penguin, 1963

Young, Patricia. "P.K. in the Classroom." In *P.K. Page: Essays on Her Works*, edited by Linda Rogers and Barbara Colebrook Peace, 31–6. Toronto: Guernica, 2001

Index

Page numbers in italics refer to illustrations

Adler, Gerhard: The Living Symbol, 193–4, 231
Alain-Fournier: *Wanderer*, 181, 193
Alice in Wonderland (Lewis Carroll), 10, 17, 25, 144, 145, 194–5, 255
Allied War Supplies, 80–2
Amos, Robert, 311
Andersen, Hans Christian, 13, 303
Anderson, Patrick: on "Another Space," 228; influence on P.K., 82–3; letter to P.K., 81; "Ours" by P.K., 247, 250; and P.K. and Scott meeting, 86; P.K. met, 73–6; P.K. on teaching, 242–3; "Poem on Canada," 78; in *Preview* group, 79; *Snake Wine*, 154; *The White Centre*, 78
Anderson, Peggy, 74, 81, 85
anthologies (with P.K.), 101–2, 106, 208–12, 222, 224, 271
Aroch, Arie, 172
art, art galleries, and theatre: in Australia, 140; of Australian Aborigines, 156–7; Brazilian painters, 164; healing role of, 307, 310–11; "intellectual" Brazil, 167–8; London 1930s, 38–40, 44; London's influence in Saint John, 48–51; Mexican schools of art, 185; in Mexico, 182, 190–1, 196–7; New York (1960), 186–7; P.K.'s comfort in, 307; in Victoria, 202, 205–7, 241, 244, 253
Art Gallery of Greater Victoria: "Print Making in British Columbia, 1889–1983," 260
Art Gallery of Ontario: *A Kind of Osmosis*, 183; *Stone Fruit*, 185; *This Church My Dromedary*, 185
Art Gallery of Peterborough, 311
Association for Canadian and Quebec Literatures, 223
Athayde, Austregésilo de, 166, 169
Atlantic: short story contest, 54
Atwood, M.A.: *Hermetic Philosophy and Alchemy*, 184, 193
Atwood, Margaret: *The Circle Game*, 213; introduction to *The Sun and the Moon*, 66; on invasion of Iraq, 296; as isolated, 205; "Landlady," 227; the Loons, 256; on P.K., 226–7, 281, 306; with P.K., 261; *P.K. Page:*

Poems Selected and New, 227–8; P.K. reading, 208; P.K. thank-you to, 227–8; P.K.'s influence on, 100, 314; in P.K.'s *Malahat* tribute, 286; P.K.'s opinion of, 223–4; *Power Politics*, 227; reading tour with P.K., 223–4; "This Is a Photograph of Me," 86, 227; in Victoria, 213

Auden, W.H.: "Elegy for W.B. Yeats," 274; "September 1, 1939," 113

Australia: Canberra, 138; decision to go, 134–5; influence on P.K., 159; landscape, 137, 140–1, 144, 148, 158; P.K.'s journals, 278–9, 286; P.K.'s public readings, 140, 142, 146–7, 154, 157, 181, 257; protocol, 138–40, 156

autobiography, P.K.'s interest in, 284–5

Avison, Margaret, 224

awards and accolades (P.K.): British Columbia Hubert Evans Non-Fiction prize, 264; for film script, 126; Governor General's, 149–50, 152, 264; Griffin Poetry Prize short list, 299; honorary degrees, 268, 287, 313–14; honourable mention in *Canadian Poems*, 116; Lieutenant Governor's Award for Literary Excellence (BC), 313; by *Malahat Review*, 268, 285, 286; Order of British Columbia, 313; Order of Canada (Companion and Officer), 244, 288, 289; Oscar Blumenthal Award (*Poetry*), 100; Page Irwin Colloquium Room, 302; reception of poetry (overview of), 245–6, 314–15; symposium at Trent, "Extraordinary Presence," 313; Terasen Lifetime Achievement Award, 313; United Nations Dialogue among Civilizations through Poetry, 298; Vancouver International Writers (& Readers) Festival, 312–13

Backroom Gallery (Victoria), 234

Banff School of Fine Arts, 272

Barbour, Douglas, 270

Bashford, Lucy, 260, 293, 315, 316

Batchelor, Rhonda: P.K.'s *Alphabetical/Cosmologies*, 298

Bates, Maxwell: childhood friends, 24; influence on P.K., 40; and Rose Page, 25, 239–40

Bates, Pat Martin: after Arthur died, 294; miniatures exhibit, 234; and P.K. after Arthur died, 293; and P.K. met, 203–4; P.K.'s comments on, 305; P.K.'s first reading, 222; and P.K.'s Sufi interests, 215–16

Bates family: "Auntie May," 12, 14; Cynthia, 24, 27; P.K.'s memory of, 24–5; William ("Uncle Bill"), 14, 25

"beam of love," 276, 308

Beardsley, Doug: "Another Space," 228; "Cry Ararat!," 228; *A Strange Bird, the Angel*, 254

Belfry Theatre (Victoria), 272; *Unless the Eye Catch Fire …*, 271

Bemrose, John, 252

Berkhamsted School and Farm (Hertfordshire and Red Deer), 5–6

Berton, Pierre: visits Mexico, 197

Bethune, Norman, 88, 123, 126

biography of P.K., 264, 284–6, 293, 297–8, 317

Bird, Florence (Anne Francis): friendship, 281; Irwins' friend, 133; Mexico visit, 197; and Pat Bates, 204; P.K.'s Australian reading, 140; on P.K.'s exhibition, 112, 184; status of women commission, 212; on "Traveller, Conjuror, Journeyman," 230; P.K. correspondence with, 224, 230, 265

Bird, John, 112, 133

bird watching, 134

Birney, Earle, 115, 122, 197, 243

Bishop, Elizabeth, 161; "One Art," 301; "Sandpiper," 276

Bishop, Jack, 62

Bishop, Roger, 201

Blackwood, David: on Brittain's portrait *Pat Page, 1940*, 63

Blake, William, 39, 40; and P.K.'s *A Grain of Sand*, 309

Blue Mountain Canadian Poetry Festival, 223, 229, 240

Bone, Eleanor ("Nell"), 52

Borduas, Paul-Émile, 84

Borges, Doña Helena (and Juan), 167–9

Bowering, Marilyn: attended launch, 282; friendship, 262, 316; glosa, 273; Hughes reading, 271; "Letter from Portugal," 273; "Me Tembro" from P.K.'s Brazilian journal, 262; "My Grandfather Was a Soldier," 262; P.K. after Arthur died, 293; on P.K. in Australia, 151; P.K. on "beam of love," 276; P.K.'s birthday, 261, 315; poetry readings, 241, 253; *A Strange Bird, the Angel*, 254–5. *See also* Elcock, Michael

Brazil: addresses, 161–2; land-scape, 163, 165, 168, 175; P.K.'s journal, 164–5, 175, 262, 263–4, 311; politics, 165–6; protocol, 165, 167; spiritualism, 168–9

Brazilian Academy of Letters: P.K. address to, 169–70

Brewster, Elizabeth ("Betty"): "Essence of Marigold," 64; "Flirtation in Silver," 63; P.K.'s friendship with, 63–5, 117, 239, 267, 318–19; P.K.'s protégé, 63–4

Briçeno, Trixie (and Julio), 165, 175

Brick Books: *Hologram: A Book of Glosas*, 274

Bridgeman, Kristi: *The Sky Tree* (with P.K.), 310

Briggs, Lucy (and Ellis), 165

British Columbia Hubert Evans Non-Fiction prize, 264

Brittain, Miller, 49, 53, 62–3, 63, 82

Brittain, Vera, 40

Brown, E.K., 115

Bryars, Gavin, 288

Buckler, Ernest: *The Mountain and the Valley*, 154

Burchett, Jim and Betty, 102

Burnaby Art Gallery: "Mystic Circles," 234; "Three Poet Painters: Eldon Grier, P.K. Page and Joe Rosenblatt," 234, 242

Burnett, Frances Hodgson: *A Little Princess; or What Happened at Miss Minchin's*, 21, 101

Butterfield, Martha (and George), 257–8, *258*

Calgary: addresses, 12, 14, 24, 28; P.K.'s description, 150, 152

Callado, Antonio: *Retrato de Portinari*, 165

Callaghan, Morley, 115, 153

Campbell, David, 146–7, 151

Campbell, Joseph: *The Hero with a Thousand Faces*, 181, 193

Campbell, Mrs Patrick, 4–5

Campbell, Ted and Rosamond, 49, 53, 62

Canada Council for the Arts, 208, 212, 223, 240–1, 242

Canada's centenary, 212–13, 304

Canadian Art: "Darkinbad the Brightdayler," 305; on P.K.'s painting, 184–5, 204

Canadian Authors Association (CAA), 55, 61, 69, 115

Canadian Club, 257–8

Canadian Forum: "Ancestors," 284; "Landlady," 106; "Melanie's Nitebook," 284

Canadian Literature: 1970 issue, 222; Brazilian journal extract, 262; P.K.'s essays, 259; P.K.'s relationship with, 207–8; "Questions and Images," 213, 259

Canadian Poems: "The Moon-Child," 55

Canadian Poetry Magazine: 122; proposed merger with *Contemporary Verse*, 115; "Reflection," 65

Canadian Studies: "Extraordinary Presence: The Worlds of P.K. Page," 313

Canadian Verse, 226

Canadian writing: 1950s new wave of, 153; academia's opinion of, 205, 212, 221, 229, 244, 268, 282; decade of, 223–4; and foreign influences, 229; P.K. Australian address on, 151; P.K.'s influence on, 100, 112, 213, 221–2, 241–2, 269, 284,

314. *See also* awards and accolades (P.K.)

Cape, Judith (pseudonym), 83. *See also* Page, Patricia Kathleen, non-ficiton

Cardiff, Leonora (and Maurice), 184

Cariappa, General Kodandera Madappa, 137, 141

Carlile, Elizabeth ("Fuzz"), 31–3, 44, 224

Carr, Emily: *Hundreds and Thousands*, 207

Carrington, Leonora, 181–6, 190–1, 196; friendship, 203, 287; *Litany of the Philosophers*, 182; *Pénélope*, 190; in P.K.'s *Hand Luggage* poems, 301; *And Then We See the Daughter of the Minotaur*, 182; *Who Art Thou, White Face?*, 182

Carter, Angela, 257

Casey, Richard G. and Maie, 135, 137, 141–2, 150, 158, 166, 186

Cavell, Nick, 133

CBC Radio: 1940s program on poetry, 122; *Art Talks*, 282; *Ideas*, 286; *Morningside*, 255–6; *What Time Is It Now?*, 306

CCF (Co-operative Commonwealth Federation), 76, 80, 88, 91, 95, 105

Chapin, Miriam, 80

Chapman, C.H., 7

Charpentier, Georges, 141

Chateaubriand, Assis, 166

Cherry, Zena (and Westcott), 196

Clarke, Arthur C., 281–2

Cleveland, Dorothy, 27

Coghill, Joy, 271, 272; *Unless the Eye Catch Fire …*, 313

Coldridge, Lynda: *The Sirian Experiments*, 266

Coldwell, Joan, 293; P.K.'s *You Are Here*, 308

Coleridge, Samuel Taylor: "Ode to Dejection," 122–3

Communists, 80, 88, 105, 125

Concordia University reading, 282

Confederation Poets, 63, 99

Connolly, Cyril, 319

Contemporary Verse, 61–2; "Ecce Homo," 67–8; Floris McLaren, 104; Jay Macpherson, 112; P.K. praises, 122; "Portrait of Marina," 119; proposal to merger with *Canadian Poetry Magazine*, 115–16. *See also* Crawley, Alan

Corman, Cid: *Origin*, 146, 314

Cost, March: *A Man Named Luke*, 30, 65

Coward, Noël, 50–1, 136

Cram, Jack, 73

Cram, Robert, 271, 272; *Unless the Eye Catch Fire …*, 313

Crawley, Alan: Canadian Poetry "Saying" tour, 116; *Contemporary Verse*, 61–2, 67–8; correspondence collection, 226; and *Cry Ararat!*, 211; elderly, 202; important contact for P.K., 71, 76; Jay Macpherson, 112; on *The Metal and the Flower*, 148, 149; P.K. letter to, 114–15, 115–16, 120; P.K. praises, 122; P.K. visit to, 122; on publishing outside Canada, 153; as reference, 201; in Vancouver, 98–9

Crawley, Jean, 114–15, 120, 122

Crozier, Lorna, 271

cubism and pointillism, 31, 84

Cuernavaca, 184

cummings, e.e., 318

Dafoe, J.W., 88

Daily Colonist, Victoria, 198

Daily Times, Victoria, 199, 207

Daumal, René: *Mount Analogue*, 195–6, 208, 211

Davies, Maggie, 83, 91, 136, 217

Davis, Elizabeth G.: *The First Sex*, 224

Day, Margaret (later Surrey), 74, 79

de Bouvier Holly (de B. Holly), Toby, 49, 58, 62

DeCastro, Robert, 216

Dee, Dorothy, 83, 106

Deichmann, Kjeld and Erica, 49, 53–4, 59, 62, 110

de la Mare, Walter: "The Moth," 43

diaries and journals. *See* Page, Patricia Kathleen, non-fiction

Diefenbaker, John, 178–9

Dilworth, Ira, 122; on *The Metal and the Flower*, 148

Dinesen, Isak, 284

divorce: British divorce laws, 51; P.K.'s thought's on, 90; in Saint John play, 58–9

Djwa, Sandra: biographical interview with P.K., 286; P.K. on "Another Space," 223; as P.K.'s biographer, 264, 285–6, 293, 297–8, 317; *The Politics of the Imagination: A Life of F.R. Scott*, 264, 284–6; review of *Evening Dance of the Grey Flies*, 248; edition of P.K.'s work, 297; Scott's illness, 252

Dominion Drama Festival (Saint John), 53, 56

Donaldson, Jeffrey, 278

Donne, John, 248, 251

Dostoevsky, Fyodor, 31, 73

Doyle, Mike, 221

Dragland, Stan: paper on P.K., 313; P.K. praise for, 279; work on *The Hidden Room*, 279–80, 283–4

dreams (P.K.): about her father, 249; "Another Space," 222–3; become poems and drawings, 232; birthing, 194–5; of book-lined corridor, 306; "Cry Ararat!," 210; "Hologram," 274; in life of the mind, 214; Scott of P.K., 209; transformation dream, 188, 191–2, 223; "Unless the Eye Catch Fire ...," 226

Dudek, Louis: League of Canadian Poets, 223

Duncan, Douglas, 179

Dunne, J.W.: *An Experiment with Time*, 30

Dunton, Arnold Davidson ("Davey") and Kathleen, 73, 133

Eden Mills Writers' Festival, 277, 281, 294

Edward VIII, 51

Egoyan, Atom, 211–12

Egoyan, Eve, 313, 316, 319–20

Egoyan, Shushan, 200, 204–5, 215, 264, 293, 311

Ehrlich, Paul: *New World, New Mind*, 269–70

Elcock, Michael, 253, 261, 271

Eliot, T.S., 75–6, 77, 155; "Marina," 119; "objective correlative," 81

Emery, Tony, 202

Emmanuel, Pierre, 134

English-Speaking Union, 38

Epstein, Jacob, 40, 67; *Ecce Homo*, 40; *Genesis*, 31

"Extraordinary Presence" (P.K. symposium), 311–12

Farquarson, Bob, 132, 133

Farrar, Lillian, 132

Fasihi, Khosrow, 315

Fenwick, Kathleen, 196

Ferguson, Maudie, 110, 128, 132, 133

Field, Joanna (Marion Milner): *A Life of One's Own*, 42, 56, 65

Finch, Robert: *Poems*, 116

First Statement, 77–8; "Landscape of Love," 86

First World War, 9–10, 72, 245

Fogt, Mimi, 183, 203

Fonteyn, Margot, 121, 175

Francis, "Dick," 99

Fraser, Blair and Jean: death of Jean, 260; friendship, 133, 136, 161, 188; P.K. correspondence with Jean, 142–3, 155–6, 170, 187, 193–4, 203, 231–2; P.K. work conversation, 203

Fraser, Sylvia: the Loons, 256

French, William, 263–4

Freud, Sigmund, 80, 116, 147

Fry, Dennis Butler, 217, 244

Fry, Thomas C., 5–6

Frye, Northrop: on "Arras," 143; on *The Metal and the Flower*, 148–9, 314; on P.K., 115; P.K. meets, 239

Fu-Shing Chinese opera, 197

Gal, Laszlo: *A Flask of Sea Water*, 266

Gal, Marika: *The Goat That Flew*, 266

Gallant, Mavis, 73, 89–90, 112

Gallotti, Antonio (and Mimi), 167

Galloway, Myron, 84, 123
Galt, George, 264
Garneau, Constance, 69
Gaskell, Eric, 61, 69
Gasset, Ortega y: *The Dehuman-ization of Art*, 164–5
Gatenby, Greg, 257
Gatineau Park, Quebec, 133
gender: in Australia, 140, 142; in Brazil, 167, 169–70; change in poetic tone, 155; diplomatic wife, 180; feminism, 224, 256; modernist debate and *The Sun and the Moon*, 66–7; women writers, 148, 212; in world of letters, 152
Georgians, 61, 71
Gerald Lampert Memorial Fund, 243
Gianelli, Shelagh (literary mentor), 30, 46
Gibbs, Philip, 39
Gibson, Shirley, 240
Gielgud, John: in *Hamlet*, 38
Gilbert and Sullivan, 44
Gillet, Vi, 62
Gilot, Françoise, 257
Glebe Place, London, 5
Globe and Mail (Toronto): A. Ir-win, 289; Canadian writing, 229; Zena Cherry, 196; P.K. in-terview, 270; P.K.'s obituary, 316; P.K.'s painting, 179; P.K.'s writing, 227
glosa, 273–8, 298, 302
Glover, Guy, 110
Godard, Barbara, 311–13
Godfrey, David, 241, 261
Gogol, Nikolai, 73
Golding, Phil, 47, 48, 56, 58–9, 62
Goldschmidt, Nicholas, 304

Gorrie, Elizabeth (and Colin), 261; *A Strange Bird, the Angel*, 253–4
Gourlay, Elizabeth ("Babette"), 234; P.K.'s story of separated lovers, 236
Governor General's Award for po-etry: 1955, 149–50, 152
Graham, Colin, 206
Graham, Gwethalyn: *Earth and High Heaven*, 98
Gravely, Mary, 27
Graves, Robert, 256; *Greek Myths*, 224; introduction to *The Sufis*, 214; "The Vow," 276; *White Goddess*, 224–5
Gray, Théa, 289; after Arthur's death, 291, 293; *The Essential P.K. Page*, 302; friendship, 272–3; P.K. near end of life, 317–18; on tour with P.K., 277–8, 281–2, 288, 294–5, 299–300; work on *The Hidden Room*, 280
Grey, Zane, 27, 31
Grierson, John, 125; *Canada Car-ries On*, 108
Griffin Poetry Prize short list, 299
Gruen, Walter, 184
Guadalajara Book Fair, 287
Gurdjieff, G.I., 183–4, 193–7, 305; *All and Everything*, 193
Gustafson, Ralph: *Canadian Ac-cent II*, 106–7; League of Cana-dian Poets, 223
Gzowski, Peter, 255–6, 281, 288

Halifax address, 93
Hambleton, Ronald: *Unit of Five* (anthology), 101–2
Harbourfront Reading Series, 257, 259, 268
Harris, Gail, 254

Harvor, Elizabeth, 53
Hatch, Ronald, 278
Hawkes, Jacquetta, 197
Hawthorne Books, 282
Hazen, Priscilla (later Prichard), 49, 73
Heaney, Seamus: *School Bag*, 271
Heilbrun, Carolyn, 1, 40
Helem, Forbes, 108–10
Helliwell, Norah, 109, 112, 129
Héloïse and Abelard story, 120, 145
Heppner, Ben, 304
Herbert, A.P., 44, 90; *Holy Deadlock*, 51
Hermes, Gertrude, 73, 217
Herrick, Robert: "Upon Julia's Clothes," 305
Hertzberg, Brigadier, 272
Hirsch, Joseph, 299
Hoban, Russell, 257
Hodgetts, Dorothy, 215
Hodgson, Gilbert, 14
Holiday, Ensor, 235
holidays: Christmas, 72, 82–3, 102–3; Go Home Lake, ON, 238–9; Great Barrier Reef, 155–6; Minas Gerais, 169; New England, 118–20; New River Beach, 46, 57, 64, 95; New Zealand, 156; Point-No-Point (Sooke), 273; West Indies tour (twenty-first birthday), 51–3, 52
Holland, 102–3, 113
Holmes, Geoffrey and Noreen, 141
Holtby, Winifred, 40
Homan, Derek: *The Invisible Reality*, 304
Hope, A.D., 146–7; "Soledades of the Sun and the Moon," 151; *Wandering Islands*, 146–7

Höstman, Anna: *What Time Is It Now?*, 304–5
Howe, C.D., 137
Hudson, W.H.: *Green Mansions*, 40
Hughes, Ted, 270–1; *Birthday Letters*, 271; *School Bag*, 271
Humphrey, Jack, 49, 53, 62
Hutchison, Bruce: assisted Irwin, 198; *The Incredible Canadian*, 154; *The Struggle for the Border*, 154; and wife Dorothy visit Mexico, 197
Huxley, Aldous: *The Doors of Perception*, 191; *The Perennial Philosophy*, 193

Ibsen, Henrik: *An Enemy of the People*, 51; *A Doll's House*, 51; *Pillars of Society*, 51
Imagists, 71
Inkster, Tim and Elke: *Coal and Roses: Twenty-One Glosas*, 302–3; copyright for "Your Slightest Look," 318, 320; P.K. praise for, 281. *See also* Porcupine's Quill
Institute for Cross-Cultural Exchange (ICE), 309
Institute for Cultural Research (ICR), 217, 237, 247
International Festival of Authors (Toronto), 268, 287–8
Irvine, Dean, 297, 313
Irwin, Alex (grandson of Arthur): on 9/11, 295
Irwin, Arthur: advice to P.K. on painting, 190; ambassador to Brazil, 162, 165–6; ambassador to Mexico, 177–9, 189–90; biography published, 274; Canadian books, 154; commissioner of

Film Board, 125–6, 133–4; death of, 290–1; as grandparent, 238; high commissioner to Australia, 134–5, 137, 155, 158–9; hundredth birthday, 289–90; illness, 156, 188, 230, 235, 242, 260, 282, 289–90; influence on A. Egoyan, 212; newspaper publisher, Victoria, 198, 199, 207; Order of Canada, 244; as suitor to P.K., 126, 127–31; "The Making of a Canadian," 239; United Nations postings, 186; work on P.K.'s Brazilian journal, 263

Irwin, Christine (granddaughter of Arthur), 290; "My Grandmother's Luggage," 286

Irwin, Neal (son of Arthur), 128–9, 132, 159, 164, 242, 288, 290, 292, 316

Irwin, Sheila (daughter of Arthur), 128, 132, 164, 238, 282, 290, 292

Jaynes, Julian: *The Origin of Consciousness in the Breakdown of the Bicameral Mind*, 236

Jeffrey, David, 244–5

Jewish people and Judaism, 21–2, 80, 171

John, Augustus, 31

Johnston, George, 270, 284, 305

Jones, Augusta (grandmother), 4, 6

Jones, Elizabeth Graham ("Lizzie"; great aunt), 4–5

Joseph, Eve, 317

Jung, C.G., 80, 147, 177; *Archetypes of the Unconscious*, 193; *Collected Works*, 181, 204; *Man and His Symbols*, 204; *Memories, Dreams, Reflections*, 192, 193, 221, 237; *Modern Man in Search of a Soul*, 77, 180–1; *Psyche and Symbol*, 192, 204, 231; *Psychology and Alchemy*, 193; *Symbols and Transformation*, 183, 232; "the Jung game," 321; "transformation" dreams, 192; "yantras," 229

Kaplan, Janet, 196

Keith, W.J., 283–4

Kennedy, John F. (and Jacqueline), 190

Kent, Stella, 194, 195, 214, 216; P.K.'s dedication to, 227

King, William Lyon Mackenzie, 44, 125

Klein, Abraham (A.M.): breakdown, 171; on Canadian art, 78; "Montreal," 78; P.K. meets, 80; P.K. on poetry of, 151; P.K.'s memories of, 305; "Portrait of the Poet as Landscape," 229; reception of, 213

Klein Symposium (1974), 229

Knight, Nora and Kit, 57, 95

Krishnamurti, 193

Kubitschek, Juscelino, 162, 165, 172

Kulyk Keefer, Janice (and Michael Keefer), 277

Lampert, Arlene, 243–4; after Arthur's death, 291; correspondence with P.K., 252, 256, 262; death of Gerald, 243; *The Essential P.K. Page*, 302; and Gerald, 242; League of Canadian Poets, 240; party for P.K., 257; on P.K. nearing death, 315; P.K.'s dedication to, 270; P.K.'s last day, 320 landscape: Australia, 137, 140–1, 144, 148, 158; Brazil, 163, 165, 168, 175; the Laurentians, 113; Mexico, 177–8; of New River Beach, 95; of prairie, 25–6, 31–2, 33, 113, 154; Rocky Mountain foothills, 33; of Sarcee Reserve, 6.

Lane, Patrick: "Albino Pheasants," 248, 271, 296

Lawrence, D.H., 40, 43, 66; *The Letters of D.H. Lawrence*, 55

Layton, Aviva, 258

Layton, Irving: *In the Midst of My Fever*, 154

League of Canadian Poets: feminist caucus, 256; Gerald Lampert Memorial Fund, 243; origins, 223; P.K. teaching for, 239; P.K.'s membership, 267; poetry festivals, 229; poetry readings, 240–1, 242; reading tour, 223–4. *See also* public readings

Leakey, Richard, 265

Leary, Timothy, 191

LeBlanc, Roméo, 288, 289

Lee, Dennis, 312–13

Lessing, Doris: *African Stories*, 218; *Briefing for a Descent into Hell*, 237, 265; *Canopus in Argos*, 296; *Canopus in Argos: Archives*, 237, 265; *The Four-Gated City*, 218–19, 265–6; influence of, 256; *Memoirs of a Survivor*, 255; P.K. meets, 257–8, 258; public reading by, 257, 259; *Shikasta*, 255–6

Lester & Orpen Dennys, 263

Letters in Canada: "Poetry," 149

Lewis, C. Day, 50

Lieutenant Governor's Award for Literary Excellence (BC), 313

Limners, 207

Lincoln, Eleanor, 183; P.K. visits, 203

A Little Princess; or What Happened at Miss Minchin's, 21, 101

Livesay, Dorothy, 98–9, 149; P.K. poem for, 283

Lofting, Hugh: *The Story of Doctor Dolittle*, 16

London: 1934, 38

London Group (sculptors and painters), 40

Long Lance, Chief Buffalo (Sylvester Clarke), 12

"the Loons," 256–7

Lord Strathcona's Horse (Calgary), 11–12, 16, 23, 47

Low, Colin, 110

McClelland, Jack, and McClelland & Stewart: *Cry Ararat!* with drawings, 208; meets Alice Munro, 201–2; *The Metal and the Flower*, 147–50; poetry manuscript, 146; rejects P.K.'s collection, 279

McCluskey, Sue, 283

McDougall, Anne: "P.K. Irwin, the Painter," 286

McGill Fortnightly Review, 130

McGill University reading, 299–300

McGlashan, Alan: *The Savage and the Beautiful Country*, 214

McKay, Molly (and Donald), 165, 172, 175

MacKenzie, David: *Arthur Irwin: A Biography*, 274

McKnight, David, 299–300

McLaren, Floris (and Mac): Australian correspondence, 140; on *Cry Ararat!*, 211; friendship,

104; on *The Metal and the Flower*, 148; P.K. sends book to, 147; submit poems for P.K., 152, 153; suffers stroke, 202

McLaren, Norman (animator), 110

McLean, Barry, 253

McLean, Ross, 125–6

Maclean's: A. Irwin, 125, 128, 129, 188, 200, 244, 284, 289, 316; rejection, 59; "Some of Our Best Poets Are ... Women," 224

MacLennan, Hugh: *Barometer Rising*, 83

McLuhan, Marshall, 115

Macmillan: *The Sun and the Moon*, 70, 82–3

MacMillan, H.R., 83

McNair, Duncan, 99

McNeilly, Kevin, 278; *Cambridge Companion to Canadian Literature*, 315

Macpherson, Dorothy, 112

Macpherson, Jay, 108, 112, 286

MacRae, Susan: on 9/11, 295; P.K.'s "Planet Earth," 298

magic realism, 170

Makosinski, Arthur: *Looking for Something*, 315

Malahat Review: "Australian Journal" excerpts, 286; "Cullen in Old Age," 303; "Hologram," 274; origins, 207; P.K. on editorial board, 260; special issue to P.K., 268, 285, 286; *Stone Fruit*, 179

Mallinson, Jean, 245

Malone, Richard S., 198

Maltwood Gallery (UVic), 260, 264–5, 311

Mandel, Eli, 228, 229, 314; on *Cry Ararat!*, 314

Mandlebrot, Benoît, 282

Mansfield, Katherine, 40; "At the Bay," 57–8; "Bliss," 57; *Journals*, 46–7, 54; *The Letters of Katherine Mansfield*, 54, 56; *Scrapbook*, 54; *Stories*, 54

Margaret Laurence Lecture (1999), 305

Marriott, Anne, 106, 149; "The Wind Our Enemy," 61

Marshall, Tom, 3

Martín, Juan: "Dreams and Superstitions," 184

Martin, Sandra: *The First Man in My Life*, 285; P.K.'s obituary, 316

Martins, Maria, 166

Marx, Karl, 80

Massey College, University of Toronto, 291

Matthews, Carol: 9/11, 295; after Arthur died, 293; P.K. near end of life, 318; P.K. on C. Rooke, 316; P.K.'s birthday, 315

Matthews, Robin, 223

Mawer, Mary, 29

Mediterranean trip (1935), 44–5

Melnyk, George: on "Preparation," 228

Menzies, Robert, 135, 137, 141–2; Petrov affair, 155

Merrill, Judith, 239

Merwin, W.S.: "Elegy," 273

Messenger, Cynthia, 270, 313

Metcalf, John, 281

Mexican addresses, 177, 186

Millay, Edna St. Vincent: "First Fig," 34

Miller, Romany, 227

Milner, Marion. *See* Field, Joanna (Marion Milner)

Mindlin, Henrique, 166

Mitha, Farouk, 297; *A Kind of Fiction* (P.K.), 305; P.K. near end of life, 319; *Up on the Roof* (P.K.), 306

Monro, Harold, 61; *Twentieth Century Poetry*, 42–3, 64

Monroe, Harriet: *Poetry* (magazine), 61–2

Montreal: addresses, 70, 83, 84, 106, 124–5; literary and artistic, 69–70, 84–5; P.K.'s description, 150

Montreal Standard, 69, 73

Moodie, Susanna: *The Journals of Susanna Moodie*, 226

Moore, Alexandra Browning, 293, 315, 318

Moore, Brian: *Judith Hearne*, 154

Moore, Mavor: death of, 302

Morgan, Charles, 40; *The Fountain*, 30, 65

Morocco, 44–5

Morris, Michael, 206

Mountbatten, Louis, 197

Munro, Alice, 201–2, 205; the Loons, 256

Munro, Grant, 110–11

Musgrave, Susan, 270–1

Nabuco, Joaquim, 166

Nash, Paul, 40

National Arts Centre, Festival Canada, 287

National Film Board of Canada: Irwin as commissioner, 125–6, 133–4; origins, 125–6; *Still Waters*, 268

National Film Commission (Ottawa), 106, 108, 117; P.K., 109; P.K. resigns, 126, 133

National Gallery, 274; *Bright Fish*, 184; *Keyhole*, 179; *Milkweed Forms*, 179

Neighbours (film), 133

Neimeyer, Oscar, 172–3

Neruda, Pablo, 298

Newlove, John, 281–2

New Provinces (anthology), 74, 151

Nicholl, Maurice: *The Mark*, 193

Nicholson, Ben, 164

Nicholson, R.A. *See* Rumi

Nietzsche, Friedrich: *Thus Spake Zorathustra*, 55

Nita Forrest Gallery, 205

Norman, Herbert (and Irene), 156, 159

Northern Review: "Lakeshore," 209; Sutherland and P.K., 116–17

Observer (London), 37, 39

O'Hagan, Howard, 223, 252

Ondaatje, Michael, 258; on Brazilian journal extract, 262; *The English Patient*, 263; friendship, 224, 257–8, 263; international reading tour, 243–4; the Loons, 256; on P.K., 270, 313, 314; P.K.'s influence on, 314; *Running in the Family*, 262, 263; work on Brazilian journal, 263; worked with P.K., 240

Orange, John: *P.K. Page: An Annotated Blibliography*, 246, 285

Order of British Columbia, 313

Order of Canada: Arthur, Officer, 244; F.R. Scott, Companion, 244; P.K., Officer and Companion, 244, 288, 289

Origin magazine, 146

Ormsby, Eric, 298

Ornstein, Robert: *New World, New Mind*, 269–70; *The Psychology of Consciousness*, 235, 242; stays with Irwins, 236, 239; on Sufi teaching story, 309; symposia, 235–7

Ottawa Citizen, 227, 281–2, 299

Ouspensky, P.D., 184, 197, 203; *In Search of the Miraculous*, 193

Outram, Richard, 283; on *The Hidden Room: Collected Poems* (2 vols.), 314

Oxford University Press: *Evening Dance of the Grey Flies*, 247; *A Flask of Sea Water*, 266; *The Glass Air: Selected Poems*, 259; rejects P.K.'s collection, 279

Page, Henry James (grandfather), 4

Page, Lionel (father), 17; childhood, 3–5; classmate, 206; death of, 97–8; engagement and marriage, 7, 9–10; heart attacks, 28–30, 34, 96–7; influence on P.K., 17–18, 26, 32, 47–8, 68, 91, 264; letter to P.K. (1934), 35–6; meets Noël Coward, 51; military career, 6–7, 9–12, 16, 21, 23, 28, 36, 46–7, 59, 72, 86, 93, 96–8; and P.K.'s suitors, 45; P.K.'s writing about, 249, 285; in Red Deer, 6–7; "Wisdom from Nonsense Land," 10–11. *See also* Page, Rose Laura, née Whitehouse (mother)

Page, Michael (brother), 17; camping, 32; childhood, 15–16, 19–20, 21–2; P.K. near end of life, 318–19; relocates to Victoria, 238

Page, Michael (nephew), artist, 312

Page, Patricia Kathleen: appearance, 31, 62, 85, 89–90, 111–12; apprentice writer, 57–8, 61; as aunt and grandmother, 238–9, 286, 288, 292, 295, 305–6, 312; autobiography, 3–4, 13, 15–16; birth and early childhood, 10–11, 14–19, 25–6; breast cancer, 315; cataract surgery, 257; circle of friends after Arthur died, 293; creates poetry contest, 63; cyst, 169, 174; as daughter, 19–21, 26, 47–8, 54, 60–1, 97–8, 237–8; death of, 320–1; death of many friends and family, 248; depression, 99–100, 104, 120, 162, 202–3, 219, 238; forgetfulness, 316–17, 318; on having children, 164, 174; hip operation, 277, 282, 294; honorary degrees, 268, 287, 313–14; on human evolution, Planet Earth, and ecology, 265–6, 269–70; identity, 17, 21–2, 144, 181, 308; illnesses, 13, 20, 26, 104, 119, 169, 174, 189, 257, 277, 282, 293–4, 315; imaginary playmate, 14; imagining life as an artist, 32–3; language: learning and losing, 162–3, 168, 178; journalism school, 38–9; "life will start," 200; maps and mapping, 5, 32, 113, 150, 154, 177, 181, 183, 193, 222, 249; marriage, 125–33; motor mechanics course, 60; not writing, 170–1, 175–6, 185; novel writing (1943), 95; on old age, 247, 315; Parents National Educational

Union (PNEU), 22, 27; as Pat, 30, 47, 63; as Patsy, 17; as "Podge," 48, 59, 101; portrait of (by M. Brittain), 62–3; "Questions and Images," 213–14; River Heights Elementary School, 17; St Hilda's, 16, 24, 26–7, 29, 31, 34; and Scott, Frank, 74–5, 86–92, 93–5, 96–7, 111–12, 161, 120–1, 225; Scott-inspired poems, 96-7, 113-14, 144, 147, 211, 225, 253, 255, 274, 276, 300-2, 321; suitors, 45, 58, 71–2, 73; as a tomboy, 17; on transformation dream, 192–3; twenty-first birthday, 51–2; work on Brazilian journal, 262; writing, again (Victoria), 208; writing and drawing process, 170–2, 230; writing group (Rothesay), 55; writing for musical compositions, 304–5, 306; writing: learning and losing language, 162–3, 168; writing process, 64; writing in Victoria, 205.
– CHILDREN'S BOOKS AND STORIES: *A Brazilian Alphabet for the Younger Reader*, 309; *A Flask of Sea Water*, 266, 310; *The Goat That Flew*, 266–7, 310; *A Grain of Sand*, 309; *Jake the Baker*, 309–10; "The Magic Wool," 56; *The Old Woman and the Hen*, 310; "Silver Pennies of The Land of Honesty," 56; *The Sky Tree*, 310; *There Was Once a Camel*, 310; *Uirapurú*, 310
– FICTION: "A Biography of You," 306; "Birthday," 306; "The Christmas Present," 54; "Crayons," 15–16, 306; "Easter Pie," 54; "Eatings," 306; "Ex Libris," 306; "The Glass Box," 106–7; "The Harp," 54; *A Kind of Fiction*, 195, 305; "A Kind of Fiction" (story), 305, "Looking for Lodgings," 70; "The Middleman," 44; "Shipwreck," 306, 307; "Stone," 306–7; *The Sun and the Moon*, 42, 57, 58–9, 66–7, 82–3, 100–1, 227; "This Happiness," 54; "True Story," 306; on two older lovers, 225; *Unless the Eye Catch Fire ...*, 271, 288, 313; "Unless the Eye Catch Fire ..." (story), 226, 250–1, 252, 255, 306; untitled story (1938–39), 57–8; *Up on the Roof*, 306; *You Are Here*, 308, 309; "Victoria," 64, 238
– NON-FICTION: Australian journal, 278–9, 286; *Brazilian Journal*, 164, 165, 173–5, 263–4, 311; in *Canadian Literature*, 222; "Canadian Poetry 1942," 78; childhood articles, 26, 27, 29–30, 34; "Darkinbad the Brightdayler," 305; duologues for radio, 49, 58; *The Filled Pen: Selected Non-Fiction*, 305; on her father, 285; "Questions and Images," 213, 259; scripts for National Film Commission, 110; on suffragettes, 56; "Teeth Are to Keep," 126; "Traveller, Conjuror, Journeyman," 1, 177, 196, 230, 235, 259; on women's inequality, 80; "A Writer's Life," 305
– POEMS: "About Death," 248–9; "Address to Simon Fraser," 269–70; "Adolescence," 113; "After Donne," 251; "After Rain," 152–3, 155, 209; "After Reading

Albino Pheasants," 248; "Ah, by the Golden Lilies," 163; "Alone," 276; "Alphabetical," 69; on "Ambition," 35; "Ancestors," 3–4, 248, 250, 284; "Another Space," 192, 222–3, 228, 232–3; "The Answer," 276; "Arras," 143–5, 147, 149, 152, 208, 209, 211, 239; "As on a Dark Charger," 283; "As Ten, As Twenty," 209; "At Sea," 248; "Autumn," 278; "The Bands and the Beautiful Children," 83–4; "Barbados Sights," 52; "Beside You," 225; "Blackout," 71; "Blowing Boy," 116; "The Bones' Voice," 75–6; "Brazilian Fazenda," 166; "Bright Fish Once Swimming Where We Lie," 147; "But We Rhyme in Heaven," 283; "A Children's Hymn," 287; "The Chinese Rug," 55; "Chinook," 270; "The Clock of Your Pulse," 283; "Conversation," 270; "Conversation with My Aunt," 238; "The Crow," 71, 282; "Cry Ararat!," 209–11, 228; "Cullen," 101–2, 113–14, 155; "Cullen at Fifty," 251, 303; "Cullen in Old Age," 303; "Cullen in the Afterlife," 303–4; "Cullen Revisited," 233–4, 251, 303; "Deaf-Mute in the Pear Tree," 259; "Death," 283; "Depression," 48–9; "Desiring Only," 72, 75–6, 90, 282–3; "The Disguises," 251; "Dreams of Caves and Winter," 209; "Each Mortal Thing," 302–3; "Ecce Homo," 40, 67–8, 71, 282; "Eden," 270; "Eighteen, Nineteen & Twenty," 61; "Election Day," 105, 116, 200, 227; "Element," 100, 208; "Emergence," 280; "Empty House Blues," 292; "Evening Dance of the Grey Flies," 247, 249; "Exile," 276; "Father," 285; "The First Part," 13, 15, 24, 26, 154, 248, 249–50; "For My Father," 96; "For V.W.," 61; "Freak," 116; "Frieze of Birds," 152; "Generation," 113, 209; "Generation (1)," 280; "The Gift," 270; "Giovanni and the Indians," 153, 155; "The Glass Air," 152; "Goodbye," 253; "Grand Manan," 280; "The Hidden Components," 270; "The Hidden Room," 33, 280, 282; "Hologram," 274–6; "I – Sphinx," 270; "If It Were You," 113–14; "Images of Angels," 149, 208, 255; "In Memoriam," 274, 276; "Intractable Between Them Grows," 147; "Intraocular Lens," 277; "Invisible Presences Fill the Air," 255; "Kaleidoscope," 270; "Landlady," 106–7, 113, 227; "Landscape of Love," 86–7, 114; "The Last Time," 303; "A Letter to K.S.," 55; "Lily on the Patio," 270; "A Little Reality," 277–8; on Louis Riel, 153–5; "Love Poem," 113, 209; "Love's Pavilion," 295, 304; "Man with One Small Hand," 149, 208; "The Map," 150; "Melanie's Nitebook," 284; "The Metal and the Flower," 147, 209; "The Mole," 82; "The Moon-Child," 55, 66; "The Moth," 37, 39, 43, 276; "Nature Poem," 152; "The Neighbours,"

17; "No Flowers," 102; "Offering of the Heart," 152; "Offices," 80; "On Being Ill," 29; "On Discussing Canada with the English," 43; "Ours," 247, 250; "Pain to His Helper," 282; "Paradise," 303; "Paradox," 86; "Paranoid," 149; "The Permanent Tourists," 209; "Personal Landscape," 89, 114; "Phone Call from Mexico," 184; "Photograph," 85–6, 227; "Photos of a Salt Mine," 148, 152, 209; "Planet Earth," 276, 298, 304, 315; "Poor Bird," 276, 315; "Portrait," 152; "Portrait of a Salt Mine," 271; "Portrait of Marina," 118–19, 149; "Preparation," 228; "Puppets," 208; "Reflection," 65; "Round Trip," 114; "Seventeen" (1933), 33–4; "Shipbuilding Office," 80; "Shipwreck," 292; "The Sick," 100; "Single Traveller," 304; "Sisters," 116; "The Sky," 270; "Sleeping on Deck," 52; "Snapshot," 101; "The Snowman," 209; "Sonnet" for Tommy Ross, 60; "Spring," 44; "Spring Tree," 278; "The Stenographers," 80–2, 86, 90, 113, 209; "Stories of Snow," 102–3, 113, 209; "Summer Resort," 101; "The End," 276, 320–1; "This Heavy Craft," 280; "To Katherine Mansfield," 56–7; "The Trail of Bread," 251; "Typists," 80; "The Understatement," 283; *Unit of Five*, 209; "Voyager," 249; "Waking," 114; "Warlord in the Early Evening," 141; "When Bird-Like," 152; "Winter Morning," 270; "Wisdom from Nonsense Land" (father's verse), 10–11; "The Woods Are Full of Them," 34; "The World," 270; "Written During Exams," 33; "Young Girls," 116; "Your Slightest Look," 302, 318, 320

– POETRY BOOKS: *Alphabetical*, 294, 298, 319; *And Once More the Stars*, 294–5; *As Ten, As Twenty*, 112–14, 209, 279, 314; in booklets with mother's drawings, 13, 52–3; *Coal and Roses: Twenty-One Glosas*, 302–3; *Cosmologies*, 294, 298; *Cry Ararat!*, 276, 314; *Cry Ararat!* with drawings, 208–12; *Cullen: Poems*, 303–4, 318; *The Essential P.K. Page*, 302; *Evening Dance of the Grey Flies*, 247–52, 255, 279, 283; *The Glass Air: Poems Selected and New*, 268, 270, 314; *The Glass Air: Selected Poems*, 259–60; *The Golden Lilies*, 302; *Hand Luggage: A Memoir in Verse*, 271, 299–300; *The Hidden Room: Collected Poems* (2 vols.), 268, 299, 314–15; *Hologram: A Book of Glosas*, 234, 268, 273–8, 279, 283, 314; *Kaleidoscope: Selected Poems of P.K. Page*, 302; *The Metal and the Flower*, 147–50, 152, 209, 314; *P.K. Page: Poems Selected and New*, 227–8; *Planet Earth: Poems Selected and New*, 298.

– VISUAL ART (as P.K. Irwin): 1927 sketchbook, 22; "Arras" as painting, 149; Australian influence on, 159; Brazil, 168–9; creative energy of painting, 172; drawing as a child, 13, 14, 22;

drawing in "Crayons," 15–16; drawing/painting compared to poetry, 234–5; etching, 187–8; exhibitions of, 179, 184, 205–6, 234, 239, 242, 260, 311, 312; learning from Carrington, 182–3, 190; learning in New York, 187; learning to draw, 164, 165, 170–1, 185–6; learning to paint, 161; on Mexican schools of, 185; mother's ability, 10; published with poems, 208–12; reception of, 179, 184–5, 206, 234–5, 311; why P.K. painted, 190; works: *Ah, Sunflower*, 234; *Aladdin's Ship*, 179, 312; *And You, What Do You Seek?*, 196, 206, 208, 276; *Arcanum*, 234; *Bark*, 179; *Brazilian Dolls*, 311; *Bright Fish*, 184, 234; *Cosmos*, 312; *The Dance*, 179, 197, 311; *Dark Kingdom*, 311; *Dark Landscape*, 234; *Desert Fantasy*, 234; *Dome of Heaven*, 312; *Doodle*, 312; *Ectoplasmic Event*, 234; *Escaping Suns*, 179; *Fiesta*, 311; *The Four-Gated City*, 232, 234, 237; *Ghost Ship*, 311; *The Glass House*, 259; *The Golden Bough*, 311; "Heart," 311; *How Is the Gold Become so Dim*, 185, 311; *Is This Gray Ash All That Is Left?*, 202; *Keyhole*, 179; *A Kind of Osmosis*, 183, 206, 307; *Labyrinth*, 179; *Little One Eye*, 234; *Milkweed Forms*, 179; *Night Garden*, 234; *Noche Levantine*, 184; octagons, 229–37, 275; *Party at Intamarity*, 311, 312; *Persephone's Flowers*, 234; *Pieces of Eight*, 234, 236; *Pink Embassy*, 264; *Red Whirling Crayon Drawing*, 179; *Sala Grande*, 264; self portrait, 312; *Shape of the Flower Is Yellow*, 206, 312; *Ship – Nocturnal*, 260; sketch of tree (Australia), 142–3; *Sky Drawing*, 185; *Spring Green*, 234; *Square*, 232; *Stairwell*, 311, 312; *Star Burst*, 308; *Stone Fruit*, 179, 185; *Striped Umbrellas*, 265; *Sun Tree*, 234; *Target*, 232; *That Which Is and That Which Strives to Be*, 234; *This Church My Dromedary*, 179, 185; *Tree of Life*, 233; *Votive Tablet*, 234; *Who in This Bowling Alley Bowl'd the Sun?*, 206, 311, 312; *Woman's Room*, 161, 170–1, 172, 311; *World Within World*, 205–6, 311; "yantras," 229, 232; *And You, What Do You Seek?*, 311, 312

Page, Rose Laura, née Whitehouse (mother), 8, 52; artistic talent, 10, 14, 25; Australian visit, 142; booklets with P.K., 13, 52–3; death of, 239; dementia, 238; engagement and marriage, 7–10; Halifax, 95; influence on P.K., 24–5, 48, 106; in last years, 284–5; migraine headaches, 119; P.K.'s marriage, 132; on P.K.'s awards, 149; riding accident, 19–20; supranormal perception, 28; visits Mexico, 197. *See also* Page, Lionel (father)

Page, Tim (nephew), 288, 289, 316

Page, Wendy (niece), 311, 312

Page Irwin Colloquium Room (Trent), 302, 316

Pages of Essex (father's family), 3–4, 5

Palardy, Jean, 84–5, 112

paranormal. *See* supranormal
    perception
Parsons, Marnie, 284
Patterson, Raymond and
    Marigold, 44
Pearkes, George, 206, 239
Pearson, Alan, 228
Pearson, Landon (and Geoffrey),
    180
Pearson, Lester B., 134–5, 149–50,
    158
Peaslee, Amos J. (and Dorothy),
    137, 141
Pedersen, George, 245
Peter, John, 207
Peterson, Oscar, 304
Petite-Rivière-Saint-François, 85
pets (P.K.): Benjamina, lion-mon-
    key, 173; Chico, dog, 184, 199,
    238; as a child, 30; dog in Aus-
    tralia, 138; Duque the dog, 175;
    Scottie dog, 104; Siamese cats,
    294, 320
Pickersgill, Peggy, later MacDon-
    ald, 49, 60
Picture Loan and Society (Toron-
    to), 179
Plumptre, Wynne and Beryl, 133
Pocaterra, G.W., 32, 224
Poetry (Chicago): "After Rain,"
    153; "Blowing Boy," 116; "Elec-
    tion Day," 116; "Freak," 116;
    "Giovanni and the Indians,"
    153; Oscar Blumenthal Award,
    100; review of P.K.'s first collec-
    tion, 113, 314; "Sisters," 116;
    submissions to, 95, 116, 152;
    "The Mole," 82; "Young Girls,"
    116
politics: 9/11, 294–6; 1945 general
    election, 105; activism of Frank
    Scott, 88, 91, 95, 123; Brazil,

165–6; Canada and Australia,
    134–5; Canada's centenary, 212–
    13, 304; Canadian nationalism,
    313; Cuban missile crisis, 189;
    ecology, 269–70; free trade, 266;
    Iraq and Afghanistan wars, 296;
    municipal water, 51; Petrov af-
    fair, 155; P.K.'s opinion of Aus-
    tralia, 159; in P.K.'s poems, 114,
    302; *Preview* influence, 76–8,
    80; Scott and Irwin compared,
    130; shared by Scott and P.K.,
    113; Suez Canal, 158–9, 186; US
    1960 elections, 188, 189
Pollock, Ann: "The White Glass:
    Conversations with P.K. Page,"
    286
Pollock, Zailig: *Complete Poems:
    A.M. Klein*, 297; "Extraordinary
    Presence: The Worlds of P.K.
    Page," 313; *Kaleidoscope: Select-
    ed Poems of P.K. Page*, 302; Page
    Irwin Colloquium Room (Trent),
    316; P.K.'s *Cullen: Poems*, 304;
    P.K.'s *The Filled Pen: Selected
    Non-Fiction*, 305; scholarly edi-
    tion of P.K.'s work, 297
Poppy Press: *Alphabetical/Cos-
    mologies*, 298
Porcupine's Quill: *The Hidden
    Room: Collected Poems* (2 vols.),
    279–80, 281. *See also* Inkster,
    Tim and Elke
Porteous, Timothy, 240
Portinari, Candido, 164–5
Pound, Ezra: "A Girl," 43, 65
Powys, John Cowper: *Wolf Solent*,
    65
Pratt, E.J.: *Canadian Poetry Maga-
    zine*, 115; P.K.'s opinion, 151;
    The Titanic, 154; *Towards the
    Last Spike*, 154

Pre-Raphaelite Brotherhood, 39
Preston, Michele (Michele Valiquette), 245–6
Preview: on Canadian art, 78; "Canadian Poetry 1942," 78; "Desiring Only," 72, 90; the group, 79, 112; Montreal avant-garde, 84–5; origins, 74–7; "Paradox," 86; P.K. essay, 80; P.K.'s dedication to, 305; "Recovery" (F.R. Scott), 89; "The Stenographers," 81, 86, 90; unknown in Vancouver, 99
Priestley, J.B.: *Man and Time*, 201; visits Mexico, 197
Proust, Marcel: *Swann's Way*, 50
public readings, 222–4, 228–9, 239, 240–3, 254, 262, 268, 277–8, 281–2, 299–300; international, 243–4; *Looking for Something* (film of readings), 315; performing "Me Tembro," 254, 262; *You Are Here*, 309
Purdy, Al, 115, 261; invitation to P.K., 222
Purley (near London, UK), 38

Quill and Quire, 245

Rasminsky, Louis and Lila, 133
reading (P.K.): 1933, 30; 1949, 122–3; 1952, 154; 1960s, 319; after marriage, 134; in Australia, 140, 142, 146–7, 154, 157, 181; in Brazil, 164–5, 172, 181; childhood, 10–11, 13, 16, 17, 21; feminism and socialism, 51; last two years in Calgary, 31; in London 1930s, 39–43, 65; on lovers, 120; Mansfield and her circle, 54–5; in Mexico, 177, 180–1, 183, 184, 193–4, 195; near end

of life, 317; in a quest for the way, 193–4, 204, 211, 214, 218, 221, 224, 231, 235–7, 255; reflected in *Evening Dance of the Grey Flies*, 251; in Saint John, late 1930s, 50, 55–6; during Second World War, 73, 77; summer 1941, 65; in Victoria, 201, 208, 213, 263
Red Deer, 6–7, 11–12
Redpath, Peter, 311, 316
Reid, Lionel, 108, 126
Reid, Stephen, 271
Richardson, Henry Handel (Ethel Florence Lindesay Richardson), 140
Richler, Mordecai: *Son of a Smaller Hero*, 154
Riel, Louis, 154–5
Rilke, Rainer Maria, 86; "Autumn Day," 39, 275–6; *Duino Elegies*, 80, 89, 254
Rittenhouse, Charles, 58–9
Robert, Dom, 117, 145
Robertson, Gordon and Beatrice, 133
Roché, Louis, 141
Romsey, Southampton, 20, 21–2
Rooke, Constance ("Connie"): after Arthur's death, 291; death of, 316; Eden Mills Writers' Festival, 277, 281; friendship, 245, 260, 286, 315, 316; and Irwin's ninetieth, 261; *Malahat Review*, 260; "P.K. Page: The Chameleon and the Centre," 246; P.K.'s dedication to, 305; P.K.'s poem for, 270; on P.K.'s poetry, 252, 284; P.K.'s seventieth birthday, 260–1
Rooke, Leon: Eden Mills Writers' Festival, 277, 281; fantasia about P.K. by Leon, 286; friendship, 253

Rosenblatt, Joe, 245
Ross, Frank Mackenzie, 50
Ross, Gertrude Tomalin ("Tommy"), 50, 58, 59–60
Ross, Malcolm, 153
Ross, Val, 270
Rossetti, Dante Gabriel: *How They Met Themselves*, 39; "Sudden Light," 39
Roszak, Theodore: *Where the Wasteland Ends*, 250
Rothesay writing group, 55
The Royal Journey (film), 133
Royal Society of Canada, 314
royal visits, 51, 133, 142
Ruddick, Bruce, 74, 78, 79, 85, 112
Rumi, 80, 204, 218, 248. *See also* Sufism
Rushdie, Salman, 257
Ruzesky, Jay: *Malahat* special issue, 286; meets P.K., 260; P.K. after Arthur died, 293; P.K. near end of life, 316, 317, 318; P.K.'s Cullen poems, 303; reads "Planet Earth," 298
Ryan, Nin, 186–7
Ryerson Press: Alice Munro, 201–2; manuscript preparation for, 146; *As Ten, As Twenty*, 112–13

Sabiston, Carole, 261
Saddlemyer, Ann, 291, 293
Saint John, NB: La Tour Hotel, 59; New River Beach, 46, 57, 64, 95; P.K.'s description, 150; Rothesay, 46–8, 51
Salaman, Merula, 31
Sandler, Linda, 242
Sandwell, B.K., 102
Sappho: "Alone," 274
Saramago, José: *The Cave*, 317

Sarcee Camp and Reserve, 6, 12–13, 25, 32, 154
Saturday Night, 54, 118, 264, 289
Schaeffer, Frank, 170
Scheier, Libby, 283
Schofield, Kit, 50
School Bag (anthology), 271
Schwartz, Harley and Nancy, 215
Schwartz, Jill, 253
Schweitzer, Albert, 172
science fiction, 281–2
Scobie, Stephen, 252
Scott, F.G. (father of F.R. Scott), 9, 91, 129
Scott, F.R.: on Canadian art, 78; death of, 252–3; League of Canadian Poets, 223; and Marian, 123–5, 127; Order of Canada, 244; P.K.-inspired poems, 89–90, 91–2, 94, 122, 131–2, 209; in *Preview* group, 79; purchases P.K.'s paintings, 179
– WRITINGS: "Advice," 104; "Departure," 89, 91–2, 131–2, 320; *Events and Signals*, 131, 149–50, 209; "Lakeshore," 209–10; "Laurentian," 78; "Message," 89, 126, 131, 209; *New Provinces*, 300–1; *Overture*, 103–4; "Recovery," 89; "Return," 121–2; "Signature," 89; Skelton's review of, 212; "Why Québec Voted No," 88; "Windfall," 94, 103–4
Scott, Marian, née Dale, 88–9, 121, 123–5, 127, 131, 244, 252–3
Second World War, 59, 72–3, 80–2, 84–5, 86, 96, 105
Seferis, George: "The King of Asine," 274–5
Seliger, Charles, 186, 187

Serpa, Ivan, 170

Shackleton, Kathleen ("Shackie"), 62

Shah, Idries: illness, 267; in Lessing's book, 219; man as multiple, 39; P.K. meets, 216–17, 235, 236; P.K. quotation of, 224; P.K.'s first encounter, 195; in P.K.'s writing, 251, 301, 305; qualities of, 220; *Recollections*, 216; "Report on Planet Earth," 265; response to *Hologram*, 277; Sufi octagon, 230–7; *The Sufis*, 204, 214–16, 218, 231–2, 265, 276–7; *Tales of the Dervishes*, 216; *Thinkers of the East*, 216; *The Way of the Sufi*, 216. *See also* Sufism

Shattuck, Roger: introduction to *Mount Analogue*, 195

Shaw, George Bernard: *The Apple Cart*, 136; *Major Barbara*, 38; *Pygmalion*, 5

Shaw, Katherine ("Auntie Kit"), 12, 13, 24, 32

Shaw, Kit, 69, 73, 79, 85–6

Shaw, Neufville, 73–6, 78, 79, 85–6

Sherman, Kenneth, 283

Shute, Nevil: *In the Wet*, 142

Siebner, Herbert, 206

Signal Hill, Victoria, 241

Simon Fraser University, 223, 239, 268–70

Simpson, Colin: *Adam in Ochre*, 157

Singh, Khushwant, 117–18, 191, 192; *Train to Pakistan*, 188

Sirluck, Ernest, 115

Sise, Hazen, 126

Sitwell, Edith, 39, 248; "Aubade," 43

Skelton, Robin: "Emily Carr Book an Insult – Don't Buy It," 207; glosa, 273; interest in Canadian writing, 212; *Malahat Review*, 207, 260; *Memoirs of a Literary Blockhead*, 226; P.K. as rival, 202, 205, 207, 226

Slim, William (and wife), 138–9, 142

Smart, Elizabeth, 258; *By Grand Central Station I Sat Down and Wept*, 258–9

Smith, A.J.M. ("Art"): on "Arras," 145; on *The Metal and the Flower*, 148; *Modern Canadian Verse*, 208; opinion of P.K., 83, 284, 314–15; P.K. correspondence, 211, 212, 223; P.K. meets, 82–3; on publishing outside Canada, 153; reads P.K.'s manuscript, 112; reception of, 221; *A Sort of Ecstasy*, 149–50; on *As Ten, As Twenty*, 114, 115; "The Archer," 192

Smith, Jori: death of, 302; friendship, 112, 281–2; holiday with P.K., 118; letter to P.K., 85; meets P.K., 69–70; and P.K. correspondence 95, 104, 116, 145, 185–6, 190–1, 202, 211, 225, 236–7, 246; P.K. on Ornstein symposium, 236; on P.K. resigning Film Commission, 126; as "tragic optimist" (P.K.), 134

Smith, Kay (writing circle), 49, 55, 56, 61, 62

Smith, Sidney, 173

Solecki, Sam, 239

Somers, Harry: P.K.'s "A Children's Hymn," 287

Spalding, Esta, 283, 312–13

Spalding, Linda, 286–7
Spanish Civil War: Guernica, 77, 86, 113
Spencer, Myfanwy (Spencer-Pavelic), 104, 202, 206–7
Spencer, Stanley: *Saint Francis*, 40
Spender, Stephen, 171, 314
spiritualism: "Another Space," 223; in art, 191; P.K. search for, 191–6; puppet play for children, 247; quest for, 204; "Questions and Images," 213; "work," 203. *See also* Sufism
Staines, David, 259, 281
Starnino, Carmine, 284, 314–15
Stein, Alan, 302
Stern, Isaac, 190–1
Sternberg, Harry, 187–8
Stevens, Wallace: "Credences of Summer," 275
Still Waters (film), 268
Strachey, John: "Digging for Mrs. Miller," 89
Strand, Mark: *Dark Harbour*, 278; "The End," 320–1
Stratford, Philip: *renga* with P.K., 294–5
Stratton-Porter, Gene: *A Girl of the Limberlost*, 27, 43
Student Union Gallery (UBC), 239
Subud, 184, 194
Sufism: in "Darkinbad the Brightdayler," 305; Dom Robert, 117, 145; in *Evening Dance of the Grey Flies*, 248, 250–1; in *A Flask of Sea Water*, 266; in *Hologram*, 276–7; octagons, 230–7, 275; P.K.'s interest, 45; P.K.'s interest "quickened," 214–20, 247; teaching story, 309; Ted Hughes, 271; in "The End," 321; in "Unless the Eye Catch

Fire …," 288. *See also* Rumi; Shah, Idries; spiritualism
Sullivan, Rosemary (and Doug Beardsley), 245; "A Size Larger Than Seeing: The Poetry of P.K. Page," 246; friendship, 257, 315, 316, 320; on *Hologram*, 286; interviews P.K., 287–8; to Mexico with P.K., 286–7; P.K.'s dedication to, 306; promotion of P.K., 247; and P.K. on Bowering, 262–3; and P.K. on feminist caucus, 256
Sumohadiwidjojo, Muhammad Subuh (and Ebu), 194
Sunshine Coast Festival of the Written Arts (BC), 268
supranormal perception: of friend after death, 59–60, 321; with mother, 28, 181
surrealism, 84, 181–2, 195–6
"Surrealism in Canadian Art," 205
Surrey, Philip, 73, 77
Sutherland, John: P.K. meets, 55–6; P.K. suitor, 71, 116; reviews, 77–8, 116–17
Suzuki, David: *A Planet for the Taking*, 265, 269
Suzuki, T.D., 183; *Introduction to Zen Buddhism*, 193
Swan Lake, 121; Margot Fonteyn, 121, 175
Sweet, Jean, 49, 55, 56, 61–3
Szumigalski, Anne, 239

Tamarack Review, 148, 171, 213
Tanner's Books (Victoria), 270–1
Tate Gallery, 39–40
Tchernakova, Anna: *Last Summer*, 288; P.K.'s "Unless the Eye Catch Fire …," 288, 313
teaching (P.K.), 241, 242–3
technology, P.K. online, 293

Teleky, Richard, 247, 259
Tenniel, John, 10, 17, 25
Terasen Lifetime Achievement
   Award, 313
theatre. *See* art, art galleries, and
   theatre
Théâtre de l'Ermitage (Montreal),
   84
Theatre Guild of Saint John, 50,
   53, 56, 58
Thomas, D.M., 257
Thompson, Francis: "The Hound
   of Heaven," 55
Thomson, David, 112; on *The
   Metal and the Flower*, 148, 150
Thomson, David and Marie, 121
Times Colonist (Victoria), 244
Times Literary Supplement, 314
Timp, Pierre, 102–3
*To Say the Least: Canadian Poets
   from A to Z* (anthology), 243
Tobey, Mark, 187
Tolstoy, Leo, 73
Toronto Children's chorus, 304
Toronto Mendelssohn Choir, 304
Toronto Star, 270
Toronto Symphony Orchestra, 304
Town, Harold, 164
Toye, William, 203, 252
Tracole, Henri, 194
Trans-Canada Trail, 304
Trehearne, Brian, 154, 282, 297,
   300, 313
Trent University, 302, 316; "Extra-
   ordinary Presence" (P.K. sympo-
   sium), 311–12, 313
Trudeau, Pierre, 213
Turner, Camilla, 315
typing and secretarial work, 30,
   46, 80–2

Unit of Five (anthology), 101–2

United Nations Dialogue among
   Civilizations through Poetry, 298
University of British Columbia,
   313–14
University of Calgary, 268
University of Toronto, 287
University of Toronto Quarterly,
   149, 284; Djwa review, 248
University of Victoria, 241, 268
University of Windsor: "Winder
   Boundaries of Daring," 313
Unless the Eye Catch Fire ...
   (Belfry Theatre), 271

Valcartier Camp (QC), 9
Valdés, Carlos, 185
Valiquette, Michele, 252
Vancouver addresses, 98, 122
Vancouver International Writers
   Festival, 268, 312–13
Varo, Remedios, 182; *Ascension
   to Mount Analogue*, 196; *Vaga-
   bond*, 196
Victoria: addresses, 99, 104; Ex-
   eter Road, 200, 264, 311, 316,
   320; P.K.'s description, 150, 200,
   202; visit to, 122
Victoria Art Gallery, 206
Victorian code of behaviour, 10–
   11
Villasenor, Laura, 183, 203

Waddell, Helen: *Peter Abelard*,
   120, 145
Wade, Mason: *The French Canadi-
   ans*, 154
Wartime Merchant Shipping, 83
Warwick, Ethel, 44
Webb, Phyllis, 100
Weisz, Emerico ("Chiqui"; hus-
   band of Leonora Carrington),
   186

Werthein Gallery, 40
West Coast Review, 245–6
West Indies "vagabond" cruise, 52
Whitehouse, Beatrice ("Bibbi";
    aunt): Australian visit, 142;
    death of, 240; dementia, 238;
    education, 8, 240; influence on
    P.K., 38–9, 240; lives with Rose,
    15, 59, 95, 98, 117, 136, 237–8;
    P.K. lives with, 34; and P.K. mar-
    riage, 132; on Scott-P.K. affair,
    97, 132; visits Mexico, 197
Whitehouse, Frank (uncle), 8–9,
    15–16, 98
Whitehouse, Robert (grandfather),
    8, 20–1, 22, 39
Whitehouse, Robert (great-great-
    grandfather), 3
Whitehouse, Robert (uncle), 8–9
Whitehouse, Rose Laura. *See* Page,
    Rose Laura, née Whitehouse
    (mother)
Whitehouse, Rosina, née Spriss
    (grandmother), 20–1, 39
Whitehouses (mother's family), 3
Whiteman, Bruce, 252, 278
Whiteside, Leon, 258
Wilkinson, Anne, 147, 148, 151,
    208
Willard (Johnston), Marian, 186–8
Wilson, Ethel: *Swamp Angel*, 154
Winchester Galleries (Victoria),
    308; "A Retrospective: P.K.
    (Page) Irwin," 311–12; "The
    Three Pages," 312
Windsor Art Gallery, 311
Winkler, Donald: *Still Waters*, 268

Winnipeg, 16–17, 21
Winwar, Frances: *Poor Splendid
    Wings: The Rossettis and Their
    Circle*, 31, 39
Wise, Jack: introduction to "Mys-
    tic Circles," 234
Wiseman, Adele, 256
Wolfe, Humbert, 40
Wollman, Maurice: *Modern
    Poetry, 1922–1934*, 43
Woodcock, George, 207–8, 213,
    228, 234, 259
Woodsworth, J.S., 88, 129, 300
Woolf, Virginia: *A Room of One's
    Own*, 40, 56, 66; *Three Guineas*,
    56; *The Waves*, 40–1
Wordsworth, Elizabeth: "Good
    and Clever," 15
Writers' Union of Canada, 243,
    305
Writers' Week (Adelaide), 257
Wunderley (Alice), 141
Wyatt, Rachel, 293, 315, 318
Wynand, Dirk, 241; *A Strange
    Bird, the Angel*, 254

Yeats, W.B., 43
Young, Beryl, 293, 318
Young, Patricia, and Terence, 253,
    318; after Arthur died, 293; at-
    tend launch, 282; on glosa, 273–
    4, 278; on P.K.'s teaching, 241; *A
    Strange Bird, the Angel*, 254
Young, Walter and Beryl, 245, 252

Zwicky, Jan, 274